The Development of Personality in the Indian Ecology

About the Author

Dr. Margaret Khalakdina is an independent consultant. She has had a long career in her area of specialisation — human development and human ecology. She completed her PhD from Cornell University, New York, US, and is a recipient of fellowships from Syracuse University, Altrusa International and Ford Foundation. She has had a long, distinguished professional career as a teacher of post-graduate student at lady Irwin College, New Delhi; and Nirmala Niketan College and SNDT Home Science College, Mumbai,

She was formerly the Executive Director of the Indian Council or Child Welfare and her last assignment was with the UNICEF in African countries.

She is the author of the books *Early Child Care in India* (1997), sponsored by the Russell Sage Foundation, and *Human Development in the Indian Context: A Socio-cultural Focus* (two volumes, 2009, 2011). She has also contributed to various publications such as *The First Five Years* (1998) and journals such as the *Indian Journal of Social Work* and *Journal of Human Ecology.*

The Development of Personality in the Indian Ecology

Margaret Khalakdina

CONCEPT PUBLISHING COMPANY PVT. LTD.
NEW DELHI

ISBN-13 : 978-81-8069-857-6

First Published 2012

Published and Printed by

Concept
Since 1974

Concept Publishing Company Pvt. Ltd.
A/15-16, Commercial Block, Mohan Garden
New Delhi-110059 (India)
T: 25351460, 25351794, *F*: 091-11-25357109
E: publishing@conceptpub.com, W: www.conceptpub.com
Editorial Office: H-13, Bali Nagar, New Delhi-110 015, India.

Cataloging in Publication Data--*Courtesy:* D.K. Agencies (P) Ltd. <docinfo@dkagencies.com>

Khalakdina, Margaret.
The development of personality in the Indian ecology / Margaret Khalakdina.
p. cm.
Includes bibliographical references and index.
ISBN 9788180698576

1. Personality development—India. 2. Human ecology—India. I. Title.

DDC 155.250954 23

To my husband Nazeem A. Khalakdina,
my grand-daughters, Isabella and Alessia,
and my grandson, Sami Khalakdina

Foreword

Human-ecology is about the way in which human beings live in their ecological spaces and the human habitat they establish; whether they continue to live in their original ecologies or whether they move from one ecology to another. Human ecology is intertwined with geo-ecology and to understand human ecology, it is necessary to know about these specific parameters of differing geo-ecologies and the effect they have on their human lifestyles. What role innovations in technology play in the process of human adaptation to his geo-ecology.

Dr. Margaret Khalakdina, who lived in different parts of the world as a social analyst, aptly explains this process involving civilization transformation from a communication and human relations perspective in India and brings out cause and effect dilemmas involved in the process of technological change.

The book analyses cooperation, co-existence and conflict and convergence aspects in interactions in the constantly changing ecological situations. The book offers insights to ponder about as environment and habitat become the agenda for all those in socio-economic and political domain. The book would facilitate in understanding the shifts in the paradigms at micro and macro levels about different phases of human ecology.

Economists and ecologists and planners and policy people alike should explore the subject matter of the book, the development of the Indian in his ecology. Margaret Khalakdina has opened up a new discipline for a holistic pursuit.

27 June 2011

N. Bhaskara Rao, Ph.D.
Chairman,
Centre for Media Studies,
Research House, Saket Community Centre
(Behind PVR Cinema), New Delhi
Tel: 011-26851660

Acknowledgements

This book could not have been written without the generous asistance of two dedicated persons, Mrs Sakuntala Dixit and Mr. Shaji. Mrs. Dixit has been very diligent and dedicated in the search for appropriate references. The putting together and the typing of this document has been mainly due to the diligent, consistent and dedicated work of Mr. Shaji who has also helped me with editing. My other helpers have been Swati Gaur and Radhika Takru. I am grateful to the above for their continued assistance. My family Ashina, Rolando, Arshad and Magda have been with me patiently throughout the writing of this document. I thank them for their caring support.

I also owe a debt of gratitude to those erudite scholars from India, whose writings on various facets of socio-psychology, cross-cultural psychology and culture, has helped me procure indigenous material.

In retrospect, I must say that whatever I have learned and gained and was able to write was due to the firm impressions left with me by my teachers from Cornell University, Ithaca, New York, namely, Dr. U. Bronfenbrenner, Dr. A. Baldwin, Dr. Harry Levin and Dr. H. Riccutti, who are erudite scholars in socio-psychology, human development and family relationships. Their long-lasting spectacular teachings have stood fast all the way through. Along the course of my teaching post-graduate students, I have learnt a great deal from interactions with them, a special gratitude is due to the many scholars who have written on the Indian culture and particularly the social psychology of the Indian.

Prologue

Human beings develop in unique and specific ecologies. The Indian is no exception. There are many varied and specific such ecologies in which the Indian lives, all over the sub-continent. The geo-ecological parameters of each ecology differ widely. It is well-known that there are two sides of the coin of the Indian psyche: The first is the individual's homogeneity in general characteristics, that all Indians possess, and the other is his heterogeneity among these ecologies. Therefore, the *Indian is socialized in the specific contextual frames of sub-societal structures: a class, a caste, an ethnic group, and a family living in a specific geo-ecology*, such as an urban area, a rural hinterland or a tribal forest, which forms his nexus.[1] (Khalakdina, M, 2008)

The second is the parameters of each ecological and contextual frame. *Each ecology has specific characteristics which consciously and unconsciously affect the individual's lifestyle* and, therefore, his traits as a person. The Indians themselves are varied in psycho-social characteristics, as moulded by their phylogenetic and ontogenetic maturation in a specific human ecological niche.

It is acceptable that as the human being develops, he acts upon his specific ecology and is acted upon by it. We observe that the Indians of Kerala, for instance, look more like Sri Lankans. Bengalis are more like the Bangladeshis and those from the North-Eastern States look more like the Burmese and Tibetans. Physionomically, features of the ethnic groups in India, indicate mixtures of races occurring over several civilizations. Yet, if we take a specific State like Kashmir, its inhabitants look like Persians, but they act like Indians, by virtue of residence and upbringing in a specific place, a given ecology.

The term ecology has come into wide acceptance in the human context since about the last century. The origin of "ecology" had *to do with the natural ecology of flora and fauna, and has gradually spread to include many other factors, the most prominent being the human ecology,* namely, those who make up various groups in terms of family and community. Ecology also includes a variety of phenomena, besides flora and fauna, like the type of air, either polluted or fresh, water, soil and, more specifically, the climate, which together contribute to the physiognomic characteristic of a given ecology and living patterns in that ecology. The specific human ecology which distinguishes groups from each other living in differing ecologies, applies to the Pigmies of Central Africa as much as it applies to the Eskimos of Iceland. Such like racial groups over centuries have adapted their living styles to their ecologies, where natural phenomena also differ.

Ecology, while an abstract concept, can be operationalised by specific attributes such as a geographical area, the type of land and the availability of basic natural 'givens'. Bronfenbrenner has incorporated the human element in such settings as human beings can make or break the ecologies in which they live.[2] (Bronfenbenner, U., 1979) For instance, the wars, both world-wide and country-wide, have depleted and depreciated the human's abilities as well as the natural ecology. World War-II has caused devastation of countries and decimation of entire peoples and traumatized children born during the war.[3] (Bowlby, J., 1998) The wars in Bosnia, Iraq and the continuing war in Afghanistan are ample evidence of the devastation caused to human and natural ecology. The secretly conducted experiments with nuclear devices in highly technologised countries have tortured the earth's surface. The increasing frequency of earthquakes and tsunamis, and more recently the eruption of a volcano in Iceland, spewing ash and disrupting air traffic, has turned nature back against humanity. These incidents form a chain reaction agitating global concerns in international fora towards recreating a 'green environment' and to curb the pollution of water, air and therefore maintain the well-being of human beings.[4] (United Nations, 2010)

Social psychology and its correlates should turn its present and future perspectives more closely to the relationship between these geo-ecological calamities and man's experience.[5] (Gruberg, Martin & Louise K. Comfort, 2009) We can very well ask the question: is there a difference in the personality formation of children born and brought up during World War-II and those children in the continuing Iraq and Afghanistan wars? There certainly is a difference. Their devastating effects are not limited to the countries involved in the strife, but the consequences of these wars are also affecting the lives of people in adjacent countries in various ways. What has the militant group of "Tamil Tigers" (now defunct) achieved in Sri Lanka after bringing misery and sorrow to civilians caught in the cross-fire? Their efforts zero down to nothing of consequence. India is continuing to quell Naxalite insurgency, which seems to be a tug of war between the insurgents and the State governments. Such human warfare only serves to destabilize harmony in the ecology adversely affecting the development of the human beings.

Academic interest in ecology has been focused on the integral and pivotal position of human ecology in its nexus. Early knowledge of elementary living was of the production and re-production of natural resources.[6] (Gadgil, M., & P. Thapar, 1990) This is not to say that all living beings in different geo-ecological areas have progressed without periods of instability, or have progressed at the same pace, along the "economic development dimension". The recent discovery of humanoid fossils indicate the existence of man about thirteen million years ago.[7] (Chakrabarti, D. K., 2004) Civilizations of human beings have come a long way since the earliest known existence of man — the Neanderthal Man.[8] (Cuozzo, Jack, 1999) This serves to illustrate that humans have lived much before those civilizations of which we have some knowledge. There is no way of knowing what their eco-systems were like. Over the years, differences have occurred in climate, in the degree of availability of flora and fauna, water and land in those zones.[9] (Dossel, D.P., & R. Gounder, 1994)

The differences in ecologies are compounded by the variations of the influential factors in the differing ecologies. If we trace humans in their ecologies along the dimension of sophisticated to elementary level patterns, we find interesting distinguishing features. For instance, the sophisticated patterns of living are more frequently observable in the Anglo-Saxon races of the western hemisphere than in the Negroids of Central Africa. The former are more acquainted with the utility of science and technology and the latter are naively innocent of them.

There is also the divide between the countries of the "North" and the "South", usually attached to the developed and the developing worlds, respectively. There is also a growing realization that development means more than economic development as it also includes social and emotional development.

However, powerful nations attempt to maintain the hiatus between the rich and the poor regions of the world. These are the self-styled developed world economies which continue to accrue to themselves power and territory.

In this century, the world is looking at the increasing development of the "Crouching Tiger", namely China, which at one time was in the netherlands of the "least developing countries", At times, westerners euphemistically equated development with democratic ideology, while communism was confined to those countries which were said to be oppressive. Currently, these beliefs are swept under the carpet, and overtly the co-existence of several ideologies is accepted. What concerns the leaders of politically powerful countries is territorial wielding authority over the less economically developing nations, so that their powerful status is retained.

In the case of India, not only has it juxtapositioned its status from the "least developed" to a growing economic power, but has also adopted a foreign ideology, namely, "democracy", after living under the aegis of several feudal regimes, the last being the British.[10] (Fuchs, Martin and Linkenbach, Antje, 2003) For a country that has been traditional for ages, the tenets of this new ideology is quite a challenge given the country's traditionality and heterogeneity.

The demographic contours of India are perhaps the major crucial factors relating man to land, where the human ecology pressurizes the geo-ecology. The major variable is, therefore, the proportion of productive human beings to the land's potentials. We have witnessed, for instance, the productivity of land in the previously arid areas of the middle-east countries. This is in stark contrast to the desert areas of Africa and, indeed, the Thar desert in India itself. Poor productivity of land tends to limit lifestyles to meeting mainly survival needs, and to nomadic lifestyles. Most western countries have more land (and that too, mostly fertile) in proportion to their human populations. One might also expect that there is more homogeneity in their living patterns with a better quality of life than those countries overburdened with high population in many differing poor-producing ecologies and with poor productivity. Additionally, poorly productive ecologies are burdened with larger masses of economically underprivileged individuals as is the case in India, which has more heterogeneity in its deprived sections in comparison with other countries of the developing world.

Why has the writer of this book undertaken to link the understanding of the development of the human personality with the staid conceptualizations of psychology and sociology and, to some extent, anthropology? This book attempts to include hitherto distal disciplines like ecology, economics, politics, and factors of globalization and national demographics, even though tangentially. These are included to put into perspective such aspects as poverty and the marginalised sections of the population, who make up at least fifty per cent of India. This book is not an esoteric attempt to emphasize mainly *emic* attributes, but is tied to ground realities of the majority, who live in the rural and tribal hinterlands of industrialized urban areas, wherein some places of the latter compare competitively well with western patterns of lifestyles. In the main, however, when describing generic psycho-social characteristics, which are the same for all human beings, examples are given mostly of the individuals living in poorer ecologies in the Indian sub-continent.

However, we do admit that in the last two decades in India, there is a discernible increase in economic productivity with the very high GDP growth of 9.7 per cent in 2007 as compared to 7.2 per cent in 2010 which shows that the Indian economic growth rate was not destabilized during the years of the global recession.[11] (Government of India, 2009-2010) But we also admit that the increased benefits of economic growth do not trickle down to the lowest rungs who are the most needy and for whom the government has chalked out specific "upliftment" programmes. These benefits get siphoned off by the top brasses in the urban and urbane segments of Indian society.

What will happen in the future considering that economic trends, social barriers and proportion of land productivity to man will continue to haunt the Indian scenario? What we do know is that, at the global level, economically speaking, China and India have better economic growth rates than do many of the Anglo-Saxon countries in this current context of economic recession. In the latter countries, their Governments have resorted to "bail-outs" for financial institutions like banks. What is hidden in the Indian context is that, about more than one-fourth of the population still live below the "poverty line" with poor geo-ecological facilities. The India Human Development Survey found poverty rates for rural areas to be 26.5 per cent and for urban areas to be 23.7 per cent.[12] (Desai, Sonalde B., Amaresh Dubey, Brij Lal Joshi, Mitali Sen, Abusaleh Shariff, and Reeve Venneman, 2010)

The India Human Development Survey finds that *Adivasis* and *Dalits* are at the bottom on most indicators of well-being, Muslims and "Other Backward Classes" (OBCs) occupy the middle range and "forward caste" Hindus and other well-to-do minority religious groups are at the top of the scale of well-being.[13] (*Ibid.*) Two factors of social groups seem to emerge: the first is inequality. This inequality stems from differential access to sources of livelihood. The second is that future generations seem doomed to replicate these inequalities of this generation, because of the continuing differences in education, income and quality and quantity of lifestyles. Added to these are the hardcore values of caste, *jat* and *jati*.

Why does a democratic country like India which has free primary education, free and/or subsidised medical facilities and several rural poverty-alleviation programmes still continue to have paradoxically a greater proportion living under scarce means. Again paradoxically, in the global scenario India is said to be economically growing at a faster rate than before. But this is obvious that the greater economic gains do not mean greater facilities for the poorer ecologies.

It is also obvious in the large canvas of other developing countries. Each has its own interpretation of what is a preferable "quality of life". To some, it means family harmony and the totality of human relationships, as in elementary societies. In other societies this means high profiled wealth and territorial power that wealth give to them.[14] (Srinivasan, T.N., 1994) If by chance, there happens to be, in a given society, the growth of economic and psychological well-being as well, then one could assume that the country is developed in these priority areas. For most poor nations of the world, their possession of autonomous territorial space does not automatically imply that they also have a well-balanced quality of life. At the same time, having a better economic status in comparison to other nations does not necessarily imply a better quality of life.[15] (Papenek, V., 1985)

The logic of the interaction of geo-ecology (autonomous territorial space) with human ecology spawns several strands of human behaviour. The more the humans utilise the earth and its products (without much effort to replace the earth's own sustenance of its geo-ecology), the more economically developed are the utilisers. This is euphemistically said to be because of their ability to accelerate the pace of science and technology. Therefore, they had to strive inevitably to climb further along that developmental staircase, utilising more and more of the earth's resources in order to remain different from those on the lower rungs of the staircase. On the one hand, human societies are at different levels of interactions with their ecologies, impacting on the differential levels of the quality of life. On the other hand, societies in their striving for economic wealth, take upon themselves greater stress to keep pace with scientific and technological development, which has its own negative consequences. The rate and quality of interaction with the environment keeps escalating, having a "domino effect". So that the higher the rate of economic and technological development, the greater the pressure to continue to do so. If we turn the scenario around, we find that in this very India, to this day, there are tribes whose lives are relatively untouched by scientific inroads[16] (Page, J.W., 1938). However, there are also tribes who are being exposed to change and represent the other end of the tribal ecological spectrum[17], (Sarkar, Amitabha, 1994). Thus, ecologies range from the economically well-developed to the economically less developed in terms of material facilities[18] (Sarkar, Q., & D.D. Dasgupta, 2000). Among the tribes in India, there are those who live physically arduous lives, hunting or gathering forest produce or as the Ao tribe of Mokokchung district in Nagaland, who live on shifting cultivation. Elementary farming societies tend to be closely tied to their natural environment. Through time and over space they develop beliefs in the supernatural powers of nature, and observe mystic and animistic types of rituals and practices, relating to the nature's benefits-giving properties. To this day, there are still tribes living at very elementary stages of civilization. For instance, the Andamanese is a tribe isolated on an island space. They are restricted in their movements, are closely related to the beliefs in the power of the elements, the transference of elements to humans and, *vice versa*, together with mysticism and spiriticism.[19] (Pandya, Vishvajit, 1993) There are other sub-societies which have learned intricately to utilise the earth's properties in a sophisticated manner, and divert their attention and money on travelling to other planets, while thousands of poor are languishing under the ravages of nature. The exploitation of the earth's resources is without thought to their rapid depletion or the need for reproductivity for a healthy balance in the eco-system. In the economically developed societies, time becomes money and money is a major criterion of who rules over whom. It is not unusual to hear that the United States is the richest and most powerful country in the world. According to the "givens" of economic, scientific and technological development, it probably is. Those societies which were previously innocent of such increased developmental indices of living, because of lack of communication, transport, education, and media, are now becoming more exposed to the higher standards of the developed countries.[20] (Sasson, A., & V. Costarini, 1991) It is not uncommon, therefore, that the peoples, especially the young of the developing nations, who live in poor conditions, experience a sense of frustration when viewing the surplus and the plenty of the developed nations.

There is a saying that "the grass is always greener on the other side", and psychological theories underscore the concept that admired models are imitated.[21] (Bandura, A., 1977) This imitation is observable in the behaviour of less developed societies. Therefore, how do economically low-profiled countries use strategies to imitate the high profiled? It is said, euphemistically speaking, that, when the rich countries sneeze, the poorer and more fragile countries develop pneumonia. This is because there is a rapid movement towards attaining riches as fast as possible, in the developing ecologies, and thus this creates pressures on personal capabilities in the developing ecologies. In the process, there is a confrontation between traditionality and modernity.[22] (Channa S.M., 2004)

The question might be legitimately asked here: What are the logical bases of attempting to relate personality types, as understood in the psycho-sociological sense, to the parameters of ecology, whether developed or developing? With reference to India as an economically developing country, we find that there are three emerging dynamic changes in the environment of the Indian.[23] (Adams, C. C., 1935) *Firstly*, the Indian is gradually emerging from his cocoon of traditionality, so to speak, and is increasingly interacting with peoples of other developed countries with the rider that this applies most especially to the urbanised industrial ecologies. In essence, the individual moves from one ecology to another. Ecologies, in our definition, are comparable to "species" of the genus, namely, the environment. This indicates specificity and a social reality. Thus, to say, for instance, that a ruralite moves from a village in Andhra Pradesh to work on a construction site as a daily labourer in Mumbai is to view the two environmental geo-ecological areas as being generically in contrast to each other. Ethnicity, sub-caste, language, food-habits and perhaps even socio-religious beliefs differ in differing ecologies in their specific parameters.[24] (Gulia, K. S., 2007)

Secondly, since we know that there is a strong relationship between the broad spectra of nature and nurture.[25] (Burks, B.S., 1942) We may surmise (although we have little data to substantiate it) that, the environment while being shaped by the human, it in turn affects the shaping of his personality. Even though phylogenetic principles indicate that human beings are generically the same in their potential generic skills[26] (Thomas, R.M., 2001), yet these are contoured by the interaction with the environment and specifically the human and natural ecology to develop ontogenetic skills.

All children learn to walk, talk and speak based on the fact that all have these inherent phylogenetic potentials. These potentials might be accelerated or decelerated by the ontogenetic potentials. For instance, the hunters and food gatherers develop perceptual, auditory and olfactory skills so as to reap their survival means from the ecology, and by deduction increases their cognitive competence.[27] (Berry, J.W., 1976) There is an increasing concern in the world's depletion of resources, and the limited capacities of the natural resources to regenerate rapidly to meet growing needs. At the same time, technologically developed countries in their industrialisation process emit polluting gases which affect the health of their societies. Currently the developed countries, aware of their transgressions in delimiting nature, are becoming more aware of the need for preservation of nature's resources.[28] (Landon, M., 2006) These concerns are to "save the planet" through remedial measures although the task is tremendous considering resources are limited and richer countries will need more from nature's resources than do the poor.[29] (Davis, M., 2006) In India, we see some glimmers of these contradictory needs. In the earlier decades, the middle class hardly had a vehicle and used public transport or lived in rented accommodations, but now many of them have at least one car and most own one house. The higher socio-economic groups have a fleet of cars and their drivers.

Thirdly, as the saying goes, "as the seed is sown so does the tree grow"; the significance of ecology is analogous to this. It is expressed by Fukuoka who describes ecological growth in simple analogies in his book *The One-Straw Revolution*[30] (Fukuoka, M., 1984). While physical sciences are galloping at a fast pace, with new discoveries and inventions, the social sciences which are trying to keep pace, are yet to discover their coordinated powers in understanding man's ability to cope with the new technologies and scientific inventions in his ecology. How the brain works despite the availability of some data, is yet not fully known, in spite of some empirical data, from the medical and neurosciences about the development of the brain and its correlative: the working of the mind.[31] (Liljencrants, J., 2007) We are beginning to perceive the need for large-scale quantitative data to contribute to theoretical conceptualisations relevant to the Indian psyche. At the same time, we know that qualitative data gives the wherewithal for stating hypotheses regarding human nature. Increasingly, the human understands more about nature through science and technology than understanding himself. There is a saying that "the mind is like a knife, it can cut others but cannot cut itself. There are, therefore, still unexplored dimensions of the science of the mind. One might say that it is easier to predict natural disasters than human disasters. As such we have the co-habitation of a dynamically developing human, namely, his personality which proceeds on hypothetical basis; and the more or less predictable events in nature due to science and technology. Therefore, the science of the mind is elusive, but the science of nature is within man's perceptual orbit. For example, currently tsunamis are predictable, but personality disorders are not, unless evident.

Therefore, human ecology has to develop as fast or at least as nearly as rapid as the physical sciences and their products, so that human coping mechanisms are in place to balance human ecology with the geo-ecology. The growing world of social reality as to what happens in a rural village, in a slum conglomerate or an *Adivasi* hamlet are not adequately amplified by empirical data. Perhaps, the closest amplification of ecology and human development is reflected in the series of empirical data by scholars who analysed economic deprivation and cognitive skills.[32] (Mishra, G., 1982) As academicians we are usually caught in their own net of unidisciplinary conceptualisations to explain human behaviour without cognition of a holistic expression. In India, human behaviour is out there in the open, and is now being monitored, modulated and manipulated by other impinging factors such as the degradation of the geo-ecology, the dissonance in human ecology, and changing negative demographic factors. Coupled with this is the growing phenomenon of agitation by tribals and villagers in the hinterlands whose lands are being grabbed by cash-rich industrialists and MNCs, such as the acquisition of village lands around large cities for industrial purposes. There are other phenomena which indicate agitation and destabilisation. These are the rapid growth of cities like Navi Mumbai and the hinterland of the capital metropolis. While the issues are large 'out there' like displacement of tribals, destabilisation of agriculturalists who have sold their agricultural lands and the in-roads of the Naxalites decimating innocent people, and the protest of the *Gujjars* for representation are indicative of dissonance between the people and the governance of the land. Questions are being asked: When will the Malthusian theory come to an end, when demand will be in equilibrium with supply and population growth will be contained?, Will population be stabilised at the end of the 21st century, as discussed by Wolfang *et al.*[33] (Lutz, Wolfang, Warren C. Sandersan & Sergei Scherbov, 2004) This intriguing theme has also been amply discussed by Cohen who uses telling predictive data to analyse this question.[34] (Cohen, Joel, 1995) If the Arctic and Antarctic circles melt down their glaciers, will there be more earthquakes, cyclones and floods? In short, how will human beings cope with the changing and shrinking ecology? This is based on the limited capacities of the peoples to cope with their ecology, given that their capacity to invent strategies to overcome these natural and contributing man-made disasters are not proactive, but are reactive.

The social sciences need to look more incisively at the specific effects of the ecology. In the past we understood environment to be a general rubric for ecology. We are becoming now more aware of its increasing parameters, influencing human habitat and, therefore, the development of the inhabitants.

This book, therefore, aims at providing a reference for understanding the relationship between man and his ecology in India. It is expected that it will be of utility to students of the social sciences, political sciences and humanistic ecological concerns. The chapters of the book relate to the importance of the development of the individual within given ecologies in India: ranging from high mountainous areas to the plains, to the large line of coastal areas, to remote rural areas and to highly sophisticated urbanites in metropolitan areas. This concern arises from the growing knowledge that *Indians while subscribing to core Indian values are as heterogeneous as varying countries in a continent*. The individuals' patterns of lifestyle are both heterogeneous at the specific ground levels and at the same time homogeneous at the generic and abstract conceptual levels. The topics of this book have been carefully structured to synchronise with the topics prescribed in major curricula for students in higher education in the social sciences. There is a caveat, however, namely, that the major concepts in their construct formulations are derived from what is available in the social sciences in India and adapting the major information by classical well-known academicians and theorists from the west. While the personality theories are scarce in the Indian context, except for a few mini-theoretical concepts like those of Kakar[35]. (1966, 1978), Paranjpe[36] (1988), Roland[37] (1980), Sylvan[38] (1981) and Neki.[39] (1976) There has been little tested theorising related to the Indian psyche. At the most there is a personality theory based on *gunas,* which is gaining popularity in analysis of human behaviour, based on the *Samkhya* concept of man's conduct in Hindu philosophy.[40] (Jerath, J.M., & Anjum Sibia, 2009). "It is difficult to identify any one person as being the average Indian since no one Indian is identical with another since Indians come from various ecologies, ethnic and socio-religious groups. The use of the word Indian here is to indicate a generic Indian personality."

The major thesis of this book is, therefore, the homogeneity of the Indian, modulated by his heterogeneous ecologies. Human beings do not grow up and adults do not become parents in a vacuum. Their development is always in a physical and social context.[41] [Bornstein, Marc H., & Michael E. Lamb (eds.), 2005: 1]

REFERENCES

1. Khalakdina, M., 2008, "Societal mores: Their implications for human development". In M. Khalakdina, *Human Development in the Indian Context*, Vol. 1, New Delhi: Sage Publications, pp. 311-338.
2. Bronfenbenner, U., 1979, *The Ecology of Human Development.* Cambridge, MA.: Harvard University Press.
3. Bowlby, J., 1998, *Attachment and Loss. Vol. 1, Attachment*. London: Hogarth.
4. United Nations, 2010, *Climate Change Conference*, Copenhagen.
5. Gruberg, Martin & Louise K. Comfort, 2009, *A Record of Natural and Social Disasters and their Political Implications: A New Issue for Public Planners*. Edwin Mellen Press.
6. Gadgil, M., 1987, "Cultural and Biological Trends", *Ecology and Evolution*, 2 (12), pp. 369-373.
7. Chakrabarti, D. K., 2004, *Indus Civilization Sites in India: New Discoveries*. Mumbai: Marg Publications.
8. Cuozzo, Jack, 1999, *Buried Alive, The Startling Truth about Neanderthal Man*, Master Books, Green Forest, AR.
9. Dossel, D.P., & R. Gounder, 1994, "Theory and measurement of living levels: Some empirical results for the Human Development Index", *Journal of International Development*, 6, pp. 415-435.

10. Fuchs, Martin and Linkenbach, Antje, 2003, *"Social Movements"*, in V. Das (ed.), *The Oxford India Companion to Sociology and Social Anthropology*, New Delhi: Oxford University Press.
11. Government of India, *Economic Survey*, 2009-2010.
12. Desai, Sonalde B., Amaresh Dubey, Brij Lal Joshi, Mitali Sen, Abusaleh Shariff, and Reeve Venneman, 2010, *Human Development in India: Challenges for a Society in Transition*. New Delhi: Oxford University Press, pp. 209.
13. *Ibid.*
14. Srinivasan, T.N., 1994, "Human Development: A New Paradigm or the Reinvention of the Wheel?" *American Economic Review Papers and Proceedings*, 84, pp. 238-243.
15. Papenek, V., 1985, Design for the Real World: Human Ecology and Social Change. London: Thames and Hudson.
16. Page, J.W., 1938, Primitive Races to-day. London: George Harrap.
17. Sarkar, Amitabha, 1994, *Industrialisation and Change in a Primitive Community*. New Delhi: Gyan Publishing House.
18. Sarkar, Q., & D.D. Dasgupta, 2000, *Ethno-ecology and Indian Tribes*. Jaipur: Rawat Publishers.
19. Pandya, Vishvajit, 1993, *Above the Forest: A Study of Andamanese Ethno Anemology, Cosmology and the Power of Ritual*. Delhi: Oxford University Press.
20. Sasson, A., & V. Costarini, 1991, *Biotechnologies in Perspective: Socio-economic Implications for Developing Countries*. Paris: UNESCO (1991), pp. 166.
21. Bandura, A., 1977, *Social Learning Theory*. Englewood Cliffs, New Jersey: Prentice Hall, pp. 486.
22. Channa, S.M., 2004, "Globalisation and modernity in India", *Journal of Urban Anthropology*, Studies of Cultural Systems and World Economic Development, Vol. 3.
23. Adams, C. C., 1935, "The relation of general ecology to human ecology", *Ecology, 16, 316-35.*
24. Gulia, K. S., 2007, *Human Ecology of Cultural Entities*. New Delhi: Gyan Book Publishers.
25. Burks, B.S., 1942, "A study of identical twins reared apart under differing types of family relationships". In Q. McNemar & M. A. Merrill (eds.), *Studies in Personality*. New York: McGraw Hill.
26. Thomas, R.M., 2001, *Recent Theories of Human Development*. California: Sage, pp. 271.
27. Berry, J.W., 1976, *Human Ecology and Cognitive Style: Comparative Study in Cultural and Psychological Adaptation*. New York: Halsted.
28. Landon, M., 2006, *Environment, Health and Sustainable Development*. London: Open University Press.
29. Davis, M., 2006, *Planet of Slums*. New York: Verso Books.
30. Fukuoka, M., 1984, *The One-Straw Revolution: An Introduction to Natural*

Farming. Rasulia, Hoshangabad, India: Friends Rural Centre (Originally published in 1978 by Rodale Press Inc, Emmaus, PA, USA).

31. Liljencrants, J., 2007, *Spiritism and Religion: A Moral Study*. Montana: Kessinger Publishing Company, p. 316.
32. Mishra, G., 1982, "Motivational Structure and Prolonged Deprivation", *Indian Journal of Social Work*, 43(1), 11-18.
33. Lutz, Wolfang, Warren C. Sandersan & Sergei Scherbov, 2004, *The End of World Population Growth in the 21st Century*. New Challenges for Human Capital Formation and Sustainable Development. London: Earthscan.
34. Cohen, Joel, 1995, *How Many People Can the Earth Support?* New York: W.W. Norton & Co.
35. Kakar, S., 1966, *The Indian Psyche*. New Delhi: Viking Penguin; Kakar S., 1978, *The Inner World: A Psychoanalytic Study of Childhood and Society in India*. Delhi: Oxford University Press.
36. Paranjpe, A.C., 1988, 'A Personality Theory according to Vedanta', in A.C. Paranjpe, D.Y.F. Ho, & R.W. Ribber (eds.), *Asian Contributions to Psychology*, pp. 185-213, New York: Praeger.
37. Roland, A., 1980, 'Psychoanalytical Perspective on Personality Development in India', *International Review of Psychoanalysis*, No. 7, 73-87.
38. Silvan, M., 1981, 'Reply to Alan Roland's Paper on Psycho-Analytic Perspectives on Personality Development in India', *International Review of Psycho-Analysis*, 8(1), pp. 93-99.
39. Neki, J. S., 1976, 'An Examination of the Cultural Relativism of Dependence as a Dynamic of Social and Therapeutic Relationships: 1. Socio-Developmental', *British Journal of Medical Psychology*, 49(1), 1-10; 73.
40. Jerath, J.M., & Anjum Sibia, 2009, *"Trends in Personality Research: An Overview"*, in G. Misra, *Psychology in India, Vol. I: Basic Psychological Processes and Human Development. Introduction*, pp. 263-306. Delhi: Indian Council of Social Science Research / Pearson Education in South Asia.
41. Bornstein, Marc H., & Michael E. Lamb (eds.), 2005, *Developmental Science: An Advanced Textbook.* Lawrence Erlbaum Association Ltd.

Contents

Contents

List of Tables, Paradigms and Flow Charts

LIST OF TABLES

LIST OF PARADIGMS

LIST OF FLOW CHARTS

Introduction

This book sets out to specify the human and geo-ecology in which the human being grows up and becomes a personality. It also seeks to find a logical nexus of the growing personality as affecting and being affected by the surroundings which make up the individual's ecology. The book also seeks to analyze the following:

- *What concepts identify the operational definition of geo-ecology?*
- *What is its importance, globally, nationally and for the individual in his family network?*
- *What are the ideational processes that take place in the individual's repertoire?*
- *What concepts influence the moulding of a personality?*
- *How does a person affects and become affected by his ecology of other individuals and the geo-ecological factors surrounding him?*

This book attempts in some measure to answer these questions. Given the fact that relating man to his geo- ecology is a philosophical idiom, operationalising geo-ecology in relation to man's development is a challenge. The human because of his continual experiences in his setting comes to know that the surroundings affect his style of living. For example, living in metropolitan cities, he becomes familiar with and assimilates the events, the relationships and the phenomena in his ecology, which consists of his family members and many others he comes in contact with. His mode of communication is both oral and written. He also uses electronic media for communication. His means of transport is usually a vehicle. If he is not an agriculturist, he does not have to farm to produce food for his daily needs. The given ecology meets all his needs for articles, artefacts and services through a process of series of interactions with the world around him. This involves industry, economic exchange of goods and services, for which he makes use of money and banking for transactions, and other facilities in his ecology which he takes for granted.

How do people perceive their environment? How do they adjust to their environment? What do they have to do to accommodate to their environment? Let us illustrate by a simple story.

A simple villager who worked as a daily labourer during harvesting was sitting by a river side, eating his simple *roti* and *sabzi* under a tree, surveying the little birds which came hopping around the gentle flow of the river. An extension worker (village level worker) who was walking along the path stopped and went up to him.

"*Bhai sahib*, why are you sitting doing nothing?"

"I am watching what is around me."

"No, no, *bhai sahib*. You should not sit idle. You must be doing something."

"What should I do?" asked the bewildered villager.

"Have you studied?"

"Yes, I have," replied the villager, thinking that this Nosy-Parker would go away. But he did not.

He persisted, "You must do more than that".

"What else should I do?" asked the now amused villager.

"You must work harder and not sit around."

"OK. After that what?"

"After that you must get a job," said the extension worker.

"OK, I will try that," replied the villager. "But, after that?"

"After that, you can get married and have a family."

"OK, after that?"

"Why", said the now puzzled extension worker, thinking, this man had no idea what to do.

"After that?"

"Then you will have money."

"After that"

"After that", said the exasperated extension worker, "Why, you will be happy".

"But," said the villager, "I am happy now. Why should I go through all that trouble to be what I am now? Happy".

The moral of the story is apparent. Each individual has his own perception of what makes for happiness.

This simple villager has found his strategy for a harmonious living. So what makes for harmony of man and nature is the capability and ingenuity of man to adjust to the habitat which he is born into. Or, if it is not his original habitat the one in which he resides: the community in which he lives; and his economic status which adjusts to the availability of goods and services. It is in that sphere that he is socialized to develop his habits and values. His main socialiser is his family, and the significant members, who tend, through the main socialiser to induct him into beliefs and values, which are societally approved, and which they themselves have been socialized into.[1] (Levine, Robert A., 2003)

Thus, *in the relevant situational framework children are taught to adapt to their ecology throughout their chronological age, so that at adulthood they achieve a fully developed personality that is uniquely their own.* Orthogenesis tells us that there is a pattern of unfolding process of inherent abilities and skills, which is a process articulated by the interaction of chronological time and chronological maturity.[2] (Misra, G., & K.N. Tripathi, 1993).

The first chapter deals with "*Ecology: Its Major Parameters*". The state of the art of how the natural environment, namely, ecology influences human development has grown in profile in the academic world. It is in consonant with the growing concerns about global warming, green-house pollution, the rising of the seas, the denudation of forests, and the changing of climatic seasons, causing devastating effects, such as increasing hurricanes, cyclones, and unpredictable floods and famine, devastating the earth's water resources. These phenomena need adaptable strategies for their sustainability.[3] (Hunt, Constance E., 2004) Gadgil, a leading social anthropologist, studied genetic lineage in human beings by assessing the lineage trees of families and found a strong correlation with the population parameters, and more especially with their language. *Brahmins* (Haviks) and *Mukris* (from scheduled castes) from Uttar Kannada district of Karnataka were interpreted from their DNA analysis that they were perhaps intermixed much before the caste system came into being some 2000 years back.[4] (Gadgil M. and Rao P.P.S., 1998) Apparently when families with similar needs and similar habits came together in clusters they tended to form clusters of homogeneous family network.[5] (Gadgil M. and Rao P.P.S., 1998). However, when they settled in scarce ecologies, their economic and poverty states became accelerated.[6] (Williams, L.K., 1973) The marginalized communities are as indicated in the table below:

Table 1: Marginalized Social Groups

Social Group	Mean Number of Social Network Connections
OBC	1.1
Dalits	0.8
Adivasi	0.6
Muslim	0.8

Source: India Human Development Survey 2004-05 data in Desai, Sonalde B. *et al.;* Human Development in India, 2010, Oxford University Press, New Delhi.

Together with these marginalized sections, the woman occupies a fragile position, although the sex-ratio is to her advantage, namely, for every 1000 males, there are only 933 females. Thus, we see that the most disadvantaged are: rural and urban poor females, the *Adivasis*, the Dalits and the poor Muslims. The poorer States are large in ecological space. It is our assumption that these large States are also those providing the most voting power for political gain of the opposing parties and, therefore, are of importance in the spheres of facilities or the lack of them, the probability of vote-catching and the attempt to retain these captive sections at their marginalized levels.

The next chapter, in our estimate, is an important one as it sets the stage for the physical surroundings, namely, the ecology, which interacts with the individual in a mutually reciprocal manner. This chapter is entitled *"The Human Ecology of the Individual*". What effect do the physical and human settings have on the individual in his development and behaviour? For example, it is known that the geo-ecology in the north Indian hill regions are devoid of iodized salt, which could lead to cretinism in physically growing children living in these geo-ecologies. Again, how does the individual adjust to his social group in a specific ecology, whether it is an urban conglomerate, or a remote isolated tribal area, where the individual pursues intergenerational habits of living, which gives him a sense of security in what is known. How does the individual act and interact with his environment of particular individual groups and institutions? What effects do they have in moulding his development and behaviour? These are themes discussed in the aforesaid chapters. These themes have immense importance in the unique Indian context, for the individual in moving towards formulating his identity is also geared towards competence in interacting with his social group, namely, the human ecology, where he learns coping mechanisms, adapted to his geo-ecology.[7] (Bronfenbrenner, U., 1993)

As such, we will first examine the conceptual underpinnings of ecology as it has developed into a science encompassing the geo-ecology and the human ecology.[8] (Marten, G., 2001) We attempt to present this analysis in relation to concepts which have proven theoretical bases, or at least rest on acceptable assumptions and frameworks. In order to understand that it is a person who is developing into a personality, we will first attempt to give the basic tenets of a theory, and the basics of important principles of theory-building in socio-psychology in the third chapter entitled "*Theoretical Basis of Personality Development*." We recognize that there are various theories of personality of specific well-constructed and tried-out conceptualizations which have stood the test of time, such as Behaviourism, Cognitive Development,[9] (Piaget, J., 1954) Psychoanalysis, and those which deal with specific domains such as needs[10] (Murray, H. A., 1938 & 1951) and motivations.[11] (Atkinson, J.W., 1964). We consider that Eriksson's psychodynamic theory of the lifecycle[12] (Eriksson, E.H., 1974) and Bronfenbrenner's theory of the ecosystems[13] (Bronfenbrenner, U., 1986) are important constructs which are relatively closer to understanding the Indian psyche in his socio-religious and philosophical frame. Eriksson's theory of the lifecycle has been used in tandem by Indian psycho-analysts like Kakar[14] (Kakar, S., 1981) and Neki[15] (Neki, J.S., 1976) as it is co-relative with the life stages conceived in the *samskaras*. In the descriptions and analyses of these theories we find a unique similarity of concepts and approaches among them, which reflect the interactive dynamism of human nature and behaviour. These are discussed in the fourth chapter entitled "*Selected Personality Theories Relevant to the Indian Psyche*". We underscore that these theories are progressions of underlying concepts of development as processes leading to a product, namely, the human personality.[16] (Valsiner, Jaan, & Connolly, Kevin, J., 2003) If there is a progression in development, admittedly there must be a relationship among the psycho-sociological events of the life span. These events of development take place during various age-related stages. For instance, the pre-operational stage of Piaget's schema occurs in early infancy, and the trait of development of identity, according to Eriksson, occurs during adolescence.[17] (Eriksson, E. H., 1965) Further, most of the biological and physical development are rooted in early childhood, starting as early as the foetal stage.[18] (Hepper, Peter, 2003) Ego and defense mechanisms are used as coping mechanisms throughout life, from conception to old age. These specific phenomena occur which influence the Indian psyche relevant to the unique society wherein, for instance, the elderly are exposed to disengaging events.[19] (Jensen, Anne-Margaret, & Lorna McKee, 2003) We also describe the *samskaras* and their philosophy as the indigenous Indian philosophical view on development. In conceptual terms, for instance, the stage of the *grihastha* is the stage at which the family of procreation begins, and there are other specific influences on the parent and child generation. The individual's growth is examined through selected major personality theories which reflect on the end product of a developed individual.

Emanating from the *Samkhya* system of thought, the theory of *guna* postulates a three-fold nexus, namely, *trigunas, as* relating to thought processes.[20] (Kulkarni, T.R., 1972) They may be hypothesized as thought processes operating at the three levels of the *gunas*, or may be hypothesized as a theory of individual differences.[21] (Paranjpe, A.C., 1998)

The relationship between the developing human being and his ecology is inextricably woven as the individual accumulates experiences from the ecological environment that fulfils his needs.[22] (Frank, N. Egerton, 1973) In the earlier seventies and late eighties, Singh in his two sociological analyses indicated the unfolding of social change affecting human behaviour in the Indian "caste society".[23] (Singh, Y., 1977; Singh, Y, 1980) In 1993, ecology began to assume greater dimensions with the growth of science and technology uncovering more of the dimensions of demographic imbalance.[24] (The Fred H. Bixby Forum, 2009) This was considered in relation to the imbalance caused by conflict and displacement of people which has risen in this century. The civil strife in Dartford, Congo, Somalia, Iraq and, more recently, in Afghanistan and the borders of Pakistan are destabilising the lives of the civilians within them where people have to live in camps.[25] (Lutz, Wolfgang; Warren C. Sanderson & Sergei Scherbor, 2001).

The fifth chapter on "*Correlates of the Developing Personality*" explores the implications of the extended parameters of ecology and culture. These parameters impact on the dynamic behaviour of the individual in the nexus of his societal frame. In a country like India, educational infrastructures are inadequate and personnel poorly trained for nearly three-quarters of the population, who mostly live in rural and tribal areas.[26] (Dreze, J. & Sen Amartya, 2002)

It also explores dimensions such as multi-culturism, ecological relativity, traditionality and scientism, as also the cohabitation of technological development with social development and ecological systems.[27] (Berkes, F., & C. Folke, 1998) In the Indian system there is a conscious effort to conserve water resources.[28] (The National Commission for Integrated Water Resources Development, 1999) As a telling point in contrasting differing societal segments, which are both developing and developed, we attempt to highlight the contrasting psycho-social elements among them. These contrasting elements are mainly in the styles of socialization and patterns of living according to their well-understood socio-cultural norms. This chapter explores the implications of the extended parameters of culture, which impact on the dynamic behaviour of the individual in the nexus of his cultural frame. What is the ecology like, which has significance on the growing individual? On this question, we depend on human and physical factors. This is related to "the deficit *versus* difference hypothesis" stated by Jensen with reference to intelligence and race[29] (Jensen, A.R., 1969) and the construct of economic deprivation and economic poverty condition in which the human lives.[30] (Misra, G., 1982) It is probable that intelligence becomes depressed when prolonged economic deprivation occurs.[31] (Misra, G., & Tripathi, K.N., 2004) What happens in the face of economic deprivation in the case of displaced families? In such situations, family disorganisation in crowded urban slums, the ravages of natural and man-made disasters are generally the spin-off effects of a deprived ecology.[32] (Papenek, 1985) Indians and their ecology are also affected by social beliefs, socio-religious norms, social and family expectations which are attributes of the human ecology.[33] (Alphale, C., 1976)

To elucidate these radial factors affecting the habitat of the social individual, these correlates are expatiated in this chapter. To exemplify differential patterns of development, four societies are examined in the specific domain of child-rearing practices and living patterns. These varying ecologies have been selected as they highlight the pattern of living in an ecology that is elementary, namely, the south sea islanders; a tribal society in transition between traditionality and modernity in India.[34] (Adams, Charles C., 1935) At the other end are, two westernised but differing ideological societies, which then indicate the positing of a different theme, namely, economically developed but ideologically different societies. These are the United States and the erstwhile USSR.[35] (Bronfenbrenner, U., 1972) The purpose of presenting these different patterns in the fabric of habitat and its related effect on the individual is to indicate that no matter what the geo-ecological territorial environment is like, the human nature has the adaptability and resilience to live in harmony with the given ecology, human and geo-political.[36] (Bennett, J.W.,1996)

Therefore, the thematic conceptualisation is a combination of psychological constructs related to the developing personality in his sociological frame, namely, the family, which is further nested in his geo-ecology. However, to the individual, the human environment around him is the most frequent and the most intense interactive process that he experiences. As a child matures chronologically, his circles of human contact increase, and he learns more about the various multiple interactive processes which impinge upon his tendencies, his nature and his attributes.

The discussions on the inclusion of human behaviour in the biological domain termed ethnology began in the nineteenth century. This may be taken to imply the beginning of human ecology which was assuming importance. Further, the concept of a holistic approach to the integration of natural sciences and social sciences was also being explored.[37] (Raghubir Singh Pirta, 2009) We have used the term ecology in its broadest sense to clearly indicate, what has also been known from ancient *Indian scriptures the relationship between man and nature*, in all things living and non-living. In the Indian culture, in growing importance, the three-dimensional effect of ecology, politics and human development are being intertwined in a highly complex manner.[38] (Spooner, B., 1984) Therefore, cognizance is also to be taken of other than socio-psychological factors affecting developing personalities, namely, the political governing structures, factions within some states such as the Naxalites, the ULFA and the Kashmir militants, peoples' movements like Chipko and Narmada Bachao Andolan.[39] (Brara Rita, 2003)

The sixth chapter deals with the highly complex pattern of the interaction of personalities in their habitats, namely their specific ecologies. The framework of the ecology and the habitat of the individual have a particular period in social historicity.[40] (Dunbois, J.A., & H. Beauchamp, 1978) This chapter is entitled "*The Interlinkages between Personality Development and Ecology*". This has been emphasized by Pirta in his analysis of the interaction of science and technology, and a holistic approach to the study of human behaviour[41] (Raghubir Singh Pirta, 2009) It deals with the changing scenario towards a 'global village' which propels the individual along the dimension from traditionality to modernity, perhaps by fits and starts, with trials and tribulations, but nevertheless moving along that path.[42] (Sharma, D., 2003) In the context of a telescoped world, these phenomena imply the co-twin of technological change and social mores. It is perhaps predictable that social and technological change will bring about challenges in human behaviour. Given the volatile situation of the nations in their interaction with the growing ecological changes, the global economic recession and global warming are affecting India, particularly in its fiscal and trade policies and programmes.[43] (Dolsak, N., & E. Ostrom, 2003) These upheavals are transitory in nature, giving rise to others, as India is moving towards a world market, a higher GDP and, inexorably, towards a better quality of life.[44] (Sirgy, M. J., 2002) These upheavals lead to both the negative and positive aspects of modernization. Therefore, proactive cognizance needs to be taken into consideration about future directions of enquiry. Thus, the social sciences need to reflect these interactions, vicissitudes and fine nuances of a changing kaleidoscope of developmental trends. For instance, schools are moving towards an understanding of an increasing technology becoming an integral part of computer teaching skills, where a couple of decades ago "chalk and board' method was the major technique for teaching in classroom situations.[45] (Srivastava, S., 2003) Now, it is becoming more possible for students than their elders to have quick access to knowledge as they tend to have greater interaction with the modern systems of information. This interactive nature of the individual with his surroundings and *vice versa* reflect the way in which the social sciences view and represent global changes.[46] (Curtis, W. E., 2004) The importance of ecological influences as affecting the development of the Indian, in his contextual situation, presents the need for a realistic understanding of the Indian in his culture *per se* vis-à-vis other cultures. Yet, the ecology keeps changing dynamically, and so does the Indian, as the global network brings about greater interaction of the Indian with the rest of the world. Social change and continuity are, therefore, not in direct opposition but complement each other.

We have expressed our concern that no longer is the Indian isolated within the contours of this country. There are many movements of the Indian from one geo-ecology to another and several protests such as the tribals in their displacement for industrialisation. We have admitted that we lack adequate empirical data regarding the development of the Indian *per se*. There are still many gaps. For example, how do we — a great nation of over 1.2 billion, a nation that has lived through the ravages of invasions, feudal strifes, a colonial overlord, becoming a democratic nation or at least espousing its principles — continue to live heterogeneously in the major poverty environments? How interlinked is India with the international world through its diaspora? We do not know precisely about these issues, although there are guesstimates galore. The last chapter entitled *"Proactive Perspectives"* essentially takes a leap forward into possible predictive areas of further enquiry. The dimensions discussed relate to both the macro and the micro levels of the ecosystems, and are expressed as challenging areas for further critical enquiry. The growing expectations of the masses who are now exposed to the electronic world of telescoped space and time have to be met with adequate facilities, services in a milieu that has a work ethic. For example, an ordinary street vendor uses a cellular with great efficiency, a tribal works on construction sites and learns about designs, physics and the combination of materials, the migrant workers live in crowded slums but have an organised lifestyle within this conglomerate. One might almost state that there should be greater academic proactive concern as to the oncoming stream of factors that will change the Indian's lifestyle in these ecosystems. This chapter underlines the yet unexplored dimensions of heterogeneity and more especially the large numbers of those in poverty and the more miniscule elite in their modes of living. This extreme imbalance causes upheaval in the movement towards a homogeneous society and, is therefore, a constant challenge.

REFERENCES

1. Levine, Robert A., 2003, ***Child and Socialisation: Comparative Studies of Parenting and Educational Change***. Washington: University of Washington Press.
2. Misra, G., & K.N. Tripathi, 1993, ***Perspectives on Human Development***. New Delhi: Sage.
3. Hunt, Constance E. 2004, ***Thirsty Planet: Strategies for Sustainable Water Management***. London. Zed Books.
4. Gadgil, M. and P.P.S. Rao, (1998), ***Nurturing Bio-Diversity: An Indian Agenda***. Ahmedabad: Centre for Environment Education.

5. *Ibid.*
6. Williams, L.K., 1973, "Some Developmental Correlates of Scarcity", *Human Relations*, 26, 51-65.
7. Bronfenbrenner, U., 1993, 'The Ecology of Cognitive Development: Research Models and Fugitive Findings', in R. Wozniak & K. W. Fischer (eds.), *Development in Cntext*, pp. 3-44. Hillsdale, N.J.: Erlbaum.
8. Marten, G., 2001, *Human Ecology*. London: Earthscan Publications, p. 256.
9. Piaget, J., 1954, *The Construction of Reality in the Child*, New York: Basic Books.
10. Murray, H. A., 1938, *Explorations in Personality*. New York: Oxford University Press.
    Murray, H.A., 1951, 'Some Basic Psychological Assumptions and Conceptions', *Dialectica*, 5, pp. 266-292.
11. Atkinson, J. W., 1964, *An Introduction to Motivation*. Princeton, New Jersey: D. Van Nostrand Company.
12. Erickson, E.H., 1974, *Dimensions of a New Identity*. New York: Norton.
13. Bronfenbrenner, U., 1986, 'Ecology of Family as a Context for Human Development: Research Perspectives', *Developmental Psychology*, 22, pp. 723-742.
14. Kakar, S., 1981, *The Inner World: A Psychoanalytic Study of Childhood and Society in India*. New Delhi: Oxford University Press.
15. Neki, J.S., 1976, 'An Examination of the Cultural Relativism of Dependence as a Dynamic of Social and Therapeutic Relationships: Socio Developmental', *British Journal of Medical Psychology*, 49(1), pp. 1-10.
16. Valsiner, Jaan, & Connolly, Kevin J., 2003, 'The Nature of Development: The Continuing Dialogue of Processes and Outcomes', 'Introduction' in Jaan Valsiner & Kevin J. Connolly (eds.), *Handbook of Developmental Psychology*. pp. ix-xviii. London/Thousand Oaks: Sage.
17. Erickson, E. H., 1965, 'Youth: Fidelity and Diversity', in E.H. Erikson, (ed.), *The Challenge of Youth*. pp. 1-28. Garden City, New York: Doubleday (original work published 1963).
18. Hepper, Peter, 2003, 'Prenatal Psychological and Behavioural Development', in Jaan Valsiner & Kevin J. Connolly (eds.), *Handbook of Developmental Psychology*, pp. 91-119. London/ Thousand Oaks: Sage.

19. Jensen, Anne-Margaret, & McKee, Lorna, 2003, *Children and the Changing Family: Between Transformation Negotiation.* London; New York: Routledge, Falmer.
20. Kulkarni, T.R., 1972, *Upnishads and Yoga.* Bombay: Bhartiya Vidya Bhavan.
21. Paranjpe, A.C., 1998, *Self and Identity in Indian Thought and Modern Psychology.* New York: Plenum Press.
22. Frank, N. Egerton, 1973, "Changing Concepts of the Balance of Nature", *Quarterly Review of Biology*, 48, pp.322-50.
23. Singh, Y., 1977, *Modernisation of the Indian Tradition.* Faridabad, India: Thompson Press.
    Singh, Y, 1980, *Social Stratification and Change in India.* Faridabad, India: Manohar Press. p.157.
24. The Fred H. Bixby Forum, 2009, *A Scientific Investigation of the Impact of Global Population Changes on a Divided Planet.* Held on Jan. 23 and 24, 2009, in Berkeley, California.
25. Lutz, Wolfgang; Warren C. Sanderson & Sergei Scherbor, 2001, The End of the World Population Growth in the 21st Century: *New Challenges for Human Capital Formation and Sustainable Development.* London: Earthscan Publishers.
26. Dreze, J., & Amartya Sen, 2002, Social Disparities in Educational Attainments. New Delhi: Oxford University Press, pp. 152-177.
27. Berkes, F., & C. Folke (eds.), 1998, *Linking Social and Ecological Systems.* Cambridge University Press.
28. The National Commission for Integrated Water Resources Development, 1999, *Integrated Water Resources Development: A Plan for Action.* New Delhi: Government of India.
29. Jensen, A.R., 1969, 'How Much Can We Boost IQ and Scholastic Achievement?' Harvard Ed. Rev., 39, 1-123
30. Misra, G., 1982, "Motivational Structure and Prolonged Deprivation, *Indian Journal of Social Work*, 43(1), 11-18.
31. Misra, G., & Tripathi, K.N., 2004, "Psychological Dimensions of Poverty and Deprivation", in J. Pandey (ed.), *Psychology in India Revisited: Developments in the Discipline* (Vol. 3): Applied Social and Organisational Psychology. New Delhi: Sage.
32. Papenek, V., 1985, *Design for the Real World: Human Ecology and Social Change.* London: Thames and Hudson.
33. Alphale, C., 1976, "Religious and Traditional Rites", in C. Aphale, Growing up in an Urban Complex. pp. 48-65. New Delhi: National Publishing House.

34. Adams, Charles C., 1935, "The Relationship of General Ecology to Human Ecology", *Ecology*, 16, pp.342-63.
35. Bronfenbrenner, U., 1972, *Two Worlds of Childhood: U.S.A. and U.S.S.R.* New York: Russel Sage Foundation.
36. Bennett, J.W., 1996, *Human Ecology and Human Behaviour*. M.A.: Harvard University Press.
37. Raghubir Singh Pirta, 2009, "Biological and Ecological Bases of Behaviour", In Misra G., (ed.) *Psychology in India,* Volume I. Dorling Kindersley (India) Pvt. Ltd., pp. 5, 6).
38. Spooner, B., 1984, *Ecology in Development: A Rationale for Three-Dimensional Policy.* United Nations University Press, UN University: New York, USA, Unipub (distributor).
39. Brara Rita, 2003, "Ecology and Environment", in V. Das (ed.) *The Oxford University Press Companion to Sociological and Socio Anthropological,* New Delhi: Oxford University Press, pp. 171, 173.
40. Dunbois, J.A., & Beauchamp, H., 1978, *Hindu Manners, Customs and Ceremonies*. New Delhi: Oxford University Press.
41. Raghubir Singh Pirta, 2009, "Biological and Ecological Bases of Behaviour", In Misra G., (ed.) *Psychology in India,* Volume I, Dorling Kindersley (India) Pvt. Ltd.
42. Sharma, D., (ed.), 2003, *Childhood, Family and Socio-cultural Change in India: Reinterpreting the Inner World.* New Delhi: Oxford.
43. Dolsak, N., & E. Ostrom (eds.), 2003, *The Commons in the New Millennium: Challenges and Adaptation.* Cambridge, Massachusetts: MIT Press.
44. Sirgy, M. J., 2002, *The Psychology of Quality of Life.* Blacksburg Virginia: Virginia Polytechnic Institute and State University.
45. Srivastava, S., 2003, 'Schooling Culture and Modernity', in V. Das (ed.), *The Oxford Indian Companion to Sociology and Social Anthropology.* Vol. 2, pp. 998-1031. New Delhi: Oxford University Press.
46. Curtis, W. E., 2004, *Modern India. Entering the 21st Century.* Washington, D.C.: Kessinger Publications; and World Bank.

1

Ecology: Its Major Parameters

This chapter consists of the following sections:

1. The meaning of ecology for human development.
2. The beginnings of ecology as a scientific discipline.
3. Attempts in India to preserve Heritage and Develop Bio-Technology.
4. The place of epigenetic rules in human ecology.
5. Ecological deprivation and its effects on human abilities.
6. The factors of deprivation: Economic and Social—and their complex interactions.
7. Relationships among caste, class and geographical areas within the ecological parameters.
8. The psychological dimensions of traditionality and modernity in the ecological framework.

1. The Meaning of Ecology for Human Development

The terms ecology, environment and culture are taken as related and in some respects are overlapping constructs when popularly used. This causes confusion, as they are actually different conceptual constructs. The "environment" as an abstract concept encompasses the totality of surroundings and may be applied as an overall term. For instance, when we say, "the environment is invigorating", it means the totality of happenings in a particular environment is harmonious, like a conference environment. *The term "culture" implies the social customs, conventions, mores and attributes of a particular civilisation*, that qualifies an individual society. Whereas, 'ecology" denotes the concrete objects, artefacts, items in the environment which are living and non-living, including the human, inclusive of air, water, land and energy.

It was Haeckel who proposed a science to study organisms in their environment and called it *Oekologie* (a Greek word for living place), where life and its development were holistically conceived.[1] (Clarke, R., 1973) Ecology was first initiated in its pristine conceptual form in the biological sciences. Ecology first evolved from a biological concept, beginning with zoology, to a bio-human ecological one. It has spread to a holistic conceptualisation in its scientific principles of human living. Added to this conceptualisation, are the principles of conditionality applied to everyday living experiences. As new discoveries occurred, they revealed many unknown areas of influence on human behaviour, such as the relevance linkages in the genome map in relation to specific human races. For, the physical and neurological sciences increasingly offer a greater understanding of the human being in his ecology.[2] (Canadian Council on Social Development, 1996). *Ecology revolves around the concepts as to what influences adaptation and survival of the organism of a particular species.* It further explored how a stable interdependence among species and their populations created and maintained equilibrium in the environment. In this chapter, the focus is on the eco-natural system interacting with the human beings living in that specific eco–environmental space influenced and influencing events in the situations.

The early years of the individual's development are the foundational bases for the maturing individual. During these years, the individual's distinct personal identity is formed through the integration of a set of unique traits. They are fostered by a set of cognitive processes, influenced by the natural setting in which the individual is placed. These combinations of relationships occur in a context which is eco-culture-specific. The context implies a specific collation of natural settings in which human development begins, proceeds and then attritions over a period of time.[3] (Gunnar, M., 1998) While there are periods of equilibrium in the pattern of living in a given habitat, it does not exist for long. Like a kaleidoscope, it changes to another sceñario, till it lasts its time span and then changes again. A child for instance is home-bound in the early years, and when of school age, the spatial boundary of his existence becomes composed of both the home and school, and is additive with increasing life experiences. The space in which the human organism lives and develops is observable from even the conceptual level when the organism is a foetus and is influenced by his mother's health status. We find that behaviour changes occur with the chronological changes in the physiological make up of the individual.

Besides physiological mechanisms, in the Indian context, the spiritual world also influences development. *According to the Vedic philosophy, the consciousness of the "self" occurs with the development of the consciousness of "being" or one's existence*. Vedic philosophy relates the "self" to the concept of the "soul", which is said to be immutable.[4] (Kak, Subhas C., 2000) After its existence in the transient life of a human being, the "soul" transmigrates and takes another life-form. Thus, the consciousness of the "self" in the working of the temporal mind directs behavioural output along with neurological mechanisms.

Humans have a longer period of developmental progression towards optimum maturity in relation to lower animal forms. In this lengthy period of time, the individual learns continuously to interact with his ecology and to direct volitional behaviour towards goals. Maturity gives the individual the ability to control inner drives. It also gives him the ability to interact with his surroundings which then influences his behaviour.[5] (Hull, Clark L., 1943)

In the ecological sense, group behaviour occurs in a certain geographical area. People sometimes are born and die in the same ecological area. Others move around several spaces in their lifetime. We will define ecology by the proportion of its natural environment, the rate at which it is utilised, the number of human beings inhabiting the geographical area and utilising its produce either in their pristine form or in modified forms with the use of technology. For example, coal is used as energy in its pristine form while the evolution of electricity is a highly developed technology of conversion of natural elements into high quantities of energy. We can at once see that discernible within these descriptions of ecology are those which range from the elementary to those which are highly developed and sophisticated.[6] (Gadgil M., and R. Guha, 1995) *If we view patterns of group living analytically, we observe that specific types of races are at specific stages of civilisation, with different levels of access to the benefits of science and technology. The latter are accepted as component parts in the explanation of the concept of ecology.*

It is within these parameters of the development of these specific human civilization, that the individual interacts with his concrete environment dynamically.[7] (Mahadevan, K., Chi Husi Tuan and V.K. Balakrishnan Nair, 1992). The parameters of ecology over the years continue to be somewhat the same, except for man's developing capacities to uncover more parameters of ecology and to modify them, the geo-ecology charts its own course of interaction with human ecology. The major parameters are given in the paradigm below:

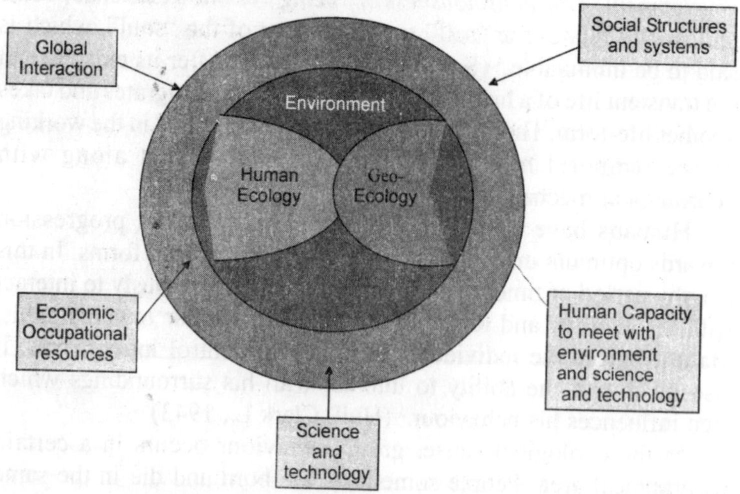

Paradigm 1.1: The Qualities of Ecology

2. The Beginnings of Ecology as a Scientific Discipline

Academic knowledge on ecology began from basic biological enquiries in the second half of the early Greek era.[8] (Egerton, F.N., 2001) Aristotle's student Theophrastus who described interrelationships among animals, and between animals and their environment in as early as the fourth century B.C. is taken to be one of the earliest descriptions of ecology.[9] (Ramalay, Francis, 1940) Humboldt with his exploratory expeditions for identifying new species of plants and his scientific description of them and their natural habitats in his mammoth works came to be known as the father of ecology.[10] (Alexander Von Humboldt, 1996). Academicians, however, speculate that the roots of documentation on scientific ecology began with Darwin's theory of the *Origin of the Species*. Tansley later coined the term e*cosystem* by analysing bio-sciences (the group of living things) and their biotope.[11] (Tansley, A.G., 2003) *The meaning of ecology moved from its original source of natural flora and fauna, geography and the time-related changes in the geo-ecological frame to centralise on the human in his habitat.* By this we mean that there are structural linkages between the human and his habitat, namely, the environment, which he acts upon and which in turn influences his behaviour.[12] (Berry J.W., 1974)

There is also an increasing interest in academics to probe further into the growing inverse relationship between human ecology *per se* and geo-ecological factors. When the relationship between the two ecologies is in imbalance, then there is loss of equilibrium.[13] (Egerton, Frank N., 1973; Egerton, Frank N., 2001) Pressures on the natural habitat, spurred on by technological changes, is adversely affecting the human in his habitat. For instance, the mechanisation of agriculture displaces the human labour which then has to resort to poorer/unstable sources of living. Again, while the use of chemicals and fertilizers boosts agricultural production, it also adversely affect human health by the emission of toxic gases. Thus, while these technological pressures are meant to increase the quality of life, at the same time they also have their 'unintended' consequences by serendipity. This creates a vicious cycle of technology being both useful and detrimental to human living. For example, technology has increased the number of vehicles on the road and, therefore, has facilitated travel between geographical spaces, but at the same time it has contributed to the emission of pollutants. This in turn is a vicious cycle, for it calls for improved medical science and, therefore, technology, to cure those diseases, which ironically have been caused by this very technology. However, it does not stop human beings from desiring more vehicles on the road and so the merry-go-round goes around. More specifically is the telling instance of the need for increasing advanced technology for procuring oil, for industry, transport, and energy for domestic and institutional purposes. This need has led to global disharmony/disputes over oil-rich territories and with oil-rich countries indulging in power-brokerage by the manipulation of their oil resources.[14] (Ramakrishnan, P.S., 2001)

How do we know about the meaning and the constructs of ecology?Briefly indicated in the following paradigm below are the following:

The tenets of philosophy, western and Indian have documented indications about the importance of the environment. The sciences on their part both biological and geographical have shown changes in human well-being, in relation to climatic changes. But most revealing is the evolutionary theory of Darwin and man's own capacity to reveal the relationship of the geo-ecology to human endeavour.

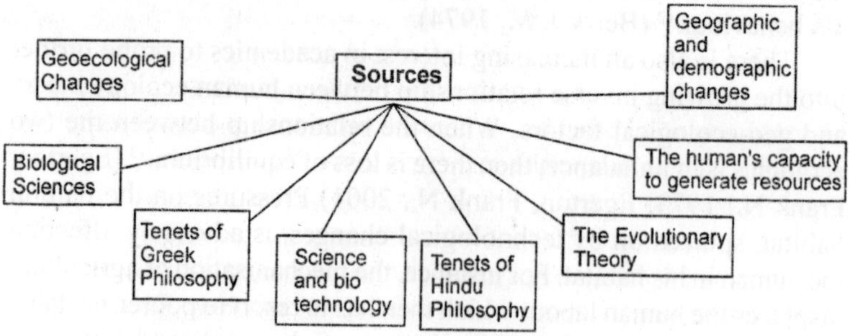

Paradigm 1.2: Sources of Knowledge on Ecology

There are several conceptualisations on the meaning of ecology as a broad generic term. The most generic conceptualisation is that *ecology is the interaction among organisms and the environment.* Basic to its understanding is the study of ecosystems in a holistic manner.[15] (Kumar, H.D. 1972) To control the environment and to articulate directional behaviour, the individual has to learn certain well-known formulae of behaviour that are categories of *routine, periodic and exigent activities,* as related to environmental "givens". It is essential to mention here that these environmental givens should not be exploited beyond their capacities. While these categories are not immutable, there are modes of behaviour, which continue to operate and to maintain these activities, such as learning to perform routine daily activities, as: a child waking up, getting ready, going to school, performing school activities, back again home; and so the cycle of routine activities continues. In the child's geoecology, he has a residence, a school, a distance for travelling, the need for obtaining school materials and, therefore, a market place, a medical centre if he falls ill and some place for entertainment, whether it is a cinema hall or a carnival or more frequently the playground. These categories of ecologically-oriented needs for ontogenetic activities are circumscribed by the potentials of the given ecology. A metropolis has better facilities than a rural village. The tribal areas have even less. The categories of behaviour are also subject to the laws of nature and ecological constructs are derived in relation to them.[16] (Krech, D. and G.S. Klein, 1952) The ecology itself has its own patterns of behaviour, sometimes predictable such as the monsoons, but not always accurate as to the timing. Events occurring in the physical environment, also have their own attributes and repercussions such as climatic changes, famines, varying energy availability and floods. These are geo-ecological events although are predictable in countries where the meteorological systems are highly sophisticated. In most elementary and primitive ecologies these events may be sensed by experience but are hardly meteorologically predictable. For instance, a nomad in the Thar desert lives with camels and sand as his environment, while, those who live in the Nilgiri hills have access to greenery of flora, fauna, adequate water supply and food produce. Unlike the nomads, they do not have to travel distances to oasis for precious water.[17] (Brara, Rita, 2003) On one hand, the limitations in deriving theoretical constructs from these realities are related to the degree of immutability of matter (organic or inorganic), such as the planetary model, the atom, and the interaction of chemicals/gases on the human. On the other hand, bio-psychological or socio-psychological information is generally not as predictable in its outcomes as in the physical sciences.[18] (Coll, C., E. Bearer and R. Lerner, 2004) This has consequences for the assessment of reliability of the human ecology *versus* the geo-ecology, where the latter has more stable processes. It is easier to predict that rain clouds will bring rain, than it is to assess the human mind whether the psyche is normally stable or otherwise. However, academic interest in human behaviour is not only confined to static behaviour of a particular event in a particular time for a particular people; but also in their negotiable behaviour with the environment, which is itself in a constant dynamic flux of changing variables. There is also the interaction with probability dynamics such as meeting with accidents, which cause injury, or neglect of hygienic principles causing diseases. It is necessary to point out here that such occurrences happen because of limited interaction in a given ecology with the availability/non-availability of facilities and the limitation of their properties. In hill tribes, for instance, where there is no such thing as treated water, there is ignorance of its properties, and action to waterborne diseases is reactive and not proactive, unlike urban areas where knowledge of water-borne diseases causes civic and peoples' activities to be proactive about disease control and the resultant epidemiological consequences.

3. Efforts to Preserve Cultural Heritage

Human beings in every era contribute to the building of their civilisation and leave behind the traces of their civilisation as, for example, in the case of Harappa valley civilisation. In India, there is an awareness about the preservation and maintenance of the cultural heritage. For instance, preserving ancient monuments as a cultural heritage for social historicity and indexing geo-ecological changes. India is a vast country with monuments of bygone civilizations dating from ancient times, many of the fortresses, temples, ancient structures of water preservation, management and wise utilization of waste products are to be seen in the arts and crafts emporia maintained to this day. Such examples are Khajuraho temple in Madhya Pradesh, Ellora and Ajanta Caves of Maharashtra, the various forts in North India and the temples still used in worship in South India like Madurai Meenakshi Temple. In more recent years, there is an attempt by social psychologists and social anthropologists to examine the documentation and preserve in the archives. This is to index resource of how the life of people interlinked with their geoecology. The purpose of the tracing back to past civilisation is:

(i) To keep the contact of the human beings with his past,
(ii) To trace the ecological changes over time so as to set the human being in a current time and a current space in social historicity.

A study by Super and Harkness,[19] (C.M. Super and S. Harkness, 1986) Murdoch's Ethnographic Atlas[20] (Murdock G.P., 1967) and ethnographic studies of small societies[21] (Elwein, V., 1947; Ghurye, G.S., 1963; Ishwaran, K., 1968; Mathur, K.S., 1964) are sources of idiographic information to generalise to a totality of a population. For this purpose, these idiographic descriptions also relate to a time and a space. By inference, the Indian of today is not like the Indian of the last century. He has become both developed in his own sphere and living in a developing ecology.

Further, there is an acknowledgement that culture-specific interpretations which are indigenous in nature may be derived from generic universalities and commonalities of traits.[22] (Misra, G., and K.J. Gergen, 2001) For instance, while Munroe and Munroe's study demonstrate the occurrence of common psychological variables like aggression, independency, cognition and sex roles, they are differentially interpreted in the three specific societies studied cross-culturally, namely, the Ainu of Japan, the Trobrianders of the islands of New Guinea and the Gusli of Kenya, who live in different ecologies and react differentially within the given ecological domains[23] (Munroe and Munroe, 1975) Margaret Mead's study demonstrate the interpretation of psychological common variables in a specific Samoan culture.[24] (Mead, M., 1930) Extrapolating these concepts of universals to the specific geo-ecological arena of the Indian sub-societies, we observe that events are differentially experienced by similar living habitats, like global warming, pollution and lessened availability of oil and food in several ecologies with a caveat that they are experienced in different degrees and different categories of people. For example, high and low caste, agriculturalists and industrialists. The current day disaster of the Haitian earthquake for example has left thousands of families homeless and hundreds of children orphans. And yet the society has to pick itself up by its bootstraps and restore its geoecology and stabilise its human ecology. In some countries, there is a proneness to earthquakes, in others, a frequency of cyclones and typhoons and in yet others, there is overabundance of rain and floods during the rainy seasons. Thus, while different experiential events occur across the globe affecting many countries and therefore their cultures, how each group interprets the ecological event is related to their living patterns where the inhabitants balance out the negative with the positive qualities of the event in a given ecology. For example, the spewing of the volcanic ashes from the arctic mountains which stopped a traffic in the northern hemisphere for many days. This one natural incident disrupted thousands of passenger schedules.

The constructs in the mentioned ethnographic studies of Munroe and Munroe, and of Mead[25] (Mead, M., 1930) is to attempt to demonstrate relationship between the laws of nature and differentially responsive human behaviour to the outcomes of such laws. The constructs of such descriptive studies have their own limitations. One limitation of this ethnographic, idiographic (emic) type of study is the probability of limited parameters. For instance, collectivism exists as an attribute in developing countries but is more individualistically oriented in the developed. However, these dimensions are not adequately over and in comparison to other society. The second limitation is that while we know that man has the phylogenetic characteristics which occur across the races, the specific ontogenetic skills differ. The latter tend to mould beliefs, attitudes and values. For instance, some practice polygamy, others disapprove of widow remarriages, some believe that inheritance goes from the mother to the daughter, such as the Khasi tribe in Meghalaya while most endorse the belief that sons inherit the family wealth.

Thus, with *the universal or the etic approach, where variables are deduced, the latter may not be interpreted in a regularised manner. The psychological constructs need to be congruent with the behaviour of the individual of a society, namely, behaviour congruent with ecological, cultural and other human structural phenomena*[26] (Dreze, J., and Amartya Sen, 2002) To illustrate this a little further, in a deprived ecology the major thought processes, congruent with behaviour, are related to strategies for survival and well-being.

4. The Place of Epigenetic Rules in Human Ecology

Epigenesis in the biological sense is the development of the individual's genes in a regulated manner, both in the phylogenetic and ontogenetic areas through orthogenesis.[27] (Thomas, R.M., 2001) In its intensive analysis, ecology, on the other hand, operationally means the relationships between the physical ecology, the psychological inner mind of the individual in his ecology and the neurological and mental adjustments required in relating to the ecology. Berry, one of the foremost academicians in the field of human ecology, has stressed that there are two basic assumptions in the concept of ecology: one is "universalism" and the other is "adaptation".[28] (Berry, J.W., 2003) The first is, those attributes shared by all human beings, which are constructs of universals/ commonalities, etic characteristics like formation of relationships between the sexes, the process of reproduction and the care of offspring by adults; and the second relates to constructs of specifics, or emic characteristics, as in the ethnographic studies, as mentioned by Whiting and Child[29] (Whiting, J.W.M., and I.L. Child, 1953) and Super and Harkness.[30] (Super, C.M., and Harkness, S., 1996)

This conceptualisation is akin to the concepts of 'etic' (universal) and 'emic' (specific), as analysed by Paranjpe in discussing positivistic notions of psychological knowledge.[31] (Paranjpe, A.C., 2003). Irrespective of the dimensions of these concepts, the immediate ecology of the human is a network, whether it is family or kin-group or caste group or other such groups, or combinations of these. They are the most intense and extensive interactive networks of the human and his ecology. We identify them by such terminology as family, kin group, caste group, ethnic group and such like. They each have their specific niches of descriptive attitudes, values and beliefs, often influenced by culture and geographical ecology.

Individuals living in a particular environment respond selectively to the stimuli of the ecology.[32] (Boyd, R., and Richerson, P., 1983) These stimuli are interpreted through personal and cultural channels, which are viewed as the eco-system approach.[33] (Moran, E., 1990) Accuracy of perception in that approach is a significant factor in the meaning and consequences of family events, such as securing family resources.[34] (Boss, P., 1987). For example, in terrains of uncertain rainfall, securing food for family sustenance is a priority whereas in urban areas securing contacts for conducting monetary business enterprises is a priority.

Therefore, it is essential to perceive the order of priorities in which an individual grows and lives, and the negotiations he makes with his ecology. For example, priority areas for a housewife is the care of children and household tasks. For her husband, it is provision for his family and his occupational tasks. These tasks tend to shape the individual's cognition as to the relative values of priority areas.[35] (Berry, J.W., 1974) Let us illustrate further: a tribal *Gaddi,* living in the *Kangra* valley, has serenity and calmness and almost a casual relationship to events that are not high profiled. If one were to ask him where a certain village was located, he would say matter-of-factly *"Oopar,"* literally meaning "on top," when it is only a few furlongs away, and when you ask him about his village that is also up, but it may be twenty kilometres away, you will be told that it is "*thodi door*" (a little distance). Therefore, geographical spree to him is a fluid perception. His cognitive interpretation of the environmental ecology is based on his unique perception of space and time. This type of cognition and its expression does not exist in the city. In the city, time is counted in minutes, directions are specific and indicated by large signposts, traffic is regulated by stop and go signs, money is transacted through micro chips and the internet and the share market, and getting to another country does not entail much effort. Given below is a pardigm of the epigenetic rules of the human parameters influenced by the environment in the human ecology.

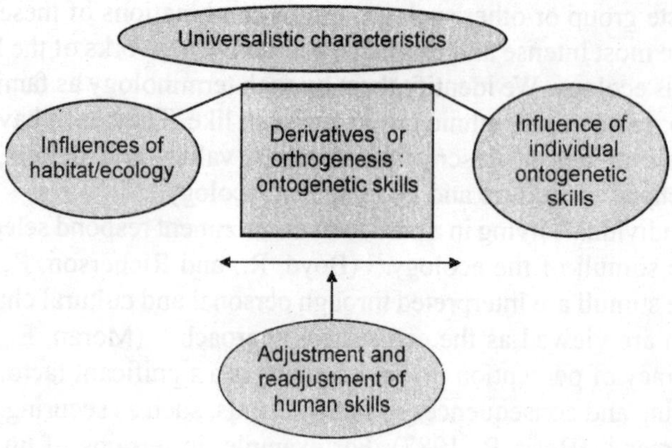

Paradigm 1.3: Epigenetic Rules and the Environmental Influences

A rural child will tell you the mark of an animal by examining the print of its paws, an urban child will know how to manipulate a computer, thus illustrating the differences in the ontogenetic characteristics as influenced by ecological parameters. A pre-school rural child will know the route that flocks of birds take; a pre-school urban child will tell you about UFOs, and uses words from the Discovery channel, such as "nocturnal animals", and "vampires that fly". The latter reads Harry Potter; the rural child tells you about the puppetry shows of the Mahabharata and how *strong Arjun* was and so on. Thus, added to the variable of habitat is education, exposure to a world vision and the pace and change of national and international happenings, which accrue to the ontogenetic characteristics of the urban child vis-à-vis the rural.

5. Ecological Deprivation and its Effects on Human Abilities

The rich individual lives in an affluent environment, which satisfies his physical needs and when surfeited usually suffers from *ennui* or boredom, and seeks more exciting exotic experiences. The deprived, on the other hand, suffers from lacunae in many spheres of physical necessities, and often due to lack of satisfaction of primary needs, a sense of apathy sets in, leading to lessened energetic and enthusiastic interaction with the environment.[36] (Misra, G., 1983; Misra, G., and L.B. Tripathi, 1976)

India has been beset by poverty affecting a large proportion of its population, especially in the rural hinterlands. Historically speaking, the existence of poverty has been due to the hordes of invaders from its northern borders, since the time of *Aryan* and *Mughal* invasions,[37] (Keay, J., 2000) which have caused fluctuations in the developmental modes. Therefore, under several feudal regimes of different cultures, for example, the *Mughals,* the warring among chieftains, *rajas* and *Nawabs*, and colonisation by the British disrupted the normal life styles of the micro systems, namely, the average family and its network. These mal-effects on normal lifestyles were more pronounced in the lower castes, the lower socio-economic classes and the powerless. There seems to be continuous and compounding of elements that complicate poverty conditions: lack of education of the masses, the rigidity of the caste system, the large areas of poorly cultivated tracts, the lack of prevention against monsoon floods or drought conditions; and the neglect of the ruled by the rulers. Even to this day, there are different garbs of the same political dynamics of governance.[38] (Ram, R., 1992) Social well-being implies a harmonious family setting and emotional well-being implies a balanced adjusted personality. All these are in combination and can shift dynamically.

The issue of this continued poverty has been high profiled in the political agenda of independent India. Analysis of this condition had initially focused on the prevalence of poverty using various indices, mainly economic in nature.[39] (Sharma, S. 1985; Pushpa, M. 1990) There have been several scattered projects in some form or the other for raising the economic status of the deprived, beginning from "Food for Work" and, the Public Distribution System.[40] (Centre for Development and Human Rights, 2004) Although the country has met its target for food adequacy, there are still pockets of inadequate food availability especially in the northern States of Bihar, Madhya Pradesh and Orissa, and in some regions of Maharashtra and Andhra Pradesh, which suffer from drought conditions in the agricultural sector. Since there are many landless labourers in the rural population, and mainly small scattered subsistence small uneconomical land-holdings, the State, district and block infrastructures are inadequate to cope with the needed assistance. Programmes like "*Garibi Hatao*", and now the "National Work Guarantee Scheme" have more or less the same flavour. There seems to be a movement by the people themselves to demand the money due to them by the scheme, and particularly women in the village communities who utilise the money for their daily living. This spurt has been motivated by the Right to

Information Act legislated in the year 2005, which encourages enlightened village communities to pursue the implementation of schemes. Earlier schemes like the National Integrated Rural Development Scheme, (NIRD) the scheme of Development of Women and Children in Rural Areas (DWCRA) and the Integrated Child Development Scheme (ICDS) while indicating some progress in some villages, for the most parts are now huge bureaucratically conducted infrastructures, with little people's participation, which was and has been the crux of the rural development ethos, but has not had the expected results.[41] (Radhakrishna, A., and S. Ray, 2005) This situation exists, since most villages were/are ruled by the political/government representatives of classes and castes.[42] (Mathew, G., 2003)

Poverty and its concomitant deprivation (whether as a cause or effect) has been a concern of social psychologists from the mid 1970s.[43] (Sinha, 1975; Shanmugam, T.E., 1975) Parameswaran and Rath examined the major variables that affect poverty, while Moullick, who followed on, analysed its dimensions.[44] (Parameswaran, E.G., 1972; Rath, 1972; Moullick, T.K., 1981) Then followed a host of academic enquiries in the psychological dimensions. One of them was on the relationship between economic deprivation and depletion of potential skills. They indicated that *poverty affects many psychological traits like cognition and its correlates such as motivation and achievement*. Tripathi and Mishra have been among the major exponents in the psychological analyses of deprivation.[45] (Misra, G., and K.N. Tripathi, 2004) The thematic concepts that have been examined were: lack of economic power, low socio-economic status and lack of opportunity for betterment, types of poverty, their measurement and their consequences in the studied ecologies, which were mostly sparse ecologies.

6. The Factors of Deprivation: Economic and Social—and their Complex Interactions

In the description of economic deprivation, what seems to have happened is that social scientists have viewed poverty from a technical aspect as an 'event out there', and so have offered erudite discussions on its existence and related classificatory variables. This perspective provides analyses different from those who actually live in poverty. To give an instance, a farmer facing ruin from the failure of his crops does not have the same perspective as viewed by the scientists who say: "the farmers are in debt due to the failure of crops". They cannot empathise with the absolute depth of despair. For these reasons, more and more *social scientists are beginning to perceive poverty from the perspective of the poor in social realities. Chambers call this perspective of the scientists as "pro-poor ideology".*[46] (Chambers, R., 1991) *From the viewpoint of the deprived, poverty is a given and evolving situation that affects groups of human beings living under sparse conditions. These conditions reduce the status of well-being of the human. Poverty is not a one-time phenomenon; it evolves from one generation to another, and over a period of time depletes the well-being of the human living under such conditions.*[47] (Mehta, Aasha Kapur and Shepherd Andrew, 2006) Deprivation is of many kinds. In modern or modernising societies other kinds of deprivation are liable to occur in the form of deprivation of social and family harmony.[48] (Furstenberg, F.F., Jr., and A.J. Cherlin, 1991) We might hypothesise that the state of economic poverty alone is insufficient to analyse the plight of those deprived. Since there is a "domino effect", poverty implies primarily and simply lack of food and water for sustenance. If sustenance is depleted, ill-health follows and ill-health is followed by lack of motivation to improve one's life, family disorganisation and social conflict, thus creating a spiralling effect of negative relativity. On the other hand, there are such ecologies where surfeit of resources also leads to family disorganisation, compounded by societal dissonance, where "too much too soon" occurs in an exponential manner. In the upper echelons in these sophisticated micro systems, parents are preoccupied with accumulating wealth, leave their children to the care of domestic staff who then become parental surrogates in the absence of biological parents. Thus, we may hypothesise that both extreme economic poverty and social disharmony may lead to destabilisation in the family ecology. Therefore, in either state, coping mechanisms of the family members are disrupted.[49] (Hofstede, G., 1984)

In the case of crises in these areas, the Indian usually reverts to his socio-religious norms for an explanation of the unexpected negative situation. It is assumed to be an acceptance of fate, and the Indian generally rationalises that it is bad karma *and resorts to ritualism and mysticism to appease the supernatural or to mitigate the "bad luck" (bad* kismat*) that has occurred.*[50] (Nandi, S., C.R. Rajalakshmi and I. Varghese, 1971) It is not infrequent that individuals facing such calamities perform *pujas,* go on pilgrimage, and appeal to special deities in a ritualistic manner. Rarely does the average Indian attribute the calamity to his personal lack of effort/achievement motivation. Defence mechanisms are often used to rationalise occurrence of the calamity through escape avoidance, or denial. It is not unusual to hear the familial rationale *"aysaay hota hai*' (it happens this way) *or "yah rahu kaal hai*" (this is an inauspicious time).

Broadly speaking, it may be said that the more dependent the society is on natural sources, the more elemental is the lifestyle, and tasks are characteristic of rudimentary forms of living. Thus, there is an interdependence of the human upon nature, where the forces of nature are modified or appeased by the human. This process of inter-dependence between man and nature may be reinterpreted in developed countries. For instance, the differences between the developed and developing countries and the relationships of their people to nature may be reinterpreted as: the less developed the country, the greater is the dependence upon nature which has a greater control over his lifestyle, whereas the more developed the country, the greater is the probability that its people can manipulate and control nature, as in technologically developed ecologies. The consequence in either case then is lack of satisfaction in having more in the developed countries, and in not having much more in the developing countries. However, the downside is that when a highly technologised country is faced with a natural crisis, the greater are the consequences in social psychological disorganisation as its people are unused to being controlled by natural events which turn out to be calamitous, such as power breakdowns in New York city and the hurricane Katrina in southern parts of USA. By inference, we may say people in developing countries have a higher threshold of tolerance to calamities than do those in the developed. For example, when there is a power failure in an Indian set-up, it is accepted philosophically, whereas in a western culture there is less philosophy and more demand for quality of services as its people, to put it popularly, "pay taxes and, therefore, demand quality".

In an analysis by Hofstede[51] (Hofstede, G., 1994) of people of different nationalities working in a high-tech corporation, comparisons were made between Swedes and Saudis. The Swedes were found to have a different concept of the role of personal relationships in business. For the former the business is with the company and for the Saudis with the person one has known and learned to trust in the company. The fundamental difference between these two societies is the role of individual *versus* group norms. The Swedes who are from the Anglo-Saxon nations were found to be more "individualistic" *vis-à-vis* the Saudis who were more "collectivistic" oriented. The family (the human ecology) being the primary collective group, was high on the list of priority concerns of the Saudis. Loyalty to the kin group, the collective "we", was the major reference group as the source of identity. If we extrapolate such concepts into the Indian situation we can identify the strong sense of "groupism" that exist in the family network and, hence, the similarity to the "integrative concept", the "collective concept" and the "group concept" which gives the members of the group their identity. The viability and the opportunity to cohere their tasks exists under the rubric of a shared empathetic milieu. In this milieu, there is more an attitude of cooperation rather than competition, which emphasises again the strength of attitudes inculcated by close adherence to the spirit of the human ecological system, namely, the micro system.

In its socio-psychological frame, therefore, how does ecology influence human perception and cognition of the environment? What interactional processes give the individual, his habitual behaviour in a given ecology (human-material)? Is it through a process of continuous and remodified adaptation?[52] (Vayda, P., 1969) Several percepts co-exist:

1. It is probable that the individual gradually acquires a perception of his status, his role (both expected and performed) in the given ecology.
2. Ecological support for survival is, possibly, the initial propelling factor on the activation of human perception of the situational determinants (availability of food, water and other resources).[53] (Barry, J.H., I. Child and M. Bacon, 1959).
3. Abilities to wrest from the given ecologies the means for existence at a tolerable degree of quality, require the development of the appropriate ontogenetic skills.
4. Appropriate skills are finely tuned to correlate within the existing limits of the geo-ecology. These are, for instance, a weavers craft community;[54] (Goodnow, J.J, 1976) the sophisticated skills in controlling drones in the sky through computerised techniques as in the current war waged by the US against the Taliban. Apart from modern technological skills, other skills such as leadership qualities are also

important. For example, an aviator requires deep and clear visionary acuity. Studies on perceptual cognitive development in Arabs, Africans, Australians, Guineans and Indians have indicated individual differences in skills in each country,[55] (Witkin, H., and J.W. Berry, 1975) mainly in relation to the ecological occupations available in their own countries.

The specific ecology needs to be viewed from two constructs. The first is the behaviour of the individual and his competence at his tasks in his given cultural role; the second is, how the individuals in the group relate their tasks to each other. One might call this ecologically related behaviour as division of labour, and indeed in agricultural families this is clearly observed from their daily lives. In agricultural India, men plough, women are not allowed to use the plough, women scatter seed and winnow the chaff, and men do not do household chores. Allotment of tasks relate to the ecological given situations of the geo-ecological contours such that it involves many separate but interrelated tasks. These may be observed in hill or plain land cultivation, plains land cultivation, cultivation by irrigation and irrigation from dams and lakes differently according to the lay of the land. Unless these tasks are well-known and well-orchestrated in terms of time and energy, the final product is less than satisfactory. There is, therefore, a cohesion of individual but related task performances. Thus, more clearly, technology mediates role prescription and role performance in the sociological sense, within the human unit: the family.[56] (English-Lueck, J.A., Dr., 1998) If the society is urban, it negotiates the roles of men and women in a typical urban family with parents working, children in school and interacting at certain times only. In rural areas, the workplace and the household are usually extensions of each other, and women in rural areas move from one activity to another, often putting in fifteen to sixteen hours of work in both home and farm.[57] (Gulati, Leela, 1970). This is an example of an ecology in which human being's behaviour indicates that the individual is either experienced or is learning through experience, to be ecologically competent. The agricultural family incorporates the occupational work and household work into a cyclic calendar of seasonal events. The urban family, on the other hand, separates the work place from the family place and from these two. Thus their differing ecologies offer them the differing parameters within which they can operate.

The concept of deprivation usually used in studies is economic deprivation. When related to social realities, the concept becomes diffused. Deprivation can be temporary and what is perceived as deprivation by one may not be the same as the perception of another, and further in its abstract conceptualisation the ranges of deprivation have relativity. Deprivation is perceived in India as being articulated by the forces of fate and nature: a philosophy of thinking also observed in most eastern cultures.

Again, we rarely see the operation of the economic variable affecting differences when the group is homogeneous. For example, there is not much difference in the economic status of tribals. They tend to be homogeneous except for the quantity of cattle/camels which indexes material wealth.[58] (Doshi, S.L., 1971)

When the programme of removal of poverty was given high profile by the politicians, beginning the slogan of *Garibi Hatao*, proclaimed in the 1971 election manifesto of the Congress party, it gave an impetus to research on deprivation.[59] (Shanmugam, T.E., 1976) However, in conducting research the operational definition of economic deprivation was used differentially by different academicians.[60] (Misra, G., and K.N. Tripathi, 2004) A related concept to deprivation in the Indian context is 'poverty'. It applies solely to economic deprivation and its consequences (mortality, morbidity, etc.) which occur because of lack of the basic necessities. On the other hand, lowered social status gives rise to social disadvantage between and among communities as, for instance, in the case of the scheduled castes and the scheduled tribes. Thus, social disadvantage and economic deprivation are correlative. Tripathi, for instance, identified three criteria for the classification of deprivation. These were: organic *vs*. environmental, objective *vs*. subjective and absolute *vs*. relative deprivation.[61] (Tripathi, R.C., 1982). There exist a few studies, which offer a factorial analysis of the interrelationships between these various differences.[62] (Agarawal, R., and G. Misra, 2002) More often than not, static classificatory discrete variables have been used, such as caste, residential area, and ethnicity. These operational definitions of the independent variables are indeed various since there is very little agreement among academicians, on a common operational definition of socio-economic status.[63] (Reddy, Sujatha B.N., 1986) Further, still, the variable 'deprivation' has been used sometimes as a cause and sometimes as an effect in research frames. For example, a hypothesis might state that deprivation causes/correlates with poor cognitive development, and another might state 'poor cognitive development is caused by/correlates with deprivation'. Over the last decade, there are several instances of disadvantaged individuals becoming overly advantaged (*nouveau riche*) and, therefore, crossing the boundaries of deprivation, disadvantage, and marginalisation. This occurs when given a pole vault of economic prosperity; a poor individual can aspire to live in a mansion, and have great wealth. which is the phenomenon of "rags to riches". There is still inadequate data in large sample studies to offer adequate reliability to these related variables. However, in spite of a few studies indicating that economic deprivation is related to lowered performance,[64] (Jachuk, K., 1993; Das, I., and P.K. Mona, 1990), the evidence is not compelling as they relate, again, to static variables such as caste and socio-economic status. Evidence indicates that genetic propensities interact with the ecological givens and that neither is preponderant over the other.[65] (Rolston, H., 1999) Bhogle and Fatima investigated quantitative thinking in children from low and high socio-economic backgrounds. The results indicated that high or low cognitive ability may not relate to being more or less economically deprived.[66] (Bhogle, S., and T. Fatima, 1981) Again, Dash and Das observed that children of low socio-economic status did not differ from the children of upper socio-economic class in the performance of tasks in the concrete operational stage of cognition.[67] (Dash, U.N., and J.P. Das, 1984) Thus, we take the stand that it is not a poverty ridden ecology *per se* that debilitates the intellect, but that it is the lack of opportunities in the ecology to utilise the individual's ontogenetic potentials that lead to greater optimal development of the given potential intellect. Further, economic status is not static and, therefore, it should not be treated as immutable. For an individual can move from one to the other category in socio-economic status. For example, a child's father may improve his economic status and, therefore, examining children at a specific age and stage in cross-cultural studies does not give adequate satisfactory information about the relationship between economic deprivation and intellectual—cognitive abilities, deprivation may be for a long period or for a short period, and a group examined at one time may not be in the same deprived state at a future stage/time. Several small-scale studies have used similar indicators of socio-economic status with permutations and combinations, studies use different operational definitions of classificatory variables, the results are unvaryingly the same, namely, the better off usually do better than the less well-off. These results are misleading, for they imply a one-to-one relationship among these categories of socio-economic statuses.[68] (Miller, C.D., and N.J. Salkind, 2002) research studies conducted on deprivation, whether economic or social, take as their subjects, such units as on individual or a family. The units are dynamically changeable. Therefore, to group them into different socio-economic classes assume that all within a class are the same in personality traits. This, obviously is not valid. Not only do personalities differ from one time to another (chronologically), but over space (geographically), and so to assess their qualities at one time may not be true at another time. For, a villager may become a rich urban magnate, or a *panchyat Pradhan*, and move from one ecology to another and become less deprived. To quote from research studies as if they were immutable and stand the test of time vitiates the very conceptualisation as to who is deprived or who is not as changes may take place from one research frame to another. We know for instance, that the middle class is growing in size as compared to the past decades.

Are personalities elastic? Do they expand and then go back to the same lines of demarcation? Or do they change entirely? *If we take the example of the micro system of the family, the ecological aspects of the boundaries can indeed change as the family grows into a unit of nuclearisation, or the members are scattered in the diasporas, or children live abroad as is currently happening. They can change not only in terms of radius of interaction, that is, a movement into the meso system and the exo system, but also that the family can change horizontally, from one geo-ecological area to another.*

To clarify this aspect of differing ecologies of the micro system of the family, we need to examine further the role-expectations and the role-performances of the members in the micro system. If the ecology is sparse, then the tasks are related to the scarcity components in the ecology. For instance, lack of water and cultivable land for subsistence farmers, limit the number of tasks that are to be performed *vis-à-vis* the tasks in an agricultural area that is rich with its properties. Further, decision-making is specific to certain age/status of the individuals. If at a family decision making situation, as to whether the daughter should marry now or study and then marry later, the participation/intervention of the young members of the family is not expected as it is not related to their role-expectations. Similarly, in sibling care of younger children, the supervising older child is not expected to make adult decisions over the ones who are supervised, but simply to do care taking tasks. With these examples, we are attempting to explain the related entity (individual) and unitary (group of entities) behaviour of the family unit in living in a specific ecological environment, such as a deprived ecology, as given in the paradigm below.

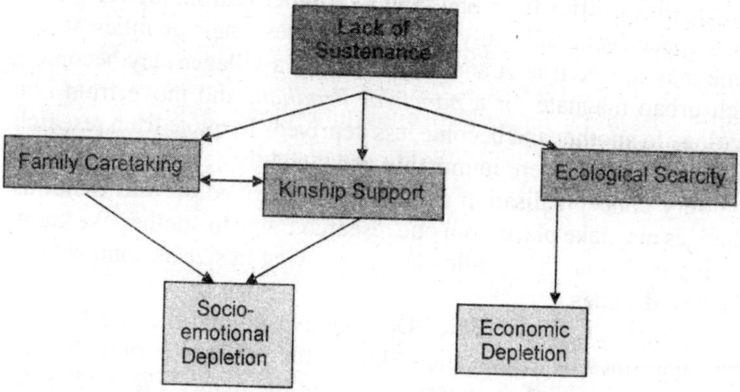

Paradigm 1.4: The Generic Aspects of Deprivation

7. Relationships among Caste, Class and Geographical Areas

India's population according to the latest census data shows that more people are living longer. In the colonial era, life expectancy at birth was about 32 years. Now it has shot up to 63 years.[69] (Cohen, S.P., 2001) The dependency rate (children below employment age) indicates that the dependency ratio is burgeoning. These have significant implications for, it means creating or expanding services for the elderly who tend to become fragile and unproductive for a longer period of time, as also providing extra familial care for the young. In a family, the income is mainly from the productive work of the able bodied young and middle aged adults. *The major thrust, therefore, for increasing productivity is threefold: increased higher education: improved technological skills, and availability of infrastructures for viable employment.* Hence, there is a vibrant movement to provide vocational and mechanical skills for the poorer section of the Indian society. This implies increased agricultural activity in the hitherto unreachable or neglected ecologies. It also implies increasing occupational avenues for entrepreneurial activities. To achieve this, it also means increased and less rigid schemes for loans to begin such activities, as in buying tractors in rural areas, and for furbishing individual in their entrepreneurial activities in urban areas.

On the other hand, the upper classes tend to accrue to themselves highly paid jobs. Professionals among them, also tend to migrate to western countries for better prospects. These Non-Resident Indians (NRIs) finance families left behind at home so as to improve their quality of life. This is obvious in the streams of people from Kerala, Gujarat and Punjab who migrate usually to the middle east for bettering the living standards for their families back home. Those who are better off live in areas of luxury apartments/houses and often usually have second homes in farm houses, in hillside resorts or luxury beach vacationing areas, or what is now becoming more fashionable is "time sharing" in resort areas. These phenomena add to the widening gap between the 'haves' and the 'have nots'.

As is well known in sociological documentation, the caste variable continues to distort community living, not only in terms of habitats, but also in terms of personal intercommunication. The "*shudh*"/"*high*" caste does not live in common residence with the "*achoot*"/"*lower*" castes. This phenomenon persists especially in traditional pockets through the 'avoidance-approach' system in the interactions of the "upper" castes with the "lower" castes, who are mostly landless labourers in rural areas, or those doing menial tasks in urban areas. It is frequently observed, therefore, that residences are ecologically separate and, therefore, limit the availability of facilities for the socially discriminated who are also the poorer in the societal framework, giving rise to differential parameter of geo-ecological living and human ecological separation. For instance, the urban migrants use public bathrooms and common water taps, while the rich have their own exclusive resources in their residential habitats.[70] (Dhesi, A.S., 1998)

As the migrant villagers return home for visits, they bring with them their savings for additional construction, for buying cattle and for items of consumer use so as to try and be at par with the rich landed in their 'visiting' ecologies. For instance, a study in the village *Rajapura* in the State of Karnataka found that what was once a sense of apathy among the lower castes towards their discrimination by the upper castes has now attritioned.[71] (Karanth, G.K., 2004) This is because most of the male members of families of such disadvantaged castes who before were dependent upon agricultural labour are, after migrating to urban centres, now earn better incomes. This phenomenon has had its repercussions in their voicing of their dissent against discrimination. They now voice their dissension and protest through the politicians they vote for. The *jajman* system, which was practised between and among the kinship groups has now shifted to a different patronage style, namely, the caste politics, where the MLA or MP is bound to his constituents for their votes and, therefore, to the commitment of their betterment which often remain near promises.

Such changes indicate the growing awareness of the lower castes that the major channels for improvement are money and political position. The signal sent to them is that if a lower caste is rich it can overcome barriers of even caste distinctions. There is a growing sense of rights among the lower castes which continues to create a schism between them and the higher castes who want to preserve this divide and resent this movement.[72] (Thornberry, P., 2005) Coupled with the growing economic power of the urban, rich residents, the divide between the rich and poor, the latter mostly belonging to the lower castes, is increasing.

Related to caste differences is the overriding belief in *karma* within each stratum.[73] (Ghurye, G.S., 1969) The inculcation of the value of *karma* during the socialisation process is so strong that in some lower caste groups, social ostracism of the lower caste by the higher caste is taken as a part of their ascriptive birth into that lower stratum. Irrespective of the traditional belief in *karma*, there is a growing and perhaps insidious movement from the lower to imitate the ritualistic practices of the higher in the belief that they symbolise higher caste status.[74] (Srinivas, M.N., 1962) In this, the twenty-first century, with the introduction of the caste-based reservation in public sector employment, there is a growing sense of the power of equal rights of all castes in the political system. Again, as with most phenomena in the Indian situation, even though social democracy is expected to have an equalizing effect, there still is inequity in social and religious relations.[75] (Adams, J.S., 1965) In absolute numbers, the lower castes are becoming aware of their power and tend to ignore the hierarchical distinction: as for instance, the *Gujjars'* reservation movement in Rajasthan, and the assertion of *Dalit* movement in Andhra Pradesh and other States to claim their legal rights. In a study in Bihar[76] (Sahay, G.R., 2004) this phenomenon appears to be so.In the context of sanskritisation, the, lower castes continue to maintain their own distinctions, but paradoxically practice the rituals, hitherto exclusively of the domain of the upper castes. The basis of relating occupation to caste is also attritioning, as also the *jajman* in the division of labour. Some controversy exists, as to whether this pattern is due to sanskritisation of the lower castes or the economic factor of increase in cash economy, which makes them deliberately increase their socio-economic status.[77] (Sipra Bose, Johnson, 1974) This confrontation depletes the erstwhile power of the higher over the lower castes. This juxtaposition and shifts in caste values and practices has a curious anomaly. For, the lower castes still live in separated residences on the outskirts of villages. Thus socio-religious beliefs and modernised beliefs cohabit in an uneasy co-existence among the high and the low castes. Such isolation of habitat tends to reinforce dependence on one's own community, a type of reaction formation which binds them closer within their own and further away from the outside communities. Yet, at the same time a *Harijan*, for instance, may be earning more than a Brahmin and is able to afford a better style of living, as happens in the industrial and bureaucratic segments of the ecologies. There is thus a growing anomaly between caste, occupation and social status, mainly destabilised by modernisation and technological inroads.

It is normally expected that when the family lives within the orbit of residences of kin groups, they are assisted in childcare routine matters. Often, they are under the care of an elderly woman, while the younger women labour at their occupational tasks outside the home. This is more so in tribal and rural ecologies.[78] (Khalakdina, M., 1979) The assimilation of deference towards authority in the hierarchical familial strata, is transferred to the occupational milieu, where there is deference towards the higher status by the lower in bureaucratic situations, where the individual is called "sahib" or if a woman "madam". There is also a tendency towards breaking away from the tradition of being group-oriented and dependent towards becoming individualistic upon the latter, this is more evident among the young who are moving up the ladder of occupational mobility in the urban areas.[79] (Kagitcibasi, C., 1994) For instance, working in informal groups tends to depress competition, but working in the corporate group tends to heighten potentials.

In geo-ecological areas the joint family eco-system, in some muted form or the other, still exists, even though as an ethic, as norms of behaviour are learned early to keep the structure intact. After six years or so a child is expected to behave like a miniature adult, especially in the performance of adult tasks in the rural and tribal habitat, like looking after sheep in pastoral families. In urban areas, he is responsible for earning a cash income at petty jobs , even though intermittent. In such ecologies, the apportioning of necessities, given the meagre amount of intermittent wages, increases the sense of insecurity within the family, which is reflected in the young inculcating a sense of low self-esteem. In times of drought and scarcity, there are few alternatives to seeking other jobs for sustenance. This sense of inconsistency in security exacerbates a sense of dependency for decision-making on the locus of authority, which normally rests with the patriarch of the family.[80] (Bhasin, K., 1994) Perhaps this engenders in the adult a sense of timidity in individual decision-making and a negative self-concept. Evidence of such behaviour is observable, where there are low levels of constructive aggressiveness and a lack of motivation to achieve.[81] (Mehta, P., 1994) Caste and class categories of differences are perceived early in childhood and this is perpetuated by adult models around the child. Several studies indicate that children in multi-caste groups like school children are less likely to adhere to caste distinctions than those living in familial and community situations.[32] (Bayley, Susan, 2001) We also find that where low caste mothers from the landless families undertake work as sweepers and agricultural labour, the non-security of regular employment and intermittent range of wages places a great strain on these females who prefer a combination of both household and occupational tasks, which bring in a regular income, either in cash or in kind, or both.[83] (Mines, M., 1980)

8. The Psychological Dimensions of Traditionality and Modernity in the Ecological Framework

The ecological situation modifies the relationship between the environmental stimulus and the human response. These relationships may occur in an overt form as the occurrence of an earthquake destabilising habitats and disorienting its inhabitants, or in a covert form as in the toxic effect of polluting gases, which bring about pulmonary diseases. There are, however, some problems in using the construct of the ecosystem as an operational unit of analysis in describing the human ecology, for it is modified by variations within the system. For example, the variable of ethnic residence may vitiate the eco-system where families of one ethnic group tend to stay together, interacting with each other, or live apart without much interaction. Whereas, in the case of the tribal group of families living together, there is an unspoken loyalty, which is heavily valued, and encompasses the parameters of tribal life. Further, the availability of and the opportunity to utilise resources is another intervening variable in such a tribal ecologies.[84] (Misra, G., A.K. Srivastava and S. Gupta, 1999) To give an example, ethnic social groups 'A' and 'B' live adjacent to each other. The social group 'A' may have poor standards of education as compared to the social group 'B'. For instance, the social group 'A' may have the motivation to achieve, but not the opportunity, while the social group 'B' may have the opportunity to achieve but may lack motivation in the given ecology. Therefore, to say that there are differences in achievement is really to compare lack of motivation and opportunity of groups in the same ecology. Such motivational levels perhaps has to do with the stimulation or lack of stimulation inbuilt in the individual human in a given geo-ecological environment.

Similarly, *the physical systems (natural, physical, biological environments) differ from one geographical area to another*. To compare such differential bases in arriving at structural relationships may give rise to spurious information. For instance, it is well-known that a child in a western ecology is influenced by psychological and sociological stimuli, which are different from those in the east, and in this instance, in India. The western ecology provides, stimulates, and encourages achievement, whereas the average Indian situation is dissimilarly positioned.

The basis of comparison among ecologies may also be vitiated by the differential adaptability of the human to changes in the ecology or the capacity towards "change proneness". Further the constancy of adaptability is unpredictable. The concept of adaptation does not fully explain its relationship between human beings and their ecologies. Some poses an inherent strength of adaptability through either intelligent cues or experimental know-how. Adaptability implies resilience or persistence or tolerance or even apathy to conditions. It is very well connoted by the saying: "*aisa hi hai, dekha jayega" (it is like this, let us see*) indicating an unwillingness to even consider self initiative in operating in either the human ecological unit or the geo-ecological environment.

When dealing with the family as the micro ecosystem in the Indian situation, it is important to realise that the concept of "family" in India is not synonymous with the concept of "household". The very nexus of the family concept is consanguinal ties, or those ties bonded by biological and mutual agreement. The former refers to biological members, and the latter to others who are treated as close family members, such as different relatives who are relatives of relatives. We see, therefore, an emphasis on the "relational network" composed of the hierarchy of those who have greater or lesser power in that particular network. For instance, if the patriarch of the family decides to change his job and to move to another habitat, possessing more power than others, he has the prerogative to decide about the relocation.

The concept of psychological parameters plays an important part in the ecological-cognitive mapping of the individual. A major concept of socialisation is to induct the child into understanding the limits of boundaries in behaviour. For instance, a primary school child cannot negotiate with adults whether he should go to school or not, a college educated child can negotiate with adults as to whether he would like to take up a job or go on to further studies. These alternatives occur against the imprinted map of the individual's cognitive perception as to what his current ecology is like, and what he would like his future ecology to be like. In other words mapping parameters keep shifting as maturity levels increase with the experience for negotiating the given parameters.[85] (Barash, D.P., 1977)

As is well-known by now, group members interact on the basis of mutual needs and services. In a sense, groups in particular societies where there are sparse services for exchange among them for fulfilling psychological and physical needs have less interaction from who have plenty to exchange from the available resources in the environment. they negotiate to distribute these services among their members. For example in times of floods, each family assist the other to combat together or flee the onslaught of floods.[86] (Bronfenbrenner, 1986)

The economic goods and services existing in a given residential area, whether rural or urban, do not normally change. They occur on a continuous basis as structured systems. In an Indian household, for instance, the services that are required on a routine basis, such as preparation of meals, care of children and such like are provided by an adult female. If she is from a poor household, she will out of necessity accomplish most of the household tasks, that are routinely and/or periodically required from the given environmental ecology. Even if the family is rich, the female head of the household is still responsible, in spite of services by servants, as this is a gender-based responsibility, normative in most traditional households. Where the family is modernised and the parents are working, it is not uncommon to observe these tasks are accomplished on a more egalitarian basis. Nevertheless, in the fast growing economy of India, whether traditional-oriented or modernising, there is little doubt that the average individual's "world vision" is increasing. Communication and media have swept over India, and are being accepted and used with surprising speed. The buzz words are 'internet', 'mobile' and "cyber cafes". Even the uneducated trundle cart vegetable vendor uses a mobile freely.

The concepts of traditionality and westernisation are still under debate as they imply several factors, such as whether they are dichotomous or continuous one-dimensional or a bipolar dimension.[87] (Lash, Scott, Bronislaw Szerszynski and Brian Wynne, eds., 1998) Again to what extent does the concept of westernisation include or exclude modernisation is still fuzzy.[88] (Shah, A.M., B.S. Baviskar and E.A. Ramaswamy, 1996) We do not know the correlation between westernization and modernization, or the implications of their operational definitions in relation to each other. For example, several far eastern countries like Hong Kong, Singapore, Malaysia and others are easily accustomed to the type of consumerism available in the west, but in their core beliefs and practices are still traditional. Traditionalism includes other factors besides the individual's covert attempt to behave like other members of the traditional family and yet, a secret yearning to initiate Western modes as observed in the social media. Does behaving in a "modernised manner" also imply thinking in terms of ethics, justice, democracy and freedom? Does it also include aspects like geographical vertical and horizontal mobility in residence? Does changing residence to well-to-do areas, affording and utilising facilities of people who are in the upper strata suggest modernisation? We suggest that what is becoming more significant is the fact, that the Indian in this twenty-first century is moving towards modernisation of ways of behaviour that are propelled by science and technology. However, for the majority of the Indians who are rural, the trend is to increase their economic status so as to become as "modern" as the upper classes, while retaining their traditional beliefs. Whether modernised behaviour implies modern or liberal/democratic ways of thinking, is not yet adequately analysed in theoretical conceptualisations through research nor are they understood by the majority who are still disadvantaged.[89] (Ravi Kumar, ed., 1999)

Another trend is the widening perspective about other societies and their cultures, which provide more knowledgeable recognition of similarities and differences. Such recognition reduces the discriminating attitude that one society may have of another or even of sub-societies within one's own culture. To put it simply, one may not have perceived other geo-ecologies of the world. Yet they may be assessed through knowledge gained from the other eco-systems: meso, exo and macro systems. Such distinctions make for cognitively mapping the boundaries of one's own ecology and its organisations for the continuance of their social group.[90] (Sinha, J.B.P., 2002) The major influences of this process as described by Berry are ecological, socio-political, and their relation to cultural and biological characteristics of the social group.[91] (Berry, J.W., 2003) *When identifying a human as a developed personality the attributes of his given eco-genetic sources, namely the race he comes from, the eco-geological group he originates* from, whether he is a Mongol or an Indo-Aryan, are the roots of the derivatives which gives him the characteristics of a similar group with whom he has a homogeneous identity. For instance, the Tamils of Sri Lanka who have originated from India and the Kurds living in a part of Iraq, are those who grew up in the socially homogeneous group, which over time contoured his identity in relation to socio-political parameter.[92] (Adelman, I., and Morris, C.T., 1967). These social groups continue to struggle to maintain an identity of their own. In spite of the fact that there are various ethnic and religious groups in India, the dominant ethos of Hinduism is imperceptibly subscribed to as it pervades all walks of life. The respect given to places of veneration of Muslim *peers*, to *Gurudwaras* of the Sikhs and to holy places of the Hindus by the people belonging to all religious denominations is because of the ingrained virtuosity of respect for sages of all religions in the context of a secular state. The most spectacular instance of veneration by people of different religions is that of *Sai Baba and Khwaja Ajmer Sharif*. Most Indians who profess different political ideologies live together in more or less peaceful co-existence because of the dominant ethos of "*ahimsa*" (non-violence) and the democratic ideology of a secular State.[93] (Dyson, T., R. Cassen and L. Visaria, 2004)

The reader may be aware that what we are moving towards, in a cohesive manner, is to place ecology on the cognitive map of the human as a powerful influence on his development. The generic term ecology may be viewed as *a package of components like nature, the moving forces of territorial institutions, the bid of countries for having control over other countries, and the individual human in his habitat.* These interweaving factors of particular ecologies are of concern in the evolving century. Whereas, previously man took nature for granted, nature is now considered a dynamic force to content with, both in its pro-active perspective (providing sustenance) and in its reactive nature (depleting natural resources). Berry proposed a one-dimensional eco-cultural model which was developed and operationalised, constructing human adaptation to environment from the era of hunting, fishing to agriculture.[94] (Berry, J.W., 1976) This concept was enlarged by Lomax and Berkowitz to include urban dwellers.[95] (Lomax, A., and W. Berkowitz, 1972) However, we would like to add that this is a fluid situation and that there are many dynamic differences from one ecology to another, dependent upon man's manipulation to change such ecologies and the forces of nature to resist such efforts.

While the development of the human is a process of change, it is explicit that not all change is development for the better. We have witnessed in this century, changes in the ecology which have brought about devastation and continual degradation of material and human resources. An example of the latter is the continual tribal warfare in many African countries and the continual threat of a nuclear war. It is no small matter that countries are forming and reforming into different international groups so as to protect themselves from other groups who threaten their existence, the most telling of the latter is the global terrorist groups.[96] (Brenda J. Lutz and James, M. Lutz, 2008) This early part of the twenty-first century has seen events compressed into time scenarios. These are of floods and fires in the west, of terrorist regimes in the Middle East, and of tribal warfare and of xenophobia decimating scores of villages in Africa. There is a continual world-wide playing of a chess game in order to procure territories and territorial rights to valued products such as petroleum and energy sources by countries which are the greatest consumers of such products.

Thus, we see that at the conceptual level, ecology and more especially human ecology relates to man's life on this planet. Just as there are different members in the family so also there are different nations, races, ethnic groups and some who have more territory and wealth than others on this planet. The latter are, are in a more powerful situation. In other words, the scenario expands from a simple sample of family parameters to that of world parameters. People who live in fertile ecologies have a greater advantage over those who do not and, correspondingly, the people in these fertile lands have greater economic command over the less fortunate and thus we have the divide between the north and the south, the Aryan and the Negroid, the well-placed in relation to the less well-placed in the same geo-ecology. *Human ecology, therefore, is an elastic concept, abstract, no doubt and when operationalised gives rise to several interpretations specifying in simple terms the place, the time the people and their artefacts.*

Translated to the Indian situation which has command over the sub-continent, territorial rights and related power, both economic and political are differentially available in the various sub-ecologies, the Indian lives in such varying ecologies and also in close proximity with others who are not of the same ethnic group, the same religion, of the same habits of living, but live in their own space, with their own unique pattern. The migrant who comes to the city for the first time is overwhelmed with the sights and sounds of the city. He lives as a transient migrant on a construction site, as a casual intermittent labourer under unhygienic conditions in congested areas where there is a high propensity for social disorganisation, usually in slum dense living conditions.[97] (Singh, M.P., 1986) Concomitant with these phenomena is chronic poverty which the government with all its policies and programmes is unable to tackle by providing for the minimum basic needs and facilities.[98] (Mehta, Aasha Kapur and Andrew Sheperd, 2008)

Gradually, the experience of the new ecology is assimilated and the urban migrants learns to adapt to it without even becoming conscious of the process.[99](Mukherji, S., 2002) But unlike his native village, such congested, lopsided living situations are a high risk factor for epidemiological diseases and social disorder.[100] (Dunn, F.L., and C.R. Janes, 1986) He exchanges one ecology of risk factors for a different ecology of differing risk factors.

Ecological changes are different for the urban migrant *vis-à-vis* the urban local resident. The former moves in wider circles while the latter moves in smaller circles within his residential ecology. It is also probable that the urban migrant does not go beyond his ecological circle, whereas the urban local may periodically move from one State to another, from his country to another. Thus, another dimension to human ecology is the radius of contact, routinely and periodically experienced. Individuals and their families have thus to build up a repertoire of adaptations to various situations in varying ecologies. Thus, adaptation is another key operational instrument of ecology and the human habitat within it.[101] (Steiner, F.R., 2002)

Table 1.1: Interactive Aspects of Ecological Living Patterns of the Individual

1. Information from documented writings by zoologists, biologists and the social sciences.
2. Enculturation of the human to his environment.
3. Dynamism of stabilisation *vs.* destabilisation.
4. Overt changes are visible. Covert changes are unexpressed.
5. The framework of societal morals influencing development.
6. Philosophical acceptance of relationship between human nature and geo-ecology
7. Geo-ecology is susceptible to human modifications.
8. Technology has both positive and negative influences on human development.
9. Human ecology has the power to change ecology, geo-ecology which however can devastate the human environment.
10. Devastation that is environmentally engendered can devastate the inhabitated geo-ecology.
11. Deprived ecology can be in many forms: economic, social and emotional.
12. Human ecology widens into micro/meso/exo/macro ecosystems.
13. The stability of the human ecology is related to the stability of geo-ecology.
14. Ecology whether urban, rural or tribal sets limits to human economic occupations.
15. Interdependence between human and geoecology is a major factor for human enterprise.
16. The occurrence of the fusion of caste and class is likely to increase with the increasing modernisation.
17. The family network originated in specific geoecologies which offered similar facilities such as for fishermen along coastlines and hill tribes in jungles.
18. The family in its ecology was originally a producer and is currently changing into an exchanger of goods and services.
19. The hiatus between the miniscule rich and poor in an already poor country like India is increasing.
20. Socio-religious norms are the core of family living in each and every ecology.
21. Divergence in lifestyles is related to availability of facilities for primary and secondary needs.

The psychological constructs of the human beings residing in a particular ecology are related to the environment, namely the geo-ecology in subtle ways which in themselves are strong attributes of the settings. These interacting aspects are given below in an interactive modular process between the human and process in his ecology.

The original meaning of ecology was related to sources of flora and fauna geo-ecologically, and its relevant aspects in the framework of change centralises the human in his habitat. As time and change progressed, so do the parameters of the natural ecology as manipulated by the human. For instance, mechanisation causes changes in the relationships of the human and his habitat.

Further the given ecology of the individual is monitored by space availability, availability of facilities such a medical services, and the opportunities in his environment to potentialise his abilities. In deprived ecologies these are sparse as, for example in far away rural scattered hamlets. Thus, India is a composite of divergent and diverging ecologies which mediate the individual's lifestyle.[102] (Pruthi, Rameshwari Devi Rajkumar, 2004)

The emanating stimuli of the ecology sets limits to the occupational tasks of the societies, living within them, such as the patterns of occupations of nomads, mining communities in Orissa, thus moulding the perception of constructing the environment in which they live.[103] (Gadgil, M., 1989)

The social sciences disciplines comprehensively conceptualised such societies in their ecological frameworks, in analyses of the strategies, which humans evolved in their habitats. Hook and Paolucci[104] interpreted these societies as being formed by clusters of families who lived in a network of exchange of goods and services, the major focus being the family network. Specified ecosystems were related to human cognitive behaviour, emphasising continuity and change over space and time (intra- and extra-familial systems), integrating the individual's phylogenetic and ontogenetic traits, and the specific skills to manoeuvre and manipulate such facilities. In this the twenty-first century the engagements of the various social sciences cohese in an overlapping fashion as affected by and affecting ecology: such as the phenomena of war and competing for territorial rights, greater or lesser access to the availability of natural facilities and such like.

From the earlier concepts of the family being its own producer and consumer of its own products, it has arrived at the present day patterns. These patterns are the availability of a sophisticated range of commerce and trade, of world policies and their concomitants, such as outsourcing and interdependency of nations. The factors of changing ecological events affect the human potential, indicative of the quality of life which has become an index of human development.[105] (Morris, David Morris, 1982)

Adaptation and survival are the combined pristine parameters in the perception of the lives of societal groups within a context, implying interdependency and creating a stability and a homeostasis. These have been interpreted in the human context by ecologists dealing with human ecology, such as by Tansley[106] (Tansley, A.G., 2003) as being the interaction between living and non-living things. This conceptualisation was furthered by Ogilvie[107] (Ogilvie, Marilyn Bailey, 1986) within the context of human science as the ecology of the human.

The striving for homeostasis in development occurs dynamically with periods of destabilisation and readjustment through change, and so the cycle repeats itself. These changes are monitored by time and chronological maturation.

Overt changes are documental, but covert are not. Physiological changes, for instance, occur even at the stage of foetal growth, which is observable, but the psychodynamics of the individual is not overtly known.

In the case of the Indian, he is bound by a strong sense of societal mores of behaviour towards his human ecology, and in many respects towards his own species such as being an Indian, belonging to an ethnic group, a religious group, a regional group[108] (Mahbub ul Haq, 1995). In fact, societal structures are changing so fast in the ecological domain that there is now a high profiling of an emerging new middle class.[109] (Scrase, Tim, 2006)

According to Hindu philosophy, consciousness develops when the self begins which is transitory during the current life and transmitted into the next. Humans live in consonance with nature and its factorial influences, such as water, air and fire (sources of energy) together with other lower forms of living organisms.

Technology, while increasing the quality of life, supposedly also causes deterioration in the environment, such as pollutions affecting health, and causing a rearrangement in the living conditions through a serendipity of unexpected intervening variables, depleting resources.

There are various other interpretations of ecology beginning with the zoologist's interpretation of the development in a triad relationship: ecology, habitat and relevant psychological behaviour. Thus we see that there is a relationship between the natural resources, the aptitude and volations of the human and their interactions which causes further rearrangements of these interactions. The relationship between man and nature was called "oekologie".

Ecology over civilisations was documented by philosophers and thinkers like Aristotle and Plato together with the knowledge of the system of evolutionary theory[110] (Hoy, Terry, 2000) with cultural themes and artefacts preserved over generations. We know, for instance, from the ruins of past civilisations, the kind of art, literature and structures about their social historicity of the human. Ethnographic studies also reveal the effect of cultural effects on human life. Given the phylogenetic traits which are universal across the human race, fissioning occurs into different cultural habitats, given the generic etic and emic epigenetic potentials.

Variegated examples of the relationships between ecology and human development exist such as reflected in the various studies on economic deprivation and psychological attributes.

The network of the human is differentiated by the various levels into ecosystems as expatiated by Bronfenbrenner,[111] (Bronfenbrenner, U., 1979) namely, the cyclic ecosystems/microsystems of the immediate family to the mesosystem as an extension to peer groups of friends and neighbours, to the mesosystem, extending to schools, religious groups and market places, where interaction is casual and informal. As the individual's experiences increase with age and maturity, the interaction increases but in a distal fashion with the macrosystem of the external world, where knowledge is gained by widening the territory of mobility and increased communication through media.

The more untouched the natural ecology, the relatively more reliable is the interpretation of the social groups living in them, in conjunction with natural occurrences, either proximal or distal. These stabilisation of relationships between geo-ecology and human ecology have given rise to animism, reverence towards mythology, spiritualism in relation to natural events, and the practice of socio-religious beliefs.[112] (Saraswathi T.S., and S. Pai, 2000: 80)

The individual is encultured to his habitat: his human and material ecology. The maturation process sets into operation a series of unique traits attuned to his environs, the context of which is culture specific.

About the 1960s, in the Indian culture, caste and occupation, for instance, were relatively structured in the social systems. With the impact of modernisation and technology these are changing their contours. The assumptions of physical and human development when perceived interactively with ecosystems of human development took on both a cognitive and a societal aspect. It included humanistic conceptualisations, in specific ecologies with their relative human interactions. Human organisations came to be foundationalised on the basis of common traits in a specific society living in a specific homogeneous ecology. This development concretised specific identities.

As elsewhere in the world, *there are continuities and discontinuities influencing patterns of life styles in the Indian context.* The sophisticated elite of India are more sophisticated than their counterparts in the west. They live in luxurious mansions side by side with shanty towns of migrant labourers. Their ecological system affects roles and tasks in the family and its community which hitherto were stable and systematic but are now changing dynamically in an accelerated fashion; systems which were diffused and rigid structures are now in a vortex of change, such as inter-caste marriages, travelling to and fro continents, and living life styles that are overly modern. For instance, in major metropolitan areas there are school children, who are given large sums of pocket money, while beggar children stand at street corners in rags, sometimes deliberately so in order to persuade rich people in rich cars to spare them a little money.

The association with nature and social religiosity continues, even in elite groups, however muted as socio-religious norms are deeply ingrained in the Indian's systemic behaviour. The phenomenon of migration clogging urban ecologies is fast becoming a predicament for providing facilities and for healthy lifestyles.

The growing individual has to increase his mobility and comes into contact and perhaps confronts increasing technology.[113] (Paboo, S., 2001) There is thus a confrontation between a growing technology and traditional structures. This phenomenon capitulates the individual towards individualization. The formation of personality which begins from early childhood in the nurturance of the child is the phenomenon of bonding, which continues to gain in strength as is spread of general effect in the kin group over a larger ecological radius. This conceptualisation is synonymous with the concept of loyalty and cooperation that exists among members of the kin group to another, which signifies an informal bonding, which is non-verbalised, but highly priced and religiously sanctioned. Thus, we find that *there is a circularity of dynamic movement in ecologies, which links the members of the extended family together. In a sense, these linkages maintain the continuity of a community of families and communities of a country* within an enmeshed network of reciprocal relationships. The growing individual has gains in majority to increase his mobility and comes into contact and perhaps has to deal with confrontation between a growing technology and traditional structures. This phenomenon capitulates the individual towards individualization and independence. Thus, the concept of ecology derived from its original basic biological foundations, has expanded in an environmental fashion to include a geo-ecology of flora and fauna and of animal and human species. The latter interacts with the geo-ecology so that the human exhibits a continual pattern of adaptive behaviour to his changing ecology.[114] (Berkes, F., and C. Folke, 1998)

With the growing recognition of the importance given to ecological influences on human life, it is essential that an understanding of ecology be explanatory not only of itself but of its network of relationships with other constructs.[115] (Robert, T.P. and M.N. Joshi, 1983) Ecological conceptualisation of the human network which began in the early nineteenth century, contoured in the late 1960s as the knowledge of social change included the dynamics of changing human relations in documentation from the West.[116] (Bubolz, M.M. and M.S. Sontag, 1993) This was followed through with the expansion of the concept of environment to include the ecology of the family.[117] (Bronfenbrenner, 1986). As technology increased, an understanding of the family further expanded to include environmentals related behaviour. There are increasing new boundaries of knowledge such as the influence of tidal waves on individual behaviour, of weightlessness in air, and more recently the prediction of undersea quakes affecting coastal living.[118] (Kanamori, H., 1972) At the other end of the spectrum, there is still belief in naïve folklore, of the influence of animistic occurrences affecting human behaviour, mysticism, superstition and exorcism, especially in elementary ecologies far removed from interaction with the scientific world.

Bronfenbrenner is one of the major experts to apply the principles of ecology to human dynamics, focusing mainly on the human being in relation to his social and physical environments.[119] (Bronfenbrenner,

1979) As indicated earlier, he notated the systematic approach to human relativity, namely, the increase in the extent of interaction dependent upon expanding mobility in his ecology.[120] (Hagen, J.B. 1992)

While providing a framework for understanding the transactions within the family, these formed the basis for the individual's psychological development. Herrin and Wright developed a taxonomy of family ecological constituents to include both material as well as non-material constructs.[121] (Herrin, D.A., and S.C. Wright, 1988) Family ecological theory has drawn upon the works of several experts, among whom are Buckley and Kuhn.[122] (Buckley, W., 1967) who discussed the relationships of the human to ecological patterns of living.

As elsewhere in the world, in India also, there are continuous and differential influences affecting the changes in family life styles. *If we assume that the family is an ecosystem, goal oriented in the creation of children, their upbringing, and guiding them towards their futures, then these different functions are dynamically related to a whole ecosystem. The father assumes the instrumental-adaptive role and the mother figure has the nurturant or expressive role.*[123] (Lidz, T., 1970) The family system has an organised hierarchy by age and sex. Roles are ascribed and actionised, with a dynamic interplay between age groups and sexes and among hierarchical systems. These are overarched by the umbrella of traditionalism, whether rigid or elastic. The changing nature of the environment (inclusive of culture and ecology) reacts upon the human nature, adapts him to changes with the underlying principle that the family energy is primarily directed towards survival, and then towards increasing the quality of this survival.[124] (Ram, R., 1982) For instance, the environment of an elementary tribal living is usually devoid of natural facilities in adequate proportions. There are many tribes who live on the produce of forests for their survival in dense jungles, like in *Yellamanchalli* in Andhra Pradesh and *Chindwara* in Madhya Pradesh. They live with the natural state of products, in untamed weather conditions in difficult terrains, whether hills or sand dunes, sea sides or unfertile plains. The physical ecology affects the style of living, particularly of those living elementary lifestyles such as traditional fishermen, herdsmen or subsistence farmers. The idiomatic form of language is frequently related to natural objects, combined with mysticism, such as deifying the earth as "*Dhartimata*" (mother earth). The wealth of the agriculturist is in the number of cattle he possesses just as the wealth of a nomad in a desert ecology is in the number of his camels. Therefore, each individual ecology seems to encompass each human ecology differentially, giving it the typical characteristics that distinguishes its inhabitants from other geoecologies as indicated in the paradigm below:

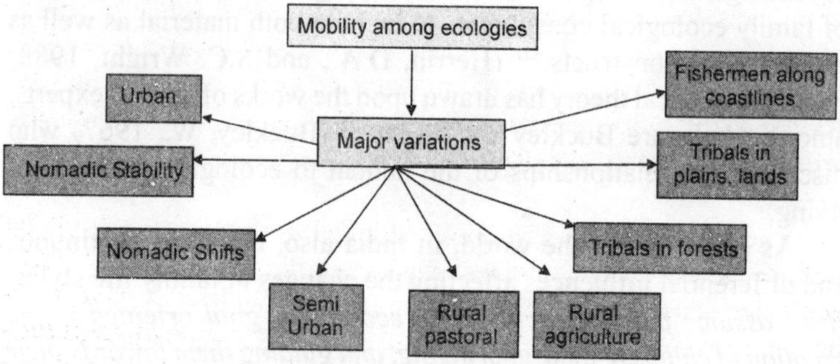

Paradigm 1.5: Major Variations of Geo-ecological Areas

Ecological factors (human and geo) contribute to economic poverty/prosperity status, chief among which is land availability, its management and enhancement.[125] (Botkin, D.B., 1990) Another factor of the geo-ecological spectrum is the massive unpredictability of geo-ecological resources, which affect the tribals or the "indigenous peoples" the most, as they are entirely dependent upon natural resources. For example, the people who live around the Amazon, the largest river in a fragile ecology, are negatively influenced by industrial inroads into their ecologies.[126] (Onser, L.E., 1995) Another example is Madagasay, the largest offshore African Island, where degradation of ecological givens, in turn create issues in well-being.[127] (Janice, Harper, 2002) Similarly, the melting ice in the North and South Pole is causing imbalances in sea and tidal waves which probably affect coastlines.[128] (Mutall, M., 1998) India has a higher proportion of poor, in contrast to many other countries. It is also affected by various heterogeneous variables within its ecologies. These variations in turn vitiate the quality of life of the people living in them.[129] (Gormely, P.J., 1998) To give a few of such countless variables are the occurrence of floods and famines during the monsoons, not only in rural areas but in metropolitan areas like Mumbai; the famine in Andhra Pradesh which cause the farmers to commit suicide, melting of the Himalayas and the flooding of the rivers, the overcrowding in slums,[130] (Jha, Lalit K., 2009) and overwhelming migration from rural hinterlands,[131] (Singh, M.P.,1986) and lack of sustainable development programmes.[132] (CGIAR, 2002) We have had such programmes of eradication of poverty like the Minimum Needs Programme in the 90's and now, the National Rural Employment Guarantee Scheme. These have had palliative effects as the population utilizing or wanting to utilize such services is beyond proportion. Unless strategies are in place, like the relationship between political and economic stability through an informed situation, such as education[133] (Uma, S. Kambhapati, 2004), a major factor in development, chronic poverty will continue to face the majority of the poor.[134] (Mehta, A.K., and A. Shepherd, 2008)

The problem of poverty has continued to plague the social and political sciences as contextual homogeneity does not exist. These ecologies have been developed or not developed due to the lack of political interest in the rural masses. For example, the inhabitants of the States of Orissa, Bihar and Madhya Pradesh are the larger and the poorer in the country. Within this nexus, except for a few industrialized cities, like Bhopal, Bhubaneshwar, Ranchi, Patna, and such others, great tracks are occupied by rural or tribal sub-cultures, which have poor ecologies. Further, their development is inversely related to the governance of the country. Programmes and policies are both central and State. Since education, health and welfare are State programmes, they are given mega handouts and, as is well-known, have poor infrastructure and personnel which hardly reach the needy.[135] (Radhakrishna, R, and S. Ray, 2005). In overcrowded metropolitan and densely populated district townships, which grow haphazardly into slum conglomerates, overcrowding is negatively related to the development of a wholesome personality.[136] (Banerjee, B., and S.M. Kanbur, 1981) *A wholesome personality requires not only a possibly re-enforcing environment of a human micro-ecology, but also adequate governance and civic facilities and a civic ethos. Within these milieus of overcrowding, the development of personality is stunted from early years of physical and intellectual development, where family disorganization is compounded by social disorganization due to few and too poor facilities for the inhabitants.*[137] (Baud, Dr. Isa S.A., and J De Wit, 2000) The most negatively affected are the fragile sections of the population: young children, women, and the elderly.[138] (Sundari, S., 2007) Drug peddling, alcoholism, family dissonance and fractions are more likely to occur in such crammed ecologies. The need for new policies and programmes for the fragile sections require serious implementable strategies. There are NGOs known for their work with street children. There are also night shelters for such children provided by the NGOs, but again, these are a drop in the ocean. The number of working children run into thousands. Gerald Merton, in his thesis emphasizes the significant role of human socialisers and ecosystems, especially the micro-system of the family, for the wholesome development of the individual.[139] (Gerald, G. Marten, 2001) which in these disorganized milieu are sparsely available. In the family micro-system, it is well-known that parental modelling is a significant aspect of the child-parent relationship.

Youth, especially females, in the inaccessible geo-ecological areas need to be provided with education even though innovative strategies have to be used. Working women in the unorganized sector need extra familial care.[140] (Mahapatra, S., 2006). It is also essential that entrepreneurial activities are provided for them for the times that are off-season in these sparse and difficult terrains. Those most aware of the plight of the inhabitants of such poor ecologies are the inhabitants themselves. Many protest movements have occurred from time to time but they die out like fizzled fire-crackers.

REFERENCES

1. Clarke, R., 1973, *Ellen Swallow: The Woman who Founded Ecology*. Chicago IL: Follett.
2. Canadian Council on Social Development, 1996, *Measuring Well-being: Proceedings from a Symposium on Social Indicators*. Final Report. Ottawa: Renouf Publishing Co. Ltd.
3. Gunnar, M, 1998, 'Quality of Child Care and Buffering of Neuro-endocrine Stress Reaction: Potential Effects on the Developing Human Brain", *Preventive Medicine,* 27, 208-211.
4. Kak, Subhas C., 2000, "On Understanding Ancient Indian Science". In A.K. Raina, B.N. Patnaik and M. Chadha (eds.), *Science and Tradition*. Simla: Indian Institute of Advanced Studies, pp. 83-107.
5. Hull, Clark L., 1943, *Principles of Behaviour*. New York: D. Appleton Century Co.
6. Gadgil M., and R. Guha, 1995, Ecology and Equity: The Use and Abuse of Nature in Contemporary India. New Delhi: Penguin Books.
7. Mahadevan, K., Chi Huy Tuan and V.K. Balakrishnan Nair, 1992,

Ecology Development and Population Problems. Delhi: B.R Publishing Corp.

8. Egerton, F.N., 2001, "A History of the Ecological Sciences, Part 1. Early Greek Origins", *Bulletin of the Ecological Society of America*, 82, 92-97.
9. Ramalay, Francis. 1940, "The Growth of a Science", University of Colorado Studies, 26: 3-14.
10. Alexander von Humboldt, 1996, (ed. and tran. Jason Wilson), *Personal Narratives of a Journey to the Equinoctial Regions of the New Continent*. London: Penguin Classics.
11. Tansley, A.G., 2003. *An Introduction to Plant Ecology*. New Delhi: Discovery Publishing House.
12. Berry J.W., 1974, 'Ecological and Cultural Factors in Spatial Per Capita Development', J.W. Berry and P.R. Dasen (eds.), *Culture and Cognition: Readings in Cross Cultural Psychology*. London: Lord Methuen.
13. Egerton, Frank N., 1973, "Changing Concepts of the Balance of Nature", *Quarterly Review of Biology*. 48, 322- 50;
   Egerton, Frank N., 2001, "A History of the Ecological Sciences, Part 1, Early Greek".
14. Ramakrishnan, P.S., 2001 (Nov.), 'Increasing population and declining biological resources in the context of global change and globalisation', *Journal of Biosciences*., Vol. 26. No. 4 (Suppl.), pp. 465-79.
15. Kumar, H.D, 1992, *Modern Concepts of Economics*. New Delhi: Vikas Publishing House.
16. Krech, D., and G.S. Klein (eds.), 1952, *Theoretical Models and Personality Theory*, p. 142. Durham: Duke Univ. Press.
17. Brara, Rita, 2003, "Ecology and Environment", in V. Das (ed.), *The Oxford India Companion to Sociology and Social Anthropology*. New Delhi: Oxford University Press.
18. Coll, C., E. Bearer and R. Lerner, 2004, *Nature and Nurture: The Complex Interplay of Genetic and Environmental Influences on Human Behaviour and Development*. Mahwah, N.J.: Lawrence Erlbaum and Associates.
19. C.M. Super and S. Harkness, 1986, "The Developmental Niche: A Conceptualisation at the Interface of Child and Culture", *International Journal of Behavioural Development*, Vol. 9, No. 4, 545-569.
20. Murdock, G.P., 1967, Ethnographic Atlas. University of Pittsburg Press.
21. Elwein, V., 1947, *The Muria and their Ghotul*. London: Oxford University Press, 1-723;
   Ghurye, G.S., 1963, *Mahadev Kolis*. Bombay: Popular Prakashan, 71;
   Ishwaran, K., 1968, *Shivapur: A South Indian Village*. London: Routledge and Kegan Paul 52-73;

Mathur, K.S., 1964, *Caste and Ritual in a Malwa Village*, Asia Publishing House, 88.

22. Misra, G., and K.J. Gergen, 2001, 'On The Place of Culture in Psychological Science', in Dalal, A.K., and G. Misra (eds.), *New Directions in Indian Psychology*, pg. 408. New Delhi: Sage.
23. Munroe, R., and R. Munroe, 1975, *Cross Cultural Human Development*. Ann Arbour, Michigan: Molly Lithographing Inc.
24. Mead, M., 1930, *Growing Up in New Guinea*. New York: William Morrow.
25. Mead, M., 1930, *Growing Up in New Guinea*. New York: William Morrow.
26. Dreze, J., and Amartya Sen, 2002, *India: Development and Participation*. New Delhi: Oxford University Press.
27. Thomas, R.M., 2001, "A potpourri of theories", in R.M. Thomas, *Recent Theories of Human Development*. Thousand Oaks, London, New Delhi: Sage Publications, pp. 188-189.
28. Berry, J.W., 2003, 'Eco-cultural Perspective on Human Psychological Development', in Saraswathi T.S. (ed.), *Cross-cultural Perspectives in Human Development*. pp. 51-52. New Delhi: Sage.
29. Whiting, J.W.M., and I.L. Child, 1953, *Child Training and Personality: A Cross-Cultural Study*. New Haven: Yale University Press.
30. Super, C.M., and Harkness, S., 1996, *Parents' Cultural Belief Systems: Their Origins, Expressions and Consequences*. New York: Guilford Publications.
31. Paranjpe, A.C., 2003, 'Contemporary Psychology and The Mutual Understanding of India and Europe', in J.W. Berry, R.C. Mishra, and R.C. Tripathi (eds.), *Psychology in Human and Social Development*. p. 25. New Delhi: Sage.
32. Boyd, R., and P. Richerson, 1983, 'Why is Culture Adaptive?', *Quarterly Review of Biology*, 58, pp. 209-214.
33. Moran, E., 1990, *The Eco-System Approach in Anthropology*. Ann Arbor: University of Michigan Press.
34. Boss, P., 1987, 'Family Stress', in M.B. Sussman, and S.K. Steinmetz (eds)., *Handbook of Marriage and the Family*, pp. 695-723. New York: Plenum.
35. Berry, J.W., 1974, Ecological and Cultural Factors in Spatial Perceptual Development", in J. Wolfenson (ed.) *Personality and Learning 2*. London: Hodder and Stoughton.
36. Misra, G., 1983, 'Deprivation and Development', *Indian Education Review*, 18, 1983, pp. 1-21;
Misra, G., and L.B. Tripathi, 1976, 'The concept of prolonged

deprivation and its measurement', *Indian Journal of Behaviour,* 1, 119-143.
37. Keay, J., 2000, *India: A History*. Harper Collins.
38. Ram, R., 1992, "Inter Country inequalities in income and basic needs indices: A recent perspective", *World Development*, 20, pp. 899-905.
39. Sharma, S., 1985 'Poverty, Health and Quality of Life', *Indian Journal of Psychiatry*, 27, pp. 3-16;
Pushpa, M., 1990, 'Social deprivation and cognitive style', in U.K Bevli (ed), *Researches in Child Development. A Book of Readings*, pp. 194-202, New Delhi: NCERT.
40. Centre for Development and Human Rights, 2004, *The Right to Development: A Primer*, p. 102. New Delhi: Sage Publications.
41. Radhakrishna, A., and S. Ray (eds.), 2005, *Handbook of Poverty in India: Perspective, Problems and Programmes*. Mumbai: Gandhian Research Institute.
42. Mathew, G., 2003, *Panchayati Raj Institutions and Human Rights*. New Delhi: PUCL Bulletin.
43. Sinha, 1975, *A Study of Psychological Dimensions of Poverty: A Challenge and Necessity*. Presidential address, 13th Annual Conference of the Indian Academy of Applied Psychology. Dharwad;
Shanmugam, T.E., 1975, 'War on poverty, role of psychologist', *Journal of Psychological Researches*. 20. pp. 1-15.
44. Parameswaran, E.G., 1972, 'Developmental Psychology', *ICSSR Survey of Research in Psychology*. pp. 56-79. Bombay: Popular Prakashan;
Rath, 1972, *Socio-psychology*, pp. 362-413. Bombay: Popular Prakashan;
Moullick, T.K., 1981, 'Psychology of Poverty', U. Pareek, (ed.), *A Survey of Research in Psychology, 1971-76*. Part 2, pp. 635-91, Bombay: Popular Prakashan.
45. Misra, G., and Tripathi, K.N., 2004, 'Psychological dimensions of poverty and deprivation', in J. Pandey (ed.), *Psychology in India Revisited: Developments in the Discipline* (Vol. 3), pp. 118-215. New Delhi: Sage.
46. Chambers. R., 1991, 'Poverty in India: Concepts, Research and Reality', in B. Harris, S. Guhan and R.H. Cassen (eds.), *Poverty in India: Research and Policy*, pp. 301-332. Oxford University.
47. Mehta, Aasha Kapur and Shepherd Andrew, 2006, *Chronic Poverty and Development Policy in India*. New Delhi: Sage Publications.
48. Furstenberg, F.F. Jr., and A.J. Cherlin, 1991, *Divided Families*. Cambridge, MA: Harvard University Press.

49. Hofstede, G., 1984, *Culture's Consequences: International Differences in World Related Values*. Abridged edition. Beverley Hills, CA: Sage.
50. Nandi, S., C.R. Rajalakshmi and I. Varghese, 1971, *Life and Culture of the Mala-Ulladan*. Calcutta: Anthropological Survey of India, Government of India.
51. Hofstede, G., 1994, *Cultures and Organisations*. London: Harper Collins.
52. Vayda, P., 1969, *Environment and Cultural Behaviour*. Garden City Natural History Press.
53. Barry, J.H., I. Child and M. Bacon, 1959, 'Relation of child training to subsistence economy', *American Anthropologist,*, 61, pp. 51-63.
54. Goodnow, J.J, 1976, 'Cultural variations in cognitive skills', in Jane Wolfson (eds.), *Personality and Learning*, pp. 97-111. London: Hodder and Stoughton.
55. Witkin, H., and J.W. Berry, 1975, 'Psychological Differentiation in cross-cultural perspective', *Journal of Cross Cultural Psychology*, Vol. 6., pp. 4-87.
56. English-Lueck, J.A., Dr., 1998, *Technology and Social Change: The Effects on Family and Community*. COSSA Congressional Seminar, June 19, 1998.
57. Gulati, Leela, 1970, 'Female Work Participation and Economic Development: A Regional Analysis', *Economic and Political Weekly*, 5, 21.
58. Doshi, S.L., 1971, *Bhils: Between Societal Self-Awareness and Cultural Synthesis*. 'Chapter 3: Occupation', pp. 54-74. New Delhi: Sterling Publishers.
59. Shanmugam, T.E., 1976, 'War on poverty: role of Psychologists', *Journal of Psychological Researches*, 20, pp. 1-15.
60. Misra, G., and K.N. Tripathi, 2004, 'Psychological dimensions of poverty and deprivation' in J. Pandey (ed.), *Psychology in India Revisited*, Vol. 3, p. 132. New Delhi: Sage.
61. Tripathi, R.C., 1982, 'The concept of deprivation: some issues', in D. Sinha, R.C. Tripathi, and G. Misra (eds.), *Deprivation: Its Social Roots and Psychological Consequences*, pp.17-23. New Delhi: Concept.
62. Agrawal, R., and G. Misra, 2002, 'A Factor Analytic Study of Achievement Goals and Means: An Indian View', in A.K. Dalal and G. Misra (eds.), *New Directions in Indian Psychology*, Vol. 1, *Social Psychology*, pp. 58-72. New Delhi/Thousand Oaks/London, Sage Publications.
63. Reddy, Sujatha B.N., 1986, 'Analysis of some of the socio-economic status scales developed in India', *Indian Journal of Behaviour*, 10, pp.1-10.

64. Jachuk, K., 1993, 'SES and time-related effects of pre-schooled education on cognitive abilities', in A.K. Srivastava (ed.), *Researches in Child and Adolescent Psychology*, pp. 24-31. New Delhi: NCERT. Das, I., and P.K. Mona, 1990, 'The effect of poverty upon intelligence', *Indian Journal of Community Guidance Service*, 7, pp. 37-48.
65. Rolston, H., 1999, *Genes, Genesis and God: Values and their Origins in Natural and Human History*, p. 94. Cambridge: Cambridge University Press.
66. Bhogle, S., and T. Fatima, 1981, 'Development of quantitative thinking in children', *Social Change*, 11, pp.13-20.
67. Dash, U.N., and J.P. Das, 1984, 'Development of concrete operational thought and information coding in schooled and unschooled children', *British Journal of Development Psychology*, 2, pp. 63-72.
68. Miller, C.D., and N. J. Salkind, 2002, *Handbook of Research Design and Social Measurement*, p. 449. Thousand Oaks, Sage.
69. Cohen, S.P., 2001, *India: Emerging Power*, p. 28. Washington D.C.: The Brookings Institution.
70. Dhesi, A.S.,1998, "Caste, Class Synergies and Discrimination in India", *International Journal of Social Economics*, Vol. 25, Issue 6/7/8, pp. 1030-1048.
71. Karanth, G.K., 2004, 'Replication or Dissent? Culture and Institutions among Untouchable Scheduled Castes in Karnataka', D. Gupta (ed.), *Contributions to Indian Sociology*. Delhi: Oxford University Press. pp. 137-164.
72. Thornberry, P., 2005, *Confronting Racial Discrimination: A CERD Perspective*. London: Oxford University Press.
73. Ghurye, G.S., 1969, *Caste and Race in India*. Bombay: Popular Prakashan.
74. Srinivas, M.N., 1962, 'A note on westernisation and sanskritisation', in M.S. Srinivas, *Caste in Modern India and Other Essays*. London: Asia Publishing House.
75. Adams, J.S., 1965, 'Inequity in Social Exchange', in L. Berkowitz (ed.), *Advances in Experimental Social Psychology*, Vol. 2, New York: Academic Press.
76. Sahay, G.R., 2004, 'Hierarchy difference and the caste system: a study of rural Bihar', in D. Gupta (ed.), *Contributions to Indian Sociology*. pp. 113-136. New Delhi: Sage.
77. Sipra Bose, Johnson, 1974, Prejudice and Caste Research: Comments on Hsu. *American Anthropologist*, New Series, Vol. 76, No. 2 (June, 1974), pp. 350-351.
78. Khalakdina, M., 1979, *Early Child Care in India*. p. 52. London/New York/Paris: Gordon and Breach.

79. Kagitcibasi, C., 1994, 'A critical appraisal of individualism and collectivism: toward a new formulation', in U. Kim, H.C. Triandis, C. Kagitcibasi, Sang-Chin Choi and Gene Yoom (eds.), *Individualism and Collectivism: Theory, Method and Applications*, pp. 52-65. Thousand Oaks, C.A.: Sage.
80. Bhasin, K., 1994, *What Is Patriarchy?* New Delhi: Kali for Women.
81. Mehta, P., 1994, 'Empowering the people for social achievement', in R.N. Kanungo and M. Mendonca (eds.), *Work Motivation: Models for Developing Countries*. New Delhi: Sage.
82. Bayley, Susan, 2001, *Caste, Society and Politics in India from the 18th century to the Modern Age*. New York: Cambridge University Press.
83. Mines, M., 1980, *Indian Women and Patriarchy*. New Delhi: Concept Publishing Company.
84. Misra, G., A.K. Srivastava and S. Gupta, 1999, 'The cultural construction of childhood in India: some observations', *Indian Psychological Abstracts and Reviews*, 6 (2), pp. 191–218.
85. Barash, D.P., 1977, *Socio-biology and Behaviour*. New York: Elsevier N. Holland.
86. Bronfenbrenner, U., 1986, 'Ecology of the family as a context for human development research perspectives', *Developmental Psychology*, 22 (6), pp. 723-42.
87. Lash, Scott, Bronislaw Szerszynski and Brian Wynne (eds.), 1998, *Risk Environment and Modernity: Towards a New Ecology*. London: Sage Publications.
88. Shah, A.M., B.S. Baviskar and E.A. Ramaswamy (eds.), 1996, *Social Structure and Change*. Vol. 1: *Theory and Method : An Evaluation of the Works of M.N. Srinivas*. New Delhi: Sage Publications.
89. Ravi Kumar (ed.), 1999, *Colonialism and Modernisation in India*. Delhi: Anmol Publishers Pvt Ltd.
90. Sinha, J.B.P., 2002, 'A cultural frame for understanding organisational behaviour', *Psychology and Developing Societies*, 14 (1), p. 155.
91. Berry, J.W., 2003, 'Ecocultural perspectives on human psychological development', in T.S. Saraswathi (ed.), *Cross-cultural Perspectives in Human Development*, p. 54, New Delhi: Sage.
92. Adelman, I., and Morris, C.T., 1967, *Society, Politics and Economic Development*. Baltimore: John Hopkins University Press.
93. Dyson, T., R.Cassen and L. Visaria (eds.), 2004, *Twenty-First Century India: Population, Economy, Human Development and Environment*. New York: Oxford University Press.
94. Berry J.W., 1976, 'Human ecology and cognitive style', in J. Halsted (ed.), *Comparative Studies in Cultural and Psychological Adaptations*. New York: Sage.

95. Lomax, A., and W. Berkowitz, 1972, 'The evolutionary taxonomy of culture', *Science*, 177, pp. 228-239.
96. Brenda J. Lutz and James, M. Lutz, 2008, *Global Terrorism*. New York: Routledge Publications.
97. Singh, M.P., 1986, *Patterns of Rural Urban Migration in India*. Delhi: Inter-India Publications.
98. Mehta, Aasha Kapur and Andrew Sheperd, 2008, *Chronic Poverty and Development Policy in India*. Delhi: Sage publications.
99. Mukherji, S., 2002, 'Urbanisation and migration in India: A different scene', in H.S. Geyer (ed.), *International Handbook of Urban Systems: Studies of Urbanisation and Migration in Advanced and Developing Countries*, p. 527. Cheltenham: Edward Elgar Publishing.
100. Dunn, F.L., and C.R. Janes, 1986, 'Introduction: Medical anthropology and epidemiology', in R. Stall, S.M. Gifford and C.R. Janes (eds.), *Anthropology and Epidemiology*, p. 20. Dordrecht: D. Reidel Publishing Company.
101. Steiner, F.R., 2002, *Human Ecology: Following Nature's Lead*. Washington, D.C.: Island Press.
102. Pruthi, Rameshwari Devi Rajkumar, 2004 *Indian Society*. Jaipur: Mangaldeep Publications.
103. Gadgil, M., 1989, "Deforestation: problems and prospects", *Wasteland News* (Supplement), Vol. 1V, No. 4 (May-July 1989).
104. Hook, N.C. and Paolucci, B., 1970, "The family as an ecosystem", *Journal of Home Economics*, 62(5), 315-318.
105. Morris, David Morris, 1982, *Measuring the Condition of India's Poor: The Physical Quality of Life*. New Delhi: Promilla Publishers.
106. Tansley, A.G, 2003. *An Introduction to Plant Ecology*, New Delhi: Discovery Publishing House.
107. Ogilvie, Marilyn Bailey, 1986, *Women in Science: Antiquity through the Nineteenth Century*. Cambridge: MIT Press.
108. Mahbub Ul Haq, 1995, *Reflections on Human Development : The Human Development Paradigm*. New York: Oxford University Press, 13-23.
109. Scrase, Tim, 2006, *The "New Middle Class in India: A Re-assessment*. The Paper presented to the 16th Biennial Conference of the Asian Studies of Australia in Wollongong, 26-29 June, 2006.
110. Hoy, Terry, 2000, *Toward a Naturalistic Political Theory: Aristotle, Hume, Dewey, Evolutionary Biology, and Deep Ecology*. Westport City: Praeger Publications.
111. Bronfenbrenner, U., 1979, *The Ecology of Human Development: Experiments by Nature and Design*. Cambridge, MA: Harvard University Press.

112. Saraswathi T.S., and S. Pai, 2000, "Socialisation in the Indian Context", in H.S.R. Kao and D. Sinha (eds.), *Asian Perspectives on Psychology*. New Delhi: Sage, pp. 74-92.
113. Paboo, S., 2001, 'The human genome and our view of Ourselves', *Science*, 291, pp. 1219-1220.
114. Berkes, F., and C. Folke (eds.), 1998, *Linking Social and Ecological Systems: Management Pratices and Social Mechanisms for Building Resilience*. Cambridge: Cambridge University Press.
115. Robert, T.P, and M.N. Joshi, 1983, *The Background of Ecology: Concept and Theory*. Cambridge: Cambridge University Press.
116. Bubolz, M.M., and M.S. Sontag, 1993, 'Human ecology theory', in P.G. Boss, W.J. Doherty, R. LaRossa, W.R. Schumm and S.K. Steinmetz (eds.), *Sourcebook of Family Theories and Methods: A Contextual Approach*. New York: Plenum Press.
117. Bronfenbrenner, U., 1986, 'Ecology as a Context for Human Development Research Perspectives', *Developmental Psychology*, 22 (6), pp. 723-742.
118. Kanamori, H., 1972, 'Mechanism of tsunami earthquakes', *Physics of the Earth and Planet Interiors*, 6, pp. 346-59.
119. Bronfenbrenner, U., 1979, *The Ecology of Human Development: Experiments in Nature and Design*. Cambridge, MA: Cambridge University Press.
120. Hagen, J.B., 1992, *An Entangled Bank. The Origins of Ecosystem Ecology*. New Brunswick, N.J.: Rutgers University Press.
121. Herrin, D.A., and S.C. Wright, 1988, 'Precursors to a family ecology: interrelated threads of ecological thought', *Family Science Review*, 1, pp. 163-184.
122. Buckley, W., 1967, *Sociology and Modern Systems Theory*. Englewood Cliffs: Prentice Hall.
123. Lidz, T., 1970, 'The family as the developmental setting', in E.J. Anthony, and C. Koupernik (eds.), *The Child in His Family*, p. 25. John Wiley and Sons.
124. Ram, R., 1982, "Composite indices of physical quality of life, basic needs fulfilment and income: a principal component representation", *Journal of Development Economics*, 11(1), pp. 227–247.
125. Botkin, D.B., 1990, *Discordant Harmonies: A New Ecology for the Twenty-first Century*. New York. Oxford University Press.
126. Onser, L.E., (ed), 1995, *Indigenous People and the Future of Amazonia. An Ecological Anthropology of an Endangered World*. University of Arizona Press.
127. Janice, Harper, 2002, *Endangered Species: Health, Illness and Death*

among Madagascar's People of the Forest. Durham NC: Carolina Academic Press.

128. Mutall, M., 1998, *Protecting the Arctic: Indigenous Peoples and Cultural Survival.* Amsterdam: Harwood.
129. Gormely, P.J., 1998, "The human development Index in 1994: impact of income on country rank", *Journal of Economic and Social Measurement*, 21, pp. 253-267.
130. Jha, Lalit K., 2009, "Indian slums represent complex political and social issues: Research", *Business Standard.* Sept. 10, 2009.
131. Singh, M.P.,1986, *Patterns of Rural-Urban Migration in India.* New Delhi: Inter-India publishers.
132. CGIAR, 2002, *Agriculture and the Environment: Partnership for a Sustainable Future.* Washington, D.C.: CGIAR (Consultative Group on International Agricultural Research and Global Environment Facility).
133. Uma, S. Kambhapati, 2004, *Development and the Developing World.* New Delhi: Wiley Blackwell India.
134. Mehta, A.K., and A. Shepherd, 2008, *Chronic Poverty and Development Policy in India.* New Delhi: Sage Publications.
135. Radhakrishna, R, and S. Ray (eds.), 2005, *Handbook on Poverty in Indian Perspective, Policies and Programmes.* Mumbai: Gandhian Institute of Research.
136. Banerjee, B., and S.M. Kanbur, 1981, "On the specification and estimation of macro rural-urban migration functions: with an application to Indian Data", *Oxford Bulletin of Economics and Statistics*, Vol. 43, pp. 7-29.
137. Baud, Dr Isa S.A., and J De Wit (eds.), 2000, *New Forms of Urban Governance in India: Shifts, Models, Networks and Contestations.* New Delhi: Sage Publications.
138. Sundari, S., 2007, *Migrant Women and Urban Labour Market. Concepts and Case Studies of Problems, Gains and Loss.* New Delhi: Deep and Deep Publications.
139. Gerald, G. Marten, 2001, *Human Ecology: Basic Concepts for Sustainable Development.* London: Earth Scan Publishers.
140. Mahapatra, S., 2006, *Working Women: Problems and Prospects.* Delhi: Rajat Publications.

2

The Human Ecology of the Individual

This chapter consists of the following sections:

1. Understanding the nature of human ecology.
2. The meaning of human ecology.
3. The family as an ecological system.
4. Human abilities and relevant coping modes.
5. Problem solving behaviour in scarce ecologies.
6. Variations in family ecological systems.
7. The psychological bases of human ecology.
8. The growing individual and his ecological network.
9. Variations in perceptions.
10. Perception of the self in the self's ecology.
11. The nature of the compact between the family and governance.
12. The changing nature of the compact between family and society

1. Understanding the Nature of Human Ecology

The socio-psychological study of human development has undergone transformation since it began a century ago in the West. There are a multiplicity of conceptual frames in studying developmental changes.[1] (Hall, C.S., G. Lindzey and J.B. Campbell, 1988) Initially, development was viewed as an orderly unfolding of predetermined genetic sequence with individual differences in ontogenetic characteristics.[2] (Watson, J.B., 1913) Such biological concepts have challenged preformationism and epigenetic views by the growing information in environmental studies.[3] (Wickew, A.W., 1992) These are engendered by the physical ecological constructs making up the human ecology. Increasingly in acceptance by the physical sciences is the importance of cognitive constructs as known by neurological investigations.[4] (Kelvin S. Hall, Gardner Lindzey and John B. Campbell, 1998) In the previous decades, scientific and technological development were high profiled, as they indexed economic development *vis-à-vis* agricultural development mostly by the rich nations. However, the recent rise in terrorism, civil wars, fragmentation of territorial rights, the threat of nuclearisation and recessionary upheavals confront the human issues of what does a tsunami, a pandemic flu, and an autocratic regime do to individuals and their societies in the various parts of the globe.

2. The Meaning of Human Ecology

Historically, works of early philosophical thinkers like Aristotle and Plato implied the variable of the environment in their concepts on the growth and development of the human ecology.[5] (Duncan, O.D., 1965) *When Darwin postulated his theory of evolution, the significance of ecology came into its own in the natural sciences, and made its* inroads *into the social sciences*. The term 'ecology' originated in the documentations of the German zoologists who explored the relationships of living things to their ecologies. Ecological psychology builds on the concepts of Lewin's life space and topology theory.[6] (Lewin, K., 1936). In the study by Barker and Wright, who followed a child's life in relation to activities during the day, they illustrated the triad relationship among a child's maturing potentials, his habitat and his wider geo-ecological environment.[7] (Barker, R.G., and H.F. Wright, 1951) Ecology is thus the mutual relationships of organisms in their given and natural physical environment.[8] (East, M., 1980) As a perspective on behaviour, ecology is of importance in analysing it, especially in developing countries/ societies,[9] (Berry, J.W., 1966) where there is a closer relationship between the individual and his natural habitat. Since societies in their ecological habitats, interpret their behaviour in relation to their ecological stimuli, such stimuli set the limits defining the potentials in their livelihood tasks, and thus their patterns of life styles. For instance, hill tribes and forest-produce gatherers in the Tehri hills of Uttar Pradesh and fishermen in the coastal areas of Andhra Pradesh or Kerala, depend upon the geo-ecological produce of the ecology for their livelihood. Analyses of such situations further imply the need for an operational definition of the contextual frame. Indians live mostly in India, in a given place; either in a city, a village or a tribal area, where interaction takes place between the human and his ecology in a reciprocal manner. Super and Harkness relate this kind of specific situation to the actuality of concrete/material surroundings of the human and their capacities for the maintenance of the group system.[10] (Super, C.M., and Harkness, S., 1986)

Human ecologists have borrowed ideas to a considerable extent from biology, including the key processes of adaptation and the concept of ecosystem, proposed by Tansley in 1935. This term as a name for the interactional system comprised living things, together with their non-living habitat.[11] (Tansley, A.G., 1935) Following on these concepts, Richards proposed a science of "home and family", similar to the ecology of the human.[12] (Clarke, R., 1973). For example, it was suggested that being a member of a particular social group does not mean that cultural traits, like achievement motivation, where some individuals become businessmen, and others carpenters, does not similarly influence the rest to move towards similar occupations. There are now several movements away from the traditional caste-group occupations, especially in the younger generation. For instance, children of the *Bania* community are becoming media professionals and financial experts, rather than tradesmen, the original occupation by caste. What this means is that dynamic interactive patterns of behaviour are changing, as influenced by ecological variables impacting upon them. There are businessmen: but not all businessmen value their profession to the same extent as the other, for example, an Under Secretary in a highly bureaucratic government job may not be similarly motivated as an entrepreneurial working in a competitive similar environment where similar goods are made and sold.[13] (Gavan, M., 1995) Some follow their parental occupations only in order to keep the business or property within the family, while others do so for security or personal reasons. Therefore, there is a leeway for humans in the same habitat to behave occupationally different in relation to their ecology. Studies of human ecology, which emerged in the late 1960s, initially were focused on the knowledge of social change, and included the dynamics of changing environments in their explanations of human behaviour. It originated with Heckel, who proposed a dynamic interaction between life and its environment and therefore included the human.[14] (Bubolz, M., and M.S. Sontag, 1993)

This interpretation was followed by Bronfenbrenner, who expanded the concept to include the family in the ecological framework.[15] (Bronfenbrenner, U., 1986)

Initially, ecology was discussed in relation to the biosphere, exosphere and hydrosphere strictly in the area of nature to study geoecology systems in a holistic manner.[16] (Kumar, H.D., 1992) The assumptions underlying this initial conceptualizations of the geo-ecology were: *(a) social and physical environments as interdependent for influencing quality of life; (b) environments are sources of available facilities; and (c) resources exist for modifying the environment for the economic and the efficiency of human efforts.* These are perceived, as a package of factors influencing cognitive life styles.[17] (Bennet, J.W., 1983)

In the early twentieth century social scientists incorporated ecology in their nomenclature as they recognised that it influenced an understanding of human organisation[18] (Bubolz, M.M., and M.S. Sontag, 1993) *and on the geographical environment.*[19] (Barrows, H.H., 1923).These concepts were the earliest to be incorporated in the ecological perspective of human behaviour. Anthropology[20] (Steward, J., 1955), political science[21] (Prout and M. Prout, 1965), economics[22] (Boulding, K.E., 1950) and human-environment relations[23] (Altman, I., and J.F. Wohlwill, J.F., 1977) were studied holistically in tandem where the effect of these disciplines on human behaviour were part of the human ecological environment. In a sense, there is close relationship in the understanding of ecology, environment and the disciplines affecting behaviour. For example, *the economic factor affects either affluence or deprivation. The political fact affects stability or instability of the governance. Anthropology is indicative of the lifestyle patterns monitored by geo-ecological facilities.* Thus, ecology as a composite of interactive factors became an academically popular and essential variable.

Human ecology as applied to the family received a boost when its theme was supported by the dynamic work of Hook and Paolucci,[24] (Hook, N., and B. Paolucci, 1970), who stated that the family was dependent on the natural environment for physical sustenance, the social environment for human interaction and the quality and meaning given to lifestyles.[25] (World Health Forum, 1996) Bronfenbrenner is a major advocate of the importance of the contextual aspects in ecological research in human development, and conceptualised the environment as being a set of nested and encapsulated structures, which he discussed in the framework of nested ecosystems.[26] (Bronfenbrenner, U., 1979)

The micro-system, is the family context, which is the proximal system acting and reacting with the family members through immediacy of interaction. The next level is relative to support systems, like education and health agencies, constituting the next capsule, which is termed the meso system. The external environment in which others participate, like market places, work settings, and social organisations, constitute the exo-system. The macro system is the world at large of norms, ideological values, their structures and institutional systems of particular cultures. These ecosystems are more or less abstract concepts converging upon each other in an interrelated form. Bronfenbrenner has also proposed the chronological system of social change and continuity or discontinuity of patterns of socialisation over time and space in the living environment of families.[27] (Bronfenbrenner, 1986) Bronfenbrenner has described the individual's environment as a "set of nested structures each inside the next like a set of Russian dolls."[28] (Bronfenbrenner, 1979) They make up the blueprint of the cultural ecology of human development.[29] (Bronfenbrenner, 1986) Thus, *the micro system is a framework for observing and analysing intra-familial interactions as influenced by extra-familial situations in a network of actions and reactions.*[30] (Bronfenbrenner, U., 1979)

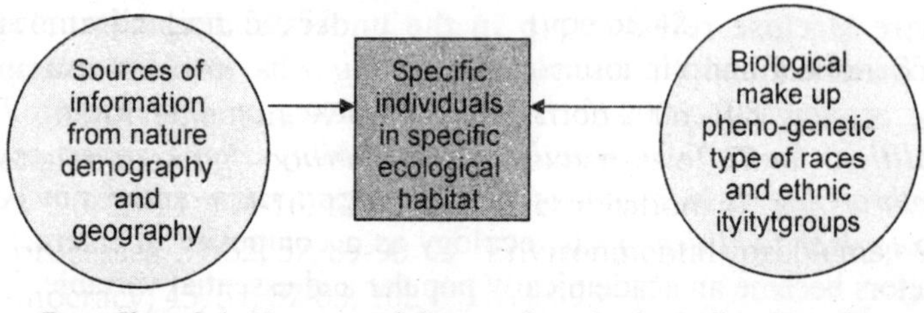

Paradigm 2.1: Human and Geo-ecology in the Indian Situation

Note: Ecological habitat implies residential living whether on an oasis, island, mountain, plains land, weather, flora and fauna are adequate in supply as related to the demand where the occupations in which the people are employed increase (scientists, technologists) improve/decrease the quality of living.

In the biological or concrete form, the visible self, the human, evolves over time, limited by his genetic determinism, which he brings into the world from his embryonic state. This epigenetic process is limited by the time factor. The individual develops at his own pace, different from others, and uses his specific ontogenetic skills, also different from others. *These skills are monitored and reinforced by his human ecology consisting of the family, the teachers, the peers and the media and others.*[31] (Bronfenbrenner U. 2005) Over generations of living in the same habitat, and because of the need to adapt to it, the human being has evolved to be physiologically compatible with his ecology, like the short-stature pygmies in the equatorial African jungles and the Nordic races of tall, large-built individuals in Netherlands, who both acclimatise their physical and physiognomic statures to the climatic givens. This is not unlike the Aryan and the Dravidian races in India, the latter having settled down in the southern peninsula, while the former have for generations inhabited the northern States and the Himalayan regions. For instance, the Aryans are said to be descendants of the race who came from Central Asia, the first being Chengez Khan[32] (Arnold, D., 1999) while the racial characteristics of the Dravidian races are more like those of the people who live in the similar tropical zones. *Thus, it seems that over time, racial characteristics attuned to the ecology of their habitat have influenced similar characteristics incompatibility with ecological conditions*. The Pygmy, for instance, is short in stature, has darkened skin, dresses scantily so as to adjust to the heat and to conserve his energy, unlike the Eskimo of the Tundra.

3. The Family as an Ecological System

As we have pointed out, ecological conceptualisation of the family began in the early 19th century in the west. Human ecology emerged in the late 60s as one of the sources for understanding social change. Human ecology included the dynamics of changing environments in its explanations of human behaviour. With the increasing pace of technology and science, and the influence of the changing environment especially the physical environs for human health and safety, ecology began to assume important variable statuses. It further confirmed the fact *that nature and human ecology are interrelated in an intricate manner; and, more importantly, they had inevitable consequences on each other. Evolving from the initial biological concept of ecology, the concept spread to a holistic approach in its scientific principles to include human living patterns and the human habitat.*[33] (Littlewood, R., 2000) Added to these concepts were the principles of conditionality applied to everyday living situations. These influences were both direct and indirect, and derived their constructs from the disciplines of economics, sociology, and psychology. Such influences conditioned the habitat lifestyles and economic opportunities essential for the maintenance of a homeostasis in living patterns. *These economic bases of human ecology are perceivable in the occupational lifestyles and the habitats, such as the pastoral and agricultural communities as well as of those living in urban conglomerates*, each differentially influenced by their specific habitats. Many remote areas are still influenced by the vagaries of climatic conditions. This ecological conceptualisation grew to include the family as a producing and consuming unit.[34] (Adam, C.C., 1935) Arising from this concept of the family, it spreads necessarily to the individual belonging to a family who also have to interact with the relational family structures which form the network. Thus, the individual is said to have both a human ecology and a geo-ecology which interact in dynamic ways. Take for instance, a farmer. He does not live alone, he lives within an environment. His immediate environment is his immediate relations, followed by the relational environment or different generations in the same physical area. He has specific tasks related to ploughing, tilling, harvesting and marketing. In this occupational enterprise, he is assisted by family members and, as a unit, they interact with other families who have or do not have similar occupations. The fact is that vicissitudes in the environment whether the residents are farmers or not, each and everyone is affected by the terrain, its fertility or otherwise. The long chain of production is ultimately successful or otherwise, dependent upon the various givens in the geo-ecology, namely, availability of water, seeds, fertilisers and tools, the market prices and the efforts of the farming family. The latter are influenced by the enterprise, the achievement motivation and the work that the total family is willing to unertake for obtaining success in their farming operations. Thus, the three aspects, namely, (1) the availability of facilities from the geo-ecology, (2) the quality of human effort, and (3) their interactions in the particular habitat, indicate the quality of life experienced in the given habitat.

Any change in any aspect of these domains has its repercussions on the other, acting like a "domino effect". For example, the tsunami in India of 2004, not only devastated land and life but also reduced the availability of the means of livelihood for fishermen along coastlines. Where there are no natural or man-made disasters, and where there is a harmonious relationship between the human and his geo-ecology, the human potential tends to increase with the increasing technology to live a better quality of life, yet there are thousands of Pacific Islands, far removed from each other where the Islanders depend upon each other for precious and shared produce. Where there is no harmony, as in some large countries such as in war-ravaged Iraq, Somalia and others, economic sevices get disrupted and lead to insecure lifestyles.[35] (Joshua, S. Goldstein, 2003) On the other hand, countries that have surplus of resources usually trade with others, thus further increasing their quality of life through an increase in their gross natural products (GNP). It is clearly visible in the Indian situation, where India is not far behind China in GNP. [36] (Guruswamy, Mohanty and Abraham, 2005) Bronfenbrenner further developed a taxonomy of family ecology[37] (Bronfenbrenner, U., 1986) which has drawn upon the work of several experts in the field.[38] (Buckley, W., 1967) In a more intensive study, Bronfenbrenner the proponent of the ecosystem influencing human ecology has investigated two different cultures in studying child-care patterns. The differentials in these patterns are dictated by the differences in political ideologies like communism in Soviet Russia and democracy in the United States. These are macro level systems and, therefore, filtrate to the various smaller systems, namely, exo, meso to the micro, where the family ideology is also permeated by the national ideologies. In this study, using the child as a focal point, Bronfenbrenner emphasises the social reinforcement through the potency of models, namely, the major source of differential childcare.[39] (Bronfenbrenner,1979)

Families as systems of relational members act and react with changing environments adapting their techniques and patterns of living suited to the changes. In India, for example, the vast variations of ecologies increased the heterogeneity in the patterns of living styles. Saraswathi has, pinpointed differences in patterns of living of average adolescents from differing ecologies, which then tabulate their life styles differently in their ecologies.[40] (Saraswathi, T.S., 1999). As elsewhere in the world, there are continuous and discontinuous influences changing the patterns of life styles in the Indian subcontinent. If we assume that the family is an ecosystem, goal-oriented creating, bringing up children, and guiding them towards their future, then we must also assume that the parts are dynamically related to the whole, where to maintain the ecological system, roles and tasks are well ascribed. For instance, the father is the head of the household and the main breadwinner, while the mother is the householder and the nurturer.[41] (Shah, A.M., 1998) The system has an organised hierarchy by age and sex. These are roles, which are ascribed and prohibited. There is a dynamic interplay between age groups and sexes and within the hierarchies. The changing nature of the environment reacts upon the tendencies of the human to adapt to changes, with the underlying principle that the family energy is primarily directed towards survival and then towards increasing the quality of life. For example, the environment of elementary tribal living is usually devoid of adequate facilities except for elementary living. For example, there are many tribes who live on the produce of forests for their survival such as villages near renowned temples like *Tirupathi* who produce leaf platters for '*Prasad*' (Temple offereings for prayer). The natural state of products, untamed weather conditions, difficult terrain, whether hills or sand dunes, seaside or plains, affect the style of living particularly of hill tribes and habitats of agriculturists., who are more closely dependent upon their natural habitats for survival than do urban populations.[42] (Ray, S., 1960)

Language and values are built around the natural milieu, as in several mini groups in India. Idiomatic language revolves around artefacts in their habitat such as land is "*mata*" (mother) and water is "*jal*" (life giving). There is a close association with nature as being animistic, a popular belief in the evil eye, ghosts and the forecast of natural events portending the coming of a good or an evil event. The rural saying, '*Ram Bharosay,*' is God is raining upon the human being as a benign sign.[43] (Ramanujam, A.K., 1994-5) There is a belief that different godheads bestow different favours and that the godhead is symbolic in animism, like the rituals performed around the *peepal* tree, which is believed to be the umbrella of the good spirits. To the agriculturalist, cattle is his lifeline and to the nomads, the camel, because they are part of the ecology which is important for their occupational tasks and survival. Natural or ayurvedic herbal medicines are used for health and, therefore, the growth of herbs is preserved. Further, water management techniques are used in many villages to harvest water, especially for the dry season. Health status is believed to be related to changes in the seasons. *Savan* is the time of harvest, *Lohri* is the time, heralding the arrival of spring (last days of winter). "*Pathjhad,*" literally means the falling of leaves (autumn). Almost every festivity which is socio-religious in nature is related to nature's attributes. Singing and music accompany almost every event in tribal life.[44] (Singh, K.S., 1972) Although attempts have been made to integrate tribal lifestyles with that of the modernising urban areas, many of them still retain dual lifestyles; one in their hinterland of origin and the other as migrants in nearby industries and construction sites.[45] (Archer, W.G., 1974) Therefore, their ecologies are both rural and urban. So, they live astride two cultural ecologies as in the case of the Bhils of Madhya Pradesh.[46] (Doshi, S.L., 1971)

What then are the routine, periodic and exigent categories of behaviours articulated by ecology? Ipso facto, it is the family itself that develops ecology of constructs, as proximal and as distal cognitive constructs. These vary in the context of the specific individual in relation to the stimuli around him. What are his routine activities which make up his work-a-day world? In India, for instance, these are proximal factors, within his life space. The tribal is occupied with his essential needs on a daily basis: females are involved in fetching wood or dung for cooking fire, and carrying water from the pond/well. This occupation of either working at a coalmine or forest cleaning or some such elementary production serves his essential needs. With the rich urbanite, proximal variables are activities like waking up to a cup of tea reading the newspapers, answering business calls on his cellular phone, rushing to work, to meet schedules. For him, distal variables are world politics and commerce and attending meetings in different cities/countries. His wife, on the other hand, has a plenty of servants, and amuses herself at the bridge club or kitty parties or goes shopping. The routine with the middle class, for example a mother of two children is different. In the morning, she rushes the children to school and to the day-care centre hoping to arrive on time at her desk as a government clerk, doing uninteresting desultory work, shopping with her colleagues at a long drawn-out lunch period, and counting the minutes while waiting for the bus to go and pick up her baby from the crèche and pick up her son from the neighbour's as he comes home early, and sets about coping to cook the evening meal and cope with the children's fussing. Thus, we see that, the concept of spatial configuration for these varying ecologies are psychologically embedded, which give rise to "spatial parameters" analysis of how work in these varying ecological areas influence lifestyles.[47] (Witkin, H.A., and D.R. Goodenough, 1981)

Periodic events are those that are generally socio-culturally operationalised, such as festivals, marriages and other family events.

Exigencies are such situations as critical illness of a family member, coping with shortage of money for essentials, bereavement, accidents and unforeseen trauma.

4. Human Abilities and Relevant Coping Modes

The behaviour of the individual changes during the years of growing up into an adult personality, and this is moderated by the geo-ecological environment interacting with the mental and physical self of the individual and relations within the family. *These material concerns are those articulated by types of occupation in which the individual is engaged. The concrete requirements are: the availability of civic amenities, services from the governance system, neighbourhood and community interactions, exchange of services and cooperation and the creation of a homogeneous human in geo-ecology*. The unique aspects of each ecology is that they exist side by side, such as the rural migrant's hut huddled against the industrialist's magnificent mansion, and yet they maintain their own spaces and lifestyles.[48] (Khalakdina, M., 1998) Each type of ecology is either favourable or unfavourable to the human being and his identified group. Again, these scenarios dynamically depend upon the changes in the socio-ecological setting and the person's ability to cognise, to prepare, to plan and to derive/obtain the means from the ecology to control and cope with his general environment. For instance, it is well known that health services in India are sparse and scattered in the outlying rural and tribal geo-ecological areas. Often, due to lack of ability to cognise, to plan and to derive the means, people in these habitats generally resort to traditional medicines as civic and government services are few and far between and in many cases inaccessible. In fact, it is not unusual for those living in far away ecologies to think that "hospitals are places for dying", simply because they resort to it as a final recourse when the illness is far advanced.

5. Problem Solving Behaviour in Scarce Ecologies

Now no longer is there a debate about which is stronger for life: "nature or nurture"; it is more of an amalgam of both.[49] (Ridley, Matt, 2003) The more that is known about human behaviour, the more apparent it becomes that interlinkages and networks, a necessary and dynamic connection. They interact as modulated by the coping mechanisms of the individual. The coping mechanisms employed by the individual relate to psychological abilities which vary from one individual to another. These abilities are related to intelligent problem solving behaviour. For example, the current lack of energy sources in the global economic downturn has provoked the search for, and the implementation of alternate sources of energy such as the production of vehicles which can use compressed natural gas (CNG) and various innovations in capturing solar energy. Depletion of environmental resources such as, deforestation and denudation of hillsides has had repercussions on the occurrence of scarce water supply. This has encouraged biotechnological experts for water harvesting such as *Tarun Bharat Sangh's* water resource development and management in the Alwar district of Rajasthan.[50] (Soni Mishra, 2008)

Human intelligence and its functionality are developed for using the resources, their allocation among members and to search for economic alternatives. Thus, it is observable that, the functionality of intelligence is related to the potential of abilities to exercise problem solving and coping behaviour. In other words, intelligent behaviour is related to the cognitive functioning of the individual's capacity and the appropriateness of strategies. For example, hunting requires appropriate perception and skill in targeting, for instance, the high perceptual abilities as in the case of the Eskimos who live by hunting. Therefore, the testing of intelligence and problem solving behaviour is more likely to be valid if it is related to the geo-ecology in which the individual live. Testing intelligence is reliable when it is related validly to the individual's environment. Culture-free tests are scarce for the use of testing IQ. If the items are unrelated to the individual's familiar ecology, there tend to be spurious results, such as testing the ability of an urban child. Naming of trees in a forest is likely to produce unreliable results. It is similar to asking a rural child to tie shoe laces. Begun in the West by Spearman in 1905, Binet developed a general test of intelligence on items familiar to western-oriented ecologies.[51] (Singh, M.V., N.K. Anand, S. Gupta and D.C. Dhingra, 1976). In India, there was a catch-up effect of adapting several tests on intelligence to assess intelligence levels of Indian children, such as Raven's Progressive Matrices and Cattell's Culture Fair Test,[52] (Desai, K.G., 1980) besides WISC,[53] (Ghuman, P.A., 1978) the Thorndike's Intelligence Test,[54] (Kakar, S.D., 1976) and the Gessell Developmental Scale,[55] (Pathak, M., 1977) to mention a few. With the adoption of constructs/concepts of human development from western-oriented literature, such tests with a few adaptations were used in the Indian situation to measure intelligence. Changing terminology was the main modification. As such, Indian experts have questioned the validity of such "transferences". Thus, social constructs developed in the west require to be critically examined when used in eastern cultures.[56] (Saraswathi, T.S., 2003: 24) More questionable is the whole range of not only measuring intelligence from a sophisticated vantage point, but also greater concern, when we should be more concerned about the validity of the contextual construct of intelligence. Individuals living in particular ecologies co-construct concepts relevant to their ecology. India is a country of many ecologies like hills, planes, deserts, snowbound areas, tropical areas and coastline areas. *It is often said that India is more a continent than a country, because of its large and varying ecologies.* For instance, the hill men in Himachal Pradesh live a different life from the hill men in the Nilgiris of Tamil Nadu. The former live near snow-clad mountains and are mainly herdsmen, while the latter are usually workers on tea plantations. These differential occupations are dictated by the specific availability of natural and material resources. This ecological perspective is essential to take into account because of its influences on living patterns and, therefore, on the family network patterns, more particular on the development of the personalities of the individual. The latter implies the need for indigenising intelligence test. In the context of these variegated ecologies, the nomadic child, for instance, is more familiar with the lack of greenery, the need to conserve food for long periods of time and the ability to survive in a desert ecology by acclimatisation and adaptation.[57] (Sinha D., 1978) There is a growing hiatus in the pattern of living between the urban and the interior rural areas mainly because urban ecologies are better equipped with technological facilities. It is fair to say, that limitations of the ecology are related to human abilities which will range from heightened cognitive processes (as in corporate organisations) to repressed or lessened expression of potentials as in sparse ecologies. For instance, the rich urbanite live in an affluent environment where physical needs are satisfied, who with a surfeit of increasing material wealth begins to experience a sense of ennui or boredom, with his cyclic events since he has most everything he needs provided by his urban industrialised ecology. The economically deprived child suffers from lacuna in many material spheres. For him, everyday is a challenge to meet basic needs; with repeated failures he might even lose the sense of challenge and fall into apathy, making do with what he has. Having said this, however, we might hypothesise that a deprived ecology could have negative as well as positive consequences. If the ontogenetic and cognitive intelligence levels are high in the individual, these might spur him on to achieve more inspite of being in a deprived ecology. In the last analysis we are implying that potentials are difficult to assess as human potentials are challenged by the relevant ecology. For example, a subsistence farmer may lack opportunities but we cannot say that he lacks intellectual potential to improve his pattern of living. We have only to observe the individual cases of persons with a high sense of challenge and ability who move from debilitating ecologies to achieve success in the competitive urban world of opportunities. On the other hand, deprivation need not cover the spectrum of emotional and social needs. In fact, it is not unusual to find economically deprived children living satisfying emotional and social need fulfilment. Poor economic status in terms of expenditure and income is seen in table below:

Table 2.1: Major Rural States, Major Urban States, Income Ranges, and Poverty Levels

State	*Income*	*Expenditure*	*% Poor*
Uttarakhand	49,892	78,387	35.7%
Uttar Pradesh	40, 130	50,313	33.2%
Bihar	30,819	47,731	Data not Available
Chattisgarh	39,198	27,972	63.4%
Madhya Pradesh	36,152	39,206	45.5%
Orissa	28,514	32,834	41.3%

Source: Indian Human Development Survey 2004-05 data in Desai, Sonalde B. *et al*, *Human Development in India: Challenges for a Society in Transition*, New Delhi: Oxford University Press, 2010.

The larger States are the poorer, and it is in these States that a large proportion of the marginalised sections, namely, the Scheduled Castes, the Tribes, the poor Muslims and uneducated females live. Interestingly these are also areas of civic turbulence such as Naxalite violence.

In terms of social realities, prolonged scarcity has adverse effects in the allied spheres. Several studies of prolonged economic deprivation, in essence, depict that the psyche of children in their

Table 2.2: Population of the Richer States and the Poorer States

State	*Whether Rich or Poor*	*Population**
Bihar	Poor	93,823,000
Gujarat	Rich	56,408,000
Haryana	Rich	23,772,000
Jharkhand	Poor	30,010,000
Maharashtra	Rich	106,894,000
Madhya Pradesh	Poor	69,279,000
Orissa	Poor	39,899,000
Punjab	Rich	26,591,000
Rajasthan	Poor	64,641,000
Uttar Pradesh	Poor	190,891,000
Tamil Nadu	Rich	66,396,000

**Source:* Census of India. Projected population of States, 2008, Census of India

ecologies are depressed, because of the deprived bare necessities, and their negative effects on the developing personality due to lack of stimuli.[58] (Krishnan, L., 2004: 47) A given ecology, however, can change its features over time. We cite a few here:

1. *The operation of a package of dynamic variables which could change the ecological scenario.* We have observed, for instance, the plough giving way to the tractor, traditional compost pits giving way to chemical fertilizers, pesticides, improved seed quality and irrigation facilities.[59] (Hull, C., 1939) An individual by nature is resilient and adaptation to change takes place fairly rapidly, especially when occasions prompt rapid adjustments to ecological changes, as generally experienced in rural India, where natural calamities are quickly overcome by a search for alternatives such as technologies like water harvesting in water scarce areas.
2. *The occurrence of differential valences (forces and energies) between proximal variables and peripheral variables.* To give an example of these, as the land yield increases the farmer is now able to free his children from farm work, to be educated. The urban worker whose wages rise is more inclined to have his children educated rather than working for petty cash in market places and such like.

3. *The occurrence of differing learning experiences during the lifespan.* Again, to continue with the same analogy, having expanded his resources, increasing his area of knowledge of other situations, the farmer may seek to become a village leader for which he has to garner votes and, therefore, travels to adjoining places learning how to persuade people. In short, he has to learn to expand his human ecology. With these experiences, his ecological sphere widens.[60] (Berry, J.W., 1974)

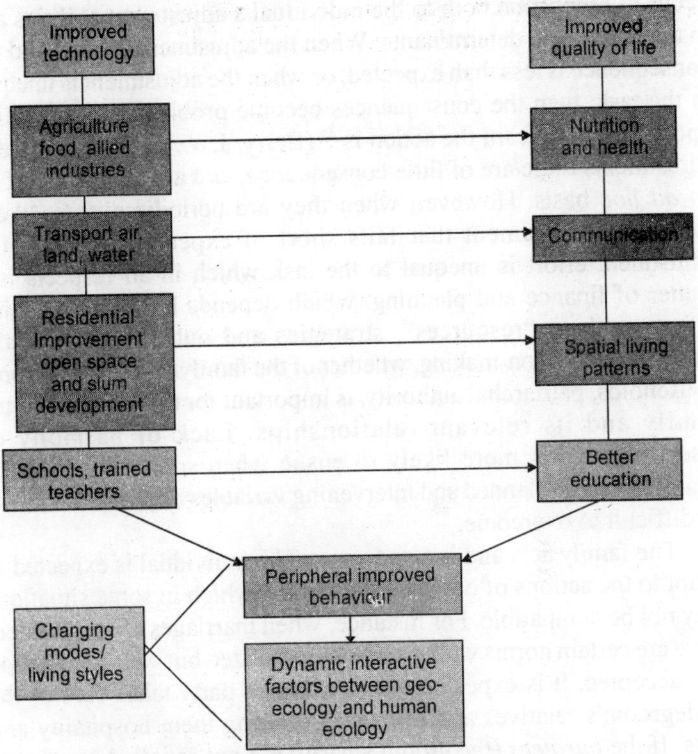

Paradigm 2.2: Factors affecting Patterns of Life Cycle

6. Variations in Family Ecological Systems

In an extensive analysis, Bubolz and Sontag[61] (1993) *conceptualise the use of a systems—analysis approach to view human ecology as a subsystem of the total ecological spectrum. This human subsystem emphasised a complex family model of living systems over space and time. These are composed of material and organic energies of morphogenetic constructs*. The human sub-system is assumed to be self-organising and self-sustaining. Families in this sub-system of human relationships are both proactive and reactive to the environment. For instance, in the routine of everyday living, there are adjustments to be made. For example, when a family member falls ill, or the maid does not show up in an urban household, adjustments in the daily routine are made. These are upheavals that occur in proportion both to the individual's adjustment abilities and to the situational determinants. When the adjustment is large and the consequence is less than expected, or when the adjustment is unequal to the task, then the consequences become problematic, depending upon how significant the action is.[62] (Berry, J.W., 1976) In everyday adjustments these are of little consequence, and are taken care of on an *ad hoc* basis. However, when they are periodic events, like a wedding arrangement that falls short of expectations, then the adjustment effort is unequal to the task which in all respects is a matter of finance and planning, which depends upon pre-planning efforts such as "resources", strategies and outcomes. Thus, the attribute of decision-making, whether of the family or, as in traditional households, patriarchal authority, is important for the harmony of the family and its relevant relationships. Lack of harmony or disequilibrium is more likely to ensue when sources are scarce, strategies are ill-planned and intervening variables are either unknown or difficult to overcome.

The family acts and is acted upon. The individual is expected to adapt to the actions of others in the family, which in some situations may not be compatible. For instance, when marriages are celebrated, there are certain norms which are non-verbalized but well-understood and accepted. It is expected that the bride's party takes care of the bridegroom's relatives and friends in offering them hospitality and gifts. If the *baratees* (the groom's party) are not satisfied or express discomfort, then it is a reflection on the status expected of the bride's party.

Thus, the human ecological framework consisting of the family and the kinship network at the micro level can structure and restructure itself according to cues either in the natural ecology or the human ecology. What composes a joint family household today, may in the next decade have members scattered over different places. The resultant nucleus left behind in the place of origin has to structure and restructure its roles and obligations towards each other and the kin group. In the past, the joint family resided in close proximity, but now, its boundaries are being elastically extended. Thus, human ecology is composed of both strategies and outcomes, the intensity of which depends upon situational factors, either permanent or temporary. Social realities are such that what is prescribed in theoretical frames might be somewhat different in terms of the ground realities in implementation. For instance, we might assume that the programme of "Poverty Alleviation" inaugurated several years ago, and at present revived as the "Minimum Needs Programme"[63] (U.N., 2002) of the Government has had the expected results. Considering the large spread of India's poverty-stricken areas, the problems of reaching them with facilities and the appropriate implementation are somewhat less than expected. And, as is true of most developing societies, where welfare and aid programmes are implemented, it is the richer slice of that poor segment that access most of the benefits. These are social realities, given the structures of continuous societies, where some have more and some have less. On the other hand, it is not unusual that individuals stimulated by the growing prosperity around them, on their own initiative, develop their own strategies for improving their status rather than depending upon Governmental poverty alleviation programmes, thus causing shifts in the human ecological network. Some poor States like Orissa, Bihar and Madhya Pradesh suffer from the lack of opportunities, political upheavals and the lashes of climatic changes more intensely than other States.[64] (Moghaddam, F.M., 1990) Thus, human ecology is subject to the effects of environmental ecology, where situational determinants dictate access to opportunities.

The family as an ecosystem consists of parts within a whole, although in a dynamic manner working together in unison, like parts of a machine. The family's physical sustenance, economic maintenance and psycho-social nurturant functions occur in conjunction with the collective needs. For instance, there are differential roles for different "actors" in a household: the mother cares for the children and the household, the father earns an income and children go to school. If the major actionisers are ill or absent, roles are redistributed and then rearranged again. For instance, if the mother in a household falls critically ill and is immobilized, other members take on her functions. Thus, an ecological perspective on the family indicates the potentials of the family roles and the probability of their accomplishment of tasks, which are interdependent. This phenomenon applies not only to single families in the micro system, but also to interlinking families in the neighbourhood system (where interactions are informal, neighbours help each other out spontaneously). For instance, the structured system in a given village is composed of elders of the village , the district *panchayat,* and the block *panchayats,* which are all represented at the State level. Originating as an informal structure for assistance to families of the micro system of villages, this network is spread through a system of governance. The family is the micro system and the family network, kinship groups and village panchayats form the meso system, while the exo system is that which occurs at Block and district levels through a process of representative interaction. What we are attempting to say here is that in social realistic situations, localities form the fundamental group interactional system, and as the interactional systems spread wider, relationships become muted or less intense and are "distal" in comparison to the nucleus (the family) within which relationships are "proximal". However, *it is necessary to point out that families who live in rural ecologies are perhaps more interactive than families in urban complexes since in the latter, there is greater mobility of geographical residence and less interpersonal interaction.* When, for instance, there are floods that affect the whole village, it affects whole family groups and, therefore, instils a sense of cooperation among neighbouring families of the stricken area to assist each other as the incident is a critical ecological one to all families. *Thus, we have a combination of (a) routine activities, (b) periodic activities, and (c) critical activities, as indicated in the paradigm below:*

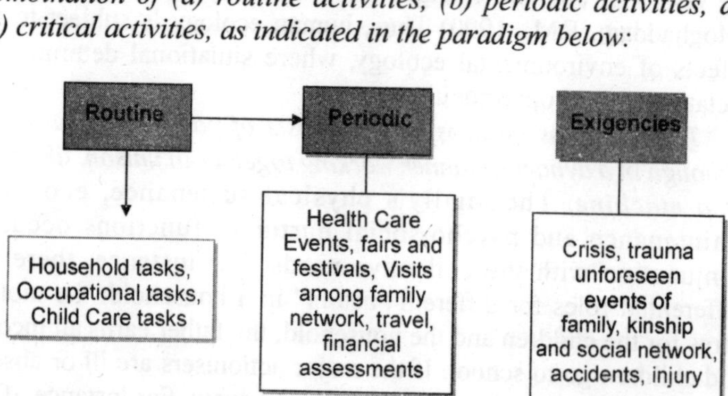

Paradigm 2.3: Categories of Types of Activities and their Related Tasks

However, situations change dynamically. There may be overlap between one set of activities and another, depending upon the type of proximal and distal situations in the given ecology. For instance, it is not unusual to observe that families in a village know each other fairly well. They visit each other informally at any time and feel free to ask for assistance, which is also many times given unasked. This type of informality of inter-relationships is unlike that of the West where families tend to stay within their own residences, eschewing the type of informality observed in the Indian situation. Families in the west tend to keep their own privacy and live in their own spaces. They interact in formal public and civic matters.

Because of these various networks of interaction, in the environment, the whole package of components, namely, biosphere, hydrosphere and ecosphere are conceptualised as an "*ecological niche.*"[65] (Bril, B., 1999) *In this niche, the components interact to develop by-products from water, wind and soil, which are harnessed for the survival of the human in his ecological context. This is especially so in rural ecologies;* for instance, harnessing wind and water for energy. Such technology affects the lives of people in different ways. In the urban areas, the easy access to the internet ties up innumerable small social groups in many ways that did not exist before. In other words, there is a crisscrossing through this electronic medium, which is changing the lifestyles of most people as it offers frequent communication across large distances of differing ecologies. For instance, nowadays, transactions regarding marriages through various websites have displaced the traditional "marriage negotiator". Further, the concern about pollution and gas emissions and the working towards a green ecology are gaining a higher profile than before, as man is more aware of his dependence upon the maintenance of nature for his sustained existence.[66] (Jain U., and Palsane M.N., 2004)

The type of population, their stage of civilisation and their access to the benefits of science and technology are accepted as a part of a modernising ecology, being very important and intricate parts of the term 'ecology'.[67] (Mahadevan, K., Chi Husi Tuan, and V.K. Bal Krishnan Nair, 1992) The following is a case study of the tribal community in its geo-ecology.

The study by Doshi, of the tribal society of the 'Bhils', examining the structure of family, kinship and personal life, states that the family system is based on individual family units and not on the joint family system, unlike the general run of structures in many tribals where the family network lives together in one residential area. An adult Bhil when he marries, sets up his own family and separates from his family of orientation. Being polygamous, there is special attention paid to the interrelationships between co-wives and their children. The large Bhil family size makes it possible for family members to engage in a variety of occupational activities, which contribute to the total well-being of the family. Most of the family agricultural activities are on little patches of manually irrigated land. Pasturing is managed by children of primary age, honey and food gathering and "mahua"—collections are activities in which all family members are engaged. The Bhils who live on hillsides come down periodically, to the plains to work as labourers on the farmlands of others. They return to their households periodically to visit and interact for a while. Thus, their ecology interacts with their familial pattern of living, dependent mainly upon their occupations, whether agricultural or any other.[68] (Doshi, S.L., 1971) *There are also several tribes where individuals live consecutively in two ecologies, one is their village of origin in the hinterland and the other is their temporary workplace in urban areas. Thus indicating that while their ecological patterns are more or less consistent, human ecology shifts scenarios from one geo-ecological area to another.*[69] (Misra, 1998)

Another example is a study of Mobile Crèches in Delhi. It is clearly apparent that the lives of construction workers in Delhi are temporary. These workers are brought to Delhi by contractors, who set up their shelters made of tarpaulin, plastics and bricks. Females do the secondary tasks of carrying and fetching for the male masons at the construction site. There are temporary crèches for the children conducted by voluntary organisations. As soon as the construction is over, they are moved to another site and live in a similar manner. Thus, the ecology, the economic sub-system, the habitat sub-system interact to influence the human sub-system in its patterns of living.[70] (Khalakdina, M., 1998)

In an insightful study, Bronfenbrenner, a major proponent of the ecosystem as influencing human ecology, has further investigated two different cultures in child upbringing systems. The differentials are dictated mainly by the socio-political ideology of communism in USSR and democracy in the USA. In this study, using the child as a focal point, Bronfenbrenner emphasises social reinforcement through the potency of models that are major sources of differential upbringing.

Thus, we see that the socio-political ideology influences the way the individual in the family reacts and is acted upon given these milieux.[71] (Bronfenbrenner, 1970)

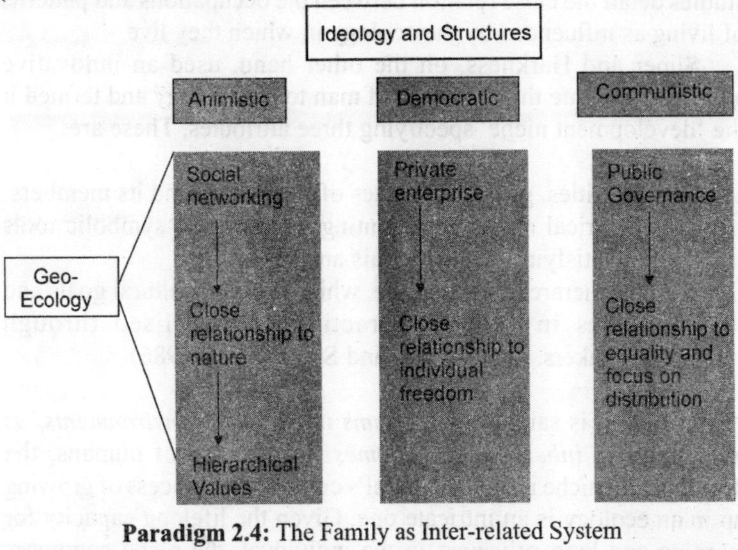

Paradigm 2.4: The Family as Inter-related System

In their description of human ecology, Bubolz *et. al.*[72] (1993) have presented *a categorisation of human ecological concepts which are as follows:—*

The qualitative aspects of human behaviour covers the spectrum of such constructs as: (a) family needs, goals, values, (b) resources, artefacts, (c) management, decision-making, sustenance activities, communication, operationalising the environmental spectrum.

However, the above categories should not be considered as discrete or immutable. These categories can interact with each other in dynamic ways, modifying each other, depending upon the individual's adaptive behaviour, which can change the state of the structure of the particular system. For example, changes in socio-economic standards can occur through a variety of permutations and combinations of the categories mentioned above. Individuals do not only have the adaptive resilience towards changes, but can also modify the environment to meet their needs, and goals. We cite here some studies which relate to varying ecological systems such as those of living in an urban complex[73] (Aphale, C., 1976) and those growing up in families whose occupation is pottery making[74] (Anandalakshmy,

S., and M. Bajaj, 1981) and to changes in a community over time in the city of Bhubaneshwar in Orissa.[75] (Seymour, S., 1986) These studies detail the close relation between the occupations and patterns of living as influenced by the ecology in which they live.

Super and Harkness, on the other hand, used an innovative approach to relate the cognition of man to his ecology and termed it the 'development niche' specifying three attributes. These are:

1. Activities, goals and values of the culture and its members.
2. Historical means representing material and symbolic tools for satisfying cultural goals and values.
3. The hierarchical structure, which initiates cultural goals and values in everyday practices, channelised through caretakers.[76] (Super, C., and S. Harkness, 1986)

In fact, it is said that *organisms inherit their environments, as much as they inherit their genomes*. In the case of humans, the development niche is the individual's culture. The process of growing up in an ecology is an intricate one. Given the lifelong capacity for learning and innovativeness in the individual, the niche composes forms of balancing structures between genetic evolution, which influence changes (both human and material) in the ecology, and the particular ecosystems. In short, this is a reflection of the interdependence of nature and nurture of the human being developing from childhood to old age. In India, the elementary environment of the farmer, the pasturer, the wood-gatherer is fast changing into industrialised and urbanised complexes, as the city hinterlands are being acquired for industrial purposes.

The genetic make up of the human through the ages has not overly changed, though it must be said that the evolutionary process of adaptation itself changes dynamically over a period of time. For instance, a productive adult in urban areas has a full work-a-day world. His ecology is wider because of his greater mobility than that of his retired father pottering around or reading newspapers and such like at home. The given genetic structure evokes a response to selective experiences from the ecology. These are phylogenetic in nature and are spontaneously active foundational potentials, for developing special ontogenetic skills, suited to the selected experiences of a given environment. For example, along coastlines the major occupation is fishing. The genetic endowment or the phylogenetic basis is the same as that of the herdsmen, or the urbanite in metropolis areas; but, for the fishermen, they develop the ontogenetic skill for the various activities involved in boating, throwing the net, catching fish, its marketing and such related activities. For instance, given the water, petrol and electricity shortage in most of India today, methodologies for water and alternative energy sources are being explored so that the scarcity in the ecology is supplemented by man's increasing ingenuity.[77] (Barkow, J.H., L.Cosmides and J. Tooby, 1992) This has led to *the transactional model proposed by Bronfenbrenner, that the family is embedded in a larger ecological framework, which should be taken into cognisance, when viewing the influences on the developing individual.*[78] (Bronfenbrenner, 1979) One might also view the ecological variable from the framework of the "givens", namely, the evolutionary adaptive genetic mechanisms in the human. Over time and space, these mechanisms are accommodated, adapted and assimilated as sustenance techniques for the developing human. Thus, the varying environmental pressures and demands lead to differential behaviour.[79] (Bronfenbrenner, U., 1989) We see that environmental pressures can lead either to reformulation of old patterns of behaviour, or to newly created types of behaviour, in order to contour behaviour to meet new cultural demands. For instance, we observe that culturally modulated food patterns are related to availability of food in the ecology.[80] (Meggars, B.J., 1954) and since the patterns are established from childhood, food habits are more or less permanent. The Middle East inhabitants are mainly non-vegetarians, the Chinese are fish-eaters, while the South Indians from a traditional environment is mainly vegetarian. These patterns have also their downside. Most of these countries have also introduced American foods like McDonalds and Italian pizzas which themselves are modulated to suit the food habits of each of these countries. We observe, however, that the new foods are more especially favourites of the younger generation, than the older generation. Given their cultural habits causes an automatic negotiable balance between the old and the young in terms of needs from the ecology. Thus, the type of food behaviour emanating from the ecology reinforces the ontogenetic skills for the readaptability of cultural habits.

Tomasello, in commenting on Guvain's thesis states, that, goals and values of a culture influence not only the individual's choice to engage in certain activities, but the very structures of the activity and what is learned from it, is a package of a number of complex activities.[81] (Tomasello, M., 1995)

Being a member of a group does not automatically reflect that the member has internalised within himself all the traits of the group culture. There is evidence to indicate that *societies whose main occupation is food producing and food gathering instil in the individuals of the community a filial sense of bonding together in shared activities of their occupations and also towards nature and its products. On the other hand, in high food-consuming societies, where collectivism is in low profile, achievement, self-reliance and independence are emphasised, since food, to give an example, is easily and commercially available.*[82] (Barry, H., I. Child and M. Bacon, 1959) In other words, where food-producing/gathering is the means for survival, there is a strong sense of bonding towards each other, but where food comes easily from other than self-produced, there are impersonal types of interaction.

This difference in collective and individualised occupational activities is dictated more especially by ecological circumstances. It is more common to observe individualised activities in urban areas where array of job opportunities is greater than those available in a peasant farming society. When we speak about the collective goal towards which Indians are frequently socialised, it perhaps has its roots in the fact, that activities in the rural and tribal areas are more homogeneous in nature than in urban areas as the Indian society moves towards urban industrialised occupations, individualised competition is enhanced if the individual is to succeed in that ecology. Yet, at the same time, there are exceptions. There is a tendency in large business managed by traditional business families to perpetuate the family lineage by working together in a collective manner in the same generational occupations.

Time is the major dynamic factor influencing change, both in the human habitat and in the lifestyle. This occurs whether progressive or regressive activities are existent in life styles, as change has to do with the movements of social mobility, both in terms of upward mobility of occupations, and also in terms of greater income, and what is more, is disposable income. Change is further exacerbated in terms of changing geo-ecological and economic statuses. These are important markers in the lifestyles of societies. Families of the middle class who two decades ago owned possibly scooters or cycles, have now cars, own houses, telephones and refrigerators. Thus, a market economy for the middle class has come into force. Rural lower classes are gradually migrating to urban areas. They are exposed to the amenities of a television and media, running drinking water and electricity, besides earning a cash income, unlike their forefathers who lived off the land where they were usually share croppers or indentured labourers of land owners. These migrant individuals still carry their traditions with them like security blankets, not losing touch with the hinterlands from which they originated.[83] (Ferrington, John and Priya Deshinkar, 2009) There is a constant state of flux in environmental support systems, somewhat unsettled in tribal and peasant populations which depend upon the vagaries of climatic conditions for their sustenance. The middle class is challenged to procure greater facilities in imitation of the upper class. In the middle class, however, the category of those who are government employees, whether teachers or clerks or bureaucrats, have several types of subsidies from the Government, the most utilitarian of which are residence and health facilities, which are greatly subsidised. The supportive network of large families, which are common in tribal/rural and poorer groups act as insurance systems during times of need.[84] (Wolpert, S.A., 2004) Talcott Parsons' theory of social interaction holds good over the years, for it states that the larger the number of members in the family (or for that matter, the group), the number of interactions increase exponentially, in that each interacts jointly and severally with each other. Thus, *the possibility of human interaction and communication increases in joint families to a greater degree than in nuclear families.* Interactions consequently are more intense in nuclear families as they are more frequent and more personalised, while in the joint family there is so much going on that there is much more cross communication and, therefore, the possibility of both miscommunication and diffused communication. Geographical space is an important factor as a part of the ecological givens. Where families are crowded in space as in the urban slums, although interaction is greater, there is also an increased possibility of miscommunication and, therefore, misinterpretation. This is reflected in the Indian television serials like *Kahani Ghar Ghar Ki* (the story of every household) watched by millions, both by upper and lower classes alike.

7. The Psychological Bases of Human Ecology

Human development is an amalgam of concepts from sociology, anthropology, more so cultural anthropology and psychology. These are the conceptual bases for understanding the relations between man and nature, in his specific environment, which can be interlinked comparatively to conceptualisations made by Erikson[85] (Erikson, E.H, 1974) and the *Vedas*.[86] (Michael, Witzel, 2005) Erikson's thesis is related to attributes developed during the chronological stages of growth as an outcome of the interaction between the individual and his human environment. The *Vedas* present a philosophical treatise on the rituals and the expectations of roles during the major chronological stages. Implicit, therefore, in these two expositions is the importance of the human environment. It is to be noted that the conceptual term of environment is abstract and generic, whereas the conceptual term ecology is more concrete and specific and is a sub-system of the environment, as the environment consists of myriads of ecologies. In the days of the *Vedas*, philosophy revolved around spirituality from which the *ashramas* or stages were elicited. Erikson's theory dealt more on the environmental sub-system of the human ecology and, therefore, much of his theoretical concepts are elicited from his experience in psycho-analysis with his clients.

At this point we must mention that *the ecological theory of Bronfenbrenner relates more to the overt situational parameters which affect human behaviour. So, while the emphasis of Erikson's theory is "inner thinking" expressed in an overt manner, the* samskaras *are directly related to overt behaviour of man in relation to societal norms and the supernatural.* In comparison, Bronfenbrenner's theory is based squarely on physical situational factors influencing human behaviour. Piaget's conceptualisation is also related to cognising the relationship between perception and interpretation of the perceived. Thus, in some way or the other, the above mentioned theories imply the intricate relationship between human thought, human behaviour, human ecology and the eco-spheres.

An indepth understanding of the writings of these experts is given in the chapter on 'Selected Personality Theories Relevant to the Indian psyche". Suffice it to say here that, from the ecological standpoint the individual is surrounded by stimuli emanating both from his undeveloped self and the ecology both human and material. In this century, with the growth of excessive stimuli suddenly appearing in a market economy based on liberalised commerce among countries, and the rapid rate of industrialisation, the variations in the environmental ecology are impinging upon the human ecology in varied, overlapping and competing stimuli. *Therefore, the more the*

modernised the ecology the greater the pressure on the human ecology for individuals to make difficult choices among the competing stimuli. For instance, in rural areas there is not much choice about transport. It is either the bullockcart, the trains in some cases or the public buses on highways or tempos that may or may not skirt villages. In urban areas, there are choices among travelling in a bus or trains, travelling by scooters and three-wheelers and most of all using owner driven cars, creating further complexities in the environmental ecology.[87] (Stephen Philips Cohen, 2002)

Geo-ecological constraints influence the family's experiences, which are passed on, from one generation to another. Erikson[88] (Erikson, E.H., 1978), based his theory on the development of traits as influenced by the human environment, emphasising for example the development of basic trust or mistrust in the environment (mainly human) in the early stages of the child's development, continuing its dimensionality along the life span, while Havighurst developed a set of expected tasks, in relation again to age groups, as stipulated by norms in the western society. These are tasks which he does due to the reinforcement or otherwise of the ecology both the human and geophysical environment and in relation to his maturational levels at different stages of development.[89] (Havighurst, R.J., 1953) Sociologically, families are said to be democratic, authoritarian or laissez-faire.[90] (Lippit, R., and R.K. White, 1958) In the authoritarian or autocratic set-up, which is more common in the patriarchal system, the child is expected to successfully complete tasks suitable to his age. When he is of school age, he is expected to help in the occupational tasks of his family, like simple agricultural and pastoral tasks. As he grows in maturity, he is expected to become responsible and accountable. The ecology also consists of forces of positive and negative energy which influence human development. These are akin to Lewin's constructs of valences in his topological theory.[91] (Lewin, K., 1936) As development chronologically increases, the complexity of human tasks also increases, where in the individual cognitively selects from among the alternative.[92] (Bronfenbrenner, 1993) Again, *viewing these theories from a holistic approach, we see that these experts attempt to offer unique views of the developing individual influenced by his environment.* For instance, if the ecology is deprived, then there are fewer facilities for the young child. We have only to review the tragedies of famine in Africa and man-made disasters such as wars, their destabilizing effects and the tragedy of families in Dafur,

Sudan, to gauge the relativity of the geo-ecological factors which devastate human life, developing mistrust in the environment. Yet, on an individual basis, we do know that a reluctant and indifferent mother may also induce emotional distrust in the child. If we accept the conceptualisations of learning theories and the concept of the "spread of effect" it is also realisable that this 'trust-distrust' dimension, which is a foundational attribute in the young, can carry over to other aspects of his personality. Where the environment is surfeit with physical facilities and emotional caring, the child tends to grow up without understanding what deprivation means. For instance, a child from the west who has a surfeit of physical facilities/ services has a cultural shock when he first comes to a developing country. He is unable to comprehend, when he is in India, for instance, how cars blow horns, violate traffic regulations, how cows are allowed to sit in the middle of heavy trafficking roads, and how jaywalkers cross roads at any time or at any place. Coming from a structured environment as in the west, the disorganization in society which the same child perceives in the developing ecology creates a sense of dissonance in the maturing individual. On the other hand, to the average Indian who is used to these ecologies, they are accepted as everyday occurrences and, in fact, it is said that the Indian lives in "organised disorganisation." Again, there are non-verbalised rules for tasks to be accomplished in specific situations. In the west, it is who does the laundry and who takes out the garbage, in the east in peasant households as in India it is who ploughs the land and who carries water. The varied forces in the psychological field as expressed by Lewin[93] (Lewin, K., 1935), indicates the nature of valences that socio-physically directs behaviour, which we surmise is differentially valued in different societies in their ecologies. While Lewin refers to mental spaces, we can easily extrapolate this concept to physical spaces which are important spatial configurations in the Indian's perception whether he is a rural, tribal, or an urban individual. For instance, it is more important for a rural housewife to conduct food activities than it is for her to gossip at the well/water pump whereas, for an urban elite housewife it becomes more important for her to go to clubs/kitty parties and such like leisure time activities, since the household is often taken care of by domestic staff.

It is apparent from the foregoing, that *human/family ecology, being a combination of genetic traits and human and physical environments, raises many questions as to its appropriate place in*

(1) the schema of related concepts, (2) that this schema raises many issues of how resources are converted, how they are transformed, what is the allocation or distribution system among family subsystems, and (3) what extra familial services are available from the given environment. More importantly, while ecology is a generic term, the abstract concept of ecology cannot be separated from its practical interpretations in real life situations. Quantitative data inadequate information about the geoecological context of living which is important in social reality situations. Therefore, ethnographic and ideographic methods of explanation are more significant in analyzing the ecological relationships of an individual. We need to clearly state the fact that the abstract term 'environment' is really an umbrella concept for other factors which can be operationalised, such as ecological situations, habitats, residences, produce of the land, utilisation of land through science and technology and ecological related occupations. Ecology, on the other hand, is limited by the characteristics of the geoecology, which the specific individual inhabits, and conducts relationships with other individuals in unique situations which change from one spectrum to another. For instance, at his work place the individual has to behave like a colleague with other colleagues. At home, he behaves like a father or a son. When he moves into public places, he is one among the crowd and, therefore, he moves from the micro to the meso and to the exo system, in his interactions.[94] (Bronfenbrenner, 1989)

We also ought to take cognisance of the term 'culture'. Culture has a pervasive social history, different from environment and ecology, which is a heritage carried from one generation to another. The concept of 'culture', while being generic is in actual fact, irrevocably tied to the geoecology in which it has existed over historical times. Ethnographic data tells us that the Incas of South America had a highly developed society living with adequate technology, which civilisation rose and fell, as known through retrospective anthropology and existent archaeological data. Thus the Incas had a culture which was erased with the depletion of their civilisation. The caves of the Ajanta and Ellora in Maharashtra also provide ethnographic documentation of the days of the Hindu dynasties. So also the ruins of the Harappa-Indus valley unfold the highly sophisticated past civilisation. In other words, a culture is bound to a specific society, while an ecology, being concrete and relatively stable, changes only if other inroads are made, such as industry in rainforest areas and denudation of hillsides in the Alwar district of Rajasthan. These are dynamic changes under the general rubric of the concept of environment, which to a layman simply means "surroundings". Thus, when we talk about ecology, we are evolving and devolving towards understanding of specific *in situ* areas of analysing the material world surrounding the human. It is now no longer valid to say that the Indian is "thus and so". We need to specify which Indian in which area, and what group is being indicated. The overly rich live in mansions with more wealth than they know what to do with it; while the poor have to scrounge for their daily food. Therefore, understanding the variations in the concept of ecology is essential for analysing specific segments of human behaviour.

8. The Growing Individual and his Ecological Network

The human during the period of infancy growth stages is dependent upon the nurturance for another individual, whether biological or otherwise. The nature of nurturance in the human structural arrangement is usually the biological parents, wherein the mother is symbiotically bonded with the child. The intrauterine environment is transferred to the outside world, where the dyad relationship of mother and child gradually expands to those of others in the familial environment. This is the child's human ecology. In India, it is rare that the environment of the child in the early years is confined only to biological parents and siblings. The child belongs to the family network of all members of the kin group.[95] (Ganesh, K., 1988)

The growing child's contact with his human ecology is an expansive network of relatives, both maternal and paternal, including their in-law relatives. For instance, a female has a different status if she is the wife of the older brother or the younger brother in a family and is differentially labelled as *jethani* and *devrani* respectively. She, in turn, has her own maternal and paternal family and their children, grandchildren, cousins and so on. It is interesting to note that whether a cousin or a biological brother, they are each called by the same label, namely, *bhaiya* (brother). Female (mother) relatives that have come into the family by marriage are known as *bhabhis* and it is customary for elders to call youngsters by one name, namely, *beta* (son) or *beti* (daughter). Thus, the human ecology in the Indian society is informal and relatively more closely knit than that observed in the West. The relationships are so close with the growing child that female adults who are married and have babies may also breast feed the infants of other female relatives in the family. In some tribal areas, the grandmother suckles the grandchild, as a substitute pacifier, while the mother works in the fields[96] (UNICEF, 1973) In the west child care nurseries are provided in factories or in offices for breastfeeding facilities. In the Indian situation, it is not uncommon for young siblings male or female to care for the younger, so that mothers can work and also take time off to breastfeed the child who is in the care of older siblings.[97] (Swaminathan, 1998) In the organised sectors, provisioning of such services is desultory and poor in quality. The upper classes, especially the educated, send their pre-school children to high-fee paying pre-schools. Therefore, *the opportunities and the facilities provided by the geoecology for the growing child are dependent upon the affordability of the family to seek such facilities*. Where parents cannot afford or do not want to take advantage of facilities for their preschool children, they are often left in the care of child-minders (usually in the neighbourhood).

In the Indian situation, a young child is helped to gradually achieve independent motor skills in the physical sphere, and is not pressurised to achieve milestones. As a result, there is little anxiety transference from the mother/surrogate to the young, especially in traditional family networks.[98] (Mandelbaum, D.G., 1968) Thus, the traditionality of the family contributes to informal care of the young child. This is an important aspect that relates to childcare being informal and because of the informality of relationships in elementary ecologies, the child is not high-pressured to achieve his maximum potential. At the same time this does not mean that there is high anxiety levels in urban children where achievement is high priced.

Further, there is an aura of deference towards age and hierarchical status, especially marked in the lower socio-economic strata and in rural and tribal ecologies.[99] (Rai, G.C., 1979) The hierarchical nature of the patriarch is so strongly embedded that, there is a formal distance between the patriarch and the younger in the family. At about the primary school stage of the child, the patriarch and other male elders interact with the child especially with the male child, in a manner that is authoritarian, with strict injunctions. Any violations in the social sense are strongly rebuked. Lois Murphy in her book says that the child is influenced to depend upon the grown-up for guidance, and is perhaps earlier inculcated with the sense of the superego dominated by authority to behave as commanded or threatened.[100] (Murphy, L.B.,

1953).Five decades after her critical work, these facts still remain as truisms in India, especially among traditional families. When we relate these concepts to Freudian interpretations and Kakar's writings in identity and self, we observe a relationship between their conceptualisation, and the development of conscience beginning in the pre-school years.[101] (Kakar, S., 1981). Any deviation is treated as a reflection upon the family reputation.

In the Indian culture, by and large, these are not high profiled in childcare practices. What is high profiled is giving enough nourishment to the child and concentration on affectional bonds. Given the fact that health infrastructures and their services are scantily available to far away villages and tribal areas, there is little knowledge of scientific childcare. Consequently, childcare is strongly related to the natural habitat. Foods which are health-giving and ayurvedic in nature are prescribed by elderly women in the family. Traditional medication, mainly Ayurvedic, is used in prevention and treatment of diseases and in general, the child is brought up like a "wild rose" unlike the scientifically nurtured rose in the sophisticated nursery gardens of the rich. There have been instances where pregnant mothers work all day and deliver a child with assistance by the casual traditional midwife (*dhai).* There are also instances where the working mother experiencing labour pains is taken behind a bush by a female relative to deliver the child. Therefore, *adaptability to nature and nurture is the pristine mode of behaviour in geo-ecological habitats that are rudimentary. Such habitats are more frequently visible in far off remote rural and tribal areas where traditional wisdom is more in use than scientific modes.*[102] (Khalakdina, M., 1979) Most of the small sample studies on early child upbringing hardly deal with the psychological aspects or their relationships to psychological theories.[103] (Sinha, D., and R.C. Mishra, 1993) These studies use classificatory variables such as age, sex, caste, indices of socio-economic class, family type, religion, urban-rural differences, and such like variables as control variables.[104] (Naidu, U.S., and V.S. Nakhate, 1985) For these reasons Indian knowledge on child upbringing practices has not gone far in creating a pool of universal indigenous and relevant conceptualisations.

Goals are embedded in the unique personality structures of the adults and the "givens" in their environment. The "givens" are the parameters of the ecology which offer or do not offer, opportunities/ facilities.[105] [Misra, G., and K.N. Tripathi, 2004) Thus, since "givens" in ecology vary from one region to another, there is a pot-pourri of variables acting and interacting. These variables change in relation to both occupational and geographical mobility within the ecology, or from one ecology to another. Since ecology is an abstract concept which is not perceived in the lifestyle of a human except at critical periods like war and famine, as mentioned above, there is almost an insidious covert ecological aura that stays with the individual over a period of time till he decides to change his ecology. A child, for instance, from urban family aspire to go aboard to "further his studies". Invariably he does so, and so his living ecologies are many. He moves from his country of origin to his country of occupation, where even there he moves from one geo-ecological area to another, comes back to visit his country men on a periodic basis, and thus is open to the influences of varying ecologies. Thus, these movements create an interdependence that implies a holistic perspective for a better understanding of the individual in his settings.

There are two spurts in the physical growth periods. These are, one during the pre-school years and another during adolescence.[106] (Bogin, B., 1988) Development itself is variable not only from one stage to another, but even within a stage. For instance, children during the pre-school years change rapidly from one year to another and even within the same family network, one pre-school child is different in personality characteristics from another. There are researches which indicate that inherited traits (phylogenetic) and inherent traits (ontogenetic) can be adversely or positively influenced by the ecological environment.[107] (Saraswathi, T.S., and H. Ganapathy, 2002) It would be simplistic to argue that variations in the environment influence individuals similarly, and that such influences are homogeneous. In fact, the theory of individual differences indicates that no one human is like another in specific traits,[108] (Eysenck, H.J., and M.W. Eysenck, 1985), even though the environment may be the same. Because of these differences, children act and react differently to the same situation. The personality of one ethnic group member is also an amalgam of different variables, some of which are known and others not known. *Ethnicity is said to be an independent variable affecting human behaviour, given that ethnicity itself is a composite of culture-specific ecologies*. For instance, a person from Haryana is usually a *Jat*, but this "*Jatism*" is a composite of related variables such as being a how caste or an upper caste *Jat*, farmer *Jat* or a labourer *Jat* and such like combinations of such classificatory variables, playing an important role in the formation of the personality, some of which are known and some are not. A *Jat* does not carry his caste as a label which is overtly obvious. It has to be inferred, and inferences are usually subjective and, therefore, are not realistic perceptions, unless reliably proven to be so.[109] (Blommers, P., and E.F. Lindquist, 1960).

It stands to reason that if the ecology is limited, two consequences affect the individual in these specific ecology. The individual may be aspiring to better his status, or may remain indifferent to its possibility. For instance, it is quite possible that a rural child when asked what he aspires to become as an adult, may either say "I do not want to do the same thing that my father is doing" such as a carpenter, or a farmer, "I want to be a doctor", while another might say, "I want to be what my father is, a farmer or a carpenter". Thus, human aspirations are potentials which can be realised, otherwise they remain dormant.

We see, for example, some professionals in business management who are unable to cope with their job tasks, while some who have risen from the ranks are able to do so effectively, because of their individual differences in achievement orientation to optimise their abilities.[110] (Ggavain, M., 1995).Thus, ecological variables interact dynamically with individual motivational levels in a specific ecology.

9. Variations in Perceptions

What are the perceptions of the major groups, such as the people in governance, the practitioners and the peoples themselves about the provision of infrastructures and services, in the State, the region, the identifiable groups living in rural hamlets, in the various tribal areas in differing ecologies and those living in slums, *bastis* and *chawls* in urban areas.

(a) National Perceptions

How has the national governance sought to modify the ecology for the betterment of the family and its individual members? We have indicated above that at the national level there is an elaborate planning and programming process, where most of the bureaucratic parameters continue from the colonial days. Take, for instance, an office structure. There are separate rooms for bureaucrats and the levels of furnishing have subtle differences for different levels of statuses. In the clerical section, there are desert coolers during summer. For the bureaucrats, there are air conditioners. There are peons (messengers) sitting outside who are called at the press of a bell to fetch and carry for the bureaucrat. This distinction between classes, however, gets dispersed in modernised private international organisations. Private corporate bodies are expected to carry and fetch for themselves, and office canteens have all types of office workers sitting side by side. These are the major organisations who supply infrastructures, like hospitals and educational institutions, and who finance, manage and maintain them for the inhabitants of the given area which is their responsibility.

Thus, *we see a swing from traditionality to modernity in offices. We also see a backward swing from modernity to traditionality when that very bureaucrat in a private MNC organisation gets back home.* He takes off his shoes before going into the *puja* room, touches the feet of his elders, and observes such like traditional behaviour. This adaptive resilience does not create pathological conditions, for compartmentalisation of behaviour is clearly perceived according to the situational determinants of the specific setting. Thus, we see ecologically influenced differential behaviour from one physical setting to another. Thus, we have hierarchies of superordinate and subordinate roles, within the socio-ecological situations.[111] (Kakar, S., 1971)

(b) Professional Perceptions

At the professional level, there is more commitment to the role performance, as it calls upon technical competence *vis-à-vis* bureaucratic administrators, whose functions are usually supervisory and organisational. This very professional depends upon his nature of rapport with the administrative structure. He is liable to be elevated or transferred or even fired. Such *political dynamics are known to exist in organisations wherein some professionals are more technically knowledgeable than are their supervisors. These two structures operate in differentially oriented frameworks or superordinate or subordinate roles*. Such professionals are goal-oriented and technically knowledgeable in their professional skills, such as teachers, lawyers, doctors, engineers and the like. Even within each substratum, there are dynamic perceptions, and interactions. Take for instance, in a large hospital said to be equivalent to international standards, there is a subtle difference in attitude between junior doctors and senior doctors, and even among the same level doctors within a department true is subtle competition. In these circles, professionalism is subdued under the aegis of the administrative superstructure. Their forte is to be known by their outcomes, such as an engineer is known for his ability after constructing a magnificent building or a lawyer who wins several important cases successfully. If they are private professionals, it requires a greater effort on their part to canvas for projects/cases and, therefore, involves greater interaction with their superiors/donors/ multinational sponsors, creating a wider network. Thus, we see the inter-mix of the eco-systems. The individual doctor from his place of work moves to his place among peers, which enlarges to attendance at national and international seminars and conferences sponsored frequently by renowned pharmaceutical companies. In ecological terms, it means that the more these professionals move from the micro to the outer ecological systems, the greater is the probability of interaction provided they are so motivated. And yet we have the one-room doctors and engineers who orbit within their own micro system. They wait for the clientele to come to them to market their skills. Further, the extent of the network is important for communication purposes. The more limited the orbit, the less the opportunity to interact with other ecosystem. In reputed business firms it is well known that there are HRD (Human Resource Development) cells specifically for the purpose of further training in updating skills.

(c) Practitioner's Perceptions

How do practitioners or actioners, interact to bring about a better quality of human development for families? For this we examine the meso system of the family. The family in the micro system moves out more frequently to interact with the meso system which consists primarily of peers/colleagues and the neighbourhood. It is from the latter sources that the micro system of the family learns to acquire the majority of goods and services. To give a few examples, in large cities, security is of concern to householders, where guards and neighbourhood watches are set up and colonies have closed access into the complex. Where domestic help is available, even if on a part time basis, most colonies are fairly well serviced, but where these are not regularly available, services are disorganised and upper class families in such residential areas find it more convenient to utilise contracted services. This is evident in the upmarket colonies of many metropolitan areas where there are common services like backup for electricity, plumbers, carpenters and electricians available for only servicing the complex. Considering the fact that demographic changes reveal an increasing proportion of the elderly, services to such senior citizens are scarce, and if prevalent, are of poor quality. Where available they are mainly for the upper classes.

While it is clear that where services of a lower order are temporary, those who substitute for parents, require to possess parenting acumen. Childcare centres, playschools, playgroups are of this type where there is expected to be a similarity with parenting practices. However, a little deeper analysis would tell us that emotional substitution for the biological nurturant is hardly possible. Administrators/organisers/care-minders do not usually have the same emotional interpersonal repertoire with the child as the biological parent. *There are bound to be differences and these differential practices between parents and organisational practitioners are frequently tangential to each other.* The same child who is taken to the childcare centre everyday by the parent, who is only at home during the weekends, is likely to develop distorted perceptions on what is right and what is wrong because of the differential disciplines between home and child care centres. The type of discipline and the type of caring is frequently not communicated between the parent and the practitioner except in the upper echelon where parent-teacher meetings are in vogue. There have been some efforts by private organisations to conduct parent cooperative childcare centres where parents are encouraged to become involved in the centre's activity. Further, *it is known that educationally the quality of services differentially available,* so that while a child from a wealthy family goes to an ecology where sophisticated facilities are offered, a child from the lower income group has to content with poor quality of facilities. At one extreme are children from wealthy families who go in chauffer-driven cars to schools which are of "the state of the art", while similar aged children from the lower classes often become street urchins, eking a living from market places, bus-stops, railway stations, working as casual labourers and rag pickers. In both ecologies, the primary school child's experience widens except that one child has access to the right facilities and opportunities, while the other does not and, therefore, is open to disruptive influences of the ecology where he is a child labourer.

10. Perception of the Self in the Self's Ecology

From the above discussion, we can deduce several sub-concepts that occur in an individual:

- Perception of the role of the self.
- Perception of the role of the other.
- Perception of tasks to be done by the self.
- Performing the tasks according to the perceptions of others.
- Experiencing satisfaction/dissatisfaction of having accomplished/not accomplished the task.
- Interpersonal perception of the competencies of each other in relation to the tasks to be performed.

It will do well to redefine the major aspects of routine and periodic tasks of living in most Indian families. Whether it is the Gaddhis of the Kangra valley of Himachal, or the *Gonds* of Madhya Pradesh, or the Marwaris in Rajasthan, or the Brahmin in Tamil Nadu. Events like birth, marriage and death have practically the same cognitive connotation and relate to periodic activities which in the main are similar but different according to ethnicity and the intergenerational values about rites and rituals. Whereas routine activities will differ from one group to another, slight variations will continue to exist in periodic activities. Religious ritualistic behaviour will continue during periodic times of life such as pregnancy, birth, weaning, etc., which are accepted as normal but significant occurrences. Frequently, low profiled attention is paid to medical or improved nutritional inputs, especially in the poorer sections of the society for the practical reason that both knowledge and facilities are scarce as compared to those who are adequately serviced.[112] (Khalakdina, M., 1979) In the study by Condominas, on aspects of mental health behaviour among Turkish, Sudanese and Indians, from developing countries, when contrasted with samples from northern Norway, and Greece, from developed countries, Condominas remarked in relation to the developing countries: "One is struck by the non-isolationism of the infant, socialisation being constant."[113] (Condominas, G., 1970) Further, consecutive and continuous childbirth for the early-wedded mother in the traditional sections of the society of India is not uncommon, and so child bearing and rearing is casual in nature, where a great deal of permissiveness and indulgence is given to the infant as the infant is considered a gift from God.[114] (Saraswathi, T.S., and S. Pai, 1997; Khatri, A., 1970) There are numerous surrogates, and the baby is handled by any and all adults.[115] (Ray, P.C., 1965) Thus, the human ecology in which the child grows is frequently informal and is enveloped in affectionate interaction with others in the family and the kinship group members. Unlike the urban areas, there is hardly any rearrangement of the ecology in rural areas, for there are inadequate facilities to interact with. The understanding is that, natural birth is the mother's natural responsibility, and if the child is destined to live he will be given the maximum care the human ecology and the geo-ecology can provide. However, in these areas the practices are elementary and based on the alternative to scientific methodology in these sparsely equipped areas and are elemental means and 'traditional wisdom' passed on from generation to generation.[116] (Swain, S., 1978) In these ecologies, natural materials through the practice of *ayurveda* and its techniques are used to prevent diseases and for curing, for example, traditional wisdom like the use of turmeric as an antiseptic during child-birth. The three *doshas* which are expected to be in harmony and balance *are: pitta, cuff and vaat* according to *ayurvedic* philosophy, are highly profiled in these ecologies.[117] (Kapur, M., 2003) The methods used by parents in elementary societies to assist the child develop naturally, relate mainly to the availability of food and medicinal sources in the natural surroundings, such sources are the scientific processes involved in physical and psychological growth are less known to them in comparison to the educated who live mostly in ecologies which provide modern facilities.[118] (Kumar, A., 1999). *Whatever progress has been made by governmental efforts to educate the illiterate and rural masses, such efforts continue to be poorly understood and implemented.* Even though, the Community Development programme began in 1952 to improve the statuses of the rural poor, oral communication and traditional sources continue to be the major modes of communication in far flung rural and tribal areas. In these groups there continues to be a valued and careful attempt not to disturb the existing conditions of the ecology, for they are to be preserved for security and the homeostasis of the progeny. The known is secure and the unknown is insecure. If, for a farmer there are no clouds at the time of the rainy season, he feels insecure and, therefore, he propitiates the rain gods as water is vital to his survival. If his harvest is spoilt by floods, he relates it to the displeasure of godhead. Such mysticism pervades the rationalisation of the deprived, so that they can cope philosophically with the disasters/trauma they frequently meet with in their frail ecologies. For the average *Indian uniquely is related to nature and the natural, as about a little less than 70 per cent Indians live in rural and tribal areas.*[119] (UNDP, 2000) *Even to this day, people who migrate to the urban areas often return to their villages for short spells* at the time of important events like *during births, deaths, and marriages*. These indicate the stronghold that socioreligious beliefs have on these transient migrating individuals.

The origin of religion has to do with the powerful influence on humans of natural forces and phenomena. Thus, the sun (*surya*), the air (*vayu*), water (*jal*) and fire (*agni*) came to be worshipped and represented in religious rituals. Since the survival of humans also depended on the harvest produced, the religious rituals also involved reverence of the fruits of the earth. Certain trees and plants like the *Peepal* and *Tulsi*, and certain fruits like banana, coconut, etc. gained special place in the ritual performances. Ecological conscientisation is, therefore, related to the veneration of symbolic plants, trees and animals,. Footwear is removed at the entrance of the house as a mark of respect that the gods dwell in the house at the entrance to the *'puja'* room or corner where the statues of gods are placed and are venerated every morning. The homes are built according to the principles of *vaastu shastra* (auspicious alignments) and auspicious timings (*muhurat*) are maintained, and propitiatory *pujas* are performed at the time of the occupation of new homes. The entrance to the house is expected to be facing the rising sun, implying auspiciousness of the sight of the "Sun God". Such beliefs are also typical of urbanised households and not just in the rural ecologies.[120] (Saraswathi, T.S, and S. Pai, 1997) Ecology also influences other aspects of behaviour like language, for instance, where the idiomatic vocabulary is related to the aspects of the ecology which gives the contextual meaning to the concept or construct to be conveyed. The ecology with which man relates assumes different connotation, and varies from one ecology to another. For example, words used in greeting are: "*Ram Ram*" which is suited to the interaction of man and nature in his habitat.[121] (Gupta, G.C., 1998) Also, if the societal and household roles are in consonance with each other, the interactive harmony tends to be in balance.[122] (Gallfather, O.R., 1973) The child, for instance, is instructed by adults to perceive their goals, in a casual manner rather than with anxiety.[123] (Misra, R, 1971) For instance, when the child is asked to perform a household chore, the intent is not to make the child a competent householder, but to initiate the child into competent complementary tasks. If the task is not well accomplished, there is only mild remonstration such as "*koi baat nahi, doosri dafah phir theek karenge*" (meaning, it does not matter, the next attempt will be successful). It is important to remember that most Indian parents generally do not convey high anxiety levels to their children, in the performance of ordinary, routine and periodic tasks. This is especially true of traditional families who live in more or less stable ecologies but this attribute is gradually being dissipated by families who live in highly complex urban ecologies, and who are exposed to many contradictory and competitive instructions about guiding the behaviour of the young. This is even more apparent in adolescents who are "betwixt and between" dependence on the family and seeking their own separate independent personal identity.

Most Indians do not live in those ecologies which are well provisioned. India lives in its villages, where according to the Census of 2001 more than 700 million people live, which make up about 70 per cent of the total population.[124] (Census of India, 2001) The other about nearly 30 per cent live in differential urban and semi-urban ecologies. Some of them are overly provided for while others just scrape through like those in the large urban slums in overcrowded metropolitan areas. About 50 per cent of the population are young people (below 18 years), implying the enormous burden placed on that populace for the care of children, women and the elderly, within their households. True, the middle class has increased almost three fold, but this does not reflect on any betterment of the huge rural population as they are mostly in districts, towns and villages. In contrast to the west, socio-demographic indices denoting physical quality of life are extremely distressing. In the Indian situation, there are scores of studies which connote concern in the numbers of maternal, infant and child mortality because of lack of medical care, malnutrition, ill health and, stunted growth.[125] (Jeliffe, 1968) In sparse ecologies, especially in areas of prolonged deprivation, children who are economically deprived, also lack activities and stimulation for cognitive and intellectual development.[126] (Dyal, R.S., 1980) Thus, there is a vicious cycle of economic poverty, psychological depression and social apathy, underwritten by lack of education and health facilities,[127] (Usha, Shree S., 1980) especially for the average poor rural female.[128] (Mehrotra, D.P., 2006)

Social history has relevance to the ecology of the family, in the sense that it facilitates or hinders human development. Environment will not change dramatically, except for the increase in population and rural-urban migrations. There seems to be a curious paradox that while it is said that there is an economic upturn, there are still about three hundred million people suffering from poverty. Though India is said to have achieved self-sufficiency in food production, continuing increase in the cost of food items, which has within a year gone up to about 14 to 18 per cent as on January, 2011, makes large sections of the Indian people live with inadequate food and nutrition. For them availability of water, power and energy are also problematic as they are more expensive or inaccessible. Such marginalized conditions of large sections of people existed for generations and is continuing even during the post-Independence period, and even after the Governments have formulated and implemented Five Year Plans for development. Unvaryingly, the "haves" tend to live in better of ecologies, unlike the marginalized poor castes.[129] (Cohn, B.S., 1996) This contrast continues to this day in the forms of social distance and discrimination. In social history, Gandhiji attempted to lift the status of the "Harijans" so that they would not be discriminated against.[130] (Pandey, T.N,. 2000). *Unfortunately, the attitude towards the lower castes tends to be more or less the same in socio-economic interactions and religious frames. These attitudes thus render it more difficult for them to climb the ladder of upward occupational mobility.* The Government's attempts to improve their status through reservation in the field of education and employment are being resented by the upper castes.

The colonial attitude towards the upper caste individuals continues to this day. Labels addressing a *sahib* and *memsahib* as Sir and Madam by the subordinates who are mainly from the lower castes indicate the subtle difference between those marginalised and those non-marginalised. However, with growing globalisation, world trade and free markets, new avenues of enterprise have been opened up even for the marginalised. The latter then have free and equal opportunity inspite of social prejudice to raise their economic status. They are now utilising and honing their skills such as working in overseas/outsourced operations like garment industry, information technology and the production of small-scale technological instruments to supply to the developed world. In the process they are reducing their social marginality in the world of caste and class in the Indian society.

One might argue that the unskilled may in the process become more marginalised than before. The fact of the matter is that opportunities are not scaled down and that these opportunities are becoming more attractive for the unskilled to become skilled. In the urban cities of today, elderly shop keepers who in their youth were unlettered except for maintaining accounts have sons and daughters who attend college and attain technical skills.[131] (Pandey, T.N., 2002)

However, except for the variation of marginality mentioned above, the general rubric is that most Indians profess similar socio-religious norms even though within fissioned communities, the types of interaction may still be one of social distance. Thus, the parameters of the general rubric are: *(1) Adherence to socio-religious norms, irrespective of caste, class and boundaries. (2) Awareness of hierarchy and locus of control, which are gradually becoming diffused. (3) Differential perspectives on gender. (4) The increasing coexistence of individualism and collectivism. (5) Values related to families of orientation are becoming loser. (6) Changing mobility patterns are increasing among ecologies and family structures.*

It is important to state that *these vignettes are not static, and, may change from time to time and from place to place. They are idiographic and ethnographic descriptions of life styles in social reality situations.*[132] (Bruner, J.J., 1991*)* A flood may wash away a rich man's mansion, a poor man may become rich, and, therefore, life styles may change, occupational slots may change, and vertical mobility may occur. These are dynamic and unpredictable changes. On the other hand, a successful CEO may shift his residence from one place to another, from one country to another, while a villager from Bihar may shift his residence from large open areas to a jhuggi in a slum area in Mumbai. Both of these movements are examples of horizontal mobility. This horizontal mobility may occur at any time with any family in India. A rider is that the rich are freer with several alternative choices, whereas those in poor ecologies do not have as many alternatives. In spite of the fact that, the per capita income has increased to $360 in less than a four-year period,[133] (Sedere, U.M., and T.C. Schmidt, 2000), the jhuggi continues to be huddled against the high rise luxurious apartment building, as commonly observable in any large metropolitan areas like Mumbai and Delhi.

The country, in the 1950s had bravely proclaimed itself to be a democratic republic with its Constitutionally mandated equality and justice for all. While these are admirably sound concepts, neither the mass of illiterates, nor the poor infrastructure in its agricultural set-up could help to sustain those high sounding proclamations, which could not be translated into reality for the masses of the people. Firstly, the human component was unprepared, with its inadequate civic services. And secondly, the country's governance proceeded on a gigantic almost overly ambitious plan. Planning Commissions set up since 1951, both at the national level and State levels, prepared Five-Year plans on the basis of estimated budgets. As expected, considering the poor revenues, most budgets worked on deficit financing. The programmes, termed planned programmes and non-planned programmes, implied that the planned programmes receive priority while the unplanned were mainly for exigent circumstances such as natural calamities. It is the responsibility of the government to give good governance by corruption-free distribution of moneys, but the programmes frequently became mismanaged at the implementation level. At the point of evaluation, it has been found that the benefits intended for the poor, have not filtered down to the neediest in the target group. For instance, the Minimum Needs Programme has not achieved its major targets due to inadequate resources, poor infrastructure, indifferent personnel and tangential perception of "who is the poorest of the poor", in such programmes.[134] (U.N., 2002) Given the paucity of revenues, and with the realisation that providing services for over 90 per cent of the population has to be subsidised, there is usually a compromise on quality. Privatisation implies that only those who can afford to pay get good quality services. For the general public, Governmental services are subsidised and, therefore, offered haphazardly, and lack the necessary personnels, skills and supplies. On the periphery of towns and cities, for example, hospitals more often than not, are state sponsored which are mainly distribution centres with scarce commonplace medications.[135] (Khalakdina, M., 1979) Often time, the health centre doctors are more busy in their own private practice.

11. The Nature of the Compact between the Family and Governance

India is fast moving towards technological patterns of living although in a lopsided manner and for the miniscule elite. In cities, cyber cafés, the cellular, new types of music systems, gadgetry from all exporting countries, especially the Far East are fast becoming common items of consumption. *With introduction of new economic policies in 1991, the per capita income has increased to $360 in less than a four-year period.*[136] (Sedere, U.M., and T.C. Schmidt, 2000) More children in absolute numbers are in school. Transport of all types has increased. People especially the salaried class are encouraged to take loans for self financed homes. The middle class is more achievement-oriented than ever before. Despite this clear movement towards modernisation, there are strands of conservatism that are deeply ingrained, like the core socio-religious values, like, for instance, the reading of *Kundlis* or horoscopes before the marriage to ascertain the match between the bride and bridegroom. *The nature of the compact implies the relationship between governance and the governed. In 1951, India had taken upon itself the ambitious programme that was essentially two-pronged: (1) to raise essential education levels through compulsory primary education, and (2) to revamp the agricultural economy.* Over half a century it has almost achieved self-sufficiency in foodgrains, due mainly to programmes like Community Development, agricultural upgrading, subsidies to farmers and spectacularly to the Green and White revolutions (Green implying accelerated grain production and White implying upgrading of cattle and their products). The first objective of universal primary school education has, for the large part, achieved less than expected results on an overall basis. While there have been rapid strides in school enrolment, there are still wide gaps to be filled to achieve universal primary education. This is seen from the fact that as of 2005, only 79 per cent of males and 58 per cent of females aged seven and older could read and write a sentence.[136a] [Sonalde B. Desai, et. al., *Human Development in India: Challenges for a Society in Transition.* Delhi: Oxford University Press, p. 76) The drop-out rate from high school was 63.88 for girls as compared to 60.41 for boys in the year 2004-2005.[137] (Planning Commission: Government of India, 2008) Thus, large numbers of uneducated youth from various rural ecologies are migrating to large metropolitan cities as casual wage labourers or as unskilled or semi-skilled workers such as mechanics, electricians, plumbers, carpenters, masons and the like. The high rate of migration towards large metropolitan cities like Mumbai, Delhi, Kanpur, Chennai, and Kolkata is bursting the seams of city limits, because these urban centres are unable to provide basic facilities for the burgeoning population, such as housing and clean drinking water. A very minimal percentage of the urban population pay taxes. Therefore, the burden of providing civic facilities falls upon the minimal numbers of taxpayers. Revenues are, therefore, short-changed. The current information on provision of facilities (health, education, welfare and other benefits) and the population surge shows a mismatch not only between their availability, but also their accessibility and the regularity of maintenance of services.

A quick assessment of the socio-demographic situation shows the following:

1. Literacy rates are poorer for females who proportionately drop out of schools more quickly and whose health status, especially in rural areas, is poorer than those of males.
2. *The urban population is closely congregated in cramped spaces especially with the influx of migrants in cities, where rural to urban flows are becoming more evident.*[138] (Cassen, R., T. Dyson and L. Visaria, 2004) Facilities like health and educational infrastructure (primary schools and health centres) are relatively less in proportion to the needs of the population, whether urban, or rural or tribal.
3. *Income per capita shows a low average increase, although hidden within this, is the fact that the bulk of the income is accessed by the minimal urban rich and some of it goes as "undeclared" wealth.*
4. While there are inadequate statistics for indexing migration and, therefore, *the numbers living in urban conglomerates, they experience greater shortage of civic amenities.* The rich, however, have supplementary sources such as generators for electricity and bore wells for water. As time increases, and as geo-ecological space becomes less available and more expensive, *the huddling of the rich with the poor reveals such glaring differences, that the possibility* of increasing resentment of the poor *is expectedly high, with the unitended consequences of social destabilisation, especially in large crowded cities.*
5. *In terms of environmental degradation there are stark cases of denudation as in the Aravalli hills of Rajasthan, in the eastern ghats of Andhra and the northern hills of the lower range of the Himalayas as in Uttarakhand and Himachal*

Pradesh. While there is adequate land for agriculture, in many places the tableland is lowered due to lack of replenishment by the perennial rivers, which go dry in summer. Thus the ratio of adequate ecological facilities to the growing needs of the increasing population is in inverse proportion .

From the above, it is apparent that two riders assume importance:

1. *Infrastructure facilities, inadequate and poorly trained staff in medical and educational institutions in rural/tribal areas is exacerbating the illiteracy rates of the young generation in these areas.* This implies the lack of readiness of the young to meet the challenges of world trade and commerce, in this era of globalisation. This is despite the fact that those in government run institutions have subsidised health and housing facilities. This is especially apparent when frequently rural youth, when asked about job aspirations, frequently say, "*hume sarkari naukri chahiye*" (I want a government job). Better-serviced ecologies are greatly prized.
2. *The proliferation of land acquisition by industries have converted large tracts of agricultural lands* and villages into expanding industrial complexes with the influx of Multi-national Corporations (MNCs). These high tech industries displace the need for manual labour and depletes the greenery of the land. Inflation had crossed the 12 per cent mark in 2008 exacerbating the crowded living conditions of the already poor strata.[139] *(UTV News*: 25 August, 2008). This does not, however, stop the influx into urban areas where, by and large, money is more accessible through daily wage labour than in the rural areas. Thus, land acquisition has spread the boundaries of the city into sprawling slums in a haphazard manner. These are dynamic changes in the ecological habitat of shifting and extending populations implying adjustments to new ecologies. These examples are increasing. Suburban in Mumbai like Navi Mumbai, industrial and residential colonies like the Bharat Heavy Electricals Limited in Delhi and in the adjoining villages of Gurgaon, Noida indicate the overflow of population from one adjacent State to another. These mobility patterns will continue in all probability so that the nexus of human ecology

and geo-ecology mix occurs in various combinations, compounding the effect of 'crowding humanity'.

Further the influx into cities of partially educated frustrated rural youth seeking greener pastures in the city life are generally frustrating, leading to the dangerous possibility of disorganised and discouraged youth, likely to become anti-social in behaviour.[140] (Madan, G.R., 1998)

There is also the Catch-22 question. Most government staff in villages are restless because of the knowledge of better pay/facilities in urban areas. They are usually on the lookout for transfers to ecologies where there are better facilities and emoluments. It is also not uncommon to find health staff and teachers at district headquarters 'negotiating' such transfers. In such situations, the quality of services also deteriorates.

The responsibility for providing facilities for the poor rests on the government. As the poor majority is vast in number, the facilities are spread thinly. Water and electricity are often erratic. The provision of facilities for the fragile population like extra familial care for the young and for the elderly are few and far between. It is apparent that the resources of the government are few, and subsidising the poor is heavy on the revenues of the government, whether Central or State.

Although, very few in number, there are many outstanding NGOs who within a very small range, live with the villagers and help develop their environment. However, they are not sufficient to serve larger populations. Some outstanding ones, to name a few out of the thousands, are: SEWA, Tilonia, Bharat Sevak Sangh in the North and in the South, the Guild of Services. Other national bodies are, for example, the All India Adim Jati Sevak Sangh and Harijan Sevak Sangh, besides the charitable missions like the Ramakrishna Mission, Brahmo Samaj and Arya Samaj. CAPART (Council for the Advancement of Peoples' Action and Rural Technology), is a semi-autonomous agency, which documents the work of several non-governmental organisations that are working for the underprivileged.[141] (Lalitha, N.V., 1987) These are but a drop in the ocean. Consequently, remote ecologies like interior rural villages and inaccessible tribal areas are innocent about such services or their availability. The general individual psyche in these difficult terrains has been short-changed mainly because of the lack of reinforcement from the human ecology around them. There are a host of ecological technologies which these neglected groups can develop in their ecologies, such as water-harvesting.[142] (Khalakdina, M. 1998) Such innovative approaches are being attempted in other far east nations, like Thailand where waste products are being recycled.[143] (Sharma, S., 1988) Given the weaknesses in the political system, though village populations are "democratically represented in village councils (the panchayats)", there is, however, the downside, that the more powerful in the representative are more prone to avail themselves of undue benefits.[144] (Dreze, J., and Amartya Sen, 2002) *In spite of being a liberalised democracy, given the mass of people, there are many difficult bridges to pass for the planning and implementation acumen of the government.*[145] (Rich, R., and E. Newman, 2004) The Government is now in the Eleventh Five Year Plan period and yet the increasing segments of the population are still poorly educated.

12. The Changing Nature of the Compact between Family and Society

In this twenty-first century there is a changing tenor in the ecology *per se*. It is apparent that there is a growing assumption that behaviour differentials are influenced by ecological and cultural contexts. Berry *et al.*, distinguish common trends from two other theoretical views: (1) absolutism which denies cultural influence on behaviour, and, (2) relativism, which denies the existence of underlying psychological processes.[146] (Berry, J.W., Y.H. Poortinga, M.H. Segall and P.R. Dasen, 2002) Irrespective of these two themes, ecology attaches itself to several other disciplines such as cultural ecology,[147] (Vayda, A.P., and R. Rappoport, 1968) ecological anthropology[148] (Moran, E., 1982) and other related approaches, each taking the line of the principles of their disciplines.

Summarising the above aspects, we can state that:

1. There is a growing understanding of human behaviour within an ethnographic/idiographic setting.
2. Providing a cultural framework facilitates an in-depth analyses of the human behaviour to be studied,
3. Ecology in India is uniquely influenced by geographical parameters such as the habitat, the natural produces of the

earth and the human's ability to cognise and use the ecology to its maximum extent possible for his well-being.

4. Ecology is relative to the psychological processes of human growth and development as it modifies and monitors human cognition and behaviour, and so the ecologies in India make for differently contoured individual attributes.
5. Ecological variation occurs significantly in India which possess all the climates from tropical to ice capped mountains, a large coastline and, therefore, variation in flora and fauna which also sets the heterogeneity of the Indian from region to region, predisposing individuals to differential consequences when living in differential ecologies.
6. Ecologies are subject to change. They modify human nature. For instance, living in West Bengal produces a human being whose style and manners are different from the product of a human in the hill ranges of western Himalayas. The individuals/groups themselves might change ecologies and, therefore, enlarge their experiential knowledge. Those who live continuously in one ecology tends to be parochial in outlook and living patterns. For instance, the urban migrant may be working at the same restaurant as the local resident. The local watches the same cricket match on his television as does the migrant on his.
7. The local living in a consistent ecology has less psychological problems to content with, than does the migrant entering the same precincts, using coping mechanisms and strategies to overcome the new problems successfully.

Thus, there is a constant dynamic interaction between the old adage that nature provides what it can, while human beings try to make their natural conditions better. Over the years, socio-economic and political history provide a basis of knowledge of how humans invent, create and rearrange their physical ecology to suit their needs. For instance, given the limited land space for accommodation, there is a necessity for architects to plan for comfort using the least space possible. This gives rise to the phenomenon of high-rise concrete jungles in urban areas. At the same time, societies deliberately for economic profit enter into processes, which are detrimental to their very own members. It is well-known that industrial effluents pollute drinking water, that belching smoke from industries choke the air and high-rise buildings overflow onto pavements where the poor homeless tend to live. Yet, when endemics and other such epidemiological diseases occur, it takes an incalculable amount of effort and money to redress the situation.[149] (Evans, A.S., and R.A. Kaslow, 1997) This conceptualisation is generic at the interactional level of ecology and the socio-psychology of the group. The individual in his own specific ecology has to deal with the various levels of differing other individuals, each with their own unique personalities, namely, his immediate family (the micro ecosystem), his school, his playground and so on (the meso ecosystem), and the world of which he has knowledge through media systems (the macro ecosystem). These interactions have their own repercussions. The individual's view has expanded. Today a tycoon whose original birthplace is a remote village has an expansive, ecological perspective. He is in Mumbai today, in America tomorrow and back in the village thereafter to visit his old parents. If he is an NRI, he makes it a point to visit his *dehat* or home town at least annually or bi-annually. All individuals, and this is true of Indians, do have a nostalgic attachment to their birthplace (*Matri Bhumi).* While in the USA he will sit at a table and eat with cutlery, when he comes home he eats with great gusto with his fingers, thus indicating an adaptive resilience to the various ecologies with which he is familiar. He is in equilibrium on a bridge between one ecology and another. He has learnt the range of expected and performed roles conditioned by the given ecology at a given time.

REFERENCES

1. Hall, C.S., G. Lindzey, J.B., Campbell, 1988, *Theories of Personality.* New York: John Wiley & Sons.
2. Watson, J.B., 1913, 'Psychology as a behaviourist views', *Psychological Review*, 20 (2), pp. 159-177.
3. Wickew, A.W., 1992, 'Making sense of environments', in W.B. Walsh, K.H. Craik, and R.H. Price (eds.), *Person-Environment Psychology: Models and Perspectives.* pp. 157-192. Hillsdale, NJ: Erlbaum.
4. Kelvin S. Hall, Gardner Lindzey and John B. Campbell, 1998, "Albert Bandura and social learning theories", in Kelvin S. Hall, Gardner Lindzey and John B. Campbell, *Theories of Personality*, New York: John Wiley & Sons, pp. 622-626.
5. Duncan, O.D., 1965, 'Human ecology', in *Encyclopaedia Britannica*, Vol. 7, pp. 923-924, Chicago Ill.

6. Lewin, K., 1936, *Principles of Topological Psychology*, New York: McGraw Hill.
7. Barker, R.G., and Wright, H.F., 1951, *One Boy's Day*, New York: Harper & Row.
8. East, M., 1980, *Home Economics: Past, Present and Future*. Boston: Allyn & Bacon.
9. Berry J.W, 1966, 'Temne and Eskimo: perceptual skills', *Journal of Psychology*, 1, pp. 207-229.
10. Super, C.M., and S. Harkness, 1986, *The Development Niche: A Conceptualisation at the Interface of the Child's Culture*, pp. 0165-0254, BV North: Holland: Elservier Science Publisher.
11. Tansley, A.G., 1935, 'The Use and Abuse of Vegetational Concepts and Terms', *Ecology*, 16, pp. 284-307.
12. Clarke, R., 1973, Ellen Swallow: *The Woman who Founded Ecology*. Chicago IL: Follett.
13. Gavan, M., 1995, 'Thinking on niches: socio-cultural influences on cognitive development', *Human Development*, 11, 35, pp. 25-44.
14. Bubolz, M., and Sontag, M.S., 1993, 'Human ecology theory', in P.G., Boss, W.J. Doherty, R. LaRossa, W.R. Schumm and S.K. Steinmetz (eds.), *Source Book of Family Theories and Methods: A Contextual Approach*. New York: New Plenum Press.
15. Bronfenbrenner, U., 1986, 'Ecology as a context for human development research perspectives', *Developmental Psychology*, 22 (6), pp. 723-742.
16. Kumar, H.D., 1992, *Modern Concepts of Economics*. Bombay: Vikas Publishing House.
17. Bennet, J.W., 1983, *Human Ecology as Human Behaviour. Essays in Environmental and Developmental Anthropology*. NJ: Erlbaum
18. Bubolz, M.M., and M.S. Sontag, 1993, 'Human ecology theory', in P.G. Boss, W.J. Doherty, R. LaRossa, W.R. Schumm and S.K. Steinmetz (eds.), *Sourcebook of Family Theories and Methods: A Contextual Approach*. New York: Plenum Press.
19. Barrows, H.H., 1923, "Geography as human ecology", *Annals of the Association of American Geographers*, 13 (1), pp. 1-14.
20 Steward, J., 1955, *Theory of Culture Change*. Urbana: University of Illinois Press.
21. Prout, H., and M. Prout, 1965, *The Ecological Perspective on Human Affairs*. Princeton, N.J.: Princeton University Press.
22. Boulding, K.E., 1950, *A Reconstruction of Economics*. New York: Wiley.
23. Altman, I., and J.F. Wohlwill, 1977, *Human Behaviour and Environment: Advances in Theory and Research*, Vol. 2, New York: Plenum.

24. Hook, N., and B. Paolucci, 1970, 'The family as an ecosystem', *Journal of Home Economics*, 62, pp. 315-318.
25. Worid Health Forum, The WHO QOL Group, 1996, *What is Quality of Life*? World Health Forum, 17, pp. 354-356.
26. Bronfenbrenner, U., 1979, *The Ecology of Human Development: Experiments by Nature and Design*. Cambridge: Harvard University Press.
27. Bronfenbrenner, U., 1986, 'Ecology of the family as a context for human development research perspectives', *Developmental Psychology*, 22 (5), pp. 723-742.
28. Bronfenbrenner, U., 1979, *The Ecology of Human Development: Experiments by Nature and Design*. Cambridge: Harvard University Press.
29. Bronfenbrenner, U., 1986, 'Ecology of the family as a context for human development research perspectives', *Developmental Psychology*, 22 (5), pp. 723-742.
30. Bronfenbrenner, U., 1979, *Ecology of Human Development: Experiments in Nature and Design*. Cambridge, MA: Cambridge University Press.
31. Bronfenbrenner, U. 2005, *Making Human Beings Human: Bio-ecological Perspectives on Human Development*. California: Sage.
32. Arnold, D., 1999, 'An ancient race outworn: malaria and race in colonial India', in B. Harris, and W. Ernst (eds.), *Race, Science and Medicine*, 1700-1960, p. 130. London: Routledge.
33. Littlewood, R., 2000 (July), 'Ecological understandings and the cultural context', *Philosophy, Psychiatry and Psychology*, Vol. 6, pp. 133-134. Maryland: John Hopkins University.
34. Adam, C.C., 1935, 'The relation of general ecology to human ecology', *Ecology*, 16, pp. 316-35.
35. Joshua, S. Goldstein, 2003, "War and economic history", in Joel M. Okyr (ed.) *The Oxford Encyclopedia of Economic History*. New York: Oxford University Press.
36. Guruswamy, M., J.P. Mohanty and R.J. Abraham (eds.), 2005 (October), *Will India Catch up with China*? New Delhi: Centre for Policy Alternatives.
37. Bronfenbrenner, U., 1986, 'Ecology of family as a context for human development research perspectives', *Developmental Psychology*, 22, pp. 723-742.
38. Buckley, W., 1967, *Sociology and Modern Systems Theory*. Englewood Cliffs: Prentice Hall.
39. Bronfenbrenner, U., 1979, *Two Worlds of Childhood, US and USSR*. New York: Russel Sage Foundation.

40. Saraswathi, T.S., 1999, 'Adult-child continuity in India: is adolescence a myth or an emerging reality?', in T.S. Saraswathi (ed.), *Culture, Socialisation and Human Development: Theory Research and Applications in India*, pp. 211-216. New Delhi, Thousand Oaks, London: Sage Publications
41. Shah, A.M., 1998, *The Family in India: Critical Essays*. New Delhi: Orient Longman.
42. Ray, S., 1960, *Aspects of Padam Minyong Culture*. North East Frontier Agency, Shillong.
43. Ramanujam, A.K., 1994-5, *Folk Tales from India*. New Delhi: Penguin.
44. Singh, K.S. (ed.), 1972, *Tribal Situation in India Today*. Shimla: Indian Institute of Advanced Study.
45. Archer, W.G., 1974, *The Hill of Flutes – Life, Love and Poetry in Tribal Life: A Portrait of the Santals*. London: George Allen and Unwin Ltd.
46. Doshi, S.L., 1971, *Bhils Between Societal Self-Awareness and Cultural Synthesis*. New Delhi: Sterling Publishers.
47. Witkin, H.A., and D.R. Goodenough, 1981, *Cognitive Style: Essence and Origins*. New York: International University Press.
48. Khalakdina, M., 1998, 'In sight, on site: a study of mobile creches', *Suraksha Series on Early Childhood Care and Education in India*. Monograph, Series No 2. Madras: Swaminathan M.S. Research Foundation; New Delhi: Sage.
49. Ridley, Matt, 2003, *Nature via Nurture: Genes, Experience, and What Makes Us Human*. New York: Harper Collins.
50. Mishra, Soni, 2008, "How Johads Bring Life and Prosperity to Rajasthan's Arid Lands". *Week* (28/12/2008).
51. Singh, M.V., N.K. Anand, S. Gupta and D.C. Dhingra, 1976, 'Intelligence and the degree of malnutrition', *Indian Journal of Clinical Psychology*, 3(2), pp. 117-20.
52. Desai, K.G., 1980, 'Comparative factorial structure of Raven's Standard Progressive Matrices, Cattell's Culture Fair Scale and Desai-Bhatt Group Tests of Intelligence on samples of various sub-cultures of Gujarat', *Journal of Psychological Researches*, 24 (1-2), pp. 8-15.
53. Ghuman, P.A., 1978, 'Nature of intellectual development of Punjabi children', *International Journal of Psychology*, 13 (4), pp. 281-94.
54. Kakar, S.D., 1976, 'Linguistic background and intelligence', *Asian Journal of Psychology and Education*, 1(1), pp. 20-23.
55. Pathak, M., 1977, 'Influence of supplied cues in human figure drawings of preschool children', *Journal of Psychological Researches*, 21 (1), pp. 45-51.

56. Saraswathi, T.S., 2003, 'Introduction', in T.S. Saraswathi, *Cross-Cultural Perspectives in Human Development*, New Delhi: Sage.
57. Sinha, D., 1978, *Perceptual Style among Nomadic and Transitional Agricultural Birhors.* Paper presented at the International Psychological Conference, *Munich.* August 1978
58. Krishnan, L., 2004, 'Attitudes, social cognition and justice', in J. Pandey (ed.), *Psychology in India Revisited, Vol. 3: Applied Social and Organisational Psychology.* New Delhi/Thousand Oaks, London: Sage Publications
59. Hull, C., 1939, 'Mind, mechanism and adaptive behaviour', *Psychological Review*, 44, 1-32.
60. Berry J.W., 1974, 'Ecological and cultural factors in spatial per capita development', in J.W. Berry and P.R. Dasen (eds.), *Culture and Cognition: Readings in Cross Cultural Psychology.* London: Lord Methuen.
61. Bubolz, M.M., and M.S. Sontag, 1993, 'Human Ecology Theory', P.G. Boss, W.J. Doherty, R. LaRossa, W.R. Schumm and S.K. Steinmetz (eds.), *Source Book of Familial Theory and Methods: A Contextual Approach*, p. 424. New York: Plenum Press.
62. Berry, J.W., 1976, 'Ecological and cultural factors in spatial perceptual development', in Jane Wolfson (ed.), *Personality and Learning,* pp. 112-123. London: Hodder and Stoughton and The Open University Press.
63. UN, 2002, *Financing Adequate Shelter for All*, p. 112, New York: U.N. Habitat.
64. Moghaddam, F.M., 1990, 'Modulative and generative orientations in psychology: implications for psychology in the three worlds', *Journal of Social Issues*, 46, pp. 21-41.
65. Bril, B., 1999, 'Dires Sur l'enfant selon les cultures. Etat des lieux et perspectives', in B. Bril, P.R. Dasen, C. Sabatier and B. Krewer, *Propos sur l'enfant et l'adolescent: Quels enfants pour quelles cultures?* pp. 5-40. Paris: L'Harmattan.
66. Jain U. and Palsane M.N., 2004, "Environment and behaviour", in J. Pandey (ed.), *Psychology in India Revisited*, Vol. 3, New Delhi: Sage Publications.
67. Mahadevan, K., Chi Husi Tuan and V.K. Balakrishnan Nair, 1992, *Ecology Development and Population Problems: Perspective from India, China and Australia.* Delhi: B.R. Publishing Corporation.
68. Doshi, S.L., 1971, *Bhils between Societal Self-Awareness and Cultural Synthesis*, pp. 54-74 and 75-114. New Delhi: Sterling Publishers.
69. Misra, S.N., 1998, *Dynamics of Rural-Urban Migration in India*, New Delhi: Anmol Publications, pp. 185.

70. Khalakdina, M., 1998, 'In sight, on site: a study of mobile creches', *Suraksha Series on Early Childhood Care and Education in India*. Monograph, Series No 2, pp. 44-59, Madras, M.S. Swaminathan, Research Foundation; New Delhi: Sage.
71. Bronfenbrenner, U., 1970, *Two Worlds of Childhood, US and USSR*. New York: Russell Sage Foundation.
72. Bubolz, M.M., and M.S. Sontag, 1993, 'Human ecology theory', in P.G. Boss, W.J. Doherty, R. LaRossa, W.R. Schumm, and S.K. Steinmetz (eds.), *Sourcebook of Family Theories and Methods: A Contextual Approach*, p. 430. New York: Plenum Press.
73. Aphale, C., 1976, *Growing Up in an Urban Complex*. New Delhi: National.
74. Ananadlakshmy, S., and M. Bajaj, 1981, 'Childhood in the Weaver's Community in Varanasi', in D. Sinha (ed.), *Socialisation of the Indian Child*, New Delhi: Concept Publishers.
75. Seymour, S., 1986, 'Changing families in India: Adaptations to urbanization in Bhubaneshwar during the past twenty years', *Proceedings of the Eighth Conference of the International Association of Cross Cultural Psychology*. Istanbul, Turkey.
76. Super, C., and S. Harkness, 1986, 'The development niche: A conceptualisation of the interface of child and culture', *International Journal of Behavioural Development*, 9, pp. 545-569.
77. Barkow, J.H., L. Cosmides and J. Tooby, 1992, *The Adapted Mind. Evolutionary Psychology and the Generation of Culture*. New York: Oxford University Press.
78. Bronfenbrenner, U., 1979, *The Ecology of Human Development*, New York: Harvard University Press.
79. Bronfenbrenner, U., 1989, 'Ecological systems theory', *Annals of Child Development*, 6, pp.185-246.
80. Meggars, B.J., 1954, "Environmental limitations on the development of culture', *American Anthropology*, 56, pp. 801-24.
81. Tomasello, M., 1995, *Human Development*, 38, pp. 46-52.
82. Barry, H., I. Child and M. Bacon, 1959, "Relation of 'child training' to subsistence economy", *American Anthropology*, 61, pp. 51-63.
83. Ferrington, John and Priya Deshinkar (eds.), 2009, *Circular Migration and Multilocational Livelihood Strategies in Rural India*, New York, Oxford University Press.
84. Wolpert, S.A., 2004, *A New History of India*, p. 40, New York, Oxford University Press.
85. Erikson, E.H, 1974, *Dimension of A New Identity*. New York. Norton.
86. Michael, Witzel, 2005, "Vedas and Upanisads", in Gavin Flood (ed,) *Hinduism*. Malden, M.A.: Blackwell Publishers.

87. Stephen Philips Cohen, 2002 (1st Oct.), *India: Emerging Power*, p. 27. Brookings Institution Press.
88. Erikson, E.H., 1978, 'Eight ages of man', in E.H. Erikson, *Childhood and Society.* Great Britain: Paladin.
89. Havighurst, R.J., 1953, *Human Development and Education.* New York: Longmans.
90. Lippit, R., and R.K. White, 1958, 'An experimental study of leadership and group life: leadership', in E.E. Maccoby, T.M. Newcomb, and E.L. Hartley (eds.), *Readings in Social Psychology*, pp. 496-510. New York: Henry Holt & Co.
91. Lewin, K., 1936, *Principles of Topological Psychology.* New York: McGraw Hill.
92. Bronfenbrenner, U., 1993, 'The ecology of cognitive development: research and models and fugitive findings', in Woznaik and K. Fischer (eds.), *Development in Context*, pp. 3-44. Hillsdale, N.J.: Erlbaum.
93. Lewin, K., 1935, *A Dynamic Theory of Personality.* New York: New McGraw Hill.
94. Bronfenbrenner, U., 1989, "Ecological systems theory", in R. Vasta (ed.), *Annals of Child Development*, 6, pp. 187-251. Greenwich, CT: JAI.
95. Ganesh, K., 1988, *Family and Kinship in India: Implications for Women.* Unpublished manuscript, The Population and Human Settlements Division, UNESCO.
96. UNICEF, 1973, *Part I. UNICEF Study on the Young Child: Indian Case Study*, p. 23. New Delhi: UNICEF SCARO
97. Swaminathan, (ed.), 1998, *Suraksha Series on Early Child Care and Education.* New York: Sage.
98. Mandelbaum, D.G., 1968, 'Family, jati and village', in M. Singer and B.S. Cohn (eds.), *Structure and Change in Indian Society.* pp. 29-50. Aldine Publishing Co.
99. Rai, G.C., 1979, 'A study of certain socio-psychological dimensions of child rearing practices adopted by Indian mothers', *Psycholingua*, 9(1), pp. 15-29.
100. Murphy, L.B., 1953, 'Roots of tolerance and tensions in Indian child development', in G. Murphy, *In the Minds of Men.* New York: Basic Books.
101. Kakar, S., 1981, *The Inner World,* Delhi: Sage Publications.
102. Kakar, S., 1981, *The Inner World — A Psychoanalytic Study of Childhood and Society in India.* New York: Oxford University Press.
103. Khalakdina, M., 1979, *Early Child Care in India.* p.25. London: Gordon and Breach.
104. Sinha, D., and R.C. Mishra, 1993, 'Some Methodological Issues related

to Research in Developmental Psychology in the context of Policy and Intervention Programmes', in T.S. Saraswathi and B. Kaur (eds.), *Human Development and Family Studies in India: An Agenda for Research and Policy*. New Delhi: Sage.

105. Misra, G., and K.N. Tripathi, 2004, 'Psychological Dimensions of Poverty and Deprivation' in J. Pandey (ed.), *Psychology in India Revisited: Developments in the Discipline,* Vol. 3, pp. 118-215, New Delhi: Sage.
106. Bogin, B., 1988, *Patterns of Human Growth.* Cambridge: Cambridge University Press.
107. Saraswathi, T.S., and H. Ganapathy, 2002, 'Indian parents' ethnotheories as reflections of the Hindu scheme of child and human development', in H. Keller, Y.P. Poortinga and A. Schlomerich (eds.), *Between Culture and Biology: Perspectives on Ontogenetic Development*. pp. 79–88. Cambridge, UK: Cambridge University Press.
108. Eysenck, H.J., and M.W. Eysenck, 1985, *Personality and Individual Differences: A Natural Science Approach*. New York: Plenum Press.
109. Blommers, P., and E.F. Lindquist, 1960, *Elementary Statistical Methods in Psychology and Education*. p. 315. Boston: Houghton Mifflin Co.
110. Ggavain, M., 1995, 'Thinking on niches. socio-cultural influences on cognitive development', *Human Development*, 35, pp. 25-44.
111. Kakar, S., 1971, 'Authority patterns of subordinates' behaviour in India organisations', *Administrative Science Quarterly*, 16, pp. 298-307.
112. Khalakdina, M., 1979, *Early Childcare in India*, pp. 29-32, London: Gordon and Breach.
113. Condominas, G., 1970, 'Introductory comment', E.J. Anthony and C. Koupernik (eds.), *The Child in His Family*, Vol. 1. pp. 354. New York: Wiley & Sons.
114. Saraswathi, T.S., and S. Pai, 1997, 'Socialisation in the Indian Context', in H.S.R. Kao and D. Sinha (eds.), *Asian Perspectives on Psychology*, p. 78, New Delhi: Sage.

     Khatri, A., 1970, 'Personality and mental health of Indians (Hindus) in the context of their changing family reorganisation', in E.J. Anthony and C. Koupernik (eds.), *Child in his Family*, pp. 391-92. New York, Wiley-Interscience.
115. Ray, P.C., 1965, *The Lodha and their Spirit-possessed Men*, pp. 94-95. Calcutta: Anthropological Survey, Government of India Museum.
116. Swain, S., 1978, 'Customs and beliefs associated with pregnancy and child birth in rural Orissa', *The Indian Journal of Social Work*, 39 (1), pp. 79-91.

117. Kapur, M., 2003, 'Childcare in ancient India', in J.G. Young, P. Ferrari, S. Malhotra, S. Tyano and E. Caffo (eds.), *Brain, Culture and Development*, p. 100. New Delhi, Macmillan India.
118. Kumar, A., 1999, *Child Healthcare in Ancient India.* Sri Satguru Publications, Indian Medical Sciences Series. Delhi: Indian Book Centre.
119. UNDP, 2000, *Human Development Index.*
120. Saraswathi, T., and Pai, 1997, 'Socialisation in the Indian context', H.S.R. Kao and D. Sinha, *Asian Perspectives on Psychology*, p. 80. New Delhi: Sage.
121. Gupta, G.C., 1998, 'Linguistic diversity, language shaping and ecology', in I. Singh and R. Parasuram (eds.), *Human Cognition*, p. 207. New Delhi: Sage.
122. Gallfather, O.R., 1973, 'Migrant labour from tribal Chotanagpur', *Indian Anthropologist*, pp. 22-444. Indian anthropological association.
123. Misra, R, 1971, *Mullukurumbas of Kappala.* Memoirs No. 30, p. 37, Calcutta: Anthropological Survey of Indian Museum, Government of India.
124. Census of India, 2001: 'Rural-urban distribution of population – India and States/Union Territories – 2001'. www.censusofindia.net/results.
125. Jeliffe, 1968, *Infant Nutrition in the Tropics and Subtropics.* Monograph Series No. 29, pp. 44-45. Geneva: WHO.
126. Dyal, R.S., 1980, 'The impact of malnutrition on intelligence', *Indian Pediatrics*, 17(2), pp. 109-116.
127. Usha, Shree S., 1980, "Social disadvantage, academic adjustment, and scholastic achievement', *Social Change*, 10 (1 and 2), pp. 23-30.
128. Mehrotra, D.P., 2006, *Gender Discrimination: Its Impact on Girls' Schooling in Four States of India*, p. 123. Plan International India.
129. Cohn, B.S., 1996, *Colonialism and its Forms of Knowledge: The British in India.* Princeton University Press.
130. Pandey, T.N, 2000, *Bose on Gandhi. The Fourth N.K Bose Memorial Lectures.* New Delhi: Indira Gandhi National Centre for the Arts.
131. Pandey T.N., 2002, 'Some thoughts on marginalisation and marginalised communities', *Journal of Anthropology: Survey India*, 51, pp. 1-7.
132. Bruner, J.J., 1991, 'The Narrative Construction of Reality,' *Critical Enquiry*, 18, pp. 1-21.
133. Sedere, U.M., and T.C. Schmidt, 2000, *Globalisation and the Low Income Economies: Reforming Education*, p. 65. Universal Publishers.
134. UN, 2002, *Financing Adequate Shelter for All*, p. 112. New York: U.N. Habitat.
135. Khalakdina, M., 1979, *Early Child Care in India.* London: Gordon and Breach.

136. Sedere, U.M., and T.C. Schmidt, 2000, *Globalisation and the Low Income Economies: Reforming Education*, p.65. Parkland, FL: Universal Publishers.
137. Report of the Steering Committee on Empowerment of Women and Development of Children for the Eleventh Plan (2008). Planning Commission: Government of India.
138. Cassen, R., T. Dyson and L. Visaria, 2004, *Twenty-first Century India: Population, Economy, Human Development and the Environment*, p. 111. New York: Oxford University Press.
139. UTV News Report at http://www.utivi.com/news, Monday, 25, August, 2008.
140. Madan, G.R., 1998, *India of Tomorrow*, New Delhi: Allied Publications.
141. Lalitha, N.V., 1987, *Voluntary Work in India*, New Delhi: NIPCCD.
142. Khalakdina, M., 1998, *Efforts to Build Trust*, Ahmedabad: Oxford India Trust.
143. Sharma, S., 1988, 'Stress and Anxiety', in J. Pandey (ed.), *Psychology in India: The State-of-the-Art*. New Delhi: Sage Publications.
144. Dreze, J., and Amartya Sen, 2002, *India: Development and Participation*. New Delhi: Oxford University Press.
145. Rich, R., Newman, E., 2004, *UN Role in Promoting Democracy Between Ideals and Reality*. United Nations University Press.
146. Berry, J.W., Y.H. Poortinga, M.H. Segall and P.R. Dasen (eds.), 2002, *Cross Cultural Psychology: Research and Applications*. New York: Cambridge University Press.
147. Vayda, A.P., and R. Rappoport, 1968, 'Ecology: cultural and non-cultural', in J. Clifton, *Cultural Anthropology*, pp. 477-497. Boston: Houghton Mifflin.
148. Moran, E., 1982, *Human Adaptability: An Introduction to Ecological Anthropology*. Boulder: Westview Press.
149. Evans, A.S., and R.A. Kaslow, (eds.), 1997, *Viral Infections of Humans: Epidemiology and Control*. New York: Plenum Press.

3

Theoretical Bases of Personality Development

This chapter consists of:

1. The meaning of a theory in the social sciences.
2. Criteria of a valid theory.
3. Characteristics of a theory.
4. Conceptual foundations of a theory as relevant to personality development.
5. The process of the developing personality.
6. A holistic perspective of personality domains.
7. Variations in the conceptualisations of personality development.
8. The progression of theoretical thinking on the development of a personality.
9. The kaleidoscope of the changing Indian personality in the milieux of science, technology and global events.

1. The Meaning of a Theory in the Social Sciences

This chapter will attempt to explain the foundations of a theory of development as it relates to the human individual. In the early days when philosophy seemed to be the main intellectual theory on the workings of the human mind, personality was viewed as a mask (Latin *personae*) akin to the verb *personae, "to speak through", referring to the mask used by an actor on stage.* Greek and Roman drama employed the use of masks extensively for the audience to distinguish characters.[1] (Harmon, F.L., 1948: 3) In Shakespearean days, while the mask did not exist, Othello was a villain and Romeo was a lovesick irrational being. Some scholars still believe that personality is a façade. Psychoanalysts believe that the ego represents the individual's face to the outer world and that, social constraints and laws cover the ego with several layers of veils which are monitored by the super ego.There are certain assumptions that form the basis of a theory.

Firstly, a theory is a collection of logically ordered abstract concepts. Simply put, a theory is a cumulative collation of relevant concepts describing thought and behaviour and/or development with special emphasis on the processes during the life span. These constructs are put together in a framework that sets limitations. For instance, the theory of Stimulus-Response sets itself to the process within the framework of an action and its reaction. It does not go beyond this set, but within this set there are various sub-concepts. A stimulus-response set of statements can be conditioned, reinforced, inhibited and retrieved. It can lead to others in a chain reaction. Socialisation practices contribute to personality development, and the developmental attributes of the individual dynamically modify each other. These constructs do not give an integrated perspective, but indicate that the whole makes up the parts and each part by itself does not represent the whole.

Secondly, psychological domains are not systemic. They vary within themselves, as for example, motivation which can be high or low, and can vacillate among the domains in a dynamic manner. Further, such domains as 'need' and 'drive' may be channelised towards negative or positive behaviour. Therefore, these domains take on differential quality when their intensity/extensity changes. The psychodynamic approach confines itself to explaining the innerself, as to how person experiences conflict and whether it is resolved. The resolution, or lack of resolution of it, of feelings, attitudes and emotions are mainly inner-directed, and do not lend themselves easily to interpretation as do overt behaviour. Therefore, *each theory has its own parameters which develop empirical evidence or try to prove the concepts of the theory evidenced through research.*

Thirdly, *a theory remains a theory, or a set of hypotheses and is acceptable if when tested they produce a factual evidence that indeed they are true.* This lends credibility to the theory when these are refined to the status of principles.

Fourthly, a theory is a disciplined approach to an enquiry. It cannot have credibility if it is an ad hoc combination of ideas.[2] (Klein, G.S., and D. Krech, 1952: 10) The approach requires to be directed towards the use of constructs that have relevance and validity to the concepts being tested. For instance, when one is putting together a set of hypothetical constructs on how children behave in conflict situations, the concepts that have relevance are proactive or reactive needs, need constraints or need fulfilment, or need reduction, anxiety, and frustration and the resolution of these.

Fifthly, most theories are at various stages of development in contributing to theory building. They must have within themselves the potential to develop further concepts which add to the meaning of a theory. For instance, frustration, which is an outcome of "need blockage," can show itself not only in progressive or regressive behaviour, but can even remain at *status quo.* A concept like anxiety should be able to demonstrate in the individual anxious behaviour where the individual has learnt to suppress frustration to various situations. To the non-achievement of the corresponding behaviour, demonstrating its existence in the individual could be lack of motivation. Most theories have an inbuilt potential to explain both development and its relevant behavioural outcomes. Concepts in defining a theory should be correlative and comparable with each other in a linking manner.[3] (Hall, C.S., J. Lindzey and J.B. Campbell, 1998: 19)

Sixthly, theories on development and behaviour advance empirical data on group behaviour in various observable situations, but rarely tackle continuity of the developmental constructs, of a longitudinal basis, such as learning and maturity, which are systemic. The latter have their own hypothesised basis of human development. They, however, have the potential to be correlated or covariantly analysed. Studies, such as for instance, investigate how groups behave when coping with crises.[4] (Maccoby, E.E., 1958)

Thus, we find there are various strands, mostly logically constructed concepts, which describe the assumptions, the reliability and, more importantly, the valid bases of the theoretical constructs. Theories are based on hypotheses, which remain valid till further knowledge adds to their validity or replace them with higher level hypotheses. Such new discoveries uncover more of the concepts of development and have within them the potential for further exploration.

2. Criteria of a Valid Theory

An acceptable theory should:

(a) define the scope of the psychological/socio-psychological domains.

(b) give a conceptual framework of it indicating linkages between their sub-concepts.
(c) offer hypothetical statements from the systems of its logical derivatives and, in the case of quantitative data, the variables can be statistically tested.
(d) have the potential to indicate further sub-areas of enquiry.
(e) lend itself to the understanding of its application to real life situations. As for example, studies on the concepts of reward and punishment in behaviour modification theory can be translated into practice.
(f) be able to reaffirm its basic assumptions when it offers postulates (statements of acceptable hypotheses).
(g) offer postulates logically compatible in reaffirming that the processes, concepts and sub-concepts are linked causally and correlatively.

Many existing theories have lacunae in adhering to the criteria specified above. Several of them are middle-of-the-range theoretical domains because they have limited boundaries and parameters.[5] (Merton, R.K., 1967)

3. Characteristics of a Theory

A theory is a set of propositions based on tentative assumptions as to the nature of the constructs devised to explain a phenomenon or a set of phenomena. These phenomena have a set of characteristics which form the concepts of the bases of a theory.

(a) A theory results from elaboration, combination and interpretation of tested data (deductive or inductive).
(b) A theory depends upon previous valid experiences which then form the foundation for later experiments/researches.
(c) A theory consists of "stimulus—response" domains of thought and action. These domains are linked or combined through discrete but related constructs.
(d) A theory links itself to the symbolic abstract concepts and is applied to sets of categories/classifications of variables which are expected to have the potential to operationalise these categories/classifications.
(e) Reliability and validity are relevant to concepts and constructs of these categories/classifications.

A theory, therefore, originates in internal selective processes of the thinking organism, which puts together ideation in creative or innovative but hypothetical ideas, and is assumed to be logically linked. As concepts become more complex in the growing arena of academic enquiry, they tend to change with a greater in-depth knowledge of these concepts. With this process of refinement, they tend to become more reliable in their linkage to the theoretical framework.[6] (Bruner, J.S., 1959) *Theories are, therefore, ordered conceptualizations, simple to complex, concrete to abstract; discrete to organised; and egocentric to socio-centric.* Their interpretation is modulated by the phylogenetic bases of the human nature and the ontogenetic characteristics pruned by environmental influences on differing individuals in different ecologies. Development occurs not only because of the increasing experience of the individual, but also by the impact of different stimuli from the environment, which in turn moderate human behaviour.[7] (Thomas, R.M., 2001: 16-18) The different stimuli of the environment (situational and ecological) reinforce or attrition behaviour.

Even if we limit ourselves to the biological and physiological sources of behaviour, such as the functioning of the endocrine glands as determining human behaviour, which are phylogenetically constant, we have not yet fully been able to identify causes or correlates, which encourage or impede such processes.[8] (Thorpe, L.P., and A.M. Schmuller, 1958). They may be suppressed by chemical ingestions, where the effects of the sources are often irreversible. For instance, brain damage is often irrevocable. There may be compensatory stimuli like physiotherapy, and drugs, but the problem is often life-long. Studies in India on brain damage where sophisticated tools are used for investigations have corroborated the relationship between brain damage and abnormal behaviour [9] (Rantkallio P., von Wendt L., and Koivu M., 1987). This is most obvious in hormone diseases such as thyroid deficiency and diabetes.

When we attribute characteristics (especially social) of behaviour to races, they are scientifically not tenable. For example, we may call an Indian superstitious, a German stoic, an Italian passionate, but these are *passé* stereotypes. Even in our society, we have stereotypes such as for miser, "*bania*", a nagging wife, "*ladaaki*", a hedonist, "*ayyashee*", and so on. These cultural labels have not been fully examined in relation to the correlates of behaviour and are mainly stereotypes. They have no genesis in heredity, or the genetic mechanisms affecting such behaviour. Again, popular generalisations do not hold good for any one person of a particular race, category or otherwise. We can still have many cold Italians, agnostic Indians, many wives who are not nagging and so on. These labels are more convenient for the biased perception of the observer to code, label and categorise his/her perceptual conclusions. Such generalisations cannot form theories. For, there are rigid and biased conditions for the acceptability of a theory.

According to Sinha, academicians are yet to offer constructs as to how and why physiology interacts with psychology to understand the concepts in the making of the personality in its fullest extent. He goes on to say that, "*even though there is hardly any branch of psychology which does not refer to the organismic variations inherent in behaviour to account for differentials in performance, we are still to investigate neurophysiology, neuro-psychology, neurochemistry and psycho-pharmacy and their influence on behaviour.*"[10] (Sinha, M.M., 1976) This is the situation currently obtained although these neurosciences are making gradual strides in relating cognitive human behaviour to the neurology of brain functions.[11] (Pirta, R.S., 2009)

4. Conceptual Foundations of a Theory as Relevant to Personality Development

Personality is the end-product of our characteristic systems. "It is the sum of the individual's total psychological assets and liabilities (actual and potential)."[12] (Wolman, B.B., 2004: 81) At the outset, *we need to differentiate between the concept of human development and that of the developing personality. 'Human development' is a product-producing process. The developing personality indicates a continuous segmented but progress process that can identify in individual as belonging to a culture, religion, ethnic group, class and caste in a country. At any time the product may be viewed as a cumulative outcome of the past experiences which are finally organised into a personality.*[13] (Eysenck, H.J., 1952). For instance, even before an infant grows into a toddler, there is frequently a comment that the child is aggressive or passive or hyper-active, indicating that the child is developing a personality characteristic which is an aggregate of characteristics making up a whole organised person[14] (Kagitcibasi, C., 1996). These characteristics during the developing years may not be stable. They may change as a child grows into adult and learns, for instance, to control his aggression.

According to Piaget, if a child's behaviour shows reasoning and logical deduction, he is in the piagetian stage of formal operations.[15] (Piaget, J., 1926). When his experiences are accumulated, he exhibits habitual expressions. What are these habitual modes of behaviour? *Over the years psychologists have centred around the explanation and justification of their views on development in a segmented fashion, such as Maslow's need paradigm,*[16] (Maslow, A.H., 1954) *Murray's psychodynamic exposition of personality development*[17] (Murray, H.A., 1968) *or Lewin's topological theory of physical forces, energy and space,*[18] (Lewin, K., 1935) *and such like theories.* Some of these theories as relevant to the developing *Indian personality will be explained in the chapter on Selected Personality Theories relevant to the Indian psyche. Most theories are based on psychogenetic and physiological conceptualisations of phylogenetic and ontogenetic regulatory mechanisms.*[19] (Thomas, R.M., 2001: 271) *However, since no man is an island, he lives in an environment of other people which reflect/deflect/deviate/modify his patterns of living and, therefore, his personality traits.*

One of the first definitions of human development was made in terms of the end-product or the person's personality. This was in 1950 expressed by the Fact-Finding Report of the mid-century White House "Conference on Children and Adults," where it was stated that "a personality is the thinking, feeling, acting human being who, for the most part conceives himself as an individual separate from other individuals and objects. The human being does not have a personality, he is a personality."[20] (Witmer, H.L., and R. Kolinsky, 1950: 3). From this definition, we extrapolate that there is a synonym between a personality and a person, except that when we are talking about personality we describe the person in a socio-psychological and physiological framework. The individual is recognised as a unique entity. The difficulty in describing personality *per se* is that it has its meaning embedded in several contexts.[21] (Sarason, I.G., 1966: 401) Following the definition by the White House Conference, there have been several definitions made by psychologists at various times. If we analyse their conceptual constructs, they remain within a specific orbit. For instance, Angyal states, "personality can be described most adequately when looked upon as a unified dynamic organisation."[22] (Angyal, A.A., 1952: 131)

In this respect, we find that out of sheer sparseness of data or theorising about personality in the Indian context, we depend heavily

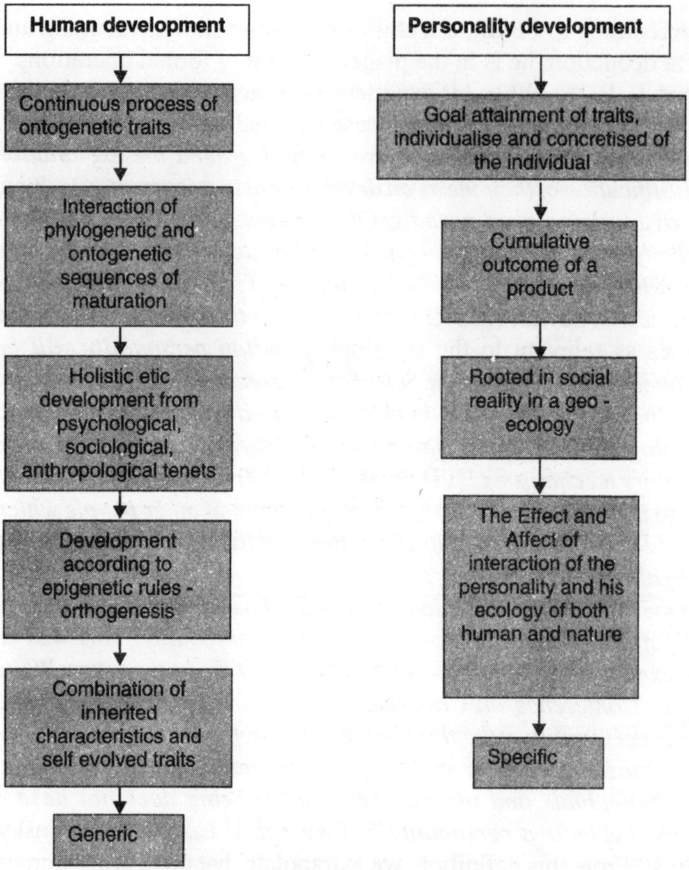

Paradigm 3.1: Differences Between Human Development and Personality Development

on the analysis of psychological and sociological theorising from the West. Some offer constructs and models based upon a western psyche. At the outset, it is essential to state that the constructs of development of the human being and the theme personality are inextricably intertwined. For, after all, development implies developing into something, and that something in this context is a person with attributes, characteristics of behaviour, attitudes and values that he grows with and into and so becomes a personality. *The closest that we can approach an indigenised interpretation of the Indian in his environment is given in a new theory advanced about personality in indigenised terms, which is called the theory of Gunas based on the Samkhya philosophy.*[23] (Uma K., Y.S. Lakshmi, and E.G. Parameswaran, 1971). It is yet in its nascent stage, and for the purpose of its development into a theory it requires empirical data.

To go back to available definitions, we find that Allport's definition is the most widely accepted definition of personality. He defines personality as "the dynamic organisation within the individual of those psychophysical systems that determine his unique adjustments to his environment."[24] (Allport, G.W., 1937: 48)

Psychology depends heavily on constructs of self-perception and the perception of others about the individual and discusses such concepts as behaviour influenced by attitudes, values and beliefs, provided they are reliable.[25] (Baldwin, A.L, 1914). Anthropology tells us that the individual is acculturated to the norms and behaves as a representative of such norms, such as conformist/non-conformist towards parental and societal belief systems, and/or parental ethnotheory[26] (Harkness, S., and C.M. Super, 1996). Goodnow refers to the latter as parents' ideas, giving it a generalistic rubric[27] (Goodnow, J.J., and A.W. Collins, 1990). *Personality traits are much influenced by the cultural communication that takes place during the socialisation process*[28] (Chaudhary, N., 2004).

5. The Process of the Developing Personality

Besides, the western theorists the Indian theorist Paranjpe discusses the developing personality using concepts of the scriptures from the *vedic* times, emphasising Vedanta conceptualisations to explain Indian behaviour.[29] (Paranjpe, A.C., 1988) *We do not have psychologically tested theory to explain human development in terms of the Indian religious belief. Perhaps, what is more telling is that the Hindu philosophy offers us markers as to the different stages of the life-span termed Samskaras. Underlying these Samskaras are traditional beliefs of the Hindu way of life,.*

The ashramas specify correlatively the spiritual and psychological maturity related beliefs and practices of the lifecycle. Samskaras denote rites of passage and rituals described in Ayurvedic paediatrics knowledge, exemplifying various childhood stages of samskaras *and their importance as the milestones of development.* The major stage from one month to the age of six is denoted below:

Table 3.1: The Major Markers of Early Child Development according to the Hindu Philosophy

Jatakarma	*After Birth*	*Rooting and suckling reflex.*
Namakarma	10th\12th day-100th day	Appropriate period for general examination of infants.
Annaprasana	6th or 10th Month	(a) Appearance of first tooth (b) Functioning of Digestive system (c) Proper time for weaning
Chudakarana	1-3 year	Care of fontanel.
Upanayana	6 – 8 years	(a) Fit for education (b) Assessment of intellect

Source: Kumar, A., 1999: 91.

Kumar states that during these stages indicated above, parents attempt to inculcate the kind of behaviour appropriate to each stage[30] (Kumar, A., 1999: 91). Since India is a patriarchy in its socio-religious frame, the parenterally required behaviour is orally communicated and monitored.

Children are guided through the above mentioned stages mainly through "love-oriented" techniques.[31] (Sears, RR, E.E. Maccoby and H. Levin, 1957) This interactive process is a continuity between the world of the adult and that of the child.[32] (Murphy, L.B., 1953 However, not all of these are marked by rituals in most families. The more traditional the family and the higher up in the caste system, more likely are they to perform these ritualistic markers at the stages mentioned in the above table. Thus, there is a traditional wisdom, an oral intergenerational communication and a structured system of beliefs and rituals that mark these stages. These rituals emphasise to impress upon the growing individual and the family network the expected maturity at each stage of early childhood development.

These stages exemplify also the continuity of the individual according to what is socio-religiously implied.[33] (Kumar, Krishna 1993: 68) *The Indian child learns more by directed imitation of the role model in the family rather than by deliberate teaching on the part of the adults*. The interaction, which begins in the family of orientation, continues into the family of procreation. It goes beyond intra-familial structure to the hierarchy of the kinship network where the child learns the value of authority and the locus of the familial power structure. Age and hierarchical positions demand deference and respect. In fact, role learning, understanding, role expectations and successful performance of the task allocated to the growing individual are parts of the development process according to the Hindu philosophy.

This relationship between the individual and the human ecology is maintained by communication from one generation to another. The continuity in development indirectly emphasises the reciprocal continuity of the human and geo-ecological systems. If we analyse some of the effect of such rituals related to the scriptures, we find that scientific knowledge is less than the traditional ways of living. The duality that exists between Indian philosophy and psychology is given below:

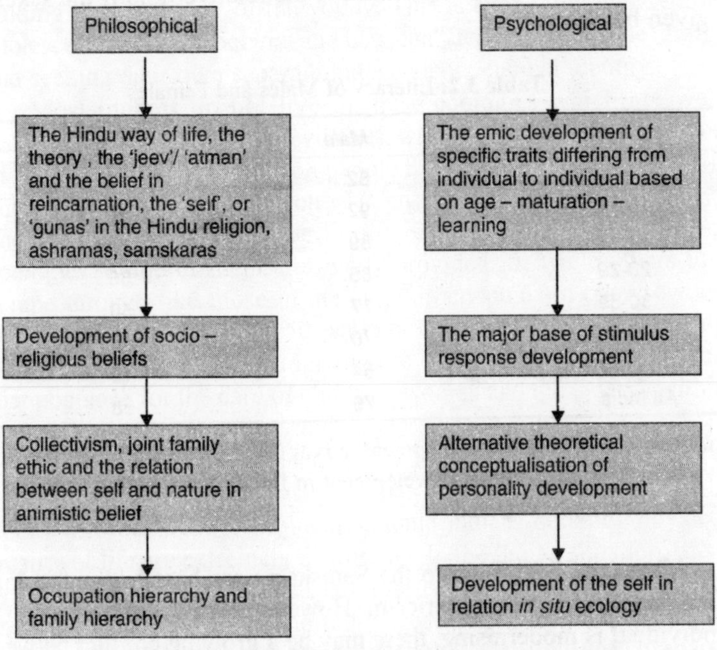

Paradigm 3.2: The Philosophical and Psychological Aspects of Personality Development

It is said that the primary aim of the finite life is to seek a relationship between this transitory world, the past and the future. *There is, therefore, a Karmic justice in the Hindu philosophy. It is interestingly related to ritualistic patterns that use ecological symbols, such as the use of fruits and earth-giving products to symbolise obeisance to the God-heads*. A caveat that is unique to many eastern cultures and certainly in India, is the duality of behaviour between the sexes (expected and performed). From the Hindu perspective, the male child is preferred to the female, and is required for the Hindu family for the sanctity of the conduct of various rituals. The low accord given to female children is observable in the daily life.

Females are less advantaged living in a patriarchal structure, where the sex ratio indicates less females to male, implying that they are at a discount in terms of health and sustenance. Being confined within the household, and, allocated household tasks earlier, with less mobility, females are less educated which further denigrates their status *vis-à-vis* males. One index is the relative ratio if the sexes as given below:

Table 3.2: Literacy of Males and Females

Age group	*Male*	*Female*
7-9	82	77
10-14	92	88
15-19	89	79
20-29	85	66
30-39	77	50
40-59	70	38
60 +	54	19
All India	79	58

Source: India Human Development Survey 2004-05 data in Desai, Sonalde B. *et al.*, Human Development in India, 2010, Oxford University Press, New Delhi.

Concepts pertaining to the Samskaras are based on a theology that is not subject to empiricism. However, as the world around the individual is modernising, there may be a growing conflict between traditional socio-religious beliefs of what influences the personality and what does not *vis-à-vis* the inherited past-oriented orally communicated habits of Indian living. Increasingly. *The Indian in his various ecologies, is learning to live in them, some modern, some traditional and also to contour his behaviour according to expected roles.*

In India, much before the age of Renaissance and the industrial revolution in the west, Valmiki and Vyasa in the early BC's, and in the seventeenth to nineteenth centuries, Gyanashwaram, Tulsidas, Kabir and Sai Baba were some of the revered sages. They expounded on the aspects of Hindu philosophy as related to the human being. *Through these sages, Indians have been handed down a tradition of the mind, the conscious, the uniqueness of being and the relationships between man, the Supreme Being, the cosmic energy and nature.*

From the psychosocial point of view, Misra *et al.* propose three axes for studying the development of the individual. Firstly, the child is considered god-given and his behaviour is channelised by his parents; secondly, the interaction of *karma* (self fulfilment) and *dharma* (the duties to others) influence behaviour; and thirdly, the child's own powers of construction and reconstruction articulate his behaviour and, therefore, his development[34] (Misra, G., and K.N. Tripathi, 1993). Thus, the basis of personality development are an inter-mix of social scientific constructs, theological thinking within an ecological framework, that is unique to each individual.

We will deal with Piaget's theory in the next chapter as his contribution to cognitive development is classic and well-known and relates to the development of biophysical and mental structures in the early years of development. This is similar to several forgoing theorists in the terminology, which is used: namely, functional invariance (Lewin's concept of habit formation).

With human nature being a dynamic entity, regulation of behaviour does not occur systematically, as the totality of variables is not under control, as in an exact science such as mathematics. Further, even with known variables such as class and class structure, there are unknown intervening variables which are psychodynamic in nature and not amenable to rigorous control, reliability or validity measures. Therefore, knowledge of how a person develops according to the whole spectrum of sciences: social, physiological, physical, theological, political, economical and geo-ecological, interact in haphazard ways, which preclude logical construction as the sciences are still reconstructing themselves continuously and progressively.

The processes of building up a personality are not monolithic. Its knowledge is gradually increased by the addition of other impinging areas of knowledge. Two decades ago, for instance, neurosciences did not have the increasing profile it does now. Since the last century, there is a growing tide of geo-ecological knowledge that is modifying the understanding of influences on personality. This era is observing the fact that Tsunamis, earthquakes, flood, failure of monsoon, rising of seas and, more recently, the blowing volcanic ashes from the mountains of Iceland have destructed normal technologically based activities of the modern world. No longer can we look askance at the destructions caused to the nature's "personality". When ravaged, disrespected and ignored, it lashes back on humans living on the earth. For these reasons, we are becoming more aware in India of the effect of geo-ecologies on our heterogeneous landscape which requires greater recognition, reconstruction and replanning of our lifestyles. *We may rejoice in the fact that we do not have to travel by bullock carts; but by this token we cannot rejoice we have more cars, less energy, greater pollution and greater frustration in travelling along congested roads that are bursting the seams of everyday urban traffic. So which is better? The untouched geo-ecology of the past or, the modified, unrecognisable geo-ecology of the present?* The wisdom of the human and the wise utilisation of time will tell.

The Indian is not an average. He is an individual and will assume forms of living suitable to his ecology, both, human and geo as future lessons will indicate.

6. A Holistic Perspective of Personality Domains

The paradigm on what makes up the concept of personality is like looking at a hilltop from different perspectives. From the viewpoint of behaviourists, there is much reliance upon chronological age maturity – observing the contour of the hill side,[35] (Hull, C.L., 1943) whereas, from the viewpoint of psychoanalysis, the interest is in delving deep into the innards of the hill.[36] (Freud, S., 1964)

In the fifties, Whiting and Child in their classic study[37] (Whiting, J.W.M, and I.L. Child, 1958) stated that "personality is the extent to which a person's characteristics differ from one to another, the extent of uniformity within oneself, the effect of different cultures on differences in personalities among different societies." This is, of course, a description related to their model of psychoanalytical theory within cultural parameters. Kardiner[38] (Kardiner, A., 1959) identifies the effect on personality in different cultures of the primary institution of the family, which produce the basic personality structure, and secondary institutions of peer group, community, classroom, world information, and such like institutions influencing the development of a personality. His conceptualisation is probably the basis of the human ecosystems. *Most theories explain segments of behaviours or development through behaviourism and limit themselves to conduct research to support their hypotheses. However, when we deal with generalisations, we find that we are caught with stereotypes, such as "he is an aggressive personality", or "she has a meek personality" and so on. But these are just clichés, which we propound by typing persons to fit into categories or stereotypes on the basis of reported behaviour or biased perceptions.* Here we evoke only what we have set ourselves out to evoke which is a professional and disciplined approach to the study of the developing personality. The behaviour theorist attempts to find out whether the child has achievement motivation or not by using stimulus-response queries and labels the overt behaviour to explain whether the child has achieved successfully or not. There is frequently little linkage from one trait to another and similarly few, if any, stated linkages among theorists. As soon as psychologists select a sample of an individual and attempt to research, for instance, whether the group can be divided on the basis of authoritarianism or submissiveness, and do elaborate analysis, all they are able to say is 'yes' or 'no', authoritarianism exists or submissiveness exists. However, individuals who are deemed to be authoritarian may be so with younger siblings and yet be submissive towards his parents. Even when we try to find some typology like Sheldon's theory on the basis of body mass,[39] (Sheldon, W.H., 1940) we are in fact bordering on the untenable. The major personality theory that has been measured in a multi-factorial design is the MMPI (the Minnesota Multi-phasic Personality test).[40] (Stark, E. Hathaway and J.C. McKinley, 1940)

From Indian sources, the major documented information on personality that has been expertly dealt with by Paranjpe is based on the Hindu scriptures. In sum, he deals with *Vedanta* epistemology and, therefore, has a place in the theoretical understanding of development[41] (Paranjpe, A.C., 1988). Thorpe, after much review of the available theories from Western sources states that, "the process of personality formation and development, though they result in a distinct unity, are integrated. Although individual variation is the basis of psychological measurement, this uniqueness must be viewed as a total process and the patterns of experience which have produced it."[42] (Thorpe, L.P., and A.M. Schmuller, 1958).

Hall and Lindzey in their monumental overview, describe in detail the psychoanalytic theory and its theorists from the time of Freud and the various mini theories on covert behaviour. They also describe the theories of stimulus reinforcement, operant conditioning, and other related behaviour theories.[43] (Hall, C.S., G. Lindzey and. J.B. Campbell, 1998) Thus, we find a complexity of conceptualisations about what comprises a personality. What do we perceive? Is it a commonality or is it an individual characteristic trade or are there combinations of characteristics which make up what we perceive, and typify. And, are these components linked in a cohesive manner to express all the known characteristics *per se*? We still are searching at the segmental level within each discipline. Sociology deals mostly with groups, communities, castes, classes and such like formations. Psychodynamic theories try to interpret inner behaviour, while those theories which depend upon observed traits do so in a limited fashion as related to a limited framework. We are still searching for an eclectic theory which has a holistic approach.[44] (Baldwin A.L., 1980)

Several experts believe that a developed human being can be only interpreted by behaviour and that theories of behaviour are really theories of personality.[45] (Klein, G.S., and D. Krech, 1952: 5) But we also know that all theories of behaviour rest on the fundamentals of the stimulus-response bond, which are only observable overtly. How then do we come to know about the inner world of the person, which is also valid but is organised in a covert fashion, such as emotions and their suppression, anxiety, conflict, and guilt. In order to find an adequacy of correlates to explain personality, some experts use the concept of "correlation of events." If the personality shows dominance, overbearingness and a tendency towards control, conflict models such as Mowrer's model,[46] (Mowrer, O.H., 1950) it tells us that the person may also have correlates of a lower order on self-esteem, self-image, self-confidence and such related correlates which have to measure either in a multiple factorial analysis or individual and are assumed to be related or not related. Psychoanalysts explain for instance that abnormal personalities may have experienced deep, intense trauma, which has become indelible or repressed. Their outcomes in behaviour are really exhibits of such correlated covert happenings in the mind. *Thus, there are very few theories which are able to preset a holistic picture. They represent vignettes depending on which theoretical model limits their interpretation.*

Given the above theoretical constructs, not all is explainable about the continuum of development. It is possible that each one of these constructs will be further examined in terms of the "surplus but unknown intervening dimensions." In other words, we underscore the conclusion that no one theory has the possibility of explaining personality through a multi-dimensional approach even though Gestalt theory attempts to do this and experts like Thorndike and Allport developed paradigms to explain as many facets/traits as possible through factor analysis[47] (Thorndike, E.L., 1920). However, their potential for further investigation continues, for a theory is credible only to the extent of the parameters it utilises and examines reliable and validated constructs/concepts. The individual Indian lives in an ecology, a family, a natural habitat, which interact to influence the development of his characteristics, as illustrated in the paradigm below.

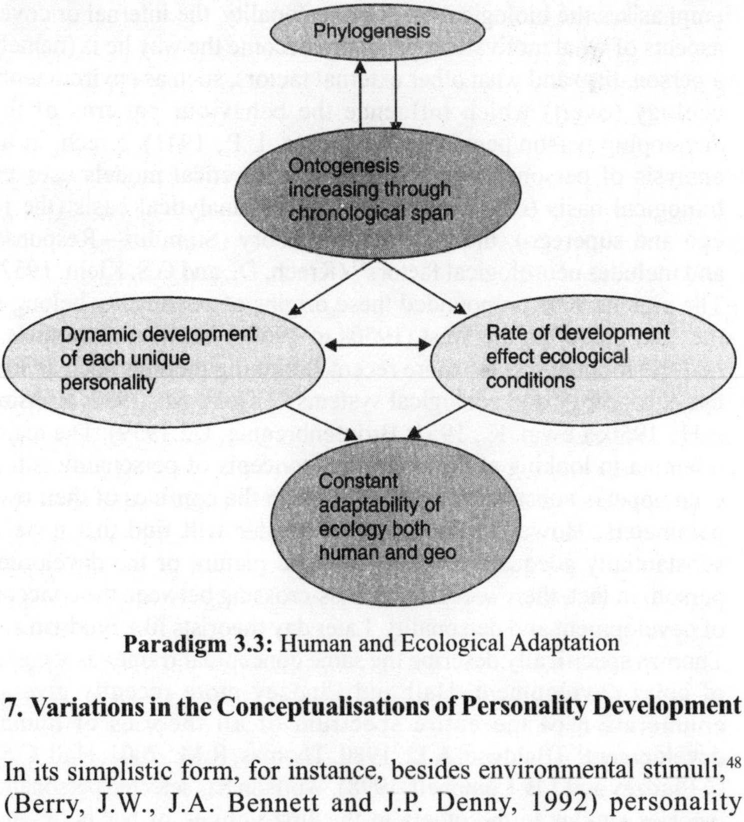

Paradigm 3.3: Human and Ecological Adaptation

7. Variations in the Conceptualisations of Personality Development

In its simplistic form, for instance, besides environmental stimuli,[48] (Berry, J.W., J.A. Bennett and J.P. Denny, 1992) personality development is viewed as an accumulation of progressively complex processes. Mental growth, for instance, is conceived as a product of learning and age-related changes and maturation. In this respect, for instance, the outcomes of inherited traits of intelligence are elicited by assessment techniques, which should be context-specific in order to be valid. Logically, this implies that there are many contextual frames comprising ecology, environment and scientific technological stimuli. Time is the major index of chronology and its relevant changes[49] (Valsiner, J., 1998). This concept implies that development is phased and that progressive development eventually evolves into a personality[50] (Valsiner J., and K.J. Connolly, 2003). Further, any one stray case does not make a whole and, therefore, an accumulation of tested hypotheses of attributes will indicate a totality of a person's attributes, which is also inclusive of his reinforcing environment[51] (Whiting, J.W.M., and I.L. Child, 1958). Thorpe, on the other hand emphasises the biological basis of personality, the internal or covert aspects of what motivates a person to become the way he is (namely, a personality) and what other external factors, such as environmental ecology (overt) which influence the behaviour patterns of this developing person/personality[52] (Thorpe, L.P., 1941). Krech, in his analysis of personality as rising from theoretical models uses the biological basis (orthogenetic), the psychoanalytical basis (the id, ego and superego), the behaviourist theory (Stimulus—Response) and includes neurological factors[53] (Krech, D., and G.S. Klein, 1952). The experts who propounded these origins of personality belong to the "old guard" in the West (1950s to 1960s) but have nevertheless laid the foundations for more recent fissioning theories such as life-cycle, topology and ecological systems[54] (Klein, M., 1932; Erikson, E.H., 1950; Lewin, K., 1951; Bronfenbrenner, U., 1979). The major dilemma in looking at these profiled concepts of personality is that each appears substantially credible within the confines of their own parameters. However, the analytical reader will find that none is substantially adequate to give a holistic picture of the developing person. In fact, there seems to be criss-crossing between the concepts of development and personality. Later day theorists like Baldwin and Thomas specifically describe the same conceptual frames as theories of child development. Hall and Lindzey more recently give an enumeration of the entire spectrum of all theories of human development[55] (Baldwin, A.L., 1980; Thomas, R.M., 2001; Hall, C.S., G. Lindzey and J.B. Campbell, 1998). Wolfson has selected personality theories similar to the others in the first volume of her book, and specified "dimensions, motivation, the developmental process, cognitive styles, intelligence and creativity," as components of a personality[56] (Wolfson, J., 1976). Thus, the reader is presented with a *pot-pourri* of theoretical concepts, their dimensions, their derivatives, and their composition, which, in effect are using similar constructs such as motivation, which is integral to psychoanalysis, and language, which is either positively or negatively reinforced in the concepts of the behaviour theories. For instance, human children left in forests were raised by wolfs and so spoke a language which was a babble, indicating the influence of ecology on language development[57] (Singh, J.A.L., and Zingg R.M., 1966).

The major writers in relating human development in the context of the Indian psyche are Paranjpe and Kakar.[58] (Kakar, S., 1981; Paranjpe, A.C., 1998) *Kakar identifies the tenets of the Hindu philosophy to the constructs of psychodynamics.*[59] (Kakar, S., 1968) *He also finds a link between them and Erikson's lifecycle conceptualisations. Several writers have "revisited" this domain of the inner world as postulated by Kakar. Some like Bhatia argue that this "old world" vision should also include concepts of globalisation and outgrow colonial conceptualisations.*[60] (Bhatia, S., 2006) The general intention is the same, from the etic (universal), one derives emic (specifics), for example, from the genus to the species, as in the biological sciences. Kakar in fact expands his arguments to include substitute caregivers and fathers in this expanding world of multiple caretaking due to modernising trends.

The criss-crossing among conceptualisations of various theories, give an understanding of the bases of a theory and its inter-linkages with ecological concepts. We present the following specific linkages that form the bases of theories:

1. 'Overt' theorising along a continuum of stimulus—response, conditioning and reinforcement, cognition, and social learning;
2. Both overt and covert concepts occur in the area of cognitive development.
3. 'Covert' and psychodynamic concepts such as the Freudian theory and the Eriksonian theory.
4. Concepts relating to stimuli emanating from the environment, such as the Lewinian theory and Bronfenbrenner's theory of human ecology.

It is important to stress here that there is a bond between the categories of overt and covert theories simply because one cannot happen without the other. Eventually, all behaviour can be only interpreted/inferred from what is perceived or communicated. Some protagonists may claim that this is finally behaviourism, which is used as the foundation of knowledge of personality development.[61] (Skinner, B.F., 1974) As such, the seesaw of contentions continues. We have arbitrarily picked upon what we think are the most significant theories in understanding the Indian in his ecology.

Before we discuss each of these selected theories, we will attempt to describe the *maturational-cum-chronological* basis of the developing human. Given the environment which acts and reacts upon the organism, changes in development are qualitatively modulated by environmental stimulation.[62] (Altman I., and Wohlwill J.F., 1977) However, the environment is not static. It changes from time to time and from one ecology to another. For instance, when an environment is deprived, it has different consequences for the developing personality *vis-à-vis* an environment/ecology which has a surplus of facilities. Again, simultaneously the individual himself modifies his environment/ecology and, as a consequence, can himself be modified in his behaviour within the given ecology from one individual to another, as each has a specific genetic arrangement of ontogenetic potentials. For example, all children learn to walk and talk, whatever the ecology. Some have the potential to become orators and others the potential to become acrobats. All depend upon the utilisation of their ontogenetic potentials.

Besides *ecology and ontogeny, another innate variable is "functional opportunity" whereby development can also be accelerated by the individual seeking every opportunity to potentialise his knowledge, and recognize his skill either physical abilities or mental traits.*[63] (Allport, G.W., 1950) We have only to observe geniuses who emerge from rural areas to realize that limiting environments also limit opportunities to maximize innate potential traits. An individual's full development can be amplified by the inclusion of further potentials. These are observable simultaneously from the viewpoints of all theories. For, such theories either lead to the perception of goals or goal-performance or to processes in the conceptualisation of thought/behaviour in a progressive manner. At the same time, there are specific strategies/techniques/methods used in each one of these theoretical constructs. For example, to assess inner dynamics in an aggressive adolescent, the strategy of protective techniques, hypothetical situations, acting out in skits, elicit the parameters as, for instance, aggressive behaviour.

In the next chapter, we will detail relevant theories and their constructs as enunciated by western theorists on personality, and attempt to relate them to the Indian situation. In the Indian context, since we have lived on socio-religious philosophy as the major fulcrum of behaviour, we note that from among the several Indian mini-theorists, the most striking which offer theoretical concepts are those enunciated by Kakar and Paranjpe[64] (Kakar, S., 1981; Paranjpe, A., 1984) from the tenants of Indian philosophy.

8. The Progression of Theoretical Thinking on the Development of a Personality

The Indian psyche is not new to the concept of testing reality. Arising from the spiritual concepts of knowledge of what is (existant), for the individual imbued with the spiritual knowledge of what exists and what does not exist in reality, for instance, the *atman* is not perceivable to the human eye but the conditions of his transient life are perceivable to the individual in his inner self. It is symbolised in forms of images, different *avatars*, but the sameness of the energy force continues like, the *Shakti* for good (*sampannata*). This fluidity of conceptualisation of the mystic world of the pantheology of the gods is instilled in the Hindu way of life. This occurs from the inception of the child's socialisation.[65] (Kak, S.C., 2000).

Through this process of induction into habitual ways of thinking and behaving in the Indian psyche, the latter has own differential developmental progressions such as a sensory perception. Perception tends to be homogeneous in the initial stages but then differentiates on maturation. For instance, the Indian child learns differentiation in the age hierarchy[66] (Anandalakshmy, S., 1998). Such like situations occur which give rise to perceptions, for example, friendship patterns. These are based on homogeneity of similar behaviours, values and attitudes rather than on heterogeneity. Such concepts are further tested on larger groups and increasing enquiries which may give rise to similar results. These may form the basis of a theory such as the theory of caste-prejudice among children[67] (Sharma A., and S. Anandalakshmy, 1981). Existing hypotheses may be challenged by further investigation into newer domains of cause and effect, or correlativity in the perception of human or geo-ecology. Caste, for instance, does not exist in Africa and class does not exist in communist countries. Proponents, therefore, do not attribute prejudice to simple socialisation processes or to political ideologies. It may be contended that prejudice may occur towards anything.[68] (Zanna, M.P., and J.M. Olson, 1994) For instance, if a group of vegetarians do not like to eat meat, this could be indicative of a form of prejudice. Therefore, prejudice is a generic term relating to how groups perceive other objects/people within their perceptual sphere of human/geo-ecology. Prejudice exist in many forms. The Ethiopian considers himself as a descendant of the Queen of Sheba. The Britan perceives himself as the original race of Australia. The Australian in turn considers the Australian aborigines as a lesser status category than himself. The Anglo-Saxon American considers the Red Indian as a race distinct from his own, although the Red Indians are the original inhabitants of America. The Brahmin in India considers himself to be more pure ("twice-born") as compared to the lower castes who are considered as polluted[69] (Carstairs, G.M., 1958; Morris, G.M., 1957). These instances illustrate how man tries to distinguish himself in a category apart from other categories. From these instances, we are indicating the existence of differential perceptions. The latter, however, does not change the contours of the given ecology. It is the same for the Brahmin as for the "lower" castes. *Therefore, geo-ecology has a harmonising effect when not exacerbated. It is the human who tries to find heterogeneity so as to outline his parameters as different from the other just as much one individual in a family will perceive himself as different from the others.* Stereotypes exist in the abstract and perceived labels are attached by the individuals in their human ecology. However, it is frequent that when individuals travel from one ecology to another, they perceive much more heterogeneity when the ecological spheres widen. Thus, geo-ecologies also moderate human perception.

Theories are, therefore, not sacrosanct. They lack in certain gaps in their explanations of human behaviour, and suffer from the age-old supposition, that what they say applies to all or at the outset to most behaviour. For instance there is criticism of the Piagetian theory that it only explains behaviour of the individual in relation to his immediate environment and does not use the dimension of language[70] (Vygotsky, L., 1962) or ecological determinants[71] (Goodnow, J.J., 1976) to complement the theorising. The same is true of neo-Freudians who amplify the classical though rigid analytical form of psychoanalysis as first conceived by Freud. Thus, theory building is a continuous process of refinement and redefinition.

9. The Kaleidoscope of the Changing Indian Personality in the Milieu of Science, Technology and Global Events

There was a popular assessment in the previous centuries that the human being, generally speaking, was able to manage and control his environment. With the growing globalisation and the various criss-crossings of national and international communications, this asssessment became untenable. For example, increased communication within the economically less developed countries where even the lower working class have cellulars, indicates a growing awareness of the outside world.

The individual the world over is able to interact successfully with his ecology. For in the twenty-first century there is a popular notion that a human being has developed well if he is achievement-oriented, competitive, politically correct and socially well-behaved. In the next century, it might be that a human being is well-developed if he can predict forthcoming events through manipulation of computerized data, can assess people's movements through spy cameras even into peoples' private homes, as is now happening in the espionage circles. He can even clone himself and others through highly developed genetic engineering. *Currently, there is ongoing research on genome typing and finding mapping programmes for different genotypes. It is also well-known that the use of stem cell research will revolutionize medicine*. When we talk of development, we also have to relate it to the impact of technological advancement, cultural realities and spiritual values. To give an instance, this generation has the burden of the upkeep of a growing geriatic population, who are losing their productivity and require huge public investment just to keep them alive. More and more institutionalisation of the aged is becoming a common occurrence. Thus, the cellular-holding villager, the migrant-urbanite have access to these events which either impact them indirectly or directly. Their major concern is increasing limitation of the world's produce, deflected away from them, whether by increased exports and decreased availability of sustenance facilities. For example, while the tribal and the poor are subject to frequent food shortages, where the PDS (public distribution system) has failed and where so-called subsidies do not reach the target group, these increased technologies are of no interest to those who are mainly concerned about survival. Poverty and its concomitant deprivation are illustrated below:

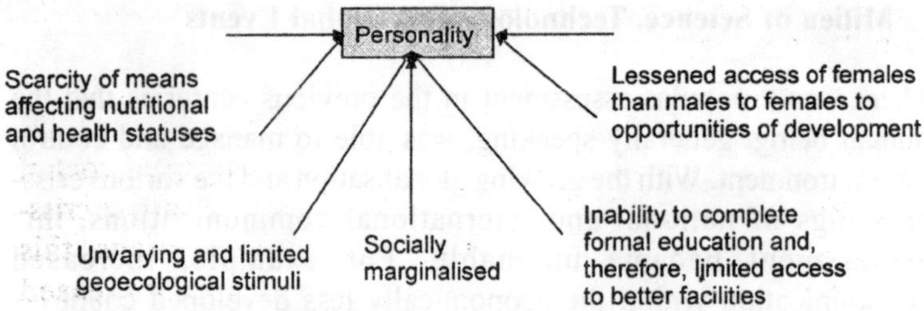

Paradigm 3.4: The Effect of Poverty on Personality Development

Although many attempts have been made by Indian experts to modify western oriented and empirical, theoretical concepts so as to make them context specific, there have been shortfalls translating them into systematic strategies and useful paradigms which are effective in the poor ecologies,[72] (Mukherjee, B.N., 1980)

If we attempt briefly to relate some constructs of some theories to the majority of Indian, we may obtain the following:

1. Limiting experiential learning in the poorer ecologies. By contrast, these stimuli are over-abundant in urban crowded ecologies. *Unvarying and limited experience also limits response to these limited stimuli* (relevant to behaviour theory). For example, the relativity of cognition of the urban migrant to a metropolis is limited. The migrants perception to stimuli in the urban metropolis is a confusion and bewilderment to the increased technological advancements in cities.
2. *Core values among the majority of the poor are more related to primary needs* (relevant to Lewinian theory).
3. The richer ecologies give access to various infrastructures and their facilities such as: professional guidance and counselling, and facilities for the disabled.
4. In poorer areas the knowledge of the inner workings of the mind is not scientific, at the most related to evil, magic and superstition (relevant to the covert theory of the Freudian school of theorising).

5. *Deprivation may also be correlated to depressed ideation and, therefore, depressed development of cognitive potentials at the stages of ideation through formal operations of mental development.* If the child is deprived of continuous of education, and lack cognitive interactions, his cognitive experience will be limited (relative to cognitive theory)
6. *The life-cycle traits as mentioned by Erikson is mainly hypothetical since the Indian is well-grained in his religious beliefs, in the stages of the* samskaras, *while Erikson marks the existence or non-existence of positive and negative traits, the* samskaras *are symbolic ritual markers (relevant to the life-cycle theory).*
7. If we combine stimulus-response concepts with cognitive concepts, with priorities in the regions of the mental field, we find that these constructs are emphasised or deemphasised by the human eco-systems as detailed by Bronfenbrenner. *For, if the micro system is static, so is its effect on the human and if the individual in the micro system lacks mobility, it lessens his cognitive experiences (relevant to the eco-systems model of Bronfenbrenner).*

Theories of personality are based on assumptions just as other theories in other fields. They are acceptable till such time as other more vibrant concepts displace their constructs and give more clear explanations of human behaviour.

There are also major disparities between the sexes in these disadvantaged sections of the poor. The female lacks opportunities and the female child is disadvantaged *vis-à-vis* the male.

Thus, the analysis given above reveals an interaction of heterogeneous variables which in and of themselves require a holistic theory for understanding the human being's development in the Indian context.

REFERENCES

1. Harmon, F.L., 1948, *Understanding Personality*. Milwaukee: Bruce Publishing Co.
2. Klein, G.S., and Krech, D., 1952, 'The problem of personality and its theory', in D. Krech, and G.S. Klein (eds.), *Theoretical Models and Personality Theory*. Durham: Duke University Press.

3. Hall, C.S., Lindzey, J., and Campbell, J.B., 1998, *Theories of Personality*. New York: John Wiley & Sons.
4. Maccoby, E.E., 1958, *Readings in Social Psychology*. Holt: Society for the Psychological Study of Social Issues.
5. Merton, R K., 1967, *On Theoretical Sociology: Five Essays, Old and New*. New York: Free Press.
6. Bruner, J.S., 1959, 'Inhelder and Piaget's 'The growth of logical thinking': A psychologist's viewpoint', *British Journal of Psychology*. Vol. 50, pp. 363-70.
7. Thomas, R.M., 2001, *Recent Theories in Human Development*. Thousand Oaks: Sage.
8. Thorpe, L.P., and Schmuller A.M., 1958, *Personality: An Interdisciplinary Approach*. p. 39. New York: D. Van Nostrand Company.
9. Rantkallio P., von Wendt L., and Koivu M., 1987, 'Prognosis of prenatal brain damage: a prospective study of a one-year birth cohort of 12,000 children', *Early Human Development*, 15, pp. 75-84.
10. Sinha, M.M., 1976, *Working Paper on Physiological Psychology*. UGC Regional Workshop on the Status of Teaching and Research in psychology. University of Allahabad, Allahabad.
11. Pirta R.S., 2009, "Biological and ecological bases of behaviour", in Misra. G., (ed.) *Psychology in India*, Volume-1. New Delhi: Dorling Kindersley, pp. 13-14.
12. Wolman, B.B., 2004, *Contemporary Theories and Systems in Psychology*. San Francisco: W.H. Freeman & Company.
13. Eysenck, H.J., 1952, 'The Organisation of Personality', in D. Krech and G.S. Klein (eds.), *Theoretical Models and Personality Theory*. Durham, North Carolina: Duke University Press.
14. Kagitcibasi, C., 1996, *Family, Self, and Human Development Across Cultures: Theory and Applications*. New Jersey: Lawrence Erlbaum.
15. Piaget, J., 1926, *Judgement and Reasoning in the Child*. London: Routledge and Kegan Paul.
16. Maslow, A.H., 1954, *Motivation and Personality*. pp. 35-58. New York: Harper.
17. Murray, H.A., 1968, 'Components of an evolving personological system', in D.L. Sills (ed.), *International Encyclopaedia of the Social Sciences*. Vol. 12. pp. 5-13. New York: Macmillan and Free Press.
18. Lewin, K., 1935, *A Dynamic Theory of Personality*. McGraw-Hill.
19. Thomas, R.M., 2001, *Recent Theories of Human Development*. New Delhi: Sage.
20. Witmer, H.L., and R Kolinsky (eds.), 1950, *Personality in the Making*. New York: Harpers and Bros.

21. Sarason, I.G., 1966, *Personality: An Objective Approach*. New York: Wiley.
22. Angyal, A.A., 1952, 'Theoretical Model for Personality Studies', in Krech, D., and G.S. Klein (eds.), *Theoretical Models and Personality Theory*. Durham: Duke University Press.
23. Uma K., Y.S. Lakshmi, and E.G. Parameswaran, 1971, "Construction of a personality inventoy based on doctrine of three Gunas", *Research Bulletin*, 6, 49-58.
24. Allport, G.W., 1937, *Personality: A Psychological Interpretation*. New York: Holt.
25. Baldwin, A.L, 1914, *Theories of Child Development*. New York: John Wiley & Sons.
26. Harkness, S., and C.M. Super, 1996, *Parents' Cultural Belief Systems*. New York: Guilford Publications.
27. Goodnow, J.J., and A.W. Collins, 1990, *Development according to Parents: The Nature, Sources and Consequences of Parents' Ideas*. Hillsdale, NJ: Erlbaum.
28. Chaudhary, N., 2004, *Listening to Culture: Constructing Reality from Everyday Talk*. New Delhi: Sage Publications.
29. Paranjpe, A.C., 1988, 'A personality theory according to Vedanta', in A.C. Paranjpe, D.Y.F. Ho, and R.W. Rieber (eds.), *Asian Contributions to Psychology*, pp. 18-213, New York: Praeger.
30. Kumar, A., 1999: *Child Health Care in Ancient India*. Delhi: Sri Satguru Publications (Indian Medical Sciences Series).
31. Sears, R.R., E.E. Maccoby and H. Levin, 1957, *Patterns of Childrearing*. Evanston, IL: Row- Peterson.
32. Murphy, L.B., 1953, 'Roots of tolerance and tensions in Indian child Development', in G. Murphy, *In the Minds of Men*, pp. 46-58, New York: Basic Books.
33. Kumar, Krishna, 1993, 'Study of childhood and family', in T.S. Saraswathi and Kaur, B., *Human Development and Family Studies in India: An Agenda for Research and Policy*, pp. 67-77, New Delhi: Sage.
34. Misra, G., and Tripathi, K.N., 1993, 'The concept and context of human development', in T.S. Saraswathi and B. Kaur (eds.), *Human Development and Family Studies in India: An Agenda for Research and Policy*, pp. 90-103, New Delhi: Sage Publications.
35. Hull, C.L., 1943, *Principles of Behaviour: An Introduction to Behaviour Theory*, New York: Appleton Century Crofts In.
36. Freud, S., 1964, *An Outline of Psychoanalysis*. Standard Edition (Vol. 23) London: Hogarth (First German Edition, 1940).

37. Whiting, J.W.M, and Child I.L., 1958, *Child Training and Personality*, Yale Univ. Press.
38. Kardiner, A., 1959, 'Social and cultural implications of psychoanalysis', in S. Hook (ed.), *Psychoanalysis, Scientific Method, and Philosophy: A Symposium*, pp. 81-103, New York: New York University Press.
39. Sheldon, W.H., 1940, *Varieties of Human Physique*, New York: Harper Press.
40. Stark, E. Hathaway and J.C. McKinley, 1940, *Minnesota Multiphasic Personality Inventory*, Minneapolis, MN University of Minnesota Press.
41. Paranjpe, A.C., 1988, 'A personality theory according to Vedanta', in A.C. Paranjpe, D.Y.F. Ho, and R.W. Rieber (eds.), *Asian Contributions to Psychology*, pp. 185-213, New York: Praeger.
42. Thorpe, L.P., and A.M. Schmuller, 1958, *Personality: An Interdisciplinary Approach,* pp. 354-355, New York: D. Van Nostrand Co.
43. Hall, C.S., Lindzey, G., Campbell, J.B., 1998, *Theories of Personality*. New York: John Wiley & Sons.
44. Baldwin A.L., 1980, "Conclusion: Toward an integrated theory of child development", in A.L. Baldwin, *Theories of Child Development*. New York: John Wiley & Sons, pp. 548-549.
45. Klein, G.S., and D. Krech, 1952, 'The problems of personality and its theory', in G.S. Klein and D. Krech, *Theoretical Models and Personality Theory*, Durham: Duke University Press.
46. Mowrer, O.H., 1950, *Learning Theory and Personality Dynamics*, New York: Ronald.
47. Thorndike, E.L., 1920, 'Intelligence and its uses', *Harpers Magazine*, 140, 227-235.
48. Berry, J.W., J.A., Bennett and J.P., Denny, 1992, *Ecology, Culture and Cognitive Processing*. Paper presented at the International Association of Cross Cultural Psychology Congress, Pultusk, Poland.
49. Valsiner, J., 1998, 'The development of the concept of development: historical and epistemological perspectives', in W. Damon and R. Lerner (eds.), *Handbook of Child Psychology,* Vol. 1, *Theoretical Models of Human Development*, pp. 189-232, New York: Wiley.
50. Valsiner J., and Connolly, K.J., 2003, 'The nature of development: the continuing dialogue of processes and outcomes', In J. Valsiner and K.J. Connolly (eds.), *Handbook of Developmental Psychology*, pp. ix-xviii, London: Sage.
51. Whiting, J.W.M., and I.L. Child, 1958, *Child Training and Personality*. "Introduction", Yale University Press.

52. Thorpe, L.P., 1941, *Personality and Life*. New York: Longman's Green & Company Inc.
53. Krech, D., and Klein, G.S. (eds.), 1952, *Theoretical Models and Personality Theory*. Durham: Duke University Press.
54. Klein, M., 1932, *The Psychoanalysis of Children*. London: Hogarth Press.
Erikson, E., 1950, *Childhood and Society*. New York: Norton.
Lewin, K., 1951, *Field Theory in Social Science*, New York: Harper and Row.
Bronfenbrenner, U., 1979, *The Ecology of Human Development*, Cambridge, MA: Harvard University Press.
55. Baldwin, A.L., 1980, *Theories of Child Development*, New York: John Wiley & Sons;
Thomas, R.M., 2001, *Recent Theories of Human Development*, California: Sage Publications;
Hall, C.S., Lindzey, G., Campbell, J.B., 1998, *Theories of Personality*, John Wiley & Sons.
56. Wolfson, J. (ed.), 1976, 'Introduction', in J. Wofson (ed.) *Personality and Learning*, Vol. 2, London: Hodder and Stoughton in association with the Open University, pp. 3-5.
57. Singh, J.A.L., and Zingg R.M., 1966, *Wolf Children and Feral Man*, Shoe String Pr. Inc.
58. Kakar, S., 1981, *The Inner World: A Psychoanalytic Study of Childhood and Society in India*, New Delhi, Oxford University Press;
Paranjpe, A.C., 1998, *Self and Identity in Modern Psychology and Indian Thought*, New York: Plenum Press.
59. Kakar, S., 1968 (July), 'Human lifecycle: The traditional Hindu view and the psychology of Erik Erikson', *Philosophy East and West*, Vol. 18, No. 3, pp. 127-136.
60. Bhatia, S., 2006, 'Reinterpreting the inner self in global India: 'Malevolent Mothers', 'Distant Fathers' and the Development of Children's Identity', *Culture and Psychology*, Vol. 12, No. 3.
61. Skinner, B.F., 1974, *About Behaviourism*. New York: Knopf.
62. Altman I., and Wohlwill J.F., 1977, *Human Behaviour and Environment: Advances in Theory and Research*. Springer.
63. Allport, G.W., 1950, *The Nature of Personality: Selected Papers*. Cambridge, Mass: Addison-Wesley.
64. Kakar, S., 1981, *The Inner World: A Psychoanalytic Study of Childhood and Society in India*. New Delhi: Oxford University Press.
Paranjpe, A., 1984, *Theoretical Psychology: The Meeting of East and West*, New York: Plenum Books.
65. Kak, S.C., 2000, 'On understanding ancient Indian science', in A.K.

Raina, B.N. Patnaik, M. Chadha (eds.), *Science and Tradition*, pp. 83-107, Shimla: Indian Institute of Advanced Study.
66. Anandalakshmy, S., 1998, 'The cultural context', in M. Swaminathan (ed.), *The First Five Years: A Critical Perspective on Early Childhood Care and Education in India,* pp. 273-274, New Delhi: Sage.
67. Sharma A., and S. Anandalakshmy, 1981, "Prejudice in the making: Understanding the role of socialisation", In D. Sinha (ed.), *Socialization of the Indian Child,* New Delhi, Concept, pp. 101-16.
68. Zanna, M.P., and Olson, J.M., 1994, *The Psychology of Prejudice*, Lawrence-Erlbaum.
69. Carstairs, G.M., 1958, *The Twice-born: A Study of a Community of High Caste Hindus*. London: Hogarth;
Morris, G.M., 1957, *The Twice-born*. London: Hogarth.
70. Vygotsky, L., 1962, *Thought and Language* [E. Hanfmann and G. Vakar (Eds.) and Trans.], Cambridge, MA: MIT Press.
71. Goodnow, J.J., 1976, 'Cultural variations in cognitive skills', in J. Wolfson (ed.), *Personality and Learning*. London: Hodder and Stoughton in association with Open University Press.
72. Mukherjee, B.N., 1980, 'Psychological theory and research methods', in Pareek (ed.), *A Survey of Research in Psychology*. Bombay: Popular Prakashan.

4

Selected Personality Theories Relevant to the Indian Psyche

This chapter consists of the following sections:

1. Introduction
2. The theory of behaviourism
3. Social learning theory
4. The Piagetian theory of cognition
5. The field theory of Lewin
6. The Freudian psychoanalytical theory
7. The Eriksonian theory of the life-cycle
8. The ecosystem theory of Bronfenbrenner
9. The cohesiveness implicit among personality theories
10. An overview indicating a possible holistic perspective of theories
11. A tentative proposal of a hypothetical theory

1. Introduction

Theories of personality as propounded in psychology are each uniquely explanations of how personality is developed. In this Chapter, we will refrain from detailing each and every theory in relation to the Indian. We have selected some personality theories to elucidate "cognitive", "social", "ecological" domains affecting the personality. The theories discussed here are :

1. The behaviourist theory;
2. The theory of social learning;
3. The cognitive theory of Piaget;

4. The psychoanalytic theory of Freud;
5. The field theory of Lewin;
6. The life cycle theory of Erikson; and
7. The ecosystem theory of Bronfenbrenner.

We may divide these theories into two categories:

(i) Where the personality of the person exhibits behaviour relevant to a theory, namely, overt behaviour.
(ii) Where the inner workings of the mind need to be extrapolated through projective strategies or communicated thinking/ feeling, where behaviour is interpreted.

Before we begin to examine each theory, there are certain general statements that need to be made:

(i) *Inherited genetic phylogenetic characteristics,* such as evident in the saying: "as the seed is grown, so the tree will grow."
(ii) *Ontogenetic characteristics* which are highly individualistic, born out of the chromosomatic and neurological qualities of each unique individual. This is evident in the situation of identical twins who although from the same genetic pool behave many times differently. This implies that each developing person from inception follows epigenetic rules in the make-up of his/her inter- and intra-cellular chromosomical make-up.
(iii) The influence of ecology on human behaviour and development, which delineates values, attitudes and practices learned from the socialisation processes.

2. The Theory of Behaviourism

The theories of personality must eventually ask the rhetorical question: "How do we know that a person is a personality unless it is observable?" *Therefore, our basic premise is founded on the concept of perception of behaviour. By the perception of the outward self of an individual, one can identify the characteristics of the entity enveloped in a personality.* Behaviour is the overt response to a stimulus whether from the internal self or from outside parameters.

Thus, a theory of personality should be able to adequately explain the characteristics that combine to formulate a comprehensive understanding of the entity observed. Each theory uses its own framework. For example, "the Theory of Behaviour" uses the stimulus-response framework; and the Ecological Theory uses the core of the influences of the human and natural environment on the development of a personality. This theory explains how the mind develops and how the developing mind directs the behaviour of the person.[1] (Klein, G.S., and D. Krech, 1952)

Personality, however, is not just behaviour at any one time at any one place in any one form. It is an observable set of related behaviours specific to a person, dynamically changing as ecological situations (both human and geo) change. This set, taking our cue from the term 'acculturation', is a series or a progression of behaviour which become habitual in nature, and are progressively limited or expanded by age, experiences during maturation and the unique ontogenetic intelligence of the individual.[2] (McGeoch, J.A., 1942) , The behaviour theory encompasses a collection of related theories, the first of which is the classical conditioning theory. It is related to a conglomerate of concepts like "reinforcement", negative and positive, "intermittent reinforcement" and "attrition".[3] (Miller, N.E., and J. Dollard, 1941) This theory is apparently the most frequently used in class-room education with the added concepts of "reward" and "punishment".

The stimulus-response theory implies a linking bridge between the growing and maturing individual and his interaction with "significant others" or significant objects. This theory is perhaps the most consciously and unconsciously used strategy by all caretakers whether in developing or developed countries, whether in abundant or sparse ecologies. In an abundant ecology, for instance, as in the West, the main vehicle for learning is the computer, while in tribal and nomadic areas, sticks, stones and other natural objects around are used as vehicles for learning. For example, a nomad will teach his child how to predict a sandstorm, a tribal mother will teach her child what kinds of produce are edible and what are not.

The basic concept of association of thought and learning began with Locke, Hume and Mill. In developing the principles of learning, they used associative thinking to formulate linkages between associated ideas,[4] (Siemens, G., 2005) like the association between the absorption of milk and the reduction of hunger in the neonate.

Ideas are formulated in a relative manner. For instance, the perception of the mother figure to a hungry infant is sufficient conditioning for the child to stop crying in anticipation of being fed (precondition to reinforcement). Watson[5] (Watson, J.B., 1928) and later Skinner[6] (Skinner, B.F., 1950) used these incidents to develop constructs about conditioning and reinforcement. Watson attempted to demonstrate the product of learning by using the data from experimental analyses of his subjects, which in essence was the imprinting of association between one idea and another from correlatives of unconditioned stimulus-response to conditioned stimulus-response. Watson dealt with static conditions of the surroundings, isolating the response to one variable and another in an experimental manner.

As a contrast, Piaget also dealt with *perception, but discussed responses by a set of schemas which involved the intervening variables of neural maturation.*[7] (Piaget, J., and B. Inhelder, 1971) Piaget's schema, discussed later, is based on accumulation of perceptions with mental imagery, which were originally biological in nature.

Hull, also a behaviour theorist, derives his principles of learning from responses which are said to be internalised. Murray's trait theory emphasises habitual response, becoming a characteristic trait of the personality. This habit becomes an automatic reaction based on a set of learned responses accumulated in memory and triggered off by the same stimuli which occurs repeatedly and, therefore, evokes the same responses. Habits, therefore, becomes sets of behaviours which typifies a personality such as "he is a miser", implying his habitual responses to be ungenerous, or he is "indifferent", implying that the habitual response is to escape responsibility. Such examples of personalities can be multiplied *ad infinitum*.

These sets of behaviours are learned either in a sequential manner or in an intermittent manner, or some aspects of the sets are suppressed while others are highlighted. The individual may, for example, be overpowering, loud-mouthed, and these behaviours may operate under different conditions. For example, when an aggressive personality is defending a weak point of view, he may be loud-mouthed, protesting and insisting that his point of view is right. This is his habitual personality which may have accumulated through a series of frustrations, thwarting of needs and lack of need-fulfilment. At other times the individual might just be orally aggressive, suppressing related physical behaviour. Yet again, at other times, he may use these aggressive actions overtly or suppress them covertly in an intermittent manner. Thus, behaviour in terms of aggression which is acted out or expressed overtly is indicative of a habitual type of person and, therefore, a habitual personality.[8] (Baldwin, A.L., 1980: 410) The example given above indicates an "aggressive personality". We observe that Piaget also uses sets of schematic behaviour progressing sequentially from sensory-motor to formalised operant behaviour. The difference is that Piaget concentrates on the mental functions of cognition and intelligence, both resting on levels of maturation,[9a] (Piaget, J., 1977) while behaviourist theories concentrate on the relationship between a stimulus and its response under sets of circumstances that may provoke such responses. For, response may be selective. It does not automatically follow either one path or another but depends upon the person's mental capacity and reasoning.

During the lifecycle an individual accumulates sets of negative or positive responses which become habitual such as the negative responses in basic mistrust and positive responses in basic trust in the lifecycle.

From the above paragraphs, we imply the following:

1. Each theory has its own conceptual framework and describes with or without experimentation the way human beings behave.
2. None of these theories attempt to interact in the conceptual framework of the others.
3. Each theory is distinctly known by either its covert form as observed or by the covert forms as inferred.

These theories explain partial forms of behaviour. The only one that goes with the whole lifecycle is that of Erikson, with the caveat that he deals with his analysis through narrative and idiographic data from life experiences of his patients and other cultures. The one that deals with the mental functions in early childhood is Piaget. *The one that deals clearly with the covert* forms *of behaviour is the Freudian psycho-sexual theory and the only one that is sufficiently generic is the behaviourist theory for it applies to human interactions at all stages.* Unfortunately, it does not allow for the influence of other than the relationship between stimulus and response. Unknown and intervening variables remain so. B*ronfenbrenner's theory of human ecology deals with the growing up processes of the child as* *his residential spaces increase from home to school, to neighbourhood, to other countries, in a progressive manner and, therefore, deals with increasing ecological areas of experience.*

Nevertheless, in the absence of other major theories, excepting the mini theories of Maslow, Murray and Allport and such like, these are the major theories that we rely upon for interpretation of human behaviour as garnered from the west.[9b] (Murray 1938; Maslow 1954; Allport 1937) Naturally, by a long stretch of linkages, we may use them as a package to explain different types of behaviour. For example, a child with the high cue grasp can have a more intelligent formulation of abstract conceptualisation according to Piaget. But, Piaget dealt with only the mental processes of the human being he studied qualitatively. Vygotsky goes further. He states that without the environmental influences on the human cognition, explanations will be short-changed. Erikson deals with positive and negative aspect of phases of development, as being "either – or". He does not describe mid-way points of this negative-positive dimensions.

Kurt Levin deals with mainly mental process and the dynamics of changes according to attractive forces from the environment high-profiling mental ideations. Bronfenbrenner deals with differential movements of the human being from one set of human-ecology to another. Bronfenbrenner concentrates on the individual's movement without much relevance to the geo-ecology in these geographical movements. Perhaps behaviourists are the overall overarching umbrella theorising framework in describing human behaviour, and yet here again the environment/ecology is relatively unknown in this theory.

It is necessary to state that none of these theories offer nomethetic explanations of developments that occur during the lifespan. Some are generically stated like Lewin, Bronfenbrenner and the behaviour theorists. Others stop at certain ages and still others offer perceived expeirences of sample subjects selected for investigating their behaviour.

Mini theories like that of Atkinson and Murray deal with specific domains of motivation and needs respectively.

We have stressed three important themes in the above paragraphs:

(i) A personality is known by the sets of behaviour which he expresses.

(ii) *These sets of behaviour are, according to behaviourist* theories, "responses" to various stimuli,[10] (Skinner, B.F., 1953) or "imitations" of an observed model, according to social learning theory;[11] (Bandura, A., 1977) or, according to Piaget, "cognitive mental functioning" or "ideation"[12] (Piaget, J., 1954). According to the Freudian theory, human behaviour occurs covertly and is only capable of being elicited on probing,[13] (Freud, S., 1962).

(iii) *These sets of behaviour can be explained by any of the theories by using concepts that exist only within their parameters* like, for example, 'stimulus' and 'response' in Stimulus-Response learning theory; 'ego', 'id', and 'superego' in psychoanalytical theory; and 'bio-physical neural maturation' and 'mental ideation' in Piagetian theory.

Under this rubric, we will put together, not in historical order, but in the order in which they logically hold together, the theoretical concepts of the several personality theories. We will emphasise the behaviourist theories since they are over-arching all other theories.

There is no behaviour without either an internal or an external, or both, stimuli. It follows, therefore, that if the environment and its ecology is sparse, there is little ecological stimulus, or if the stimulus exists, it is unvaried as in tribal areas. If the stimuli are full of crowded human beings, it follows that human ecology is surfeit, while the geoecology is limited, for example, urban slum dwellngs. If one ecology is imbalanced without the other, it makes for a treatise on balanced harmonised living of the growing personality, for example, the fragile ecology in the Kashmir valley where terrorism exists.

Although it has been said that the human mind in its pristine stage is a clean slate[14] (Locke, E.A., and G.P. Latham, 1984) phylogenetically, *according to pre-formation and pre-determinism* concepts, *epigenetically the potentials of habitual thought exist from the early stages of development.* As the child grows in maturity, he begins to selectively respond to selected stimuli. Skinner has been the chief proponent of the conditioned response theory.

Logically, interaction with other families is dependent on geographical access. Encompassing these vignettes is the theory of learning whose initial major proponents are Watson and Pavlov, continued by Skinner in his classical theory of conditioned response (stimulus and reinforcement). Skinner's theoretical explanation is termed 'instrumental conditioning' because there is a deliberate attempt on the part of the conditioner to repeat the stimulus to obtain reward.[15] (Baldwin, A.L., 1980: 423) For instance, a child learns that he will get a reward only when he says 'please.' The probability of the child saying 'please' in anticipation of a reward is the stimulus technique to reinforcing the directed expected behaviour. Therefore, the concept of reinforcement adds to the strength of the stimulus. The appearance of the expected behaviour is, however, not automatic; it is intervened by other variables like lessened motivation, non-interest and apathy towards behaving in the way expected. For example, a child ontogenetically might be more interested in sports than in studies and, therefore, the effort on the part of the re-enforcer is likely to be more frequent. It may be more insistent and will perhaps lead the child to study reluctantly because at the end of it he is usually promised a prized possession. For example, a child uninterested in studying may be persistently reminded by adults to do his homework and, where affordable, tutors are engaged to reinforce the child to study. Therefore, the child internalises the set of stimulus response behaviours in their reinforced context. He, therefore, attempts to perform to achieve, receive rewards. This is more especially parental and peer approval, which raises his self-esteem. The recurrence of the expected response may be reduced and may even attrition. Attrition however might also occur if there is opposite sets of reinforcement, namely, continuous negative or dual reinforcement. When a child responds to a stimulus which is painful, the response is likely to occur less often and in fact may not occur at all after a while. We often hear parents complain that the child is not studious perhaps because the child is reinforced negatively by threats, by punishment and by withholding what he prizes. *Thus, reinforcement relates to attached internal or external pressures to the original stimulus and is termed secondary reinforcement patterns. They may also be positive or negative and depending upon the response pattern inherent epigenetically in the child, the responses are likely to be in compliance or in contradiction to the expected outcome.* Thus, the behaviourists' conception of reinforcement is parallel to the conceptualisation of Freudian principles of pleasure and pain where there is avoidance of painful experiences and a positive reaction to pleasurable experiences.[16] (Freud, S., 1922) This configuration of stimulus-response (unconditioned and conditioned, reinforced/not-reinforced) and the Freudian principle of pleasure-pain are perceptually similar to the theory of Miller who explains avoidance approach behaviour towards or against an experience "(negative or positive)".[17] (Miller, N. E., 1944) Miller states that the closer the individual is towards an attractive object/experience, the greater is the gradient of approach and conversely the more unattractive the object or event the slower is the gradient of approach. We might derive many illustrations which confirm the symmetrical stances of these theories. However, a caveat is that the behaviourists do not interject the element of emotion or feeling. To them, the stimuli and its responses are seen as automatic. Whereas the attached stimulus are the emotions of persons which direct his attention to stimuli and the feeling of being rewarded, or negated when he responds. Similarly, Piaget's theory is said to lack the concept of language and social environments influencing the schema and neither Lewin or Bronfenbrenner deal with the whole array of emotions, intelligence, social norms and societal expectations in becoming a person. The closest theory which is more likely to reveal traits of a personality is relatively easier to understand in terms of the Eriksonian theory. Erikson illustrates domains mainly through his interactive experiences in his clinical work. These experiences, however, are not related to the social or ecological networks.

Let us take an example: a primary school child in an agricultural farmer's family is expected to assist in the care of cattle and small animals, to fetch and carry water, and assist in the agricultural activities in general. From Skinner's point of view, he is constantly being conditioned through positive reinforcement and may in fact accomplish these activities without much pleasure according to the Freudian principle because they are unattractive, and so according to Miller these unattractive activities are slow in performance.

Thus reinforcement, negative or positive, has an emotional context when used by the elders in the family to whom a child is emotionally attached, and it is perhaps to this that the Indian child responds to in the context given above. This secondary reinforcement is often just as powerful as the child's original unconditioned response and unconditioned stimulus. We see, however, a progression in the learning process from unconditioned response theory to conditioned stimulus response theory to reinforcement theory of a secondary type where other sets of behaviour are attached to both the stimulus and the response. For instance, the love reinforcement by elders in the family. Therefore, in an accumulation of complexities of behaviour patterns, *the learning child responds to not only the original stimulus, namely, the task, but also a host of others such as parental approval, expected reward, rise in self-esteem and, most importantly, a homeostasis between the needs of significant others and his own needs.* The main strategy for the interaction to take place is the classical operant conditioning theory, namely, instrumental learning by setting up the sets of reward when the goal is attained.[18] (Skinner, B.F., 1953) Thus, learning eventually becomes habitual. For instance, a child of a nomad who is constantly caring for the camels learns to repeat such caring activities so that, as classical conditioning theory states, he is rewarded by adult approval and so the addition of the stimulus of adult approval, admiration of peers, accomplishment successfully of a task and love reinforcement by parents raises his self-esteem as a personality. This habitual repeated pattern of internalised learning can also be made explicit, inhibited or be responsive to secondary reinforcement as just explained and can also attrition due to negative responses from his environment. If a child is continuously and constantly being rewarded for his behaviour through love-oriented techniques as described by Sears and Macobby, it generalises to other types of behaviour which he recognises as having adult approval. For example, a child of a carpenter in helping his father might also learn wood work and if he does so efficiently he receives adult and peer approval and it raises his self-esteem. On the other hand, in rich families children tend to get substantial pocket money which then they use as stimuli for attracting friends, who may or may not be genuine.

This is generalised stimulus for a generalised response. It is to be noted that there are no barriers between the two. The stimulus, however, can also be discriminatory. The child may be allowed to swim in the children's pool but not the adult pool, so that he responds to a fractured/discrete stimulus where he is allowed to enter one place but not another although both have the same general parameters. *The formation of a habit is, therefore, a basic premise of the developing personality and can be traced throughout the maturational process in a given ecological environment.* A habit can also be conditioned as has been observed through further experimentation by the use of intermittent reinforcement.[19] (Baldwin, A.L., 1980: 423) Intermittent reinforcement is a strategy where the same behaviour is sometimes rewarded and sometimes negated, so that it increases the motivation to achieve / being rewarded when this contrasting reinforcement occurs. We see the similarity to the theoretical construct of need reduction. Need reduction relates to gradience.[20] (Miller, N. E., 1944)

For example, the closer one approaches the goal the speedier and the quicker is the reaction to its positivity. On the other hand, the closer one approaches a goal that is feared, the less speedy is the gradient to reach that goal of need-reduction as we have indicated in the theoretical constructs of Miller above.

If the child is intermittently rewarded and intermittently punished, not knowing when he will achieve and be rewarded, his responses are expected to go stronger. It is akin to target shooting, if the first time the target is achieved, there is a reward and the reduction of the need. If the target is not reached, the child is likely to try repeatedly. He may not be rewarded one 'next time', but will be rewarded thereafter and so this increases his drive, namely, his motivational level to achieve. This explanation may be simplistic, but we can find similar more complex instances in the behaviour of motivation to achieve as explained by Atkinson[21] (Atkinson, J.W., 1958) in his theoretical construct of need achievement and such like other needs.

In the context of habit formation, it is essential to relate it to the Hullian concept of learning. *Hull rested his thesis on the basic assumptions of operant conditioning and developed a series of principles of learning.*[22] (Hull, C.L., 1943) His postulates are based on mathematics applied to psychology. According to him, very much like operant conditioning, he exemplifies how a set of orthogenetic individualised traits can evoke a hierarchy of responses either sequential or intermittent, one linked to the other. For instance, an intelligent/mature person can respond to a stimulus in a linked manner through logical, sequential reasoning using relevant premises. He observes rain clouds the consequence of which is expectedly water. He is also aware through a linked thought process that if it rains too much it will cause flooding and affect crop production, insufficient food and deprived conditions. Thus, from observation of rain clouds, he can foresee the future possibility of food scarcity or otherwise. Through this process, the child learns formal abstract reasoning as in doing mathematical experiments. For instance, one cannot force a three-year old to learn the relationships among numerals, he might repeat them by rote, but he has not developed chronologically the ability to recognise their abstract formal operations.

The occurrence of a continuous set of stimulus responses, sets up a chain reaction of logically related behavioural units. For instance, a child initially begins with learning alphabet, grammar and comprehension and these over time with chronological maturity lead to a set of responsive ideas which might make him a poet, a philosopher, or a scientist using logical and creative thinking processes of stimulus and response. The intervening variable of motivation in the stimulus response is such that it can either increase or decrease the strength of the response. For instance, if the anticipated response of a teacher to class behaviour is poor understanding of the psychological makeup of that age, this situation indicates that the lack of motivation in the class is probably due to poor teaching quality. This implies a poor quality of understanding of the students' psycho-social make-up and, therefore, poor motivation to teach.

(a) The Place of Motivation in Behaviour

Motivation is an inner-directive drive that begins in early childhood and can be either reinforced by positive encouragement or deflected by negative reinforcement. The aspects of ecology tends to influence motivation either in the direction of positivity or negativity. A nomadic child finds little motivation to do other than the routine tasks of survival, but an urban child has a great deal of stimuli in his ecology to motivate him to experience further situations.

Motivation is propelled by the inner-directedness of the individual either to achieve or not to achieve. *However, motivation can be barriered or deflected by other high energy needs for self-satisfaction.* These barriers may be the lack of the artefacts to achieve such as a poor child may be highly motivated to achieve but does not have the opportunity. For instance, a poor but highly motivated child in a class room may not have the necessary books or mechanical devices as does his rich classmate sitting beside him in the class room. This situation may lead to either alternative anti-social behaviours or it may lead to the sense of apathy and pessimism reducing his motivation to achieve or to compete The latter is propelled by a sense of frustration which may also lead to aggressive behaviour.

Again, motivating adults both in the home and school usually propel the individual's motivation. However, the human ecology in the home and in the environment may not be conducive because of disharmony and poverty in the home ecology and/or poor school infrastructures and teachers, which then deplete motivation. For instance, many rural schools have poor infrastrcuture and poor staffing which depletes the child's motivation to achieve academically.

Motivation is a strong factor in personality development. Atkinson describes the need to achieve as being an inherent drive and the need for affiliation as being the need to be with others. The concept of motivation is also akin to the psychoanalytic theses of Freud where he describes the id as being strongly motivated, but barriered by the super ego. This is also akin to the psychodynamic theorising of Murray, Maslow and Erikson. According to Murray, motivation is volition which is a combination of both conscious and unconscious drives and their related effort to reach a homeostasis through satisfaction of needs (self and others). In a sense, this describes how habits are formed which then become observable traits. If repeated, they cohese to organise a personality. *What then are needs, which are necessary for satisfaction in the development of the personality? Kurt Lewin in his theory of topology represented a need as "a system in a state of tension" and the satisfaction of that need as a release of the tension within the system,*[23] (Atkinson, J.W., 1966). This reduces the need energy. Motivation is that energy or drive, unconscious or libidinal (Freud's analysis) or conscious (ego-driven), which energises the individual to move towards need-reduction and towards the anticipated experience of the goal. Frequently, an individual is faced with conflicting needs which then causes a disequilibrium in his personality till he satisfies priority needs to reach homeostasis.[24] (Miller, N.E., 1944)

(b) The Place of Reinforcement in Behaviour

The type of reinforcement increases or reduces motivation levels to achieve. In relation to motivation in completing a task in time, if more attractive the incentive, the shorter and quicker will be the time taken to respond. In other words, the stimulus enhances the strong need to achieve. The response to a stimuli may not always be completely expressed. For example, it is rare that students reach the maximum scoring of the exam in test situations. Therefore, there is a residue of the potential of an individual's response to achieve. By inference, we might assume that children in deprived ecologies are less motivated, perform less adequately to successfully meet the experience either formal or informal in their daily life. *Conflicting needs may detract the performance of an individual by the varying strengths of the competing needs.* An industrialist has many priorities at the same time, whereas a rural farmer usually does not. Instrumental conditioning as in behaviour theories is said to relate to mainly the 'S-R bond'. Instrumental learning as explained by Skinner can be used as a technique for inculcating behaviour.[25] (Skinner, B.F., 1974) Intermittent reinforcement in the learning process is also called a perceptible behaviour modification.[26] (Bandura, A., and R. Walters, 1963)

Thus, added to motivation, *attention is an important variable in the process of learning*. In a classroom, for instance, it is usual that a few children are listening and working attentively whereas the others are not. Attention is not the same as motivation, for motivation is an emotive inner feeling whereas attention implies the attentiveness of perceptual acuity of the mind to the response like the waiting for the signal to start in an athletic race. *There is a relationship between reaction potential and the threshold of tolerance.* This is evident in feats of strength where one who holds out and endures the longest is the one the most successful. In a competition, it is possible that not all individuals respond to the same stimulus in similar capacities.

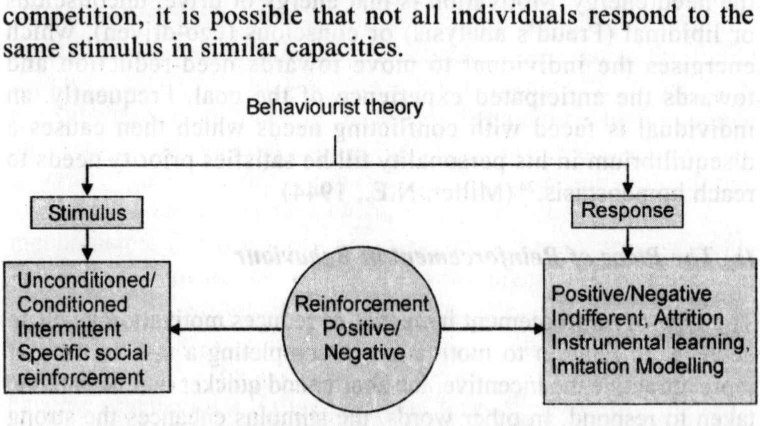

Flow Chart 4.1: Major Characteristics of Behaviourism

It is evident that there is no one-to-one relationship between the stimulus and the response, either conditioned or unconditioned, either reinforced or non-reinforced. There are intervening variables unique to an individual situation which generally is unknown as they operate in the mind of the person and may not be expressed in behaviour. That is why behaviourist theories are limited to observation of overt behaviour. At times such techniques like surveys and interviews conducted by urban individuals in rural areas might elicit 'halo' responses as the ruralite may give such responses which they think the researcher needs such as "Are you pleased with your political leader?". The answer generally to this question is "yes", because that is generally expected. Therefore, to elicit response that is valid in reported behaviour, one might assume that there are intervening unknown variables not observable in reported behaviour. Assessing observed behaviour by sheer perception of the incident can also be biased by the perceiver's own interpretation. Therefore, the stimulus-response theory is limited to the extent that the responses are validly and reliably assessed.

Basic behaviour explainable by any theory is based upon stimulus, external or internal, and behaviour, external or mental. This suggests comparability of the theories of social learning through imitation, cognitive theory and psychoanalytical theory. In the latter, behaviour is covert and has to be inferred. In the social learning theory, there needs to be a model, abstract or concrete. *Stimulus-response theory is perhaps the most fundamental theoretical construct in assessing personality and behaviour. The major tenet here is a combination of genetic potential, human and material reinforcement and the opportunity to respond or express oneself truly.* Where there is economic scarcity, it does not imply lack of motivation but lack of opportunity to increase one's potential.

Early behaviour theorists who contributed to the systems of education which came to be labelled behaviour modification techniques were James Dewey,[27] (Dewey, J., 1891) Angell[28] (Angell, J.R., 1904) and J.M. Baldwin.[29] (Baldwin, J.M., 1897) The latter drew a parallel between the phylogenetic development of human species and ontogenetic development of children who were taught the necessary behaviours to comply with the norms of the society in which they lived. There was little room for individual experimentation or innovative expression. These theorists believed in the strict learning principles of "teacher" and the "taught".

We have refrained from using the term "principle" as it connotes being mandatory. We know that the human being's behaviour cannot be fully predicted. It varies from time to time and from situation to situation and, therefore, even when we make certain conventional statements as related above, there is always the caveat of "other things being equal." For, it is necessary to state that stimulus response implies learning, and learning is only observable by its outcome that is, behaviour.

(c) Differential Behaviour in the Heterogeneous Indian Context

In the Indian situation, there is no one homogeneous explanation of learned behaviour. Perhaps the most applicable model is the social learning through imitation of the models.[30] Miller, N.E., & Dollard, J., 1941. Children in the Indian situation come from myriads of family lifestyles. It is easy to make general statements that the majority live in similar deprived ecologies. However, while the geo-ecology may be sparse, the human ecology may not be so. For example, in tribal areas, there is much interaction among the families of the tribes where homogeneity of behaviour occurs. This is unlike urban families where even in one residential area, there may be much heterogeneity of behaviour in living styles. Sparse ecologies with homogeneous human interactions, for example, of the tribals, may lack opportunities. However, we have to ask the question, opportunities for what? A tribal or nomadic child who goes to a simple one-room, one-teacher classroom will only learn what is taught and, therefore, has a limited world vision. His teacher might talk of television, of metros, of malls, but they make no impact on motivation levels as, for him, they exist in another world. The child is quick to learn how to count by looking at the sheep and goats as he is part of a pastoral nomadic family or if a rural child, he knows about clouds, rain, fertility of the agricultural land, the possibilities of famine and flood and to count how many kilos of rice or wheat or maize can be harvested. Therefore, his motivation to learn is mainly towards the goal of survival. Therefore, the nomadic or tribal individual deals with the satisfaction of primary needs where behaviour is learned in relation to his ecology. The urban child, on the other hand, has not the slightest clue about agricultural produce, what goes to make fertility of land, or what is a lowered watertable for agricultural needs, as happens in ecological places in Haryana and Rajasthan. What he knows is that the produce is sold in the urban market. Therefore, his motivation to learn is within the parameters of the stimuli in his urban setting.

The behavioural context is not general, but specific to a cultural context. Behaviour modification is, therefore, a part of the socialization process moderated by parents, teachers, peers, and relatives and other significant adults. The examples we have given above relate to learning behaviour in different geo-ecologies moderated by parental kinship, school and other social factors in his human-ecology, which we call the micro eco-system, according to Bronfenbrenner.[31] (Bronfenbrenner U., 1979)

3. Social Learning Theory

The Indian, no matter what his ecology is like, learns certain value systems of behaviour, passed down from generation to generation. He learns deference to elders. His behaviour is moulded in a patriarchal system where the eldest male is most respected and where he abides by the social norms of his given society, whatever the ecology, whether it is an urban milieu, a rural interior village or a remote tribal hamlet in the forest. These attitudes arise from the inculcation of socio-religious norms of values of behaviour, accepted and approved.

We need to ask at this point further questions about the theoretical underpinnings of behaviour theory in relation to unique settings, both contextually and content-wise. How does the individual move towards social interaction and what processes are involved? *If we look at the writings of early psychologists, James was one of the first to indicate that experience gives rise to habitual action. His thesis is based on neural pathways, where repeated actions and reactions automatically trigger off the same cyclic events on the basis of cues in the environment.*[32] (James, W., 1890) For instance, it is habitual to greet people on meeting them. There is no deliberate or conscious effort: it is a part of the automatic (habitual) response of the individuals to the social norm.

The social learning theory emphasises the environment, namely, the different geo-ecological areas in which people live, learn, work and try to fulfil their aspirations. Social learning, therefore, implies learning in a social environment of the nuclear family or the joint and extended family, existing in a supportive network (human ecology). The social learning theory emphasises the observation and imitation of others in the "micro" (family) and "meso" (neighbourhood, school and such like) systems. The individual is encouraged or reinforced by his caretakers to imitate models. Such models are usually elders in the family or revered high-profiled individuals. More often than not, therefore, the model is an "admired model". This model is usually highly respected member in the micro system, or the teacher in the meso ecosystem. We often hear a mother say to her son, I want you to be a big, successful man like your father, or to a daughter, that she should behave in a feminine manner and prepare herself for a married life as observed in families where the mother is a successful housewife. The reinforcement of imitation is more encouraged in the male than in the female since the male is expected to become a wage-earner for his family of procreation. Further, social media like the television which is watched by millions in India have many channels for broadcasting social and family events.

Theoretical concepts have been explained by Miller and Dollard. In their explanation, they emphasise the basic stimulus-response conceptualisation in their theory. They, however, proceed further relating the S-R theory to the environment consisting of the human ecology. In the socialisation process, children are reared towards perceived goals of the parents. The strategy used by parents is to emphasise imitative behaviour. In fact, imitative behaviour, initially occurs from childhood where children learn to walk, talk and use the language of the adults in an imitative fashion. For example, when children play, they have imaginary role-playing as part of their play behaviour. These are the initial beginnings of social learning.

The mini theory of conflict and its resolution is central to the theme of social learning theory. The basic assumptions of the concept of conflict in relation to psycho-dynamic satisfaction of needs and need reduction are as follows:

(i) *The tendency to approach a goal is stronger, when the subject is nearer to (gradient of approach).* For instance, an athlete in a race when approaching the winning post increases his speed.

(ii) *The tendency to avoid a feared stimulus is stronger, when nearer the subject is to it (gradient of avoidance).* For instance, the nearer a child approaches a testing situation, the more he is likely to approach it at a slower pace than when he is being awarded a prize at his school function.

(iii) *The strength of avoidance increases more rapidly with nearness than does the strength of the approach (gradient of avoidance is stronger than gradient of approach when they occur simultaneously).* For example, when there is a treasure hunt, excitement builds up when the situation is a garden vis-à-vis a dark and frightening looking cave.

(iv) *The strength of tendencies to approach or avoid varies with the strength of the drive/motivation upon which they are propelled (increase in drive raises the height of the entire gradient).* For instance, when there is competition between two individuals for a coveted goal, the motivation of one may not be the same as in the other in achieving the goal.

(v) *When two incompatible responses/needs are in conflict, the stronger one will tend to be realized.*[33] (Miller, N.E., 1952)

In the societal environment, primary needs are usually the first to be satisfied. Sustenance or survival is one of the primary needs. Therefore, primary need-fulfilment has the highest motivation as man cannot do without the means for survival. In a sparse ecology, to learn to find the means for survival is a primary need.

The social situation acts as a conditioner of social propriety (social norms) which define primary and secondary needs. The secondary needs are so called because, unlike primary needs, an individual can survive, if necessary, without them. For example, Robinson Crusoe survived for a long time on his own, on his lonely Island where he could meet his primary needs. The secondary needs relate to the needs for security, for achievement, for belongingness and for esteem. These needs form the "warp and woof" of socially approved behaviour in the nexus of social learning in a particular geo-ecological area. For example, tribal children are occupied early in life in the family trade as in Yellamanchalli in Andhra Pradesh, where the tribal people weave leaves from the forests into leaf-plates and give them to middlemen for use in the revered Tirupathi temple where they are used for distributing *Prasad*, and the potters' children produce clay utensils for sale in urban areas. For these children, both tribal and urban poor, their secondary needs are met from their circumscribed environment, namely, the forest for the tribal and the slum-dwelling for the urban poor. These are in sharp contrast to the ecologies of the middle and upper classes who have a wider circle of stimuli to meet their secondary needs.

In terms of conflict of varying needs simultaneously, the individual has to make a choice, dependent upon the greater need. In the expectancy model, there is the interaction of the need to achieve for oneself which is also compatible with the needs of admired individuals and the individual more frequently than not make his choice upon the expectancy of reward and the avoidance of punishment. It is but natural to assume that the greater the child's fear in this socialising situation, the greater the avoidance of the situation for fear of punishment. On the other hand, the greater the need to please the adult socialiser, the greater will be the child's tendency to approach the goal, namely, compliance with the norms communicated, indicated or directed by the socialiser; in other words, to comply with the aspirations of the elders. This occurs even though there are other priority needs competing for satisfaction and other compelling drives. It is clear, therefore, that through this process of a paradigm of need reduction, self satisfaction, other's satisfaction, and the expected behaviour processed according to social normative needs, interactions take place in various combinations. These interactions depend upon self-drive, drive to please others, motivation to advance. Other feelings that operate in its activity are frustration, conflict, guilt, repressed behaviour, introversion and/or projection which are a combination of feelings and coping mechanisms as described in Freudian theory.

At times, the inability to resolve a situation leads to a requirement for assistance in decision-making. In the West, professionals are sought for counselling and guidance,[34] (Dollard, J., and Miller, N.E., 1950) while in developing countries, the advice and direction of elders is the usual trend.

The basic premises of learning societal mores which form habits are as below:

(i) The process is a link between sources of secondary reinforcement and its relevant secondarily conditioned response.
(ii) The process emanates from an individual towards his environment and is not necessarily an inherent transaction within himself.
(iii) Social learning is in a context-specific environment which reinforces with social norms.
(iv) The purpose of learning is to arrive at socialised goals as monitored by the elders.
(v) The process is inhibited/barriered/contravened by conflicting needs to reach the goal.
(vi) The more pleasurable the connotation of goal-attainment, the less is the conflict within the individual. The strength of the conflict is mediated by the strength of other competing needs.
(vii) *The strength of the need is reinforced or not reinforced by the individual's motivational levels and the sources of reinforcement in human/geo-ecology.*[35] (Mowrer, O.H., 1950: 29) *The learning process is mediated by extraneous variables such as cultural norms, social relevance and overall need*

to be an approved member of the society.[36] (Hall, C.S., and Lindzey and J.B. Campbell, 1998: 557) *The momentum of conflict is related to varying strength of conflicting needs.*

(viii) The continual and progressive performance of the link between the secondary stimulus and the secondary response is contoured into social habit formation based on conditioning.

Given the above assumptions, social realities reinforce that the process of social learning be relevant not only to the ontogenetic capabilities of the individual to be motivated or otherwise by the 'inner' environment of the self and also the 'outer' environment of the human and geo-ecological system.[37] (Baldwin, A.L., 1980)

Hall and Lindzey[38] (Hall, C.S., Lindzey, G., and Campbell, J.B., 1998) *expand the theoretical dimensions of social learning to include four other areas of relative interaction: Unconscious Processes, Conflict, Acquisition of Neuroses and Psychotherapy.* We give below a flow chart indicating the developmental progression from stimulus response concepts through various additive concepts inclusive of the adjunct theory arising from it, namely social learning theory.

These concepts encompass both normal and abnormal personality behaviour. The implication here is that, the process of learning socially approved behaviour can also backfire. For, in the individual's inability to meet his goals successfully, he tends to become anti-social as a form of ego defence of reaction formation as stated by Freud.[39] (Freud S., 1953).

Hall and Lindzey put into perspective the additive theorising of social learning which complements behaviour theory. The major points are:

(i) the event/situation to be solved confronting the individual.
(ii) the socialiser's strategy to resolve the situation.
(iii) the availability of the model
(iv) the ability of the socialisee to imitate the model.

The Process of Imitation in the Ecological Situation

The concept of model here implies either an individual who is revered in the human ecology or a specific goal to be attained such as becoming a doctor which is an imitation of an abstract concept. The

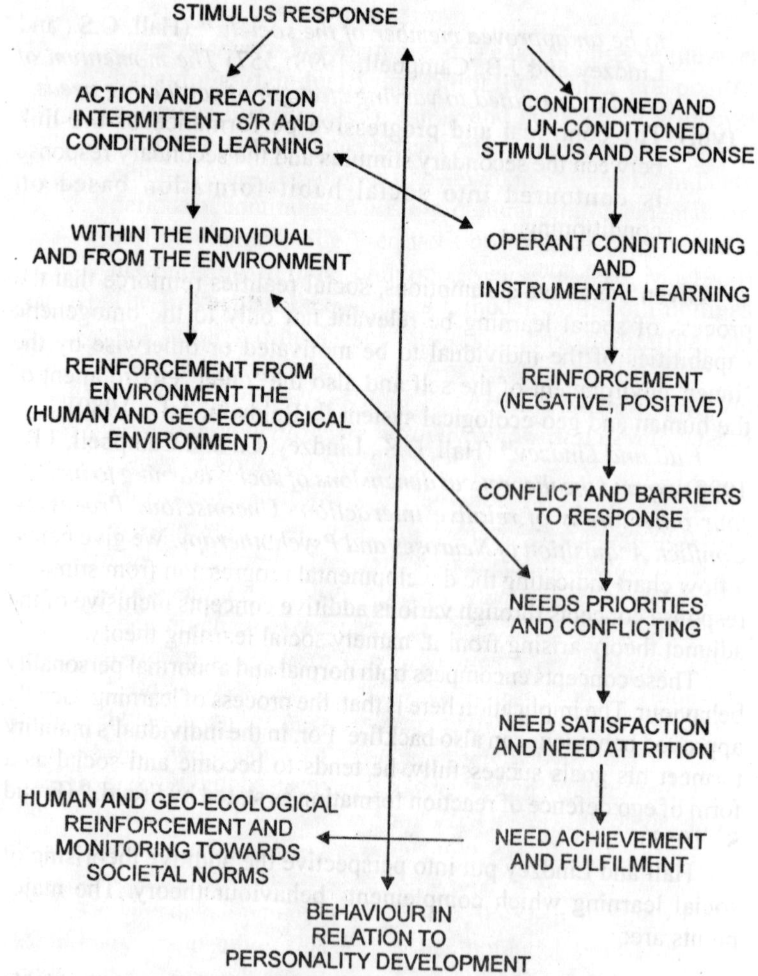

Flow Chart 4.2: Developmental Progression of Stimulus-Response (S/R) Theory

major sources of imitation are: (i) relatives and siblings, (ii) the mythological forms depicted in the Indian epics or current day "heroes" and "heroines".

Imitation can be spontaneous and immediate or secondarily reinforced to bring about the expected response. Primates use imitation constantly, hence the term 'to ape.' For example, it is frequent that the younger sibling is prone to doing exactly what the admired older sibling or adult does. Over time and through maturity, the younger sibling branches out to finding other sources of imitation in order to establish his own identity. Further, an individual internalises selective modes of experiences which meets his needs. By such repetitive experiences, behaviour patterns become habitual responses and, therefore, sets up an organisation pattern of a personality. For example, children about the age of three or four are known "to want to be seen" as little helpers to parents who they imitate to meet their own needs and for being praised/rewarded by elders.

Bandura's contribution to social learning theory expands the theoretical concepts of imitation and describes it as a form of cognitive functioning.[40] (Bandura, A., 1962)

In social learning, imitation begins early in life when the child copies gestures and idiomatic utterances of the adult, especially that of the nurturer. The idiomatic expressions are usually culturally toned and often refer to the geo-ecology. For instance, children learn the first utterances *mama* or *papa* and other relational names like *didi* (sister) or *bhaiya (brother),* which are reinforced by the adults. These are consciously enunciated words by the nurturant in an exaggerated fashion, so that the child follows the movement of the nurturant's lips to enunciate the word initially, one syllable at a time, which rapidly increases during the second and third year, by which time the child acquires a substantial vocabulary, often in the language used in the household. Differential reinforcement or positive responses by the nurturers guide the process of social learning.[41] (Bandura, A., 1969: 213) The facets of social learning have several interpretations. One interpretation is that it is based within the phylogenetic circuit and the child does the act of imitation automatically, which is what was known in early psychology as "instinctual behaviour". It is now more acceptable to view this behaviour as "spontaneous learning behaviour' as evident in primates.[42] (McDougall, W., 1908). This type of behaviour is frequently observed in the play of infants where each one will copy the other in repetitive patterns, such as hitting, banging, or some contraption of noise-making (known in cognitive theory as "circulatory response reactions"). As the child progresses chronologically he learns rapidly from his environment. An urban child, for instance, is attracted to telephones and computers as they are part of his surroundings which attract his attention, especially since they are the sources of imitative behaviour of the adults.

In the formal learning school system, learning of contextual information is considered as embedded processes in the constructs of learnng of self and other directed behaviour.

The child through this continued imitative process learns the differences between role expectation and role performance and in the learning process attempts to bridge the gap. *The potential to* display *imitative behaviour is said to be the part of the epigenetic ability residing in orthogenesis of the individual.*

Thus, in the last analysis

(i) Drive and motivation are the major internal reenforcers towards social learning.
(ii) The stimulus is intermittently provided by the caretaking adult.
(iii) The stimulus is directed towards a model admired by the care-taker.
(iv) The imitator should feel a high need/motivation to imitate.
(v) The imitation may also have other than self motivation such as pleasing the caretaker or the peer group.
(vi) The imitative behaviour should be in consonance with the geo-ecological surroundings of the imitator so that there is harmonious equilibrium.
(vii) All imitation is not motivated by a positive drive. Frequently, a child is threatened or punished if he does not follow the directed imitation such as in school drills of physical exercise, such described in Whiting's study of children in the traditional society of Kwoma of New Guinea.[43] (Whiting, J.W.M., 1941)

The most popularly recognised theorising of social learning has been presented by Bandura, who emphasized mainly the cognitive process in a social milieu.[44] (Grusec, J.E., 1994) The social learning theory is thus an expansion of the original stimulus-response theory. More recently, cognitive theorists have emphasised the more enduring aspect of the mind and necessarily the brain which has a memory track through which neural messages are received and responses sent back in order to de-emphasise the argument that imitative behaviour is not only an automatic physical response but is cognitively conceived and enacted.

Models are not static. They change as the individual matures through the chronological age-span and as his world expands from the micro ecosystem into the meso and exo ecosystems where he finds more appealing models to imitate.

Imitative behaviour is not a perfect one to one relationship. The imitator tries to mould his behaviour as nearly as possible to the model, but because of his own ontogenetic tendencies there will be deviations: slight or expanded.

4. The Piagetian Theory of Cognition

Piaget's theory focuses on fundamental logic in thinking and behaviour. Throughout this theory, we will observe that there are concepts repeated from the fundamentals of neurobiology and the neuropsychology of the individual. The innovative expressions of developmental thought through innovative experiments are explicit idiographic writings in Piaget's cognitive theory.

(a) The Bases of Cognitive Logic

Piaget emphasises two primary concepts, assimilation and accommodation, which form the construct of the adaptive development of the personality. *Adaptation occurs when there is a coordinated and reciprocal relationship between assimilation of external reality in the individual's mental schemata, which become enactments of schemas of progressive thought in social reality.*[45] (Piaget J., 1954) Over a period of time, the perception of external objects/persons are accommodated in the schema without assimilation having to occur repeatedly. This is because assimilation has already been mentally patterned and cognitively mapped for retrieval. Adaptation forms the foundation for further complex cognitive mapping. A young child who has learned to fold his hands in greeting others need not internalise the meaning as they are related to social learning tenants. For mental processes reveal that unless comprehended, assimilated and adapted into thought (covert) or enacted through behaviour (overt) the learning process is not stable. The accommodation, assimilation and adaptation become a schematic pattern in early childhood, which is recalled on the visual presentation of the object or the person already perceived.

During the sensory motor development schema in early childhood, child is first exposed to interactions with external stimuli when he tends to repeat an activity for its own sake which is *circulatory* in nature. For instance, accidentally hitting a rattle yields a sound, and on discovering this, he repeats this action over and over again without the need for attentive cognitive perception, namely, the activity has already been assimilated in his cognitive map as a repetitive "*circular reactive behaviour*", to which he has adapted.

It is important to recognise that the cognitive ability depends upon the concept of perception (accuracy, range of field of perception, figure ground perception, figure embeddedness and intensity of the visual ability)[46] (Ramesh, C. Mishra, 2000). *This perceptual ability is based on biological maturation of the synapses, receptivity and messaging to and from the brain.* When the maturational abilities reach their potential, cognitive ability increases progressively. The schema of cognition develop sequentially, the first being circular reactive movements as explained above. Each schema is dependent upon the successful assimilation and performance of the previous. The regulatory mechanisms underlying the schemata foundationalise behaviour. This process occurs by repeated exposure to a series of events which increase in complexity. Usually this takes the form of repetitions of the same acts till it is completely assimilated. The schema proceeds to the skill of sense and sensory-motor adaptation.

(b) The Place of Perception in Cognition

Before we begin to describe the schema, it is important to describe briefly the concept of perception, and its neural functions. Neural perceptors *of the perception faculty can vary according to the perceiver's innate abilities and motivation (ontogenetic)*. Initially, a sensory perception is an image of the factual object. This occurs more frequently in infancy. However, *perception assumes varying attributes, reformulated by other intervening and stronger perceptions, distracting attention from the original perceived object.* This distraction of the perceptual attention is usually used as a source of deflecting attention from related disapproved behaviour. For instance, if an infant is crying incessantly, the mother finds alternative strategies to distract the infant from his already imprinted cognition of the object that makes the child to cry. Perceptual ability, depth or intensity of perception and perceptual acuity control contribute to the 'saliency' of the perceived object. Singh and Misra in their study using pictorial depth cues on children's painting as related to near space and distant space, found that with increase in age, children not only indicated that they used a greater variety of the cues, but also that, when each cue was more frequently used, there was an increase in the saliency of cues depicting depth.[47] (Sinha, D, and Misra, P., 1975). For instance, if a driver while watching the road in front is distracted by other objects and is not focussed on his driving, he is likely to meet with an accident. In the lack of focus of the driver on the perception of his vehicle to the road, to the speed, to the other vehicles around him, it is reasonable to assume that acuity of perception is lessened, that depth of perception is amorphous and that the range of perception is dispersed in perceiving different objects. Thus, distraction emanating from other objects is likely to lead to lessened accuracy of the perception of the objects focussed upon and, therefore, lessened cognition. For instance, a tennis player can be distracted by emotional feelings of anxiety while playing, which might defocus his attention. Therefore, focussed and controlled attention of perception is foundational to the accuracy of cognition. Thus, perceptual ability and attentiveness are necessarily linked adjuncts of cognition. *At the stage of primary school development, a cognitive pattern is linked to cumulative experiences, the object* needs to *be perceived concretely, but can assume abstract cognitive parameters and functions.* For instance, when a child comes late to class, he tries to avoid perceiving the looks of the teacher, the looks of his classmates or even the classroom clock to cognise that he is late, for these experiences are internally perceived in an abstract manner.

The following are the significant aspects of perception:

(i) The intensity of the perception of an object depends upon the motivational level of the perceiver.
(ii) Perception is focussed on the object or is dispersed through distracting other intervening objects or objectives.
(iii) Perception is either selective and biased or non-specific and without emotional energy attached to it.
(iv) The ability to perceive moves along a continuum of dynamically restructuring the perceptions as the human being interacts with his ecology in greater complexity, accumulating further experiences, perceiving new objects and ideas tempered with concurrent emotions.
(v) *The process of cognising implies many factors.*
The major one is coding and decoding the stimulus, whether

the object is internal such as a memory or external, i.e., the object outside the individual. There is, however, no adhocism in the coding and decoding process. It is the logically ordered process of thinking. How can one explain, how this logical ordering (cognitive states) appears and develops in the early stages of life?

(vi) In order to recognise an object it has to have a symbol or a label, which constantly (consistency of perception) appears the same.

(vii) Such constancy of perception is stored for retrieval so that like a library it can be retrieved and recalled.

Perceptions cumulate into a package of connective ideations and chronologically assume more complicating dimensions, such as finding a familiar face in a crowded market.

The theory of cognition since the last fifty years or so has become the most substantive credence in the observation and recording of early childhood behaviour and the relative complexities of thinking.

Piaget's major thesis is the amplification of cause and effect, through inductive and deductive reasoning in the child. This process grows in complexity as the child matures chronologically. Therefore, cognitive theory is a dynamic intermix of logical thought, accuracy of perceptual abilities, and the reasoning ability of finding out relationships between ideations. The latter occurs primarily based on the ontogenetic intelligence of the given individual.

Piaget is said to be the father of the theory of the most widely used interpretation of cognitive development. Piaget has also emphasised a theory of play whereby the child learns his role and its performance by acting out perceived thematic constructs.

(c) The Piagetian Stages of Cognitive Schema

The cognitive schema as unfolded by Piaget in his experiments and documented in his idiographic observations and qualitative narrations are as follows:

(i) *Sensory motor stage*: This stage occurs through sensory perception and the acquisition of motor skills. For example, smiling on recognition of the nurturant, and acquisition of early language syllabic pronunciations and the coordinated skills between sensory perception and the voluntary activity that follows such as the infant stretching out his hands to his nurturant.

(ii) *Objective permanence*: This stage refers to the child's perceptual direction of an object on which his perception is fixed and internalised in his cognitive map. Even if the object does not exist, it continues to have permanence in ideation. For instance, a ball may disappear behind a wall; the child cannot perceive it, but it exists in his mental imagery. He regains the visual permanence of it when he goes around the wall and recognises it. We observe this commonly in play situations of "peek-a-boo' ('hide and seek'). Even when non-observable, the child goes through a process of circular reactions (primary, secondary and tertiary) in order to regain permanence and visualisation of the object. Thus, the child acquires knowledge that action begets reaction in relation to his initial attempt. Repetition brings about experimentation and clarity about the attributes of the items in the experimentation and gives cognition that the process of *A* leads to *B*, implying that *A* occurs before *B*. Thus, storage of these sequences occurs in memory. During the self-initiated experiment, the child learns the use of the object in relation to his physical skills and in repeating sequences which also improves the skill performance such as the skill to scribble with crayons.

During this stage rudimentary thought occurs of the relationship between the self and the object and the physical manipulation of the object in relation to the individual self and physical reality. This stage occurs during the first-two years.

(iii) *Pre-Operational Stage:* This stage occurs at about 3 years and is a period of imagery and memory imprinting. There is an increase in the use of perception without a precondition of a stimulus occurring. Cognitive ideations are internalised and they can be recalled volitionally. This process is similar to conditioned behaviour and rote-learning in the behaviourist theory. Thus, repetitive action and reaction for routine recall of increasing and complex concepts occurs progressively. At this stage, egocentric behaviour and conceptualisation through the use of rudimentary language is fairly apparent.

(iv) *The concrete operations stage:* This stage occurs when objects form relational concepts to the perceiver in an elementary and causal manner. Knowledge is assimilated about the physical properties of other individuals/objects and the process of labelling. For example, the process of conservation of volume occurs at this stage and is termed invariance. Such cognitive developments take place as conservation of mass, cognition of size, distance and relationships of weight to mass. Such abilities are obtained through simple experiments like floating a rubber ball in water vis-à-vis attempting to float a weighted ball in water. These attributes are understood through self-initiated experiments to concretize objects so that later on they can form the basis of abstract operations which is the next stage.

(v) *Formal Operations Stage:* This stage occurs between 6-12 years. In this stage, there is a reduced dependence on concrete objects for problem solving and innovative thinking. These become assimilation of logical constructions and mathematical abstractions, and the use of symbols to find relationships and to predict effects based on causative factors.

However, *Piaget's theorising is an approach that is heavily based on perception of concrete and abstract attributes of objects, places and people.* This reveals Piaget's tendency of assessment of the growing individual's capacity to *use the themes of biological limitations and/or abilities as well as individualized approaches observing child behaviour in informal situations.* Such theorising does not include the effect of the socio-emotional influences which could also cause variations in the expressed outcomes of perception and logical analysis. The perceptions occur, relating to the natural processes, as they happen in the normal chronological development of the individual. *Consequently, there is not much stated in terms of children who have abnormal development or are underprivileged or apathetic to a normal empowering mind.* Much of Piagetian research has been made on middle class intellectually and physically healthy children in the west.

The following paradigm illustrates the various aspects of perception and cognition in Piaget's theory (Paradigm 4.1)

In describing these schematic stages, it is essential to give a few examples so as to clarify their abstract meanings. In the circular

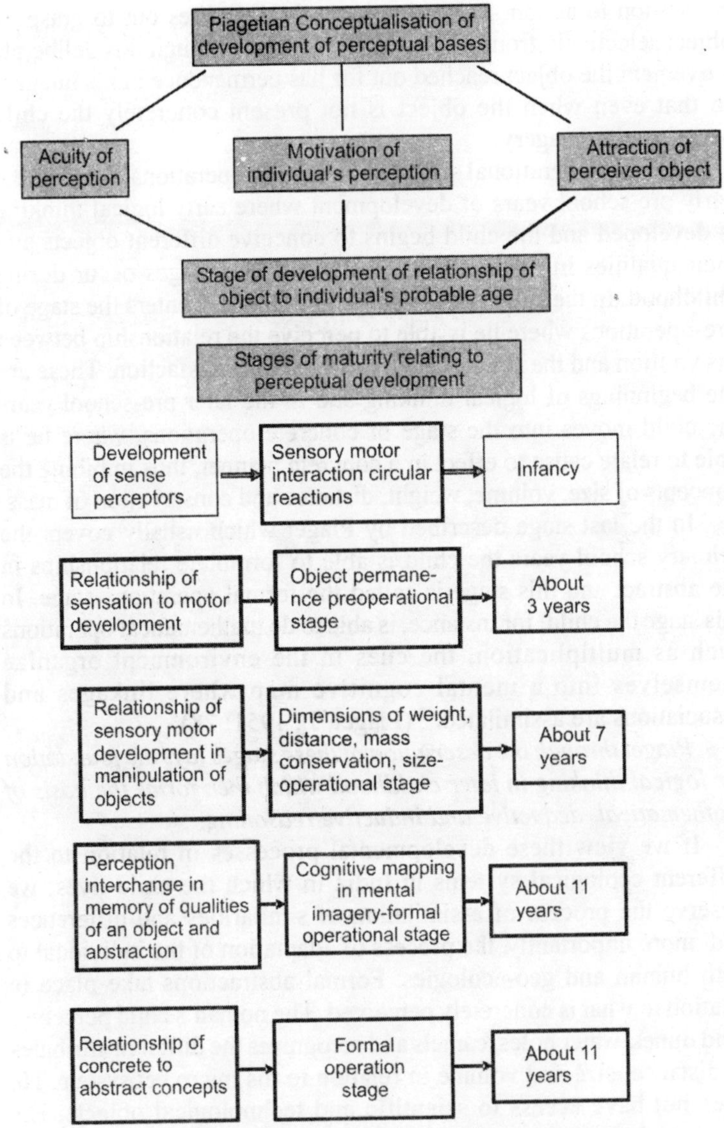

Paradigm 4.1: The Piagetian Theory

reactive stage the child repeats the same activity so as to imprint the circular movement in his cognitive map just as a child banking a rattle repeatedly. In the sensory-motor stage the child learns to relate perception to action. For example, a child reaches out to grasp an object selectively from among other objects. Through this deliberate movement the object reached out for has permanence in his imagery so that even when the object is not present concretely the child perceives its imagery.

The pre-operational stage leads into the operational stage in the early pre-school years of development where early logical thinking is developed and the child begins to conceive different objects and their qualities in relation to each other. These stages occur during childhood. In the early pre-school years, the child enters the stage of pre-operations where he is able to perceive the relationship between his volition and the action which brings about satisfaction. These are the beginnings of logical thinking and in the later pre-school years the child moves into the stage of concrete operations, where he is able to relate cause to effect in a concrete manner, thus imbibing the concepts of size, volume, weight, distance and conservation of mass.

In the last stage described by Piaget which usually covers the primary school years the child is able to formulate relationships in the abstract and this stage is called the formal operations stage. In this stage the child, for instance, is able to do mathematical operations such as multiplication, the cues in the environment organize themselves into a mental cognitive map where linkages and associations are assimilated.[48] (Piaget, J., 1951: 78)

Piaget through the description of these stages lays the foundation for logical thinking in later childhood which then forms the basis of mathematical, deductive and inductive reasoning.

If we view these developmental processes in relation to the different ecological systems in India in which the child lives, we observe the process of assimilation of similarities and differences and, more importantly, the process of adaptation of the individual to both human and geo-ecologies. Formal abstractions take place in relation to what is concretely perceived. The nomad's child perceives sand dunes, water holes, camels and recognizes the different attributes of distance, size and volume in relation to his micro ecosystem. He does not have access to scientific and technological objects. His perceptual cognition is limited to the parameters of his micro system. On the other hand, the urban child has a surfeit of stimuli and his cognition during the concrete operations stage impels him to make selective choices. Obviously, what is most attractive to him in his unique individuality will differ from one child to another because of the breadth of selection. Correspondingly, the rural child will develop through the concrete operational stage dependent upon stimuli in his environment which he then uses for mental abstractions in the formal operations stage. There are myriads of examples among these ecologies. The major thesis here is the effect of the different geo-ecological settings on the human in his micro-system.

(d) Critical Analysis of the Piagetian Schema

Theoretically, an understanding of the lifespan is not available in the Piagetian schema as the schema covers only the childhood stages with some guess estimations as to where one stage ends and another begins. Piagetian concepts are not as rigid as the schema would have us believe. There is considerable overlap in the stages, so that one cannot categorically affix a conceptualised behaviour to any one chronological stage. *Development at these stages is circumscribed mainly by the neuro psychological mechanisms of perception, motor development and mental imagery. It is circumscribed by the boundaries of the individual child's perceptual abilities, intellectual capacities to deduce through reasoning and the absence of socio-emotional intervening variables; in other words, perception of other ecological considerations in the understanding of the schema.* There is a gap of the outcomes of influential variables, such as the child's self-emotionality and the influence of social relations. Piagetian schema are also limited by the lack of its relationship to cultural relativity.[49] (Vygotsky, L.S., 1978)

The theorising of behaviourist theory seems to overlap Piagetian theory, in that stimuli and response are also basic to cognitive processes also. Piaget argues that the stages of development are based on the concept of the third kind of development, namely, equilibration. Piaget also contended that the learning theory is passive, namely, environment impressed behaviour which when repeatedly emphasised becomes the behaviour itself. He emphasises the conceptualisations related to the child's seeking and curiosity behaviour. Critiques stressed that the natural environment if thoroughly explored are relevant to the Indian context conditioned by the specific ecology which can be both a stimulus and a response This, therefore, could influence Piagetian cognitive behaviour schemas. For instance, children in the early stages in rural and tribal areas learn about the causes of weather changes through formal abstractions. The child's progressive cognitive development is related to the ecology, which conceptualisation is not fully explored in the Piagetian schema.

There are interesting researches on the relationship of cognitive thinking to brain processes. In fact, modern knowledge in physical sciences, such as the association of neurological development with cognitive processes, which is a further scientific development, that is not fully reflected in Piagetian schema .

Because of the long-standing popularity of the Piagetian theory, interest in it over the decades has widened. *Yet, as with all theories, Piaget's limited boundaries have been questioned and have been expanded by other neo-cognitive theorists like Vygotsky who included in the analysis of cognition themes of social historicity such as language and culture.*[50] (Vygotsky, L.S., 1962) These cognitive developmental processes are further expanded into cognitive styles by later day cognitive theorists.[51] (Bruner, JS, J.J. Goodnow and G.A. Austin, 1956) There is no further knowledge as to how formal operations are furthered, which when reflected in the Indian context might have different outcomes given the differential ecologies in India. For instance, children who are brought up in close proximity to the family occupation such as agriculture, basket weaving among tribes, might develop these differential stages of schema earlier than given in the Piaget's chronological stages.

The Flowchart 4.2 gives the relationship among the constructs occurring during the mental processing theory.

Piagetian theory is also the basis of understanding the psychometric development of intelligence, singularly and in its multiple dimensions. Piaget used the biological basis in the acquisition of maturation in relation to mental processes. He hypothesized that biological maturation of the growing child to develop the structure of conceptualisation occurred where the child tests his thinking on the basis of reactions in the environment and its feedback. Piaget used an idiographic method of observation, hypothesising and inventing problems for solutions related to how they provoke cognised reactions. He also used puzzles and games to observe and note the detailed manner in which the child's mental ability was translated into behaviour. His unconventional ways of assessing mental development, his extensive idiographic descriptions and frequent generalisations, which were non-quantified, were viewed skeptically as they did not provide empiricism. For example, the relationship between cause and effect were not tested. For a long time, his

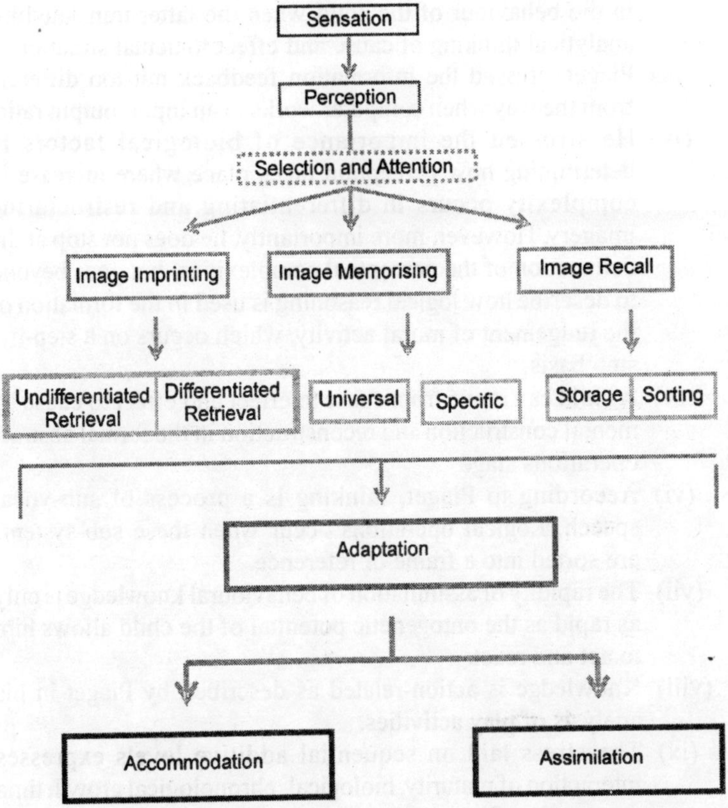

Flow Chart 4.3: The Processes from Perception to Cognition

hypothesising remained in the doldrums, till in the late 1960's his qualitative theoretical statements were tested empirically by his colleagues, giving his theory a credible status as regards reliability and validity from the 1970's onwards, mainly in the areas of early childhood. The major emphases of the Piagetian theory are:

(i) Piaget has aptly described the logical process in thinking as related to neurological maturity in the child's progression from sensory motor development to abstract formulations.

(ii) He explained the progression of logical thinking wherein his subjects used deductive and inductive processes to arrive at linking constructs. These linking constructs were apparent in the behaviour of the child when the latter translated his analytical thinking of cause and effect to actual situations.

(iii) Piaget stressed the information feedback not too different from the way when computer works in an input- output ratio.

(iv) He stressed the importance of biological factors in determining how perception takes place where increase in complexity occurs in differentiating and restructuring imagery. However, more importantly, he does not stop at the delineation of the perceptual complexities, but goes beyond to describe how logical reasoning is used in the formation of the judgement of moral activity, which occurs on a step-by-step basis.

(v) A child can move from cause to effect and effect to cause by mental construction and reconstruction in the formal abstract operations stage.

(vi) According to Piaget, thinking is a process of sub-vocal speech. Logical operations occur when these sub-systems are sorted into a frame of reference.

(vii) The rapidity of assimilation of behavioural knowledge is only as rapid as the ontogenetic potential of the child allows him to act and react.

(viii) Knowledge is action-related as described by Piaget in his analysis of play activities.

(ix) The stress laid on sequential additive levels expresses interaction of maturity, biological, chronological growth time sequence and innate genetic abilities.

(x) Piaget's conception of schemas is mainly related to mental growth. The analysis of pre-conditions or post-conditions in his descriptions of the acquisitions of the schemas are, however, not clearly defined.

5. The Field Theory of Kurt Lewin

Understanding the concepts which make up the domain termed personality implies a knowledge of how the human organism meets its needs and how these are hierarchically organised. As such, the behavioural constructs of field theory seem to emanate from the original theory of Darwin.[52] (Darwin, C., 1859) In his relationship within a social group, the individual strives to arrive at a stage of homeostasis. *Leuba has suggested that man's actions are directed by forces in the environment which he terms "topism."*[53] (Leuba, C., 1955) Lewin followed on by his thesis on natural teleology – a science which affirms the biological and/or psychological needs of the human organisms. He comments that the occurrence of needs triggers restlessness or a tension in the organism in such a way that this tension thereupon assumes control over motor behaviour.[54] (Lewin, K., 1951) *Lewin's major principle revolves around the function of valences in a system of tension between the drive arising from the need, and the self-seeking reduction of the need.* According to Lewin, behaviour is a total process where the goals are in direct relation to the needs. All features of the tension situation are related in an equational manner. These are: the intensity of the need, the drive-strength of the need, the obstacles/barriers present in the pathway of need fulfilment, and the forces that operate in the field situation where these tensions exist and where needs remain unfulfilled. Thus, we observe that his theory is an intensification of behaviourism, for, while behaviour theorists stay within the limits of stimulus and response, he goes further to describe the intensity of the stimulus (energy of the drive) and/or other emotional or interactional variables which are not amplified in the behaviourist theory.

Lewin adopts a model of physics where the dynamism of the vectors or valences determine the interaction between the human and the field of forces or vectors at any given time or situation. These vectors are akin to a circle, its circumference and its radii. The radii emanate from the circumference of the circle to the midpoint. The space within the circumference is occupied by organised field spaces pertaining to domains of needs and their fulfilment. Thus, Lewin attempts to relate development to needs, drives, energy, forces of attraction or detraction of other variables, giving a more or less physical contextual mapping of development.

Since field theory implies space and within that space are organised sets of needs which are unfulfilled, these vectors/valences are the radii within the circle (the strength of the need). These are dynamically and constantly being re-organised as their fulfilment occurs and other needs take their place for fulfilment during the process of development. *Therefore, the field theory implies dynamic changes within the circular circumference as needs are constantly changing towards fulfilment to reach a stage of homeostasis.* These change dynamically within a cluster of needs and their forces for fulfilment.

According to Kerékjártó, topology can be defined as "a part of geometry which investigates properties of figures which remain unchanged under continuous transformation".[55] (Kerékjártó, V.B., 1923) *Lewin thus formulated his theory on the basis of mathematical principles and represented relationships as a set of geometrical equations. These relationships could be cognised against an abstract space which he called life space, indicating that the perimeters encapsulated the experiences over a certain period of time (chronological) and over space (differing environments, both human and material).* The life space was theorised as being the sum of all experiences[56] (Lewin, K., 1951).

However, there is no one-to-one relationship between the individual's needs and the attainment of goals. *Vectors or radial influences from the perimeters which impact upon the individual's core needs (centrifugal), at any one time,* at any one of the regional spaces within the life space. The force of the valence/vectors either becomes tangential or well-targeted. However, if one were to imagine a person composed of competing needs, and levels of motivation to meet them, then the imbalance attracts the vectors to find equilibrium among the individual's needs and his goals (satisfaction). However, those needs that are core/deep-seated or pristine/primary, are deeply lodged in the centre and are more resistant to change, than those needs which are on the periphery. For instance, food habits are more difficult to change than apparel styles. Using the analogy of physics, Lewin formulated equations such as $f_{pg1} > f_{pg2}$ where 'f' represents the force or drive motivation and 'g' represents the goal. When the force of attraction to one goal (f_{pg1}) is greater than the force of attraction to another goal (f_{pg2}), it implies conflict as in Miller's theory of social learning[57] (Miller, N.E., 1944), where conflict is a core concept. We observe in Lewin's theorising the utilisation of the original concepts of James who discussed how behaviour was energised, directed and reached a point of satisfaction in attaining a goal.[58] (James, W., 1890) The field or the life space causes the individual to be in a state of conflict in meeting with competing needs and/or needs of different strengths. These needs may be impeded by forces such as lack of reinforcement, lack of opportunity or inaccessibility. For instance, given the large numbers of deprived ecologies in India, it is fairly easy to understand that the energy towards meeting the core needs for survival, namely, food, shelter, clothing and sex, are more important or centrifugal to the individual in such deprived ecologies than the peripheral or centripetal needs such as changing apparel according to fashion designers. By contrast, the ecologies of the developed and rich people are replete with stimuli which have easier paths to meeting goals for realization. In the latter, there is a surfeit of need fulfilment which are peripheral and centripetal. For example, in the Western world, there are varieties of ice-creams and a child can only eat that much till he is satiated or reaches the over-fulfilment point of a need. In some countries, it (peripheral need) is taken to the extreme so that, in Japan, for instance, having facial cosmetic surgery is a popular need, sometimes with drastic results after its achievement.

Thus, we find that *the topological mapping expressed by Lewin is well-suited to describing proximal and distal variables affecting human beings in relation to peripheral and core of their ecology,* such as human ecology in relation to needs. Sometimes needs overcome rational boundaries. Such is the case with nations embarked on waging war in other countries with little consideration for those in the war-torn areas, especially civilians as in the civil strike in Dafour, Sudan and the loss of life in Afghanistan and Iraq where drones (spy planes) are employed.

Lewin's concept of drive is akin to that of Atkinson's conceptualisation of motivation[59] (Atkinson, J.W., 1964), *as also to drive-reduction in Miller's thesis.*[60] (Miller, N.E., 1951) *All three imply an impelling force or energy towards equilibrium in relation to need satisfaction and these are also akin to the concept of homeostasis in field theory.* Therefore, to go back to the three axes, force may be equated to the inner strength/rate of behaviour, namely motivation. Its strength radiates from a centrifugal core in a centripetal direction. For example, there must be a strong need felt by the individual in order to move him towards fulfilment of the need through a set of forces/valences. It is, therefore, logical that primary core needs are to be met first, before secondary needs. Therefore, Lewin's theory emphasises the following:

(i) The human being at any one time has a set of needs. These needs are of varying strengths.
(ii) The strategies to meet these needs, namely, need fulfilment, need reduction, need attrition are by the motivating forces or drives of human intentions.
(iii) These forces have varying strengths or valences, some greater than the other as propelled by the need whether weak or strong.

(iv) The human system is in a state of restlessness or tension till the needs meet their goals, namely, satisfaction.

(v) This restlessness, or the state of disequilibrium, tends to restructure need fulfilment by its innate disposition to satisfy first primary needs and then secondary needs so as to reach equilibrium in the regional spaces of the circle. These areas of disequilibrium are in an abstract form within the life-space of the individual and form different regions composed of needs and their valences.

(vi) The more heightened the need the greater is its force and valence towards goal-attainment.

(vii) When goal attainment occurs these regions being satisfied give place to other which are next in the line of priority. Thus, the human life-space is in a continuous state of dynamism, meeting some goals and not meeting others, but in the larger context of survival first meeting the primary needs and related goals.

(viii) If the need is primary, like hunger, and the longer the state of tension, it follows that the greater will be the flow of energy from the centrifugal nexus.

(ix) The frequency of the pathway towards goal-satisfaction if repeated becomes a habit.

(x) When the strength of the drive is optimal and the goal is not attained, the organism is deflected to find another pathway to attain the goal. For this reason, we find that where there are elementary ecologies, with little sources of sustenance, human adaptability is so configured that with resilience to deprivation, the individuals living in such ecologies tend to find alternate means for sustaining their core needs.

Thus, the field theory proposes a mathematical environment where forces are constantly in conflict in order that their related needs are met. When needs are met the regions of the life-space are said to be in equilibrium. But when they are not, the personality is said to be in a state of disequilibrium. For instance, in Jharkhand and Chattisgarh, where the livelihood of the people depend upon the produce of the land, there is little land for agricultural produce and, therefore, the *mahua* tree is nurtured for its flower and seed, some of which is used to brew a mild alcoholic drink which is nutritious and most of it is sold to *mahajans* who are commercial contractors, but recently due to the vagaries of the monsoon the *mahua* tree production has become limited and so, for about six months of the year, these tribal seek casual labour in the adjoining city areas or work on agricultural land of wealthy farmers.

Thus, we see that goal-directed behaviour is both personally as well as socially motivated. This phenomenon is not unlike the other theories such as the social learning theory. Stimulus: drive: energy: imitation and modelling and formation of cognitive abstract ideations as in cognition are not unlike the concepts in field theory such as valence/vector/priority-regional spaces and the dynamic changes from the fulfilment of one priority need to another. If we translate this model with its theoretical assumptions and the various aspects that make up its totality to a culture, we may observe three distinct patterns:

(i) The major additional value of this theory is its description of forces of different needs and the movement towards equilibrium;
(ii) The dynamism of changing priority needs;
(iii) *The occurrence of core needs, peripheral needs and the relationship between highly valued behaviour at the centrifugal point of the regional topological map.* This phenomenon is concomitant with the occurrence of less profiled need, lesser valence and lesser force which usually occur in peripheral or centripetal needs of the life-space.
(iv) Assumedly, *therefore, the most valued becomes the most habitual core behaviour of the individual such as socio-religious habitual beliefs.*

Thus, we find the importance of this theory to that of ecology, especially human ecology, in relation to the processes of accommodation, assimilation and adaptation, to the given geo-ecology.

This movement/energy/dynamism as variously interpreted by social learning, cognitive theory and the theory of psychoanalysis, indeed assume a state of conflict between the human being's needs and their source of fulfilment.

In the Indian situation the environment is composed also of the culture and its cultural artefacts. The human being has individualised traits, as seen in Lewin's theoretical assumptions, where these traits are differentiated not only among individuals but even among groups

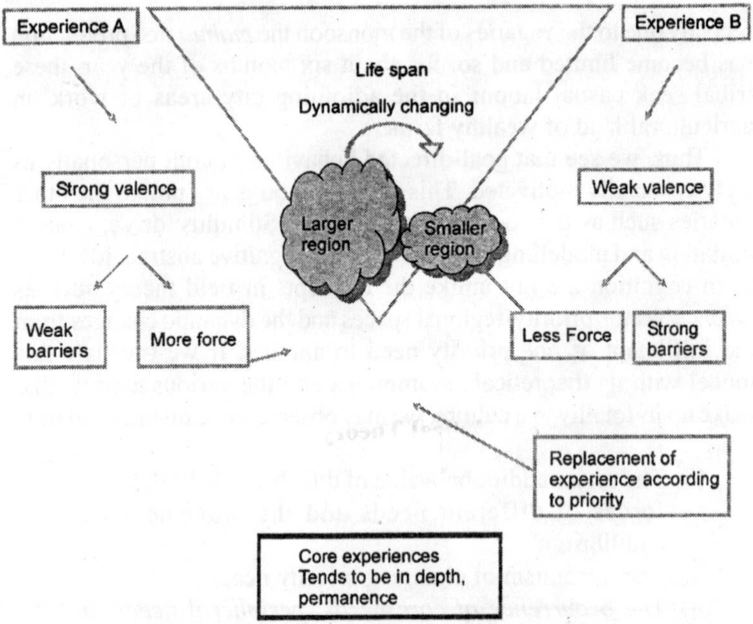

Paradigm 4.2: Topological Interaction of Valances, Periphery/Core, Field-Space Regions, Centrifugal and Centripetal Force

and among sub-cultures. The life-space begins with early childhood experiences and, over time, by virtue of being lodged deeper into the inner space, core traits like interdependency, collectivism, non-violence and adaptive resilience are highly valued.[61] (Verma, J., 2000) With the movement towards modernisation, other experiences, which have their own value, accumulate like change in leisure-time activities and changes in aspirations towards a better quality of life (mainly health and educational betterment). These are centripetal types of behaviours which change over time as their valences are weaker in comparison to the valences towards core values. Thus, we see that this physical model of the relationship among energies, vectors, valences and interaction of regional attributes, among and between spaces, offers a configuration of the cognitive mapping of man's changing needs. The search for need-satisfaction is triggered off by internal disequilibrium and conflict, within oneself and the human and environmental ecology in the external world. Viewed as a constellation of constructs, these constructs indicate the individual's attempt to select experiences, to accumulate experiences and to modify them into a state of equilibrium.

According to evolutionary theory, behaviour becomes adaptive to its environment due to the process of selectivity. This adaptation occurs on the basis of the biological needs of the organism which vary in relation to both ecological functional changes. Changes in the organism appear as overt responses, and occur primarily as an intrinsic reaction to major primary and secondary biological needs. This recognition of biological needs is stressed in all theories of behaviourism, social learning and cognitive development. We may observe from the field theory relationship to the cognitive mapping emphasised in Piaget's theory.

6. The Freudian Psychoanalytical Theory

The Freudian theory of psycho-analysis is a covert theory whose concepts are constructed on the observance of behaviour and/or of reported inner feelings, thinking and constructing ideas. It is perhaps the most relevant theory of the workings of the inner mind.

(i) Origin

The psycho analytical theorising was first evident in nervous disorders exhibited by individuals unable to cope with their problems. Freud and his associates discovered the relationships expressed by their patients using free association to uncover their deep-seated problems. *Freud on the basis of his observation of hysterical behaviour in his clinical patients developed the concept of the unconscious as being of greater importance than the conscious.* The latter was reported to keep the former at bay. In other words, the conscious layer of mental imagery barriered the unconscious from expressing itself in an overt manner in normal behaviour.[62] (Freud, S., and Breuer, J., 1953-74) *Between the conscious and the unconscious is an area of transaction which Freud called the preconscious.* These three layers were linked in mental imagery. This theory rests on the implicit assumption that the individual has a complex of primitive and irrational desires that reside in the unconscious. The unconscious is mediated by the conscious which attempts to reach a homeostasis. *Both the conscious and unconscious are superimposed by the construct of the super ego.* Freud's findings are documented in his writings based on the analysis of dreams and mental states of people whom he treated clinically.[63] (Freud, S., 1960) His theory, although dynamic, is based on physio-psychological structures. It is based on biogenic determinants similar to the theory of motivation of the individual's motivation towards need satisfaction/reduction and Lewin's concept of forces and valences motivating the individual towards goal-attainment and equilibrium.[64] (Atkinson, J.W., 1964; Lewin, K., 1935) In Freud's discussions, he used the *'pleasure-pain' principle as related to the reality principle about which he said "Sufficient discernment to perceive when it is opportune to stifle passions and when it is opportune to either face or fight the realities of the outer world, is after all, the alpha and omega of practical wisdom."*[65] (Freud, 1941) *His main constructs are the id, ego and superego.* What is overtly observable is the workings of the ego. Mental imagery, however, is in a dynamic flux. An analogous illustration might offer further clarity to these three major constructs.

Covert behaviour can be explained with an anology of a house. The ground floor of the house is akin to the ego (the ordinary, everyday normal person, who funciton on the basis of the ego). In the attic lives superego (the authoritative layer figuratively implying the super conscious and the overlord). The superego represents the moral layer of thinking, overlords the individual's human ecology and oversees the activities of the ego. The superego expects the ego to differentiate and act on the basis of what is right or wrong, morally and according to the social norms of his human ecolgy. In the basement exist the id which is strongly barriered from entering the ground floor by the ego which is expected to keep a stranglehold on the unconscious from getting out of the basement and occupying the ground floor. However, figuratively speaking, when the ego sleeps at night, the id, again figuratively, unlocked the basement door and occupied the ground floor satisfying the primary and almost primeval needs, and crept back slowly into the basement at the break of the dawn and were known as the 'rat in the basement'. During the day and when in control of the self, the ego, through various mechanisms (which we shall describe later), controls the situation so that only those needs are expressed and fulfilment sought which met with the approval of the super-ego. The ego is, therefore, in a position to adhere to the instructions of the superego to do what is morally and normally approved and to control or so to speak to keep a lid on the libidinal energy or the energy emanating from the id. The superego generally presides over the behaviour of the ego. While the ego is awake and alert, it keeps a balance between the id and the superego in balance.

Thus, when Freud analysed his patients' expressions when they were in a hypnotic state, he discovered that the emotive irrational desires were not overtly expressed. For, *Freud's interpretation was: the personality who is not expressing his irrational desires could live in a socially acceptable overt manner*. When the unconscious was overtly expressed in aberrant behaviour, it indicated the individual's inability to cope with his libidinal energies.

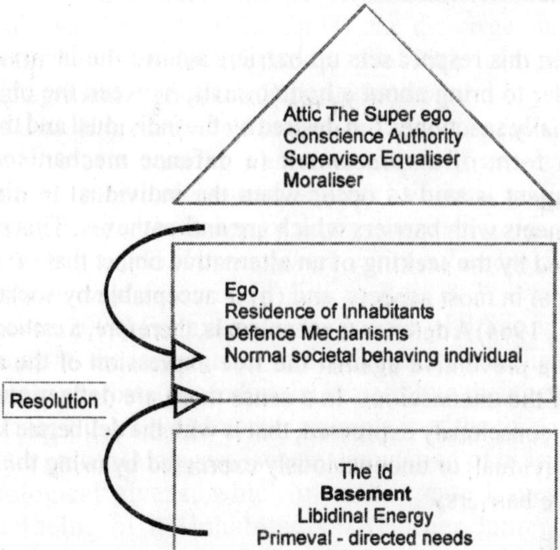

Paradigm 4.3: The Freudian Analysis

The principles of the psycho-analytical theory are:

1. the pleasure-pain principle,
2. the dynamic strength of the id, namely, libidinal energy,
3. the moderator of the area, namely, sanctions and prohibitions expressed in culturally normative prescriptions.
4. the attempts of the ego to keep a balance between the superego and the id or the inconscious.
5. *Cathexis is also a construct for diverting the energy of the id. The cathexis*[66] (Baldwin, A.L., 1980: 335) *deflects the*

abnormal behaviour through the operation of ego defence mechanisms. When the object is unattainable through the process of instinctual cathexis, then the ego seeks another mode by which it can derive need-satisfaction by focussing on an alternative object which has a compensatory value.

6. Finally and most importantly, the ego is the preservator of the self in the socio-cultural framework.[67] (Hall, C.S., G. Lindzey and J.B. Campbell, 1998: 43)

(ii) Defence Mechanisms

The ego in this respect sets up barriers against the incursions of the id. In order to bring about a homeostasis, between the object which is not socially sanctioned but desired by the individual and the personal desire, a form of *displacement* (a defence mechanism) occurs. Displacement is said to occur when the individual in his adaptive process meets with barriers which are anti-cathexes. This situation is determined by the seeking of an alternative object that (a) resembles the original in most aspects, and (b) is acceptable by social norms.[68] (Freud, S., 1964) A defence mechanism is, therefore, a cathectic barrier acting as a preventive against the free expression of the anti-social desires of the unconscious. In a sense these are deflections and they are either consciously expressed, that is with the deliberate knowledge of the individual, or unconsciously expressed by using the following preventive barriers:

(a) *Conversion:* The individual unconsciously develops some physiological malfunction that automatically removes him from a recurrent source of frustration such as the commonly used expression of feeling unwell when faced with a test situation or an unpleasant confrontation.

(b) *Displacement:* The individual unconsciously displaces an unacceptable idea or action by another that is more acceptable. For example, when the individual finds he is unable to satisfy his need, he offers to accept a deferred gratification instead of its immediate gratification.

(c) *Identification:* The individual unconsciously attempts to emulate the psychological characteristic of some person or persons to whom he is emotionally attached. This form of behaviour is commonly observable in "hero-worship" and is akin to the concept of imitation in the social learning theory.

(d) *Introjections:* The individual unconsciously incorporates the demands of the external environment into his own personality. For instance, although not socially acceptable and cannot be openly expressed, an individual, for instance, incorporate a desire within himself but he suppresses its open expression as it is socially not acceptable.This is commonly observable in young children who unconsciously imitate the villains' roles.

(e) *Isolation/ Withdrawal:* The individual teaches himself to withdraw from experiencing the pleasure of possessing the object or expressing the type of behaviour socially prohibited. For instance, when a group of children are playing and a strange child wishes to also enter into the gang spirit but knowing that he is unwanted, excuses himself by saying he is not interested in that gang.

(f) *Projection:* The individual unconsciously projects his own wishes or desires onto objects or persons in the external world. This kind of behaviour is frequently observed especially during the early years of socialisation which often unfortunately continue into adulthood. When a child does not want to admit that he is a cause of a mistake or socially objectionable behaviour, he leaves the blame on others/ unknown events and, therefore, extricates himself from blame.

(g) *Rationalisation:* The individual unconsciously attempts to make his inconsistent behaviour appear consistent to both himself and to others by verbalizing socailly acceptable explanations. For example, when a child is caught doing something wrong, he absolves himself from being the perpetuator of the deed by saying "I thought I was doing the right thing" or "I did not know".

(h) *Reaction-formation:* The individual unconsciously responds to the demands of society by doing the opposite of what he was formally expected to do. Again, in the transparency of childhood, this is also frequently observed when a young child is told "don't hit the cat." And the child defiantly continues to do so.

(i) *Repression:* The child unconsciously excludes unpleasant ideas from consciousness and behaves as if the unpleasant/ unapproved behaviour is of no consequence to him when actually he has repressed it into his unconscious. Most of these ego-defence mechanisms are covert form of behaviour indicating the defence barriers held up by the ego in order that his behaviour complies with societal norms. For example, when it is well-known that children love sweets and a child says that "I don't like sweets", he is repressing his real need, offering a rationalisation for this behaviour. If he goes on to say, "my mother says that I should not eat sweet", he is projecting the cause to another. If he moves away from the friends eating sweets, he is exhibiting withdrawal behaviour and, further, if he wishes to exhibit a highly acceptable defence mechanism, he will use sublimation, which is the most profiled system of socially and even socio-religiously accepted form of behaviour.

(j) *Sublimation:* The individual unconsciously denies the gratification of abnormal needs in favour of good deeds, bordering on the sublime.[69] (Thompson, G.G., 1952) In other words, a child may say I do not want this toy, please give it to the beggar child on the road. In adults we observe this form of sublimation when an adult who likes gambling turns around and says "I'd much rather stay at home and read a book." We see this heightened form of behaviour in sages who deny themselves even of primary needs, thus, sublimating their desires from earthly wishes/goods.

We ought to differentiate between defence and self-control at this point. The former is a barrier so that the originally intended expression is barred either consciously or unconsciously in order that conformity to norms is practised. On the other hand, control implies conscious modification through strategies like planning and programming oneself in a socially acceptable manner, where the ego is fully in charge, like motivation to achieve success. The libidinal energy in the case of defence mechanisms is completely barriered while in the case of control it is consciously inhibited or modified. Control implies conscious effort and, therefore, is ego-directed behaviour according to societal mores.

Using ego defence mechanism is an unconsciously learned behaviour towards socially approved norms. This is observed transparently operant in early childhood behaviour as the child is socialised towards socially approved goals by modulating the inner needs of the id.

(iii) The Stages of Psychosexual Development

Understanding the id and the role that it plays or is deterred from playing, is to understand the barriers that divides normal behaviour from non-normal behaviour. There is a rider to this statement. *All human beings use defence mechanisms in everyday life. It is only when such ego defence mechanisms are used in a heightened, consistent and severe form that they accrue towards non-normal behaviour*. For example, an individual may be observed as being particularistic and systematic in behaviour in the same way everyday and say consciously: "I am a structured person. I cannot deviate". If this structured behaviour is done in a heightened manner, it may be identified as "compulsive behaviour".

The Id is the unconscious motivating force behind primary needs such as hunger, sex, power, control and domination. Living in social groups, adhering to social norms is a primary requirement for the membership of the human group. When these norms of behaviour are violated, there are various levels of confrontation with the self, and, therefore, conflict exists within the individual. The acceptable form that happens in everyday normal life is the milder forms of expressed defence mechanisms. There is within all human beings a sense of libidinal direction: an urge to control and to be acceptable as a member of the group. What we observe here is that the ego mechanism comes into play. If the libidinal energy is allowed to go scot-free, it converts the ego into many forms of abnormal behaviour, the most common being depression and often maniac depression. There are still more severe forms such as catatonia, dementia but, more often than not, they are mild psychotic behaviours which appear infrequently. It is not unusual in cases of behavioural problems in children for child psychologists/psychiatrists to use doll play techniques to elicit libidinally repressed behaviour.[70] (Thompson, G.G., 1952: 322). Some other methods of testing such behaviour are the *TAT (thematic apperception test) and the CAT (children's apperception test). There are various manifestations of the ranges in neuroses and psychoses, some of them are indicative of a permanent split between reality and non-reality, where a strong defence mechanism becomes permanently organised in mental imagery.* This is a form of escapism, where the individual completely disengages himself from reality. Freud equates libidinal energy to sexual energy. However, there is a reinterpretation of this energy by later day neo-Freudians. This energy relates to gratification of the erogenous zones – the pleasure of biological excitation whether it is eating, expelling and/or experiencing sexual or anti-social drive satisfaction. Because of the uncontrollable nature of these drives, the ego has to keep the libidinal energy constantly at bay. Secondary needs like belongingness and achievement also come into play but with lessened libidinal strength to overcome the ego.[71] (Baldwin, A.L., 1980: 331)

The ego, the controller, has three functions:

(i) To prevent drive discharge even when the drive object is present.
(ii) To control the access of anti-social ideas through conscious behaviour, whether it is by using ego defence mechanisms, or a socially motivated self control.
(iii) To guide the behaviour of the person towards those goals that are acceptable by family and society.

Therefore, with this background of the tri-axes of the id, the ego and the superego, the importance of the gate-keeper, namely, the ego, is significant. This role of the ego is to express socially approved behaviour and supress socially disapproved behavour. It also directs the individual to move from ego-centricism to socio-centricism as expressed by Piaget in his analysis of play.[72] (Piaget, J., 1951)

We turn now to the stages of development as delineated by Freud. *The understanding of the use of psycho-sexual conceptualisation in Freud's theory is not that the humanity is crazily driven towards sex-drive and its fulfilment, but that at every stage of development from early childhood to adolescence the child is stimulated by erogenous physical features.* For example, one of the most obvious types of behaviour we see occurring in infancy is that the child learns to suck at the mother's breasts for nourishment or the child is comforted when ill by the close physical proximity of the nurturer. As the child grows into pre-adolescence, he or she experiences sexual urges as also prompted by the development of sex-related organs such as the growth of breasts in female and the growth of hair around sexual organs in the male. From adolescence, the male experiences erections and nocturnal emissions, and the opposite sexes are attracted to each other for intimacy and satisfaction of sexual urges. The tendency for the female to look physically feminine and for the males to look muscular by developing biceps and sporting a beard are all symptomatic of the development towards adulthood.

Freud used this psychosexual conceptualisation as the main pivot for describing the stages of development from birth to adolescence. Like Piaget, and unlike Erikson, he does not extend the stages into the years of adulthood and old age. He has characterised the period of childhood as being the foundation period of the homeostasis between psychosexual demands of the libido and its adjustment to social reality. In essence this implies the attainment of psychosocial adjustments, through control of the self by successful passage through the pre-genital and late genital periods. It is interesting to note here that Piaget also concentrated on internal mental reasoning and adjustment in the development of the stages of his schema, while Erikson's stages are parallel observations made by him in relation to identity development in a psycho-social dynamic manner through his stages of development. The control of libidinal energy, whose aim is irrational pleasure, is through libidinal object searching. This phenomena has been aptly elucidated by Healy, Bronner and Bower.[73] (Healy, W., Bronner, A.F., and Bower, A.M., 1930)

It has been commented that *Freud has also used his initial data on the "Interpretation of Dreams" as basic to the concepts of these psychoanalytical techniques of readjustment.*[74] (Freud, S., 1953) The major basis of these techniques of attempting to readjust to the parameters in the process of personality development is catharsis. This catharsis in simple terms implies the technique of unravelling man's adjustments in the personality of development so that it conforms with societal expectation of role-performance at every stage of development. For example, in the Indian society it is not expected that the adolescents should indulge in pre-marital sex, nor that the Indians should indulge in anti-collective behaviour. These are well-understood norms. Transgression brings about dissonance of the self with his society. What is expected is the individual's behaviour according to social norms.

Behaviour that exceeds the limits of normality is erratic. *Normality is a relative term. What is normal in one society may not be so in another, as cultural norms differ.* We have several examples in different societies, which are traditional or modern or in-between, where confrontation to ideologies occur. For example, in the Indian society, eating meat is abhorred by the highest caste, namely, the

Brahmins who are the Pundits or '*puja* performers' at rituals which are expected to be performed by those who are ritualistically more pure or as Carstairs points out are the "twice-born".[75] (Carstairs, G.M., 1957) There are also clear food prohibitions among cultures. The eating of pork, for instance, is sacrilegious to the Islamic faith, while eating beef is similarly sacrilegious to the Hindu faith.

Each of Freud's psychosexual stage is characterised by a different erogenous zone like from where the individual derives maximum pleasure. *An erogenous zone does not imply the literal meaning of an area which if stimulated satisfies sexual desires. Its meaning is symbolic. It relates to the physical drives primary among them being the basic drives of hunger, thirst and sex.* If we relate these primary drives to the fact that Freud has postulated the id as being the central figure of an energy which is irrational and only knows a straight-line relationship between a primary need, need-reduction and, therefore, satisfaction, we can compare this frame originating to physiological development. This is where certain stages of sexual drive are more prominent than others.

This dimension is related to the major gratification of an erogenous zone like sucking of the breast by the infant in order to satisfy the libidinal drive to ingest food. It is by the sucking reflex that the child initially ingests his primary food so that the act of sucking becomes a secondary source of gratification. Accordingly, Freud named this period which coincides with infancy as being the stage of oral development or the grutification of oral needs.

We digress here to cite the classical study by Whiting and Child who developed a set of hypotheses based on the psychoanalytical theory. They focused on the first-two psycho-sexual stages, considered foundational for later development. These stages are: the oral and the anal. This gave the platform to be able to identify behaviour operationalising the stages. Based on gratification and non-gratification as concepts used in Whiting and Child's study, i.e., if fed orally, the child is satisfied and gratified, if not, gratification does not occur, which leads to other forms of deflected behaviour termed "fixation", literally meaning that the individual is fixated or overly focussed on this need. Similarly if the child does not wish to part with his treasured possessions and displays anti-social behaviour for a longer period of time than expected, he is said to be anally fixated. These concepts arise from early infancy where the child resist defecation as a symbol of retaining what he possesses.

The concept of "displacement" utilised by Freud was modified by Miller by relating it to general social-learning concepts.

Most behaviour is built around the concepts of gratification or non-gratification of these pleasure zones in early childhood. In popular parlance, we often hear the term "he is an oral character or he is an anal character." This construct connotes that the oral character is more frequently fond of pleasurable events / things greedy, wishing to ingest food more often, and is expectedly garrulous. On the other hand, the anal character is supposed to indicate that he is mean, miserly and does not wish to part with any of his possessions, however non-functional they might be. In other words, the personality is fixated to the expressions of frustration of these stages of oral and anal non-gratification related to severity of training in these two areas in early childhood.

In the Indian situation, these types of fixation do not generally occur because in infancy, children are freely breast-fed with little severe frustration. They are also not prevented from freely excreting as happens in western cultures where feeding and toilet are disciplined.

In the next stage, the pregenital stage, *the child's genital area becomes the focus of libidinal energy where the child seeks physical pleasure and avoids pain in seeking self-eroticism*. During this stage the child develops an interest in his sexual physical features and evidences exploratory activities such as masturbation. *Social norms dictate that this is a taboo area and may lead to severity or negative adult reinforcement thus creating a complex in the child and the fear of castration with a morbid anxiety about his genitals*. On the other hand, if the exploration is not severely reprimanded and the child is treated as if exploring a curious area, this phase is likely to arrive at a plateau of homeostasis. The next stage, namely, the phallic stage is symbolic of reproduction which is the source of ultimate sexual pleasure and, therefore, is significant in this stage as it is here that the individual learns that sexual drives are normal – that, nocturnal emissions for boys are accepted and that the differences between himself and the adults in physical characteristics are a course of normal development and, therefore, the growing adolescent does not normally develop obsessive sexual tendencies.[76] (Freud, S., 1955) The phallic stage is symbolic of the phallus or the penis of the male, but there is no explanation about the female genitals in relation to sexual drives.

It is also in this stage that psychoanalytic theory tells us that the child develops a peculiar psychological trait, *acceptable as normal behaviour, in that the child develops an emotional admiration for the opposite sexed parent.* Such traits, based on Greek mythology, are known as "Oedipus" and "Electra" complexes in male and famale children respectively. *At this point in time of development, the domain of displacement as a defence mechanism takes place.* The libidinal energy of the daughter is directed towards the father just as it is of the son to the mother. These phases are called complexes and have their origin in Greek mythology as the Oedipus and the Electra complexes.[77] (Freud, S., 1953) When ego defence mechanisms are vibrant at this phallic stage, they either have to be curbed or deflected or displaced by conscious controlled ego defence mechanisms. In the Indian culture, in most sub-societies, whether tribal, rural or urban, adolescent sexual behaviour is curbed and negatively reinforced by deflections into other socially approved spheres such as sports, drama, and other forms of impressive behaviour.

The next stage is generally a period of organisation and setting of priorities between the id and the ego. In this phase, the superego is the main play-actor. The superego functions to create a plateau of a positive interface between the individual's libidinal energy and the confrontation with societal norms. This stage is, therefore, called the *latency* period where the individual learns about the expectations of society through imbibing cultural norms of behaviour and internalising their values at about the point of reaching adolescence. The individual at this stage enters enthusiastically into peer group relationships.

The next stage is termed the genital stage, where the adolescent reaches the potential of awareness of his ability to cohabit with the opposite sex or in some cases with the same sex (homosexuality) in order to gain the full experience of erogenous sexual pleasure. This genital stage is of importance in the study not only of normal development, but also aberrant development. The conceptualisations during this period are interpreted as follows:

(i) This period, we may hypothesise, corresponds to the life-cycle stage of intimacy and generativity of the Eriksonian lifecycle theory.

(ii) It is at this stage that the tendency for attraction towards the opposite sexed parent reaches its potential libidinal expression in cases of abnormal behavioural disorders. In normal individuals, this tendency is controlled and deflected to attract an attractive opposite sexed individual. Thus, it is in this stage that normal individuals tend to enter into consanguinal heterosexual relationships

(iii) If the tendency of attraction towards opposite sexed parent persists and results in sexual relations between son and mother, or daughter and father, these are termed incest relations, which are considered taboo in almost all societies, and socially prohibited.[78] (Hall, C.S., G. Lindzey and J.B. Campbell, 1998)

Beyond this stage, Freud does not theorise on further stages, unlike Erikson who develops a life-span conceptualisation. The phallic symbol, namely, the "*lingam*", is profiled in Hindu rituals as the symbolic representation of fertility, and in some sub-cultures, especially in South India, the phallic symbol is venerated to appeal to the godheads for bestowing fertility upon married females, especially those, and more especially for the procreation of the sons.

Psycho-sexual developmental constructs are mainly qaualitatively derived in this theory. In the psychoanalytical frame of personality development, and the development of inter-personal relations in the family, these conceptualisations of the theory are at best covert. As such, data are mainly idiographic and narrative, and do not lend themselves to quantitative analyses as empirical data. The data are qualitative on a case analysis basis, and as such they are perhaps the only handle to analyse covert personality dynamics, and to elicit over expression from the client through projective techniques, that is, interpretation/ inference from free associative behaviour or reported communication, where the behaviour of the communicant is assessed in a non-ego threatening environment. At best, they are explainable through case history methods applicable to individual differences.

It is necessary to emphasise that the superego is viewed as the parental authoritarian symbolic figure which continues to monitor and evaluate the ego's directional tendencies. *This representation of authority in the Indian context is best illustrated by the patriarchal system. It is said that the superego is the repository of generation of moral values imbibed and transferred from one generation to another through socialisation according to patriarchal norms.* If there are

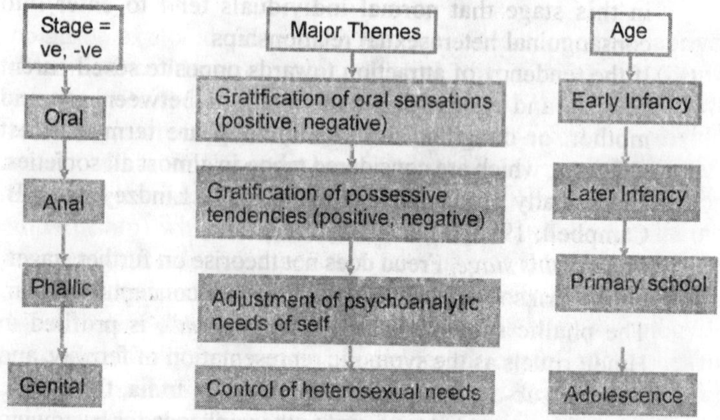

Paradigm 4.4: Psycho-Sexual Stages, Positive Outcomes and Negative Outcomes of Each Stage and the Interaction with Either Sexed Parents in Guidance and Counselling of their Children

negative dispositions in the early stages of infancy and are not re-organised either through the patriarchal system or by the voluntary effort of the ego, bcomes aggravated in later psycho-sexual behaviour.

The harmonious interactions among family members, both in the nuclear and extended family, strengthens the positive characteristics of the child's developing personality, according to the psycho-analytical premises. On the other hand, family disharmony such as domestic abuse might affect the developing child's personality negatively. We observe the existence of family disharmony in the West although not much evidence exists to establish such hypotheses conclusively, we might assume that there are also negative influences on the child generation. Where parental deprivation exists, we might assume that it has negative effects on the adolescent and the youth behaviour.[79] (Misra, S.S., 1977) The absence of parental guidance and counselling in the middle and lower classes is apparent because of poor infrastructural facilities, yet the extent is not empirically evidenced except in some case studies mentioned by NGOs, who have desultory counselling services within their organisational portals. As a result, children in these classes are being gradually exposed to anti-social experiences. These experiences are aggravated through the social channels of the electronic media. Rural and tribal ecologies are less exposed to the latter and, therefore, tend to be less deviant and more conforming with evident social norms.

In all communities, the individual has to come to terms, irrespective of caste, class or ethnicity, with the expectations of the given culture. How is this done? This takes us to the next stage of the operation of the major psychoanalytical dimensions of the sources of ego defence mechanisms. Primarily, they occur when there are gaps between a need, the drive to satisfy the need and the quality and quantity of goals to be attained. Operationally, this statement implies that when there is a barrier to libidinal energy, especially where primary needs are barriered, the tendency towards either repression and a parental conformity occurs or libidinal force breaks the barriers of the ego and allows the individual to express himself in deviant behaviour. In the Indian culture when an individual exhibits abnormal behaviour, we tend to say "*is pe bhoot chada hai*", also rationalising that it is not the individual, but a devil that is prompting the abnormal behaviour. Otherwise, in rural areas especially a *jharra (sweeping away of the evil by a medicine man. Sant/peer)* is brought in to sweep away the devil with incantations or a *Puja* is performed or some rituals are undertaken in order to drive away the evil spirit and to restore the individual's sanity.

In relation to the defence mechanisms, Freud was aware of the cognitive aspects of behaviour. *The transaction from the elementary principle to the reality principle was an acknowledgement that it was not necessary that there should exist a dichotomy between pleasure and pain, but that there is an intervening principle called the reality principle.*[80] (Freud, S., 1941) According to him, the latter is when the ego discovers an alternate way of ensuring gratification, with its relationship to the outer world. In relation to the reality principle recognising the affiliation of the ego to the outer world, psychoanalysis also includes the constructs of cognitive styles. Freud laid the groundwork for constructs in cognitive development in the recognition of the extending parameters of the ego in the cognitive operation that takes place in behaviour ramifications. In fact one of the more modern techniques used in mild cases of depression is called cognitive behaviour therapy.[81] (Andrew C. Butler, Jason E. Chapman, Evan M. Forman and Aaron T. Beck, 2006) To give an example of a treatable psychological disorders, we refer to *the Compulsive Obsessive Behaviour Personality*. This type of personality is a person who is sharply focussed, given to particular detail, is always concentrated on paying particular attention to the task at hand. This type of person also shows rigidity and is very similar to a 'repetitive 'human machine', a person dominated by what ought to be done, not what he would like to do, if his defences were down. This type of personality, appears constantly harassed, excuses himself from leisure and is only at balance in terms of his ego and libido when he is performing and is in control of his environment; very much like a workaholic who is completely tied down to his alcoholic occupation.

The second style is *the hysterical type.* The hysterical person is one who is always on the edge of anxiety and is liable to explode on the slightest provocation. Hysterical patients, for instance, behave histrionically, play-act, build up attentive audiences and are not happy unless emotions are displayed in an exaggerated high-pitched theatrical manner. This type is usually attributed to those in the fields of expressive arts who are high-strung, highly emotional and super-sensitive. These two styles, briefly touched upon, occur in all societies dependent upon the strength of the barriers they meet in the realisation of their needs. They are as much observable in our society as in any other. While the range of behaviour may be from minimal to severe forms of outward behaviour, they nevertheless exist; and in some, they exist as latent potentials. It is evident that both these types exhibit behaviour related to their ability/inability to control their frustrations/ libidinal energy.

In the field of abnormal psychology, there are severe cases of neuroses which are more frequently a part of the personality. Extreme forms of psychosis such as schizophrenia and multiple personality disorders, are not amenable to retrievable strategies *in the field of normal behaviour.* By 'normal', we imply that which is considered normal in a particular socio-economic ecology, where socio-cultural and religious beliefs are strictly adhered to. No religion condones a man who kills another. No social group approves of annexing another's property. Such anti-social behaviours are penalized by the governing laws of the society. In some instances, high-profiled positive behaviours are recognized and approved like, for example, the awards given during the Republic Day where bravery citations are mentioned. In traditional societies, where abnormal behaviour of an individual might provoke resentment and protest from the social network, the individual is protected from the public by being kept indoors.

7. The Eriksonian Theory of the Life-cycle

Erik Erikson developed the theory of the stages of the human being's life cycle. He stated in his book "Childhood and Society" *published in 1963, his theory on the "historical processes", which according to him is written from his own experiences, "a conceptual itinerary."*[82] (Erikson, E., 1963: 14) His thematic conceptualisations which originally dealt with the eight stages of man later includes a ninth stage.[83] (Erikson, E. 1987: 134)

The original thesis arose from the practice of psychoanalysis on children wrought by anxiety and apathy, with neurosis and conflict being the most studied aspects. He underscored that, the psychoanalytic method is mainly a historical method. *The life cycle of the individual is based on case history data, with little attempt to derive empirical generalisation, and in a sense* the theory *is ethnographic and ethnocentric in nature.* The dynamic processes in this theory are closely related to the ecological characteristics in which the individual grows throughout the stages of his life cycle.

The emphasis is on the growth of the ego beginning with early childhood and with assessing behaviour through the play culture of childhood.[84] (Hoare C.H., 2002: 118) It is to be noted here that Erikson was not a 'desk writer'. *Erikson's thematic constructs arose out of his experience in psychiatric practice, his interaction with ethnic communities like the American-Indians,and his* exposure to *Martin Luther's and Mahatma Gandhi's teachings*[85] (Erikson, E., 1958; Erikson, E., 1975). His major thesis revolved around ego identity and its seeking of *homeostasis*[86] (Erikson, E., 1956). The search starts from the beginning of early life. The categories he has developed cover infancy through gerontology, and is a co-joint of physical and mental maturity constructs. *Erikson made no attempt, unlike Piaget, to divide these stages chronologically. He observes a continuum without definitive stages of chronological development*. In a sense, this offers various interpretations that differ from one culture to another, as to when for instance, childhood ends and adulthood begins. *In primitive cultures, societies make their own traditionally normative* assessments *as to when one stage begins and another ends.*[87] (Mead, M., 1927) However, there are continuities and discontinuities between the childhood and adulthood stages in most cultures. In most elementary societies, pubertal rites are performed for girls who reach the age of menarche and "rites of passage" for testing adulthood qualities in young males.[88] (Benedict, R., 1956) Thus, we see that *Erikson uses an intricate mix of social anthropology with his expertise as a psychoanalyst in his writings*. Early childhood is a period of nurturance, but old age is a period of unavoidable degenerative diseases, which do not receive the same quality of nurturance. *This is also exacerbated by the phenomenon of children being orphaned or* abandoned. In these situations, the child tends to develop *a traumatic personality:* together with *fear, neurosis and other psychosomatic disorders as observed by Bowlby of children separated from mothers in the post-war situation in Britain.*[89] (Bowlby, J., 1969) *Erikson* intermixes several disciplines which give a sequential picture of the child's transition toward identity in young adulthood.[90] (Erikson E. 1950)

The theory centralises the themes of bipolar or contrary dimensions of a developmental process. These processes are not exactly anti thesis to each other, but they represent positive and a negative concept of a chronological developmental age.

(i) Basic trust *vs.* basic mistrust.
(ii) Autonomy *vs.* shame and doubt.
(iii) Initiative *vs.* guilt.
(iv) Industry *vs.* inferiority.
(v) Identity *vs.* role confusion.
(vi) Intimacy *vs.* isolation.
(vii) Generativity *vs.* stagnation.
(viii) Ego integrity *vs.* despair.

(i) *Basic trust* versus *basic mistrust: This stage is a clear uni-dimensional construct indicating that the dependency status of the infant is open to negotiation by the caretaker.* Generally, in most cultures there is a heavy input of positive reinforcement by the caretaker in establishing a foundational base. (Mead, M., 1964)[91] Dependency, may through the infancy period develop further to *generalised trusting responses towards other figures and to the general environment* (human and material), arising from the initial bonding between parent and child. *This period is called 'Numinous Ritualisation' where the perception of the child during this period is to recognise his mother as the major source of comfort.* This sense of security generalises to others in the environment, and if not thwarted, contributes to the fulfilment of the need for succurance. This process is similar to the Freudian principle of "pleasure-pain". The concepts of need fulfilment and need reduction are correlative, and their development during infancy indicates a development of the "trusting

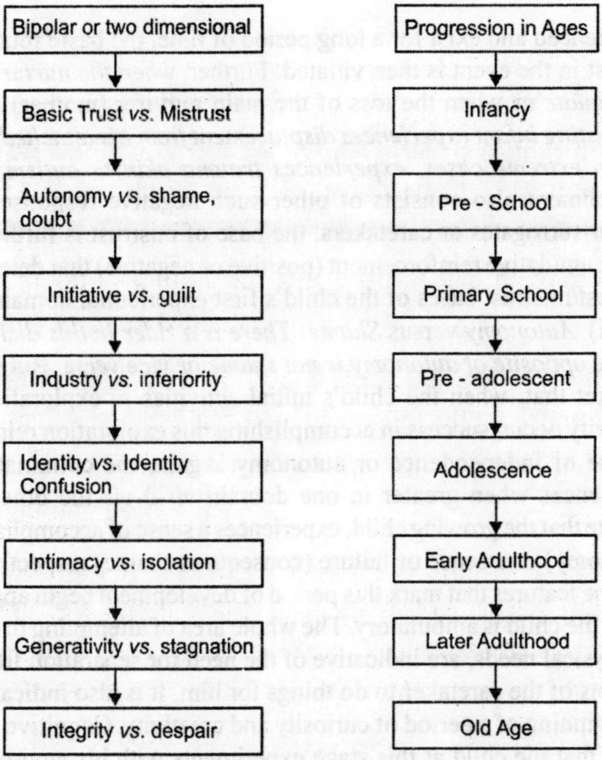

Paradigm 4.5: Eight Stages of Life Cycle – Eriksonian Conceptualisation

response" from the child. We have indicated in the previous chapter of" Environmental correlates of personality" the findings of a classical study on animal behaviour where a child monkey deliberately kept hungry demonstrates his need for security by reaching first for his mother rather than the feeding bottle, to which he was previously accustomed. Thus, the formation of a trusting relationship with the first nurturer is deemed an important step in the formation of the initial responses of the child to his environment. The positive reinforcement of this response releases the tension in the life space of the growing infant. On the other hand, the influences that generate mistrust are the intermittence and inconsistency of care, especially in the satisfaction of the child's primary needs for food and safety. However, if painful experiences are prolonged and intense, the infant experiences lack of need fulfilment. If these lacunae are repeatedly experienced and exist for a long period of time, the basic foundation of trust in the event is then vitiated. Further, *when the nurturance is inadequate* or when the loss of the main nurturer (mother) occurs, *the trusting infant experiences displacement from his attached figure, and in extreme cases, experiences trauma akin to autism.* If the environment also consists of other such negative responses from mother surrogates or caretakers, the base of mistrust is furthered. It is the cumulative reinforcement (positive or negative) that determines the trust/mistrust bases of the child's first experiential domain.

(ii) *Autonomy* versus *Shame: There is a rider in this dichotomy for, the opposite of autonomy is not shame or vice versa*. But we can interpret that, when the child's initial activities in exploration and creativity occur, success in accomplishing this exploration reinforces a sense of independence or autonomy. Again, the culmination of experiences when greater in one domain *vis-à-vis* the other, may indicate that the growing child, experiences a sense of accomplishment (autonomy) or a sense of failure (consequent shame) respectively.

The features that mark this period of development begin apparent, where the child is ambulatory. The whole area of attempting to satisfy his physical needs, are indicative of the need for separation from the attempts of the caretaker to do things for him. It is also indicative of the beginning of a period of curiosity and creativity. Cognitive theory states, that the child at this stage experiments with his environment continuously from a sensory-motor stage to a pre-operational stage according to Piagetian theory. *The distinguishing features of this* Eriksonian *stage is, the child's initiatives into using relatively self-propelled activities. This stage is termed the "judicious stage"*. It marks a period where the child begins to develop a sense of what is right and what is wrong (conscience or the beginning of the activity of the super ego). In relation to Freudian psychosexual stages of development it is related to overcoming anal inhibitions or anal related tendencies such as suspicion, excessive jealousy, a tendency to hoard possessions and such like negative behaviour. *The increase in autonomy increases* self-directed *behaviour*. For instance, at meal times, the child stubbornly refuses to be fed and wants to feed himself on his own in a haphazard manner, much to the distress of his nurturer. His ambulation increases his awareness of the world around him and in a sense, propels him into the Piagetian stage of concrete operations where he examines the relationship between objects or events and begins to question the causation of happenings in his environment.[92] (Piaget J., 1973)

A sense of shame on the other hand is not observable as is autonomous behaviour, as it is more covert than overt. It is an inner feeling, an emotion that cannot be precisely inferred from consequent behaviour. *The reprimand of the adult might instil* in the child *a sense of self withdrawal and hesitancy in attempting this task for fear of further negative reactions.* It might become apparent that these repeated actions cumulate and generalise to other actions, such as withdrawing from becoming social with other children and/or in becoming restrictive in attempting to do creative or innovative tasks. The appearance of withdrawal behaviour might be misread by adults, that the child is being non-compliant and lacking discipline, whereas the child cannot express his behaviour conceptually at this stage. The usual reaction as we see frequently is "I do not want to," meaning not wanting to implement an adult directed command/demand. A discerning and sensitive adult may be able to decode such behaviour as the child's lack of confidence in attempting such directed behaviour or lack of self confidence. In a sense, this period is moving from that of ego-centricism to socio-centricism. In this transition, children while playing together make up their own "jingles", stories, and fantasies, indicative of creativity. On the other hand, a child who is constantly negatively reinforced may withdraw from such interactions for fear of failure. *This combination of self negation and restriction from the outer world might result in a lack of performance in relation to the performance of his peer group.* If this behaviour continues, it may bring about a loss of confidence and self esteem, and indicates the beginning of a period of conflict between the id and the ego, between self and the needs of others. We observe such happenings in traditionally-oriented families, where children are only told to do what is expected without offering any reasons or explanations. Whereas, in a democratically-oriented non traditional family, nurturing adults tend to use persuasive encouragement and offer explanations so that the child's curiosity for knowing the relationship between cause and its effect is understood and then the response is internalised, differentiating between right and wrong behaviour.

(iii) *Initiative* vs. *guilt: This period, which probably coincides with the later pre-school years, emphasises the potential of becoming not only independent, but also that the child looks forward to cumulative experiences which widen the horizons of child's experiences*. He moves into the socio-centric world of interaction with peer groups in various situations, such as on the playground and in informal situations, thus moving towards socio-centricism. Firstly, the child learns to behave according to adult rules and regulations and the ways to comply with them. Secondly, this is a period of dramatic ritualisation where the child shows an exceptional interest in stories such as 'teacher-teacher' among girls and Tarzan like behaviour among boys. Thirdly, this is a period where the child begins to take a self directed interest in gaining new experiences. Fourthly, in relation to the Freudian theory, this is a pre-genital period. Frequently, there is an innocent exploration of the other sex in order to learn and understand anatomy and other sex related behaviour that are not socially sanctioned. Fifthly, there is a more clear distinction between right and wrong than in the previous period.

On the other hand this period is also described as one where negativism seems to have a stranglehold. Clearly, the formation of guilt is not only covert as in shame in the previous period, but perhaps is a further complex development of shame and other attributes. For, shame has overtones of not performing according to sanctioned norms, leading to a sense of guilt. Guilt is also a component of the further development of the ego, which as is now known, is superimposed by the superego by cognitively amplifying behaviour which is correct and permissible, and negating behaviour, which is non-permissible.

Firstly, the attribute of guilt, like shame, is an internal emotion, which may be interpreted by its related exhibitions of defence mechanisms. For Secondly, there is increasing awareness of the contravention of norms, especially in the presence of others, who abide by such norms. The comparison between his and others' behaviour gives rise to a sense of guilt that his behaviour is contraindicative. He may also become rebellious and in extreme cases become revengeful a form of reaction formation. Thirdly, the sense of inadequacy increases. *Such a sense of inadequacy, if internalised and if extended over a long period of time may evolve into loss of self-confidence and deplete the self-image*. The feelings of guilt are experienced at this stage where the child's conscience is fairly well developed as to the value of justice, morality, and conformity with normative behaviour.

(iv) *Industry* vs. *inferiority: This period of industry* vs. *inferiority is usually apparent during the primary school years, wherein normal behaviour, a great deal of activity is observable. This is a period of formal ritualisation* according to Erikson, akin to the formal operational stage of the Piagetian schema. A child for instance, becomes interested in sports like playing cricket. The interaction with the same sex increases. If boys are not interested in boys' activities, they are apt to be called *sissies*. Where girls want to climb trees or play with toy guns and so on they are apt to be called *tomboys*. On the other hand, in gender theories this is a period where activities take place within the same sex while activities with the other sex are discounted.[93] (Inhelder, B., and J. Piaget, 1958)

Firstly, there is an increase in formal learning in knowledge and abilities and to imbibe abstract conceptualisations. It is also a period when competition in the arts, sports and academics is normally heightened. *Secondly, according to psycho-sexual developmental stages, there is a fear of genital castration, "castration anxiety" perhaps for this reason we may assume, that the type of activities are more same sexed than heterosexual* at this stage[94] *(Erikson, E., 1950).* At this stage the child is increasingly aware of sexual differences and his/her biological potential. The individual is given to the fantasies of heroes, heroines and admired models such as film stars. Therefore, we may also take a leap in the theorising aspect and may relate this imitation to tenets of the social learning theory, where imitation of admired models is incorporated into the activity repertoire. Such comic strip figures like "The Hulk" become admired models to imitate for boys and "Barbie dolls" for girls, especially in fantasy imagery. *Thirdly*, there is an almost insidious and deliberate separation of the child from his family in order that he intuitively relies on his own capacities. In other words, the child continues to move along the pathway of independence.

The origins of inferiority are derived along the line of mistrust, shame and guilt in the previous periods. The previous negative stages become more strongly entrenched in his personality, if he moves towards the negative of this stage. *Fourthly,* this is also a period when the child from the industrious positive dimension begins to confidentially envision what he would like to be as an adult and displays vocational interests. As we have observed, the favourite aspirations are pilots, engineers, and doctors for the males and teachers and nurse for the females, as frequently reinforced by the socialiser/s into masculine and feminine role behaviours. These are the beginnings of the sociological roles of instrumental activities for males and nurturant activities for females. *Fifthly, this is also a period when the child attempts to compete earnestly, especially in the academic sphere.* Therefore, academic achievement becomes a priority. This is more especially in the Indian situation because of the 'home work syndrome' pursued by the school and the parent, wherein the upper and middle class parents are themselves tutors, or employ tutors for their children. Correlatively, examinations become a frenzied activity for parents who identify with their children's abilities. It is also in these years especially, during pre-adolescence, where the child consciously or unconsciously grooms himself to be an adolescent, and attempts to control his frustration, guilt and conflict by entering into activities more vigorously such as drama and athletics so as to divert his libidinal energies into socially approved modes of behaviour.

The opposite of this process of development, is a period of experiencing inferiority or a depleted self image. *Firstly, the individual gradually falls into a mode of non-competitiveness and lack of self-confidence* and apathy. *A large part of this has to do with physical appearance. This pre-adolescent stage is concerned with dealing with awkwardness.* Awareness of sex differences and their relative physiological changes which take place, during this period. *Secondly,* where there is already a negative build-up towards an adult personality, from the earlier foundational period of mistrust, shame, guilt and now inferiority, *the child tends to regress into himself. He becomes unsure of his capabilities, and is hesitant and non-confident about his sexuality. Thirdly, this negativity tends to increase withdrawal behaviour*, from competition where competencies are observable in the public eye. *Fourthly*, in this technological arena, the individual at this stage is expected to publicly display his skills. If he is suffering from a sense of inferiority, he tends to withdraw from such "testing situations." *On the other hand, experiencing a sense of inferiority does not necessarily imply regressive behaviour. On the contrary, in not being able to adjust realistically with institutional norms, the individual might overreact and behave in an exaggerated manner*, such as, bullying and boasting. *Fifthly, these forms of negative behaviour, which if excessive, may culminate into neurotic/ psychosomatic behaviour* such as an imagined stomach aches, asthma attacks or other symptoms of ill health at the time of public performances.

(v) *Identity* vs. *Role Confusion: The importance of this stage cannot be over- emphasised, because it demarcates the period, when the child is about to enter adulthood.*

(a) *The ultimate aim of the individual in this stage is to find and consolidate his identity as a unique person in his given environment.* His perceptions become sharpened, so as to be able to assess the quality of relationships, which surround him.

(b) *The individual becomes more acutely aware of his sex-role, his tendencies may be either toward hetero-sexuality/ homosexuality/ambivalent self-sex identity.* We may assume that this period may be compared with the Freudian psychoanalytical stage of latency where the individual is gearing up his concept of sexuality, potential abilities, and his place in the family as an individual and in the institutional framework. In the latter he is expected to possess a personality apart from others.

(c) *In relation to the theoretical underpinnings of social learning and cognitive theory, it may be assumed that, working towards an identity, helps develop the cognitive parameters of the individual to perceive himself as being different from others.* The stage of identity *vs.* confusion is a period where the ego or the self develops behavioural traits in consonance with what the super-ego dictates, or falls into a state of confusion, as to what is expected of him. Adolescence is a period which is fragile, during which he can easily become a delinquent. He may, at *this stage,* develop *an awareness of his multifarious roles and an internalisation of societal values and mores.* He also learns to cope with barriers of conflict, using a range of ego defence mechanisms which are socially acceptable.

(d) *The adolescent becomes serious about his vocational plans and begins to prepare for them in earnest. In the understanding of his role in the family,* he attempts to achieve a healthy perspective in the control of his libidinal energy, especially in relation to the opposite sex. Finally, he learns to or is encouraged to interact in groups on a team spirit basis seeking a more permanent place in his preferred group structure.

The opposite of identity formation as noted by Erikson is confusion about the self not only in terms of identity but also intra- and inter perceptions of him as an entity. Firstly, he may be *ambivalent about his sexuality*, and vacillates between being an assured person, who does not know how to project his/her sexuality in a confident manner. *Secondly*, if we compare this experience of the diffusion of the self with that of Freudian conceptualisation, *we may hypothesise that this diffused inner feeling of the self is related to the ego's inability to control the libidinal energy and also the inability to follow the directions from the superego.* He may become ambivalent about his sex role. This ambivalence may generalise to other areas such as in heterosexual relationships, where he may be awkward or overbearing. It may be assumed from such behaviour that positive learning of socially approved behaviour has not been fully incorporated into the self's identity. It is not unusual to find young people become infused with varying ideologies from Buddhism to Communism, or some such form of idealism. We might also assume that in relation to Freudian terminology which is symbolised by the phallic stage, that this confusion about his sex identity might also be diffused in his interaction with others.

Therefore, we interpret confusion to mean a lack of appropriate knowledge as to the individual's status in his familial kinship, peer group and community and, therefore, a lack of social identity. If his experiences have been positive and he has had a supportive network (both human and concrete), he is likely to develop a sense of positive identity of himself.

(vi) *Intimacy* vs. *isolation: This stage deals with the young adult through the period of pro-creativity*, when the individual makes choices about whether he should or should not marry and have a family. It is also a period where he has to make choices about his occupation and cement his responsibility towards others.

Firstly, this is a period where his heterosexual adjustment is determined and the young adult moves to the status of being a husband and a father and, therefore, extends his life space to attain more permanency in social *relationships. Secondly, this is a stage where the individual makes commitments to others, and is willing to share his identity with them. Thirdly, his attitude towards societal roles and role performance become more stabilised. Fourthly,* whether he gets married and, therefore, becomes the patriarch of the family, or whether he remains single and, therefore, more committed to his family of orientation, *he begins to develop a sense of moral and economic justice. Fifthly, by now he also integrates his ego to be in control of his future destiny,* and learns to resolve issues and barriers that arise in domestic work and social spheres, in the various ecologies in which he has made commitments, such as in his professional sphere having a steady job for a steady income to support his family of procreation.

On the other hand, isolation is also observable as a negative attribute in contrast to being in close relationship to others. In this dimension, there is a lack/inconsistent process of sharing and behaving responsibly towards others. Also, there is a tendency of moving towards being anti-social, and there is a trend towards becoming a recluse. *The individual* in this respect *exhibits a sense of incompatibility with other individuals in his immediate micro system.* As compared with cognitive processes, in this isolation period, he is unable to adapt successfully and accommodate to his human ecology, beginning with the micro eco-system.[95] (Piaget, J., 1965). He tends to become incompetent in positive relation, more especially individual and perhaps exhibits inconsistent relationships with the opposite sex. There is also a *probability that the individual lacks productivity and creativity. He may return to egocentric behaviour, as in childhood.* It is not uncommon to find spinsters and single old men becoming fussy and attention seeking, a carry over into these later years from the years of confused identity in adolescence.

(vii) Generativity vs. *stagnation:* The next stage is an outcome of the previous ones in almost a vertical lead process and occurs when the individual progresses into the stage of being middle aged. *At this stage, we find that both the attributes, generativity and stagnation, are covert inner feelings, difficult to operationalise in outcomes of behaviour.* The following features may distinguish this period as follows:

It is the marker of a lifestyle, which normally is the period of productivity in heightened potentials in one's abilities. The individual generates or produces outcomes like success in business activities, heightened status of being a professional or in the relative spheres of continuous successful activities, even if being a householder/wife/mother. It seems that the potentials from the previous chronological ages come into full effect. This is the period in which the instrumental role of the husband is fully "exercised," and the wife's role fully "expressive" in terms of generativity. *It is also a period where through socialisation the parent generation transmits values to his progeny,* which is a *transmission of the cultural heritage he has imbibed.* It is a period where sex relationships are either stabilised or there is dissonance in inter-spouse relations and even perhaps a change in heterosexual relations.

On the other hand, the individual at this stage may lack initiative and competence, and, therefore, does not proceed further, but stagnates. *On this negative side, the individual lacks motivation to achieve because of the cumulative loss of self-esteem, initiative and innovativeness, arising from the experiences of the earlier stages of the life cycle.*

(viii) *Ego integrity* vs. *despair*: The next and the last stage as conceived by Erikson, relates to a period where there is integration of the self concept. The individual is able to look back objectively and assess his accomplishments and failures, and accepts them as such without being overly regretful. He tends to retrospect his past experiences and may not feel a sense of guilt or conflict.

From the positive aspect of generativity, it *is a period of consolidation of* the individual's *worldly affairs.* As an adult, he has now settled in his life as a householder and, perhaps, he has already made financial provisions for his old age. Further, his role responsibilities as a worker and provider for the household are delegated to the next generation. *He tends to generally occupy a position of supervisory activities and becomes a guide and counsellor for the young.* He generally thinks more in terms of non-worldly affairs, of spiritual values, and is given to philosophising and acts as a role model for the younger generation.

On the negative side, there are feelings which destabilise his self image as he descends into old age. If by this time, he has been unable to cohese his personality into a stable figure, he isolates himself from others, and is given to phases of conflict, guilt, and depression. He begins to develop a feeling of loneliness. This feeling could exist even though he might be in the midst of his family members. Being distanced *this is a period, when he realises that he could have accomplished more than he had, and suffers from a lack of security in his familial environment. He exhibits inability to delegate authority and, therefore, is separated from relationships by his own feelings of inadequacy from human interaction.* He may also want to keep all his possessions for himself, not wishing to part with any, as they represent his 'security blanket'. Elderly *people who feel that they are still indispensable, although retired from active work, frequently exhibit these feelings* of a negative self image. At this stage he may begin to *experience physical disabilities and diminishing of mental capacities*, like different forms of Alzheimer's disease or dementia and finds that he, so to speak, is "losing the grip on his lifestyle". This *is also a period when the individual seems to regress into a "dependency relationship", with those around him, especially the progeny.* Seeing no future, except perhaps the end, the elderly fall into a sense of despair, aggravated by lack of emotional support in his micro ecosystem.

The following are the Significant Markers of this Theory

(i) *There is no indication in Erikson's schema of intervening variables, which influence overt attributes*. The development of positive identity could be due to many factors: the individual's own volition to have an identity or reinforcement from his human environment or from both.

(ii) *The described stages do not elaborate upon the cognitive processes that take place during the transformation from one stage to another*. What Erikson has done is to put together different personal clinical experiences to sum up different conceptualisations.

(iii) We need to take into account individual *differences based on cultural norms, which differ from one society to another, unavailable in the Eriksonian schema.*

(iv) What seems to be appropriate to the Indian culture is the interweaving of the societal norms impacting on the particular system, whether of identity in the adolescence (positive development) or isolation in the middle years. *What is of importance is a life span perspective, which is of growing interest in social psychology*. For instance, the religious connotation of old age is intervened by the concept of '*vanaprastha*' (an individual, who has accomplished his duties and tasks) and is culturally approved for exhibiting the trait of asceticism at this stage.

(v) Erikson constructs each stage as being an "*either, or*" attribute with little indication as to whether there are dichotomous or continuous bipolar dimensions. The categories relate more *to the exhibition of frequency of these traits in Erikson's interactions with his clinical patients*.

(vi) *Perhaps, what is unclear is as to how one could measure opposing traits within each stage when one is overt and the other is covert.* For example, it is easy to observe the overt behaviour of industry and initiative which are positive attributes than to assess shame and guilt which are covert attributes. For example, Mead's ethnographic study is on how cultures reinforce themes of behaviour. She clearly indicates periods of continuity in positive cultural reinforcement during early childhood. She then goes on to describe a period of discontinuity in older childhood years.[91] (Mead, M., 1964)

(vii) The Eriksonian theory offers a model, with both unilinear and bipolar dimensions. Its content is qualitative, and inferences made are based on psychoanalytical deductions.

(viii) *There is a similarity in conceptualisation with the psychoanalytical frame of the psychosexual developmental stages of Freudian theory.*

(ix) The theory emphasises *the importance of proximate relationships, more especially in the micro ecological system.*

(x) *This model emphasises early bonding of the mother and child in a symbiotic relationship. This bonding and its effects have been much debated upon, as also its gradual or abrupt weaning away from this dependency relationship in the Indian context.* Early dyadic relations are the fulcrum of the development of interdependence in the growing individual. This then becomes a bonding in interdependency.

(xi) *Erikson* emphasises *the ego interaction* within *the cultural context. He also incorporates Hull's learning theory in the process of the child's socialisation.*[96] (Hull, C.L., 1943)

In viewing development throughout the life span through an inter-disciplinary perspective, this theory has potential significance for contextual analysis, which could be further amplified. In other words, this theory has potential for its empiricism in the Indian context. We have scant research which traces the development of such attributes through the life span especially in the adulthood years. Since, gerontology is becoming an area of increasing interest, there is considerable concern, especially in India, that we do not have adequate data to contextualise this geriatric period.

8. The Ecosystem Theory of Bronfenbrenner

When the study of human ecology was being profiled in the West,[97]

(Cohen, R., 1985) interest in specific situational contexts of the human habitat also gained importance. Knowledge of human behaviour from the writings of Behaviourists, Social psychologists and from the earlier days of psychoanalysis is well entrenched in documentation. *Stalwarts like Karve, Dube and particularly Marriot's study of great traditions and little communities, in India, are well-known classical sociological writings on the Indian in his indigenous ecologies and the social realities which are aptly described by Iswaran's contributions of lifestyles in different ethnic communities.*[98] (K. Ishwaran, 1970) In the psychological writings of experts, the potential impact of the ecology on human behaviour was given scant attention except in the abstract constructs of culture and society. *Bronfenbrenner's theory is the most closely related to the geo-ecological system, as it takes its conceptualisations from the gene construct of geo-ecology.* For example, several studies on deprivation referred to ecology, specifically economic deprivation, a facet of the interaction of the human with his geo-ecology, both in proactive and reactive manner. The perspective on the importance of the geo-ecology as related to the human being, was initially of an ambiguous nature. These facets were only discussed in historical annuals when floods and famines occurred in the country, giving glimpses of the interactive nature of the human with his natural environment: the geo-ecology.[99] (Basu, S.R., 2002)

Bronfenbrenner stated that there is a mutual accommodation between the complex bio-psychological organism and the changing properties of the immediate natural *setting in which the organism lives.* He further stated that the individual is affected by the relationships between the immediate ecology and the contextual settings[100] (Bronfenbrenner, U., 1993: 7). This concept of the spatial interrelationships is akin to Kurt Lewin's life space constructs, where human events, overt or covert, interact dynamically with events in the outer world[101] (Lewin, K., 1951). *Bronfenbrenner's theory is also similar to Murray's mini theory where the individual is said to transact* with the conditions in his *environment to satisfy his needs.*[102] (Murray, H.A., 1938) This concept of human interaction is also a construct of cognitive theory for in simple terms, cognition is the transference of the outer world into an inner mental mapping of processes and products. As such, the human being in Bronfenbrenner's ecological theory, also uses the cognitive structures to map the positioning of human beings in their ecological frames. *Bronfenbrenner has in a very innovative manner cohesed ecology and human beings, as one not being able to act without the influence of the other*. The implication is that human beings act and react on their human and geo-ecology simultaneously with one influencing the other. *Bronfenbrenner used a set of inter-related ecological variables, in relation to their intensity and extensity of impact on the human being.* Extensity refers to the extending contacts in concentric geo-ecologies where humans are differentially moulded by the geo-ecology in which they live. For example, the individual's family members are more familiar than his peer group and his peer groups are more familiar than strangers in the outside parameters of unknown ecologies. The latter may be also less frequently visible, cognised, or understood. For example, to the traditional Indian villager, the moon is the repository of the super-natural and a symbol of romanticism, whereas scientists and technologists know that it is only a planet devoid of water and living beings.

Correlatively, the further away ecologies exist in the individual's context, the less is the influence on the individual's lifestyle. *As such, Bronfenbrenner constructed concentric circular interactive cognitive mapping of these various layers like that of an onion: the most proximal interactive construct being the family. These systems moving from the centrifugal to the centripetal circular systems vary in order of intensity.* Their intensities vary from the micro ecological system namely the family, to the meso system namely neighbourhood and peer groups. From the meso-system, interaction moves to the exo-system, namely organisational institutions and public places and to the macro system, namely the outer world, which is less frequently and less intensely interacted upon by the individual in his family nexus.

Elder, furthered this conceptualisation in his analysis of the relationships between the individual and the environment, to propose the following bases of his theory :

(a) *The stability and change of a society:* It is well known that societal structures may have an enduring quality like the caste system, but over time its contours of being a discrete entity are slowly blurring. Positions of super-ordinate and subordinate statuses may be juxtapositioned, whereas "Scheduled caste" individual may be an employer of a Brahmin individual who is his subordinate.

(b) *The dynamic tendency of events:* Events, whether stable or in a flux, are examined as to how they are articulated in time and space. Stability and change are in opposition to each other, for stability is a fixated term but force of time does not allow for the stability of an event to maintain its contours indefinitely. Civilisations of societies rise and fall like the Mauryan dynasty, and systems of rule may attrition over time, like the feudal kingdoms and the British colonial system, while others may restructure themselves such as the nuclearisation of the joint family system. Whereas, before formal education seemed to have been a prerogative of the upper classes, but in independent India it is now focused on the inclusion of the lower classes in providing at least a free elementary education.[103] (Elder, G.H. Jr., 1996)

We have discussed human ecology in great depth in the chapter on "The ecology of the Individual in the Indian context". To present Bronfenbrenner's model we recapitulate the following parameters:

(i) The individual has a centrifugal position in his cognitive life map.
(ii) As the ecological distances increase, there is less frequent contact, and lessened intensity in interaction with the increase in the extent of the adjoining ecologies.
(iii) Variations occur in these special phenomena dependent upon whether the individual's needs are satisfied or otherwise.
(iv) The emotive context of the interaction decreases the relational bond, that is, the further away the individual is from the other, the less is his emotional involvement.
(v) Interaction is initiated by the individual or by his environment. *The individual in his centralised centrifugal position can initiate the interaction. He can also react to stimuli from others in varying degrees of contact.* The more centripetal is the position of other ecosystems, the more emotive is the content.

Given the above parameters, one might envisualise the actors being placed in different boxes one nested into another, with the centre most being the individual himself. *We might assume a likeness between this cognitive ecological model and that of Kurt Lewin's topological model who viewed the individual as having a life space, with different regions from where forces impact upon him and where repeated interactions bring about a habit forming traits.*[104] (Lewin

K., 1936) These interactions through frequency of impact, create more habitual traits which are more or less permanent characteristics of the personality. Lewin's life spaces overlap each other, similar to the "adjacency" of the ecosystems stated by Bronfenbrenner. However, the ecological theory stays well within the boundaries of the circular interactive human system. The main *themes are the intensity and extensity of interactions affecting the personalities in situ. It is essential to indicate that these are generic frameworks and do not focus entirely on the individual's inner cognitive mapping as did Kurt Lewin in his theory where he used the gestalt approach.*[105] (Lewin, K., 1951; Wolfgang, Kohler, 1959)

As the individual moves out of the micro ecosystem to other ecosystems, *the frequency of mobility impels the frequency of interactive processes to other human beings in their social networks. The individual's second layer of interaction is the meso system which is his first level of interaction with these social networks outside the micro eco-systems*. These contacts are usually integrative community networks, and intra-village and inter-village oral information, which provide residential, regional and ethnic areas of interaction[106] (Desai, Sonalde B. Amaresh Dubey, Brij Lal Joshi, Mitali Sen, Abusaleh Shariff, and Reeve Venneman, 2010). For instance, it is fairly well known that the individual has more contact in frequency and intensity with his family living in the same vicinity, than with those members living abroad. *This frequency of proximal contact evolves into micro-level analysis, which is more thoroughly understandable than with those in ecosystems further away from the individual's centrifugal position.* For example, intensity of interaction is more with family members than with the peer group. This interaction is even less than with the people in the institutional framework like administrators and businessmen in their workplaces.

Further, experiences increase with age even within the proximal membership of the family. Perhaps, it is this type of framework which gives expression to the phrase that the person has a "world vision" depending on his enlarging experiences and avenues in furthering interaction with other macro ecosystems.

The third layer of interaction is the exosystem. As the individual's mobility increases, he does not stay confined to his little neighbourhood but occasionally ventures out into public places where his contact with individuals is either indifferent or is based on acquaintanceship. There is, therefore, hardly any emotional interaction or impact of the others from the exosystem as compared with the individual in his micro ecosystem, and consequently the individual is more secure in his familial network.

This extensity and intensity with other human beings also implies that the effect on him, his actions, his feelings, and his attitudes are tangential, in relation to individuals in the meso, exo and macro eco-systems. Individuals are like "ships that pass each other in the night". This does not necessarily imply that the outer centripetal systems are not as essential for meeting his needs, or for influencing his personality. What it simply means is that in an indirect way they may or may not influence his perspective, or cognition either positively or negatively. For instance, the shortage of petrol in the macro system is something that the individual does not have a one-to-one relationship with. But indirectly, it affects his family budget and spending patterns.

According to data recently collated by NCAER and University of Maryland, there is much enlightening information either directly or by inference or by both that it is possible to cite specific geo-ecologies which relate to the *micro system in which the individual* lives. *In a sample of states, it was found that poverty, for example, ranged from 33.2 per cent in Uttar Pradesh to 63.4 per cent in Chhatisgarh.* High percentage of poverty is also more especially found in the relatively neglected States like Orissa, Jharkhand and Madhya Pradesh according to the India Human Development Survey 2004-2005 data.[107] (Desai, Sonalde B. Amaresh Dubey, Brij Lal Joshi, Mitali Sen, Abusaleh Shariff, and Reeve Venneman, 2010) The similarity in the economically deprived conditions in these States relate to the similarities in their deprived ecological systems, both human and geo. More telling *is that economic deprivation measures by these poverty lines is more especially related to lessened opportunities for quality education.* In these States of deprived ecologies, the primary, middle and higher-secondary level education is done through State run schools which are typically poorly managed and run. These forms of deprivation seem to have a spiralling effect. *Poverty is more pronounced in those which are historically disadvantaged.* These sections consists of Scheduled Castes, Scheduled Tribes and other Backward Classes including such communities among the Muslim religious community. There is a vicarious experience for the individual through the communication brought to him *via* the electronic media, where he views or hears of experiences that are far removed from his personal perspective.

In sum, therefore, Bronfenbrenner's ecological model gives an understanding of a system of interaction in a structure that is dynamic. Parsons deals with the concept, that the greater the number of people interacting in one space, the greater the multiple frequency of the interactive processes of communication. For example, in the current phenomena of the exodus of young males from rural areas to urban conglomerates in search of work, the male leaves behind the single female-headed householder. It is not unusual, for instance, to find young men from the rural areas of Uttar Pradesh, Madhya Pradesh, Bihar, Orissa and Rajasthan (the poor States) flocking to metropolis areas in search of casual labour or work on building or other construction sites. Thus, the frequency of communication depends Upon:

(a) The value of oral communication which happens most amongst adults and which is stylised by the hierarchical lines of communication.
(b) The type of family structure whether there is autocratic interaction or patriarchal lines of interaction between and among generations in the family. These situations are especially aggravated in poorer geo-ecologies.

It is the cognitive map of the individual that expands along these concentric lines of ecosystems, from the micro to macro. If an individual in a remote rural area is confined to the parameters of his village distant from other hamlets in the village, he is cocooned and knows only what he sees while the rest of the world goes by.

Thus, *Bronfenbrenner's analysis of the ecological systems implies development of cognitive abilities to be able to identify similarities and dissimilarities in the ecological spheres*. These cognitive abilities are also able to comprehend the forces that push and pull competing needs/activities for priority fulfillment in the system. These dynamic strains create, conflict and anxiety about the outcomes of the individual's specific interactions. It follows that the more well-developed the perceptual abilities to anticipate outcomes, the better prepared are the individual's strategies to be successful in the attainment of goals. In other words, *implicit in the cognisance of the variables in the ecosystems is the understanding of role expectations/ performances.* Where this cognition is inaccurate, the relations might be perceived in a distorted manner.

The "systems model" provides several strands of possible theoretical assumptions. For instance, group formation, organisation, familial and social networkings, the inherent nature of selectivity and chance, and decision-making abilities of the actors are developed in specific individual cognitive maps. There is also an inherent dynamism of differential interactions mediated by time and space. If ecological environs are more nearly similar, they facilitate adaptations more readily than when they are different. *As the individual moves dynamically through his life span stages, the contacts, experience, and learning from the interactive context may vary over time within an ecosystem. The individual may also vary his interaction from one system (peer school group) to another (professional group) dependent upon his reactions to the variables affecting his personality development.* Again, we come back to the basic tenets of social learning theory whereby increasing and complex stimuli when rewarded and reinforced bring about the expected social behaviour. This conceptualisation we may *assume could be similar to the Freudian conceptualisation whereby as interactions increase the individual learns that his ego can control his overt behaviour and that his libidinal energy can be repressed and can divert its energy to other forms of approved behaviour by selective ego defence mechanisms.*

Bronfenbrenner's Model is Illustrated in the Paradigm Below

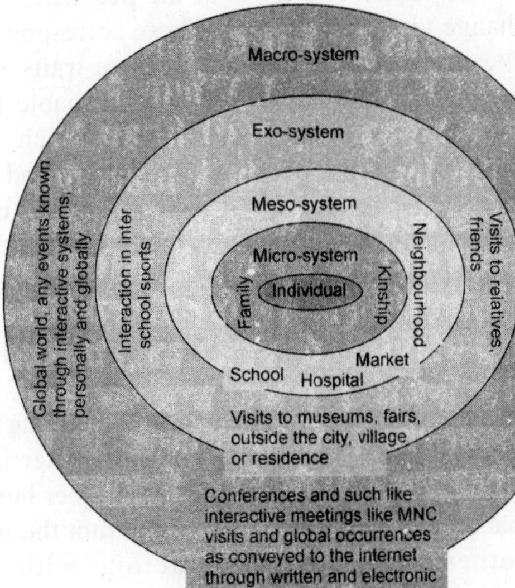

Paradigm 4.6: Relationships Between Frames

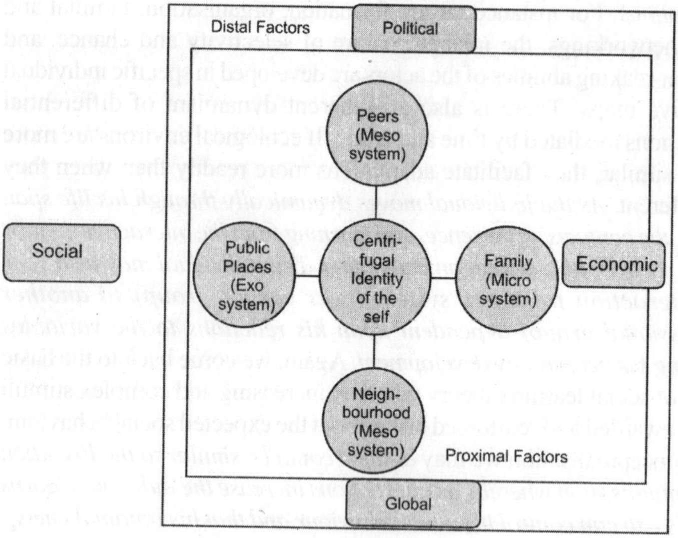

Paradigm 4.7: A Modified Ecological Paradigm

We have also used in the paradigm above the Lewinian concepts like centrifugal (core), centripetal (peripheral) to illustrate those habits and values which are rooted and those at the perimeter, which are more likely to change vis-à-vis the core. These correspond with the distance from the individual at the core. Those traits which are proximal are close to the individual and less amenable to change than those which are far or distal. Again, those which are in the immediate vicinity, like family, peers, or neighbourhood are more proximal than those which are far out of contact, such as economic, social, global, and political events which in the larger context are not within the micro system of the individual, but are at the level of macro influences. Thus, we see that the configurations offered in this model are constructs of space (geo-ecology) and individuals other than the self (human ecology).

They set the stage for the type of interactions connoting relational systems in the ecosystems. Thus, these concepts offer intriguing hypothesis such as the closer the interaction with other humans, the more likely is change to be affected, not only within the individual but also the other individuals interacting with him. In Bronfenbrenner's ecological model, the spaces form concentric circles called ecosystems, which also indicate hypothetically that the actors and the happenings within these systems can vary from one culture to another. For instance, for the nomad these varying systems offer little human interaction, as other ecologies are not within his purview, whereas in a teeming metropolis, the stimuli not only provoke various types of interaction but criss-crossed interactions in permutations and combinations of relationships.

9. The Cohesiveness Implicit among Personality Theories

Compacting the seven theoretical models which have relevance to the development of the personality in India, namely, stimulus-response, social learning, cognitive theory, field theory, psycho-analytical theory, life cycle theory and the ecological theory, we find that there is a mixed bag depending upon the perspective taken by each individual interpreter. *These theories in and of themselves are incomplete pictures of the total personality. Objectively, they overlap in some respects and diverge in some others.*[108] (Hall, C.S., G. Lindzey and John B. Cambell, 1998) A couple of decades ago, Baldwin touched upon the interaction by proposing an eclectic theory of human development.[109] (Baldwin, A.L., 1980) Strides have been taken at intermittent times to view personality development through a multi-disciplinary approach. Again, here the approach is usually to describe a unified personality along the constructs of parallel disciplines. *Their interactional aspect* is yet not fully evident. Different theories are comparable to horses running along a race track with blinders on. Science and technology have opened up realms of what make up the human development process, by introducing more variables like genetic engineering strategies and bio-technological manipulations which modify behaviour, or technologically devised manipulation of the human mind through electrodes or medication. *Man is moving more towards a computer mind, but he has to compete against the stresses of fast moving technology.* The more computer-chip-minded man becomes, the more he has to cope with stresses, time changes and the quick interactive effects of events which require accurate and effective thinking on his part. It is fair to say that science and technology are making accelerating inroads into the lives of people. We have only to view the displacement of people from their geo-ecological habitats like the displacement of tribals by the process of expansion of industrial projects into their ecologies, to understand the dissonance caused by displacement through technology.

10. An Overview indicating a Holistic Perspective of Theories

In the above paras, we have attempted to interlink one personality theory with another so that we could emphasise similarities in conceptualisations. We need to stress some conditional statements. Firstly, according to a recent analysis, there are now scores of theories, hundreds of models and theoretical concepts even around limited aspects of behaviour, such as values like loyalty, justice and morality. *It is evident that the theories are disparate, viewing development from different angles*. They all move towards describing how a personality develops and sustains itself through organisation of attributes within itself. *The basis of all this theorising is the Stimulus—Response bond, for it shows interaction of a living organism*, which is the human and, in this case, the Indian. The other mentioned theories in developing their premises are not complete in relation to the totality of the developing personality. Mini theories like those of Murray, Maslow and Allport offer snippets of detail but only in selected conceptualisations. The Eriksonian theory offers a narrative descriptive scenario of the lifecycle based on subjective narratives of a psychiatrist. The slant of analysis is, therefore, psycho-analytical without much empiricism as it is idiographic in nature. *Piaget stops short at the formal learning stage in early primary school years. Lewin describes the relationship between priorities in the mind and the effects of the environment and is a physical, mathematical design. Bronfenbrenner assumes that the individual either crosses or does not cross the range of eco-systems and, therefore,* is exposed *to relevant experiences* within the given ecosystem. *Freud delves into the inner mind* where *inner data can only be elicited by trained professionals and used as case studies.*

Thus, in the last analysis, we are still searching for completeness of information on the developing personality. True, we might and rightly state that the Indian really exists on the conceptualisation of the platform of his religious beliefs as we have indicated in the previous chapter. But these are spiritual and not amenable to empiricism and, therefore, evade the principles of reliability and validity in fact finding, which is the essence of theorising.

However, turning to widening horizons in the twenty-first century, we see the appearance of such *newer additional concepts to understand the growing personality such as political science, physical sciences and now genetic implications of the DNA, the genome mapping and modification of human behaviour.* This does not mean that human ingenuity is not required, but that ingenuity is required at a much accelerated and complex level.

In the expanse towards understanding human development globally and internationally, we observe the inter-positioning of social, political and such like variables in depicting the nations of the world, thus underscoring the psychological and sociological elements that relate to the economics of global human development reports.

11. A Tentative Proposal of a Hypothetical Theory

We present a tentative conceptualisation of aspects of a hypothetical theory, which we assume may be relevant to the Indian situation. It is essential to give a few conditional statements here:

1. The picturised view of a holistic integrated understanding of personality as relevant to the Indian is based mainly on a collation of hypotheses.
2. These hypotheses take from the generic etic characteristics of human development to focus on the emic characteristics as they apply to the Indian in his habitat.
3. Necessarily, the intervening of concepts from the above detailed personality theories are woven into a contextual frame, namely, the Indian frame.
4. The general idea is not to abandon what is known but to learn further, from what is known.
5. Therefore, these hypotheses/suppositions/assumptions have a theoretical base but not an empirical base in the Indian context. They are, therefore, challenges to theorising about the Indian in his ecologies.

Given the emic characteristics of the various Indians in the Indian States and now even abroad, we need to look squarely as to how personality development in ecologies affect differences in personality. The fact remains, as we have said before, in the prologue, that the majority of the Indians are economically poor, educationally short-changed and socially discriminated. It is essential to tie theoretical constructs to the majority of Indians. Necessarily, we need to demystify the psychological context of understanding personality and balance it with social reality so that we obtain a balanced, equilibrated perception of the heterogeneous Indian in his homogeneous society. We present the various theories described above in a holistic manner together with the proposed concepts, given in the paradigm below. These are put together to make up a hypothetical theory.

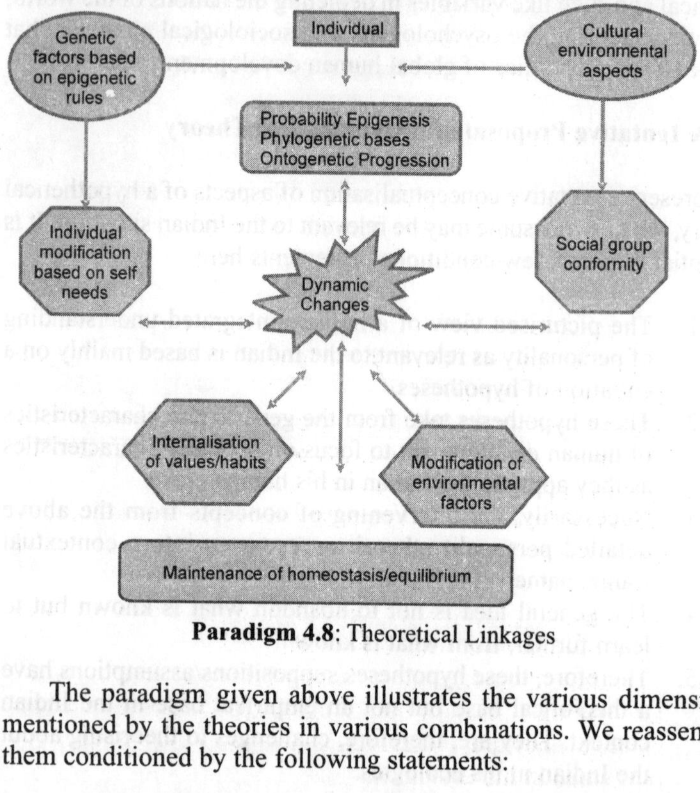

Paradigm 4.8: Theoretical Linkages

The paradigm given above illustrates the various dimensions mentioned by the theories in various combinations. We reassemble them conditioned by the following statements:

1. *The individual comes into this world with the potentials for an orthogenetic development.* The phylogenetic base applies to all individuals and ontogenetic potentials vary from one individual to another. These variations apply to the different individuals in differing ecologies, both in the human and the geo-ecology. These characteristics are both etic (universals) and emic (specific).
2. A personality *proceeds to develop on the basis of epigenetic rules of organisation of characteristics at a given time in the chronological stage and during chronological* stages *of*

maturity. Behaviourists emphasise the psychogenetic attributes of the individual in relation to his ontogenetic abilities in a stimulus-response framework.
The individual, therefore, is regulated by epigenetic factors which monitor orthogenetic processes. The degree of individual conformity displayed towards his social group is an outcome of the influences of his cultural ecology as modified by his inherent traits. He responds positively to some of the various criss-crossing influences from his cultural ecology, negatively to some others. He also ignores some of the influences. As an individual, he learns a unique way of balancing his needs with those of the outer world and attempts to maintain an equilibrium between himself and his situational determinants. If successful, he is said to be a well-adjusted personality and has acquired the benefits of successful modelling. A further caveat is that in the Indian situation, knowledge of such scientific development does not exist in the acumen of tribal and rural ecologies, and perhaps even poor urban ecologies. For, the principles of development documented and communicated are understood by the minority upper classes who form about one-third of the total population, living mostly in urban areas.

3. *Orthogenetic characteristics arise from the inherent genetic traits as well as those nurtured by the environment. In the Indian context, this nurturance is the socialisation process which in the majority of families is traditional, authoritarian—oriented towards patriarchy and embedded in socio-religious beliefs*. These are variegated by the differing geo-ecologies in which each specific individual lives. The developing personality in a tribal area will develop differently from an urban elite individual as the processes of stimulation and responses form different organisations of traits.
4. *The processes of stimulation and relative responses do not proceed in an ad hoc manner*. The environment which consists of the human and geo-ecology and the specific situations and settings modify the expression of responses. They are further modified by a host of other variables; the chief among which are the socialisers: both proximal and distal. By proximal we mean the centripetal forces, which

are self or other motivated and form the micro system, namely the family. The forces from these various sources have an energy of their own, dependent upon the motivational drive of the individual. A sparse ecology, provides routine invariant stimuli as compared to a fast-moving urban high-tech metropolis. Therefore, variations by ecology, both human and geo, mediate responses.

5. *Human needs are either covert or overt. The covert needs are existent usually in the unconscious propelled by the* libidinal energy. *The unconscious is the repository of primeval needs.* These primeval needs are barriered by the ego, which is authoritatively controlled by the superego. In the Indian context, the superego is reposed in the major patriarchal authority, who is usually the eldest or the most powerful male member in the family network, both nuclear and extended. In a few cases the power resides in the matriarch as in some North Eastern States and is still existent in some parts of Kerala. This symbolic authoritative figure is also the communicator of societal norms. In traditional families, this communication is oral from generation to generation evolving from the years of the epics, related in the courts of feudal kings and maintained by the highest castes, the Brahmins. The Indian from his early years is also nurtured to perceive and internalise caste discriminations, reinforced by normative prescriptions and prohibitions. Thus, not only are stimuli intermittently reinforced but are also conditioned to create conditioned responses. These processes are engendered mainly by positive and negative reinforcement from the human and the geo-ecology. For example, tribals living in jungles are attuned to the features symbolic of the animal and the natural environment to which the urbanite is clueless. These positive and negative sources and reinforcements bring about socially learned behaviour, namely, behaviours which should be adapted and internalised and behaviours which should be avoided and made extinct. Through this process the years of early childhood consist of phases of social learning and imitation of models, modelling the perceiver's behaviour according to the model to be imitated. Again, through the socialisation of avoidance and approach to disapproved and approved behaviour

respectively, repetition makes such behaviour habitual. Throughout the process of informal and formal learning whether in the micro ecosystem or the meso ecosystem, habits become valued behaviour. Valued behaviour exhibited by a personality becomes characteristic of that personality. In Freudian terms the personality may be an oral or anal one; in Lewinian terms these values are called core values if deeply embedded in the personality like food habits or peripheral. In other words, core values are values which are centrifugal and cannot be easily discarded such as deference to elders or peripheral values which can be easily discarded and are centripetal to the personality such as the adherence to the caste system in a traditional individual vis-à-vis a modernised individual.

6. *Overt needs are those easily exhibited such as expected role performances,* to which there is *little resistance, or negative responses. These are societally expected forms of behaviour, although different from one ethnic group to another and in relation to sex roles related to instrumental and expressive role tasks.* When known norms are violated such as in delinquent behaviour by adolescents, the ego defence mechanisms lose their power to barrier the Id' s energy and, thereby, the repressed anti-social libidinal driven behaviour is expressed.

In the Indian context, early childhood is a period when the child is considered God-given and child rearing is generally informal and casual. A boy is more welcome than a girl. In the Indian context, all human beings *have their destinies written even before they are born.* There is thus, an intermix of causality and mysticism. If the child lives or dies, it is rationalised as the wish of the Godhead, and becomes an accepted eventuality. The young child is considered amoral. Such assumptions are related to the fact that the majority are poor, live in poor ecologies, have poor facilities for health and education and, therefore, tend to be less literate and less healthy than those where such facilities exist as in urban areas. This majority is really what makes up the face of India and reflects the great extremes between those who have and those who have not: between the economically well-off and the economically deprived. At the base of these two extremes are the constructs of perception and cognition. In a deprived environment the stimuli are usually repetitive and, therefore, do not stimulate acuity of perception related to stimuli ranging from the micro ecosystem through the meso ecosystem through the exo ecosystem and providing a window on the world through the macro ecosystem. The individual might have the potential to hone his perceptual skills, but he can only do so in relation to the habitual ecology, his habitat. The fisherman is highly perceptual about the sea, fish, waves and such like; the Pangi of the Himalayas is attuned to snow, ice, lack of greenery and existence on pasturing where his skills of perception relates to such landscapes. As perception is the basis of cognition, therefore, cognitive skills are dependent upon the stimulation from the ecology and the habitat. This is to say that since cognition is related to the ecological and the cultural environment, being economically deprived does not mean being cognitively deprived. What is deprived is the opportunity to be stimulated and to develop high cognitive skills when barriers exist in the process of such attainment. We may assume a repression of need-fulfilment, consequent frustration and either repressed behaviour or aggressive behaviour, given the facilitating or non-facilitating human ecology. In those families who are economically poor and socially unaware, these indications are bypassed by ecological factors.

The life cycle of the human goes through a phase of over-protectionism in early childhood, where the child learns to trust his environment, to become autonomous, industrious, find his identity and adjust to the problems he will face in his family of procreation, as delineated by Erikson. This life cycle may have a different turn. The individual may not trust his environment. He may become too dependent. He may not be need-achievement oriented. He may become a confused adolescent if the socialising trends influencing him interacting with his inherent tendencies which may cumulate in negativism. We may assume that the Indian child goes through a period of casual, informal care-taking processes from his traditional caretakers given the fact that India is mainly a traditional society. Most parents transmit inter-generational values of obedience and deference to the hierarchy. If the child's ontogenetic propensities are such that he is in confrontation with family and societal demands, most of his experiences may be negatively toned. We may assume that this negativity continues from infancy into old age that the personality is somewhat disorganised in relation to societal norms. In this assumption, we may discern the operation of Freudian principles of "pleasure-pain" and relative to negativity or positivity of development according to the Eriksonian model of the life span.

The Indian's ecology over civilizations, feudal upheavals and now in these centuries of democracy and secularism has undergone many changes. Change is time; and time is change. Due to political and social policies the individual is moving from his micro systems to other ecosystems surrounding him. It is natural that his experiences will expand. Expanding experiences is expected to improve his cognitive skills, his cognitive mapping of similarities and differences. But, topologically his socio-religious beliefs which are traditional, learned from early childhood, remain core and centrifugal. In the dynamics of changing ecologies to which the individual is exposed, as he moves from one ecosystem to another, centripetal values and regional areas of need might cause conflict and tension in the topological modular sense.

Who is an Indian? Can we hold on to an Indian personality at random and say that this individual is a representative of an Indian? Certainly not. There is no average Indian. For instance, a Punjabi is not like a Bengali. He is also not like an Andhraite. If he is a Hindu, he is not like his Muslim friend living next door. Also, he cannot relate in the ways of behaviour, values and attitudes to a tribal in Madhya Pradesh.

Intuitively and logically there are differences in behavioural characteristics of Indians living in different geo-ecological States some of which are known to be productively fertile like the Punjab while others are sparse ecologies like Rajasthan. Yet all who live in them are Indians. If we analyse the qualitative behavioural characteristics of an Indian, all that we can use to identify the individual is: whether he is a Bengali on the east coast or a Gujarati on the west coast or a Kashmiri in the northern hills or a Keralite at the southern tip of India. All have socio-religious core values irrespective of caste, class, region or religion. Again, within a State, like Gujarat, for instance, the Gujarati Brahmin is different from a Gujarati Harijan just as much as a Kshatriya is different from a Scheduled Caste in Madhya Pradesh. Thus, the homogeneity of social religious values is attuned to the type of ecology, the economic situation and the adherence to community values and as to how collectivistically or individualistically oriented he is. All we can say is that the better off he is (socially in terms of class and caste, economically in terms of wealth and power), the more differentiated is he from the class above or below him. This rootedness in core values is what distinguishes an Indian from a non-Indian, living heterogeneously in a homogeneous society. This conceptualisation is so beset with unknown variables, that like a changing kaleidoscope the picture of the given Indian changes and yet paradoxically does not change. This sounds contradictory, but may be assumed as logical if we view a given heterogeneous Indian in his micro system as encapsuled in a macro ecosystem where he adheres to both systems simultaneously.

In the above framework, as such the principles of Erikson's lifecycle and the constructs of Bronfenbrenner's ecological systems theory, are more amenable to the Indian psycho-social system and structure. The major reason is that these two theories besides having psychological conceptualisation also weave in sociological constructs. The justification is that without a totality of understanding of the individual in a societal framework, comprehension of a personality goes short-changed.

REFERENCES

1. Klein, G.S., and Krech, D., 1952, 'The problem of personality and its theory', in D. Krech and G.S. Leon (eds.), *Theoretical Models and Personality Theory*. Durham, North Carolina: Duke University Press.
2. McGeoch, J.A., 1942, *The Psychology of Human Learning*, New York: Longmans.
3. Miller, N.E., and Dollard, J., 1941, *Social Learning and Imitation*. New Haven: Yale University Press.
4. Siemens, G., 2005, 'Connectivism: a learning theory for the digital age', *International Journal of Instructional Technology and Distance Learning*, 2(1), pp. 3-10.
5. Watson, J.B., 1928, *Psychological Care of Infant and Child*, New York: Norton.
6. Skinner, B.F., 1950, 'Are theories of learning necessary?', *Psychological Review*, 57, pp. 193-216.
7. Piaget, J., and B. Inhelder, 1971, *Mental Imagery in the Child*, New York: Basic Books.
8. Baldwin, A.L., 1980, *Theories of Child Development*, New York: John Wiley & Sons.

9a. Piaget, J., 1977, *The Development of Thought: Equilibration of Cognitive Structures*, Oxford, England: Blackwell.

9b. Murray, H.A., 1938, *Explorations in Personality*, New York: Oxford University Press.

Maslow, A.H., 1954, *Motivation and Personality*, pp. 35-58, New York: Harper.

Allport, G.W., 1937, *Personality: A Psychological Interpretation*, New York: Holt.

10. Skinner, B.F., 1953, *Science and Human Behaviour*, New York: Macmillan.
11. Bandura, A., 1977, *Social Learning Theory*, Englewood Cliffs, N.J.: Prentice Hall.
12. Piaget, J., 1954, *The Construction of Reality in the Child*, New York: Basic Books.
13. Freud, S., 1962 (ed. by James Strachey), *The Ego and the Id*. New York: W. Norton & Co.

    Baldwin, A.L., 1980, *Theories of Child Development*, p. 413, New York: John Wiley & Sons.
14. Locke, E.A., and G.P. Latham, 1984, *Goal Setting: A Motivational Technique that Works*, Englewood Cliff, N.J.: Prentice Hall.
15. Baldwin, A.L., 1980, *Theories of Child Development*, p. 423, New York: John Wiley & Sons.
16. Freud, S., 1922, *Beyond the Pleasure Principle*, New York: Boni and Liveright Publishers.
17. Miller, N.E., 1944, 'Experimental studies of conflict', in J.M. Hunt (eds.), *Personality and the Behaviour Disorders*, pp. 431-465, New York: Ronald.
18. Skinner, B.F., 1953, *Science and Human Behaviour*, New York: Macmillan.
19. Baldwin, A.L., 1980, *Theories of Child Development*, New York: John Wiley & Sons.
20. Miller, N.E., 1944, 'Experimental studies of conflict', in J.M. Hunt (eds.), *Personality and the Behaviour Disorders*, pp. 431-465, New York: Ronald.
21. Atkinson, J.W. (ed.), 1958, *Motives in Fantasy: Action and Society*. Princeton: Van Nostrand.
22. Hull, C.L., 1943, *Principles of Behaviour*, Appleton Century
23. Atkinson, J.W., 1966, *An Introduction to Motivation*, pp. 79-80, Princeton, NJ: D. Van Nostrand Company.
24. Miller, N.E., 1944, 'Experimental studies of conflict', in J.M. Hunt (eds.), *Personality and the Behaviour Disorders*, pp. 431-465, New York: Ronald.
25. Skinner, B.F., 1974, *About Behaviourism,* New York: Knopf.
26. Bandura, A., and R. Walters, 1963, *Social Learning and Personality Development*, New York: Holt Rinehart and Winston.
27. Dewey, J., 1891, *Psychology*, 3rd ed, New York: Harper Press.

28. Angell, J.R., 1904, *Psychology: An Introductory Study of the Structure and Function of Human Consciousness*, New York: Holt Publications
29. Baldwin, J.M., 1897, *Social and Ethical Interpretations in Mental Development*, New York: McMillan Press.
30. Miller. N.E and Dollard, J., 1941, *Social Learning and Imitation*, New Haven: Yale University Press.
31. Bronfenbrenner U., 1979, *The Ecology of Human Development*, Cambridge, MA: Harvard University Press.
32. James, W., 1890, *The Principles of Psychology*, Vol. 1, pp. 114-116.
33. Miller, N.E., 1952, 'Comments on theoretical models', in D. Krech, and G.S. Klein (eds.), *Theoretical Models of Personality Theory*, p. 90, Durham: North Carolina: Duke University Press.
34. Dollard, J., and N.E. Miller, 1950, *Personality and Psychotherapy*, New York: McGraw Hill.
35. Mowrer, O.H., 1950, *Learning Theory and Personality Dynamics*. New York: The Ronald Press Co.
36. Hall, C.S., and Lindzey, G., and Campbell, J.B., 1998, *Theories of Personality*. New York: John Wiley & Sons Inc.
37. Baldwin, A.L., 1980, *Theories of Child Development*, New York: John Wiley & Sons, p. 411.
38. Hall, C.S., G. Lindzey and J.B. Campbell, 1998, *Theories of Personality*. New York: John Wiley & Sons Inc.
39. Freud S., 1953, "Three essays on sexuality", in J. Strachey (ed.), *Standard Edition of the Complete Psychological Works of Sigmund Freud*, Vol. 7, London: Hogarth.
40. Bandura, A., 1962, 'Social learning through Imitation', *Nebraska Symposium on Motivation*, 10, pp. 211-269.
41. Bandura, A., 1969, 'Social learning theory of identificatory processes', in D.A. Goslin (ed.), *Handbook of Socialisation Theory and Research*, pp. 213-262, Chicago: Rand McNally.
42. McDougall, W., 1908, *An Introduction to Social Psychology*, London: Methuen.
43. Whiting, J.W.M., 1941, *"Becoming a Kwoma": Teaching and Learning in a New Guinea Tribe*, New Haven: Yale University Press.
44. Grusec, J.E., 1994, 'Social Learning theory and developmental psychology: The legacies of Robert R. Sears and Albert Bandura', in R.D. Parke, P.A. Ornstein, J.J Riesar and Czahn-Waxler, *A Century of Developmental Psychology*, pp. 473-497, Washington D.C.: American Psych. Association.
45. Piaget J., 1954, The *Construction of Reality in the Child*, New York: Basic Books.
46. Ramesh, C. Mishra, 2000, "Perceptual Learning and Memory Process",

in Pandey J. (ed.), *Psychology in India Revisited*, Vol. 1, New Delhi: Sage, pp. 95-150.
47. Sinha, D., and P. Misra, 1975, 'Use of pictorial depth cues in children painting', *Indian Journal of Psychology*, 50 (3), 222-231.
48. Piaget, J., 1951, *Plays, Dreams and Imitation in Childhood*, New York: Norton.
49. Vygotsky, L.S., 1978, "The development of higher mental processes", in M. Cole, V. John-Steiner and S. Scribner (eds.), *Mind in Society*. Cambridge, MA: Harvard University Press.
50. Vygotsky, L.S., 1962, *Thought and Language*. Cambridge, MA: MIT Press.
51. Bruner, J.S., J.J. Goodnow and G.A. Austin, 1956, *A Study of Thinking*. New York: Wiley.
52. Darwin, C., 1859, *On the Origin of Species by Means of Natural Selection, or the Preservation of Favoured Races in the Struggle for Life*. London: Murray.
53. Leuba, C., 1955, 'Toward some integration of learning theories: The concept of optional stimulation', *Psychological Reports*, 1, 27-33.
54. Lewin, K., 1951, *Organisation and Pathology of Thought: Selected Sources*. (Trans. by Rapaport, David). New York: Columbia University Press.
55. Kerékjártó, V.B., 1923, Vorlesungen über Topologie, Springer.
56. Lewin, K., 1951, *Field Theory in Social Science*. New York: Harper and Row.
57. Miller, N.E., 1944, 'Experimental Studies of Conflict', in J.McV. Hunt (ed.), *Personality and the Behaviour Disorders*, Vol. 1, pp. 435-465, New York: Roland.
58. James, W., 1890, *Principles of Psychology*, Vols. 1 and 2, New York: Holt.
59. Atkinson, J.W., 1964, *An Introduction to Motivation*, Princeton, New Jersey: D. Van Nostrand Company.
60. Miller, N.E., 1951, 'Learnable Drives and Rewards', in S.S. Stevens (ed.), *Handbook of Experimental Psychology*, pp. 435-473, New York: Wiley.
61. Verma, J., 2000, 'Social Values', in J. Pandey (ed.), *Psychology in India Revisited — Developments in the Discipline*, Vol. 3, pp. 69-117, New Delhi: Sage.
62. Freud, S., and J. Breuer, 1953-74, '*Studies on Hysteria*', in J. Strachey (ed.), *Standard Edition of the Complete Psychological Works of Sigmund Freud*, Vol. 2, London, Hogarth Press.
63. Freud, S., 1960, 'The Interpretation of Dreams', in J. Strachey (ed.), *Standard Edition of the Complete Psychological Works of Sigmund Freud*, Vols. 4 and 5,London: Hogarth Press.

64. Atkinson, J.W., 1964, *An Introduction to Motivation*, Princeton, New Jersey: D. Van Nostrand Co.;
Lewin, K., 1935, *A Dynamic Theory of Personality*, New York: McGraw Hill.

65. Freud, S., 1941, 'Basic Conceptions of Psychoanalysis', in R. Waelder (ed.), *The Living Thoughts of Freud*, pp. 59-60, New York: Longmans, Green & Co.

66. Baldwin, A.L., 1980, *Theories of Child Development*, New York: John Wiley & Sons.

67. Hall, C.S., G. Lindzey and J.B. Campbell, 1998, 'Sigmund Freud's classical pychoanalytic theory", in C.S. Hall, G. Lindzey and J.B. Campbell (eds.), *Theories of Personality*, pp. 30-77. New York: John Wiley & Sons.

68. Freud, S., 1964, 'Civilisation and its dscontents', in J. Strachey (ed.), *Standard Edition of the Complete Psychological Works of Sigmund Freud*, Vol. 22, London: Hogarth Press.

69. Thompson, G.G., 1952, *Child Psychology*, New York: Houghton Mifflin & Co.

70. Thompson, G.G., 1952: 322, *Child Psychology*, New York: Houghton Mifflin & Co.

71. Baldwin, A.L., 1980, *Theories of Child Development*, New York: John Wiley & Sons.

72. Piaget, J., 1951, *Play, Dreams and Imitation in Childhood*, New York: Norton.

73. Healy, W., A.F. Bronner and A.M. Bower, 1930, *The Structure and Meaning of Psychoanalysis: As Related to Personality and Behaviour*, New York: Knopf.

74. Freud, S., 1953, 'The Interpretation of Dreams', in J. Strachey (ed.), *Standard Edition of the Complete Psychological Works of Sigmund Freud*, Vols. 4 and 5, London: Hogarth Press.

75. Carstairs, G.M, 1957, *The Twice-born: A Study of a Community of High Caste Hindus*, London: Hogarth.

76. Freud, S., 1955, 'Totem and Taboo', in J. Strachey (ed.), *Standard Edition of the Complete Psychological Works of Sigmund Freud*, Vol. 13, London, Hogarth Press.

77. Freud, S., 1953, 'Three Essays on Sexuality', in J. Strachey (ed.), *Standard Edition of the Complete Psychological Works of Sigmund Freud*, Vol. VII. London: Hogarth Press.

78. Hall, C.S., G. Lindzey and J.B. Campbell, 1998, 'Sigmund Freud's classical psychoanalytic theory", in C.S. Hall, G. Lindzey and J.B. Campbell (eds.), *Theories of Personality*, pp. 30-77. New York: John Wiley & Sons.

79. Misra, S.S., 1977, 'Juvenile delinquency and parental deprivations', *Indian Journal of Clinical Psychology,* 4 (1), 69-73.
80. Freud, S., 1941, 'Basic Conceptions of Psychoanalysis', in R. Waelder (ed.), *The Living Thoughts of Freud*, pp. 59-60, New York: Longmans Green & Co. Inc.
81. Andrew C. Butler, Jason E. Chapman, Evan M. Forman and Aaron T. Beck, 2006, 'The empirical status of cognitive-behavioural therapy: A review of meta-analysis', *Clinical Psychology Review*, Vol. 26, Issue 1, pp. 17-31.
82. Erikson, E., *Childhood and Society*, New York: W.W Norton.
83. Erikson, E., Life-Cycle Completed, Chapter 5 (extended version with new Chapter on "The Ninth Stage"). New York: W.W. Norton.
84. Hoare, C.H., 2002, *Erikson on Development in Adulthood: New Insights from Unpublished Papers*. Oxford University Press.
85. Erikson, E., 1958, *Young Man Luther: A Study in Psychoanalysis and History*. New York: WW Norton;
Erikson, E., 1975, 'In search of Gandhi', in E. Erikson, *Life History and the Historical Moment*, pp. 111-189. New York: Norton.
86. Erikson, E., 1956, 'The problem of ego identity', *Journal of the American Psychoanalytic Association*, 4, 56- 121.
87. Mead, M., 1927, *Coming of Age in Samoa,* New York, Blue Ribbon Books.
88. Benedict, R., 1956, *Patterns of Culture*, Boston: Boston Press.
89. Bowlby, J., 1969, *Attachment and Loss,* Vol. 1, New York: Basic Books.
90. Erikson, E., 1950, *Childhood and Society*, New York: Norton.
91. Piaget J., 1973, *The Child and Reality: Problems of Genetic Psychology*, New York: Grossman.
92. Inhelder, B., and J. Piaget, 1958, *The Growth of Logical Thinking from Childhood to Adolescence*, New York: Basic Books.
93. Erikson, E.H., 1950, *Childhood and Society*, New York: Norton.
94. Piaget, J., 1965, *The Moral Judgment of the Child*, New York, Free Press.
95. Mead, M., 1964, *Continuities in Cultural Evolution*, New Haven: Yale University Press.
96. Hull, C.L., 1943, *Principles of Behaviour*, New York: Appleton Century Crofts.
97. Cohen, R., 1985, 'What's so special about spatial cognition?' in R. Cohen (ed.), *The Development of Spatial Cognition*, pp. 1-12, Hillsdale, NJ: Erlbaum.
98. K. Ishwaran (ed.), 1970, *Change and Continuity in India's Villages*, New York and London: Columbia University Press.

99. Basu, S.R. (ed.), 2002, *Changing Environmental Scenario of the Indian Subcontinent*, Kolkata: ACB Publishers.
100. Bronfenbrenner, U., 1993, 'The ecology of cognitive development: research models and fugitive findings', in R.H. Wozniak and K.W. Fischer (eds.), *Development in Context: Acting and Thinking in Specific Environments*, pp.3-44. Hillsdale, N.J: Erlbaum.
101. Lewin, K., 1951, *Field Theory in Social Science*, New York: Harper & Row.
102. Murray, H.A., 1938, *Explorations in Personality*, New York: Oxford University Press.
103. Elder, G.H. Jr., 1996, 'Human lives in changing societies: Life course and developmental insights', in R.B. Cairns, G.H. Elder Jr., and E.J. Costello (eds.), *Developmental Science*, pp. 31-62. Cambridge, UK: Cambridge University Press.
104. Lewin K., 1936, *Principles of Topological Psychology*, New York: McGraw Hill.
105. Lewin, K., 1951, *Field Theory in Social Science*, New York: Harper; Wolfgang, Kohler, 1959, *Gestalt Psychology Today (1)*, First published *in American Psychologist, 14, 727-734.*
106. Desai, Sonalde B., Amaresh Dubey, Brij Lal Joshi, Mitali Sen, Abusaleh Shariff, and Reeve Venneman, 2010, *Human Development in India: Challenges for a Society in Transition*. New Delhi: Oxford University Press.
107. *Ibid.*
108. Hall, C.S., G. Lindzey and John B. Cambell, 1998, 'Personality theory in perspective", Chapter 5 in Hall, C.S., G. Lindzey and John B. Cambell, *Theories of Personality*, New York: Wiley & Sons Inc., pp. 630-651.
109. Baldwin, A.L., 1980, 'Towards an integrated theory of child development', in A. Baldwin, *Theories of Child Development*, New York: New York, pp. 537-538.

5

The Correlates of the Developing Personality

This chapter consists of the following sections:

1. Biological bases of development and cognition;
2. Cultural systems of behaviour;
3. The social structure of valued systems of behaviour;
4. The dynamics of consistency and inconsistency in behaviour;
5. The maintenance of identity in the Indian Structural System;
6. Modes of normative behaviour;
7. Communication and societal ethos;
8. Cultural relativity;
9. Multiculturalism in India;
10. Cross eco-cultural considerations;
11. Selected parameters among selected varying cultures;
12. The kaleidoscopic development of the individual in varying cultural ecologies;
13. The lifestyles of the majority;
14. Traditionalism and Scienticism: A pot-pourri of relational systems; and
15. Acceleration of socio-cultural change.

1. Biological Bases of Development and Cognition

There is a growing emphasis on studying individual differences. Amplified, it means that developing organisms of the same species use different pathways to reach the same point in development. For example, children of the same chronological age who are twins can grow along the continuum towards adolescence but exhibit differential attributes.

The simple cellular organisation as ordered at birth change dynamically as development progresses, through complex intercellular integration, which occurs throughout life[1] (Weiss, P., 1959). During the physical development process, some groups of cells may get mutated or degenerated. Some of the major diseases that deplete intellectual development like Alzheimer's and dementia occur due to cellular degeneration in the old age.[2] (Knight, R.G., 1992) However, congenital mutation, due to lacunae in chromosome patterns, may occur in early childhood, such as autism, mongolism and sensory defects. These and increased senility due to sensory degeneration occur during the development period. These are apart from traumas experienced by individuals during the lifespan like loss of close relatives and unexpected physical incapacitation due to accidents. Besides genes, individuals inherit not only a standard embryonic and foetal stimulating environment but also the effects of the human situations they encounter. *Parents, relatives and peers modify the orthogenetic niche (the development of phylogenetic and ontogenetic traits).* These influence the stimulating effect of the outer sensations on the development from the early childhood through adolescence. After adolescence it plateaus out during adulthood and decelerates as old age occurs.

The psychogenic basis provides a linkage between behaviour and the influences of heredity, and the ways diverse individuals develop the unique differences they exhibit. The laws of heredity are also evidences of the intermix of inherited genetic traits and one's own epigenetic development of psychological domains based on inheritance of dominant genes. For instance, it is not uncommon that individuals look very much like one parent and not the other, or the grandparent. They exhibit different physiological attributes and psychological traits. These depend largely upon the arrangement and potentials of the genes[3] (Jennings, H.S., 1930: 3). This theoretical concept is by far one of the most promising. As more medical and scientific data indicate the close relation between the mind and the processes in the brain, the utility of examining phylogenetic and ontogenetic sources of behaviour is essential. *Greater importance is increasingly being given in the neuroscience, to the relation between the mind (abstract) and the brain (concrete) aspects of thinking.*

The recognition of the operation of genes transmitted from one generation to another is still evident in commonplace sayings like these children have similar values as they come from the same family or boys are more aggressive than girls as boys are taught to imitate their fathers and girls to imitate their mothers. The most prominent evidence is defective physical and mental characteristics. It is said that because of the doubling of genes in the formation of a new foetus and their transmission of physical characteristics, including defects, to the young generation, further research is important for the future generation as they are influenced by the pairing of parental genes.[4] (Jennings, H.S., 1930 : 3) These are clearly apparent in cases of brain damage leading to retarded intelligence of various degrees, or in the case of sensory defects. It is also evident in hormonal imbalances causing disorders like cretinism.[5] (Merke, F., 1984)

Factors such as pregnant mother's smoking, use of alcohol, and maternal illness may act upon a developing foetus to result in Mongolism, stunted growth and mental retardation.[6] (Cullen, J.F., and H.G. Butler, 1963) Cognitive abilities are attuned to the recognition of one's abilities and the cognition of others.

In the past three decades or so, tomes have been written on the effect of control and experimentation with animals in these areas of enquiry.[7] (Singh, M., 2000) Animal experiments have been attempted by psychologists in the laboratory and the field situation[8] (Singh, M., 2000: 34) and the results have been used as possible extrapolations to humans in the biological and physiological domains. Such extrapolations are still debatable in terms of cognitive and human behaviour development. Manual states that the limbic system plays an important part in motivation, learning and memory, however, few experiments have been done on humans to substantiate these findings adequately.[9] (Singh, M., and 2000: 34)

In most research on the central nervous system and the autonomic nervous system, electrophysiological methods have been used to measure minute imbalances or aberrations (EEG/EMG/DGR/IMR/ECG). These changes indicate the neural and synaptic systems, impacting on psychological characteristics which are clearly detected through visual imagery.[10] (Mandal, M., 2000: 80) Electrode positioning gives encoding of behaviour through radio telemetry. These methods assess neurological diseases related to pathological conditions: dementia, epilepsy, atherosclerosis and intracranial infection. These can be detected at early stages for their control. These findings, however, are restricted to clinical experiments and cannot be extrapolated to the normally functioning human brain. The linkage between foetal injury and performance deficit of the individual is not fully known. These latter are related to maladaptive behaviour and give scarce information about normal personality development in the behavioural domain. The biological and physical sciences have worked closely in evidencing such relationships, as depicted in the following paradigm:

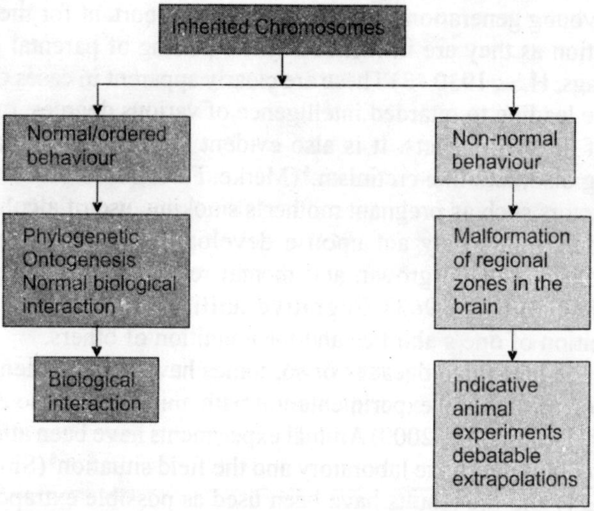

Paradigm 5.1: Biological and Physiological Bases of Development

2. Cultural Systems of Behaviour

In India today, at all levels, most of the attitudes and behaviour of the younger generation, to some degree or the other, is changing. These changes are in confrontation with the societal norms, prevalent in the different ecologies. We may cite a few examples that have risen over time and space, in the last two decades. There are more family disorganisations, growing in complexity, such as premarital sex, drug addiction, dangerous sex (occurrence of HIV/AIDS) and distancing between parental and child generations.[11] (Moorthy, K.S., 2008) Even after marriage, marital conflict, separations and divorce are beginning to surface more frequently, especially in urban areas. While these phenomena are more or less accepted in the West, in India, socialisation during childhood does not equip the younger generation to deal adequately with such types of traumatic experiences. With the *stress on achievement and being competitive, especially in the upper classes, more youngsters are becoming less able to cope with crisis situations such as educational and professional examinations*. India represents several layers of culturally tinged families, from the very elementary in the untouched and inaccessible forests, to the overly sophisticated elite in metropolitan cities. Pressures to conform to modes at each level are affecting the different age groups within each ecology differentially. The tribal adult wants to become an urbanite. The urban adult wants to become an international figure. On the other hand, each group tries to retain the identity of its members as a whole, leading to a "conflict zone" between the old and the new. Adolescence and young adulthood are becoming increasingly concerning areas of academic enquiry, as these are stages where there is much pressure and turmoil.

Irrespective of the generational pressure to conform, the gap between westernisation and traditionalism is gradually becoming wider between the elite and the poor. In western cultures, children are cognitively attuned to deal with such pressures. In western ecologies, there are many support systems in their ecologies, such as the school and neighbourhood, the community and even on a psycho-clinical services. In India, unfortunately, adherence to these societal norms is becoming distorted without adequate compensatory support systems. For example, more abortions of unmarried college and, sometimes, high school girls are occurring, without a network to support young females in these traumatic situations. In the upper echelons, pre-parital sex and live-in partnerships are also creating inroads. The existence of some drug de-addiction centres only touches the tip of the iceberg of the need for rehabilitation in India. Suicides in cities and even in semi-urban ecologies are on the increase due to intergenerational conflict, youngsters wanting to marry outside their normative caste and class, depression due to the indiscriminate use of drugs, and also failure in academics. Therefore, it is stressed that traditional norms of behaviour are losing their "rootedness" in this century and the struggles to attempt to preserve one's cultural heritage are becoming weak in the face of the influences from western cultures. It appears that the strong advertising and social media channels are drawing the adolescents and young adults towards imitation of western cultures. The ways of the westernised ecologies seem to have a stronghold than do adults in their ecologies. Although the attempts to retain the cultural heritage are slipping away, mostly in the modernised elite, the "rootedness" still prevails in some form or the other. One might also say that there is a conscious movement for revival of the Hindu cultural norms, especially in terms of socio-religious ritualism as reflected in media and the celluloid world.

Social structures are based upon the individuals' functionality in society, their configurations through social modes of behaviour, and "system maintenance" efforts. In all societies of the world, whether primitive or modernised, there is a system of social organisation based on regulatory mechanisms. What are these regulatory mechanisms in differing cultures? We have attempted to illustrate them in the following flow-chart:

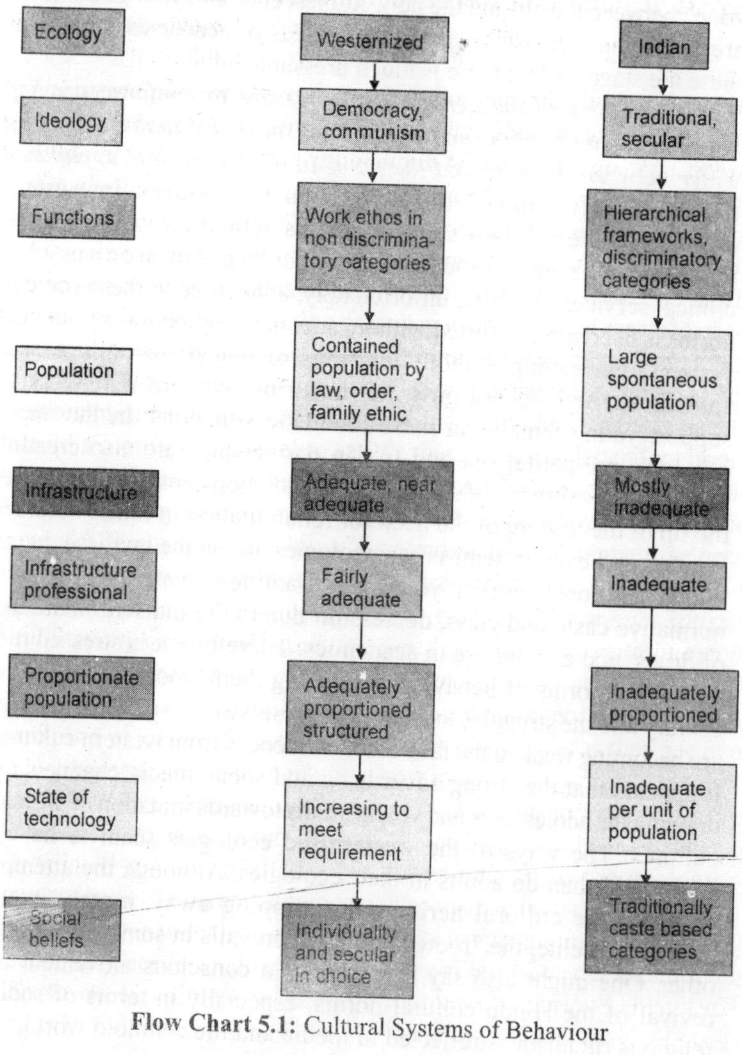

Flow Chart 5.1: Cultural Systems of Behaviour

In the western ethos, it is anti-social adult behaviour to physically punish a child, whereas in eastern countries, it is common place in rural areas. In the west, reaction to a child's behaviour is through "love withdrawal techniques"[12] (Sears, R., E. Maccoby and H. Levin, 1957: 443-486) and "time out". In the Indian situation, the parent may not use "love-oriented techniques" but may use threats and physical punishment. It is not yet clear as to why the child is more attuned to material things, when we say that the child is brought up according to the Indian philosophy, to the spiritual aspects of life. It is possible that the experience of deprivation in most of our families is so strongly ingrained, that the acquisitive nature of children during their growing years is high profiled due to lack of need satisfaction.

In the Indian societal structure, *law refers to two aspects: (1) the religious mandates or the laws set down in religion, and (2) the laws of the secular state*. Through a process of elaboration such events as division of property rights by lineage, and by sex are determined by the Hindu law.[13] (Stork, H., 1980) So is the distribution of property in the Muslim religious law where usually the male is the privileged. But in cases like marriage, divorce, and the custody of children, the secular law assumes predominance. Its implementation however is weak, many cases do not appear in court. Honesty and justice, are tendencies influenced from birth, by the human and material environment. For instance, studies have shown that children will cheat in the absence of supervision, which implies that unless the authority is physically present, children attempt to achieve through dishonest means.[14] (Hartshone, H., and May, M.A., 1928) The frequent reason given as to why a person does not come to work on time is because "his grandmother has died" or he has "to take his wife to the hospital" or some such, and often times elaborate excuses which in our culture compels us to overlook, although we know it may not be entirely true. The Indian *dharma*, compels us to be compassionate or to behave compassionately when another is in distress. On the other hand, a child who is constantly in a disorganised family situation, learns also not to abide by the rules of right behaviour, for his anxiety and conflict over his parental quarrels, his father's alcoholism or infidelity, and the distress caused to his mother may lead him to anti-social behaviour and delinquency as a protest against conformity. In this case, wrong becomes right, and his sense of superego is blunted, since he knows no other way of castigating his parents. *Therefore, internalising the values of right and wrong are learned behaviour either from the scriptures or from behaviour of those socially valued models surrounding the individual, and the reinforcement to internalise what is right or just and what is wrong.*[15] (Deutsch, M., 1975) There are, of course, many forms of redress of such dissonance. In the main, when there is a transgression against societal norms, damage to civic property or to another human being, then justice is meted out according to the law of the land. More serious transgressions such as rape, incest and physical abuse of children and wives generally go unnoticed in most developing societies, as there is no freedom given to females/children to protest or to be heard. This is not to say that such situations are tolerated. There are many movements, by several NGOs who take up the cause of the unjustifiably treated women and children. Especially those who live under poor ecological conditions. But, these happenings are part of the ingrained ethic of the society, or the sub-society to which the individual belongs, where he is expected to tolerate others' wrong doings. To put it succinctly, a child in an upper income group who goes to a good school, who is not economically deprived, is likely to know and practice right from wrong. A child who lives in an overcrowded *jhuggi* area in close geo-ecological proximity to other familes[16] (Pandey, J., 1987), where social disorganisation tends to prevail, is likely to turn out to be aggressive, crafty and almost like an adult in his behaviour, trying to snatch any opportunity to better himself. This is not to say that children from the upper elite do not, therefore, turn out to be non-conformists. Their deprivation which drives them to non-conformity is mainly emotional such as neglect of the family, indifference to their needs and lack of communication between them and the older generation.

In a brief review of the conceptualisation of justice, western experts such as Adams,[17] (Adams, J.S., 1965), Levinthal[18] (Leventhal, G.S., 1976) Greenberg and Cohen[19] (Greenberg, J., and R.I. Cohen, 1982), have commented that *the equity theory is based on the individual's expectations, and that there is a proportionality between rewards, costs and their investments*. In the mandates of developed countries, these are reflected in the ideals of democracy and justice in their political histories. In short they imply that rules are to be followed equally by all, irrespective of the status of the citizen, and that reward and punishment are equitably meted out.

3. The Social Structure of Valued Systems of Behaviour

The previous chapters on ecology dealt with the paradigmatic variations in the configuration of the Indian ecology. *This chapter will move into the relational aspects of the ecological systems impinging on developmental behaviour, psychological, sociological and cultural affiliatives.*

(A) Psychological

In the psychological domain the major configurations are two:

1. Congruence of behaviour with ethical values in the sub-culture.
2. Congruence and continuity with socially approved behaviour.

(1) Congruence of Behaviour with Ethical Values in the Sub-cultures

The concepts of ethical values and justice have received much attention in the area of cross-cultural research.[20] (Kagitcibasi, C., and J.W. Berry, 1989) Morality has high profile in the Indian's psyche, and is related to the value given to justice from the Hindu philosophical viewpoint. These concepts were originally from the epics of the *Ramayana,* the *Mahabharata*, and from the *Dharmashastras*, *Manusmriti,* as also from the later writings like Kautilya's *Arthashastra.* The major concepts, as commented upon by Krishnan,[21] (Krishnan, L., 2000: 186) are as follows:

(a) "*Vyavahara*" (behaviour) as observed in *laukik* (worldly) manifestations.

(b) "*Nyaya*" which is the most commonly used term for "fairness'. This most closely meets the concept of justice/ equality. *Nyaya* is one of the main Indian philosophical systems dealing with logic, argumentation, and such like.

(c) "Justice" as we know it in the everyday world of communication, is mentioned, alluded indirectly in aphorisms, codes in various texts, anecdotes, parables and dialogues on the self. These are interpreted from the scriptural texts. "*Nyaya*", however, is the Hindu philosophical concept of the term "justice" (fairness), in the context of spiritual ethos.

(d) *"Neeti" is an expression of justice. This term implies policies which are broadly ethical or moral codes.* Such concepts in the Hindu philosophy are perhaps based on the epics and the *Shastras.* The major theme is that equity, as enjoined by religious injunctions, should supersede man-made codes based on civil laws, where, one gets what one deserves which is implicit in the relationship between thought and action.[22] (Krishnan, L., 2000: 119) These are important markers in the constructs of the Indian value system, as they are implicit in the scriptures. They arise from the interpretations of sages who explain morality and justice and indeed are alluded to in the democratic principles enunciated by governance. *Equity, however, comprises a host of in-depth meanings which may not be similarly understood by a non-Indian. To the latter, equity might mean that everybody has access to the same opportunities and facilities.* However, in the Indian context it has a philosophical meaning, that everybody is born to seek his own opportunities, which are equally available to all. But in the interpretation of this aspect of the Hindu way of life, the Hindu society through the ages has gradually allocated different status to different social groups. In this division, we may interpret equity within the group but not among different groups. Thus, these groups were formally composed as caste, class and ethnicity. The individual does not choose his position, it is allotted to him at birth wherein the tasks socially ascribed to the position he occupies are pre-formulated. If each individual performs according to his pre-formulated position, he then is equitable with others, who themselves are expected to also perform their allotted tasks equitably. Translated into religious thought, *"vyavahara"* is the *karma* of the caste in which the individual is born. It is predestined by the former incarnations and the labeling of groupism (caste, ethnicity) has been given by leaders and overlords from early civilization. *"Nyaya" or distributive equity does not imply homogeneity of behaviour,* but that the particular expected behaviour is *attributed to one's 'sthiti" or position. As* such, behaviour is interpreted by the caste, ethnic group and the cultural ascribed role performances, like the Brahmin is the priest, who is the highest in the caste system and, therefore, begets the highest reverence for his purity status. The *kshatriya* is expected to be warrior like, the *vaishyas* should be business minded, and the *shudra* are lower in caste positions and are allocated lowly occupations.

(e) *The individual's behaviour according to religious philosophy:* The characteristic relationship between action and outcome is observable in everyday life. *The average Indian is habitually prone to attribute the outcome of his actions to causes other than himself: a* dharmic *attitude*. For instance, if a person is late to work, he rationalises, as follows: "there was a traffic jam" or "I had to take my ailing child to the hospital" or some such reason outside himself, and is not attuned to relate the cause to himself. Otherwise, the usual refrain is "I thought I should do it this way" *(hum ne socha aise karna chahiye*), but "I did not cause the situation to occur" or " *hum ne nahin kiya"* meaning I am not responsible for the way in which the action has had this consequence. In psychology this behaviour is termed as "evasion", "rationalisation", "projection", and "such like the ego defence mechanisms detailed in the chapter "Selected Personality Theories relevant to the Indian Psyche".

"Justice" or "*nyaya*" is the acceptance of crises as being destined. Perhaps, it is this attitude which gives the Indian a greater tolerance and resilience to mishap, or the occurrence of a negative experience or unintended consequence. The usual saying is "it happens this way" (*aisa hi hota hai*). When one experiences tragedy, one attributes it to destiny or *karma,* even if the individual could have done something to avert the incident. The individual's perception, is of experiencing a sense of justice. According to Hindu philosophy, the event was inevitable as the consequence of an act (*karma*). This, therefore, contributes to a sense of equanimity in the face of a crisis or tragedy. Indians by and large, tend to accept everyday happenings in a casual manner as routine happenings. It is only when there is mass meeting where he is like one of the others, that he cognises that he is also responsible for the event/ action, with the others as in protest marches.

(f) *Socio-religious value systems:* Even the aphorism of saying: "you reap what you sow" in the biblical sense is equivalent to the idiomatic saying *of "jaisa boya waisa paya"*, meaning as you sow, so you reap, implying that the reaction is caused by an action. Perhaps this attitude tends to colour the collectivistic tendency of the Indian and to downplay individualism where normally as in the west "one is responsible for one's own actions". Thus, the individual acts and reacts to events sequentially, and often in a circular manner, akin to the saying "what goes around must come around". *Piaget's writing on the development of morality, and Kohlberg's thesis on honesty and justice in children, look at these concepts purely in terms of the individual's perception of the action and its consequence*[23] (Piaget, J., 1930: 309; Kohlberg, L., 1981 and 1984). *For* instance, according to these concepts, "If I hit someone, it is wrong", "If I help some one, it is right". *The individual's super-ego or the voice of conscience, translated into reality terms, the voice of the authority*, the repository of which is usually the patriarch in a family. They simply follow instructions from their own parental generation as a traditional habit, assuming that authority cannot be wrong. This oral tradition is richly imbued in the Hindu way of life. They influence the individual's feelings and, therefore, behaviour regarding what is right or what is wrong, and what deserves punishment or reward is inbuilt in the developing personality. Valued behaviour such as morality righteousness ethical and, charitable acts sharing and compassion and a sense of empathy for the other's troubles are transmitted orally by traditional modes.

In the paradigm above we have delineated several strands of sources of socio-religious beliefs, both those which contribute to a nexus of socio-religious codes of behaviour and those which negate them. *The amalgam of socio-religious values and their relevant behaviour arise out of the context of a package of sources, as given in the paradigm above, which together allocate a status for the individual in the social system.* Value systems arise out of the context of the human ecology. These consist of the family, the kinship group, which are the closest groups to the individual in influencing his value systems in the given micro-ecosystem.

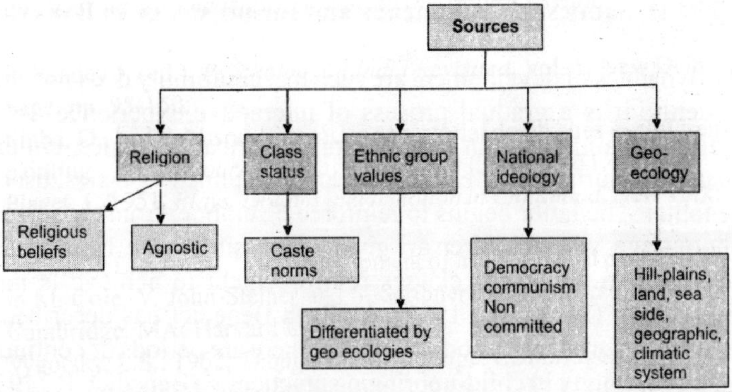

Paradigm 5.2: Sources of Socio-Religious Systems

(2) Congruence and Continuity with Socially Approved Behaviour

As a corollary to the co-existence of homogeneity and heterogeneity in the Indian culture, there are also the interactive concepts of continuity or discontinuity, and conformity or non-conformity in societal norms. On the one hand if one is attuned towards homogeneity of behaviour in the generic Indian culture, it follows that there are more conformist than non-conformists to socially approved behaviour. On the other hand, it is well known that there is no one homogeneous pattern overriding the Indian in his various ecologies. *Socially approved behaviour is differentially perceived from one sub-cultural stratum to another, each is related to its environmental ecology of humans and their interaction within their geo-ecological spaces*. The Indian psyche is crisscrossed by several intervening factors like ethnicity, socio-economic class and the like, which mediate the dimensions of continuity and conformity, as they occur in the interactional process. For example, in the early years of childhood the caretaking practices are mainly for physical well-being. In the primary school years, however, there begins to be the practice of inculcating valued behaviour and, therefore, a discontinuity in the casualness of care taking in the previous pattern. Now the child is given responsibilities according to traditionally known ways, such as helping in household chores for the girl child and helping in the occupational tasks for the male child in rural and tribal areas. The pattern changes for the urban child who is expected to attend formal school and to take responsibility for his actions.

4. The Dynamics of Consistency and Inconsistency in Behaviour

The dynamics of development are such that conformity does not occur suddenly. It is a gradual process of interactive experience. In the traditional family, and in remote rural and tribal ecologies, children are usually nurtured by females, but are disciplined by males, usually the father. The latter begins to reinforce discipline, from the primary school stage, when children are given responsible tasks, in increasing measures. In the upper classes reinforcement to achieve is more observable[24] (Misra, R., 1971). As Ruth Benedict has described in her writings on "Childhood in Samoa", there are periods of continuity and discontinuity in child-upbringing practices.[25] (Benedict, R., 1938) Discipline is the crux of the adult reinforcement techniques to conform the growing child's behaviour to societal norms.[26] (Khalakdina, M.,1979: p. 212) *Kakar has referred to this phenomenon of discontinuity at the psycho-clinical stage of abrupt weaning and its possible consequent trauma.*[27] (Kakar, S., 1981) *Bowlby has elaborated on this dependency behaviour between the mother and child in his classical exposition of "attachment and loss".*[28] (Bowlby, J., 1981) Thus, the individual, at the stage of about primary school years, when his ability for cognitive formal operations in cognition appear, is expected to suddenly conform to adult behaviour roles through imitative learning. In rural ecologies, this adherence to responsibility-taking emanating from the adult, is expected to continue well into adulthood, where the male child is expected to be responsible for the welfare of his family of procreation and elderly relatives. The tendency in such ecologies is that family members in the same occupation tend to live together in a joint household dividing the tasks and sharing each other's experiences. In urban ecologies, in deprived sections, the individual procures his means of livelihood from petty tasks, like selling newspapers or working at stations or market places, and such like. In this ecology, there is a mixture of joint and nuclear families living side by side. In local residential urban areas, there is almost always nuclear families as occupations differ and interests are separate. So, we observe here a clear relation among ecology, occupation and type of family. *The sudden thrust of responsibility and accountability at about the primary school stage, often leads to unpreparedness on the child's part, and he, therefore, tends to develop resistance to conformity and yet conforms because social norms dictate this.* He either conforms by force which is against his natural tendencies, or conforms apathetically, or even worse is in a conflict situation, becoming dangerously close to being 'street smart', or is close to being exploited or criminalised in these deprived sections. It appears that conforming to socially approved and expected roles is not easy for the male, but is easier for the female who is discouraged from the normal avenues of enterprise given to male children. Cultural norms of a given human ecological system, dictate that anti-normative behaviour is not condoned. *Since most families live in poor sections of the society, in deprived ecologies, they are more preoccupied in eking out a living for their daily needs. Therefore, the upbringing patterns of their children are unrelated to considerations of the psychological impact of socialisation techniques.* The major objective is to structure the child into behaving in a culturally approved manner. These may be identified as performing chores and following instructions, participating in family occupations and/or younger siblings during later childhood. Males are expected to earn a living, carry family responsibilities and observe the household of the wife, children and the elders. For females, cultural norms dictate that they be brought up as respectful, obedient, feminine, good at house keeping and be deft in caring of children but, most of all, to be submissive towards her in-laws and loyal towards her husband. *In this entire rubric, however, and in the dynamics of social change brought about by high-tech ecologies, both sexes of children are beginning to break away from these longstanding traditional bonds. Their influences are more those that emanate from their peers and social media, and less from parental sources.*

5. The Maintenance of Identity in the Indian System of Policy

After Independence, India framed a Constitution based on the principles of democracy, secularism and justice for all. To implement these complex Constitutional principles in a generally illiterate and traditional society, various barriers are experienced. This occurs as there are many bifurcations along religious, caste and community lines. The vast majority of the Indian people little understood the mandates of the Constitution. In the main, however, the major precepts are now somewhat understood and abided by. True, there are many aberrations along the way, but by and large the courts are seen as the seat of dispensing justice, even if delayed in action. However, as said before, *a society in transition takes a long while to adjust to new statements and policies of governance*. While there are many infrastructural and personnel inadequacies in policies and programmes, law and justice and their implementation is generally respected by the public. However, ethical ethos has yet to take a stronghold in everyday interactions, as many forms of corruption, both overt and covert, exist. What we are implying is that intuitively these rules are understood and accepted, but when we observe the implementation of justice the consequences get diffused. Subsidies to government employees, and credit schemes for the poor and the disadvantaged are in place in theory, in practice the population is so large and dispersed and revenues are scarce, many goals are underachieved, especially among the under privileged.

India is a land of people who live in village ecologies, and live under the poverty line and in deprived economic conditions. With the large gap between the rich and poor, and the size of the population that lives in economically deprived conditions, the concept of equity at the level of social reality in terms of policies and privileges is indifferently understood by the poor and what is more is dealt with greater corruption with the poor than with the rich.

Cognisance should be taken of the socio-political system, where higher rewards go to those who wield a higher power, have a higher authority figure, and have greater control. Chatterjee has studied the rewards systems among Machiavellian and non-Machiavellian males and found this to be a consistent factor.[29] (Chatterjee, L., 1984) It is easy to observe that this rewards system is related to the traditional *jajman* system where relatives in higher power structures such as being a politician brings about higher rewards which in turn is redistributed among the kin group and *biradari:* a kind of political nepotism prevailing. We see the operation of this behaviour, for example, in the superordinate-subordinate relationships among employers and employees in the Indian system. However, criss-crossing the system are interactive variables such as caste, class, ethnicity and regionalism. It is not uncommon in these intra-relationships for a *Harijan* (now called a member of a Scheduled Caste) to take a backward step in relation to a person belonging to the Brahmin caste at a temple ceremony, although these two persons may be of equal status as employees in a factory. These differing ecological situations contour behaviour in favour of the identity required in a given ecology. In the example above, the caste structure is adhered to in traditional ecologies, and diffused in the modernising trend, which causes disorganization among castes and classes. In the former situation identity is well pronounced and in the latter it becomes diffused.

The identity of the individual in such changing systems to which he has to adapt from the traditional mode to the modernizing mode of democracy and secularism diffuses his identity. Such is the case of the migrant who works temporarily in urban areas. He has two identities, one in his village and the other in his place of work. New systems and structures taking place in the attempt of India's participation in globalisation and as a member in several international forums, has its feedback in media both national and local. These happenings affect the individual's psyche at different rates at different times, in a given geo-ecological place. These influences occur at all levels. In his adjustment, the individual sometimes reverts to his old habits of behaviour in the traditional milieu. Such is the behaviour of a typical urban youth in India who is traditional in the family circles, the micro ecosystem, and modern in his interactions with members of his peer group.

6. Modes of Normative Behaviour

Culture is an abstract term, but its operationalisation does not occur in a vacuum. *The modes of behaviour accepted as normative are transmitted from one generation to another as cultural heritage.* It may be reasonable to assume that the primary source of communication is the parental generation, the kin group structure, oral traditions and media. These may be also assumed to be representative of modes of behaviour that are significant in a given society at a given time. *We are not implying that modes are static. They themselves vacillate from time to time, and so each individual has to extract from these modular expressions, as to what is sanctioned behaviour and adapt them to his own personality structure within his given ecology.*

Thus, communication and its variations are the major mode of cultural transmission on patterns of living over generations. The value of retaining such cultural modes of communication, helps document the past eras preserved as heritage in museums, architecture and historical monuments, so that the national identity is profiled constantly. Such communication through visible signs of heritage link the current culture with the past in a continuous chain for posterity.

As societies move along the dimension of social change, some sub-strata discard some cultural forms, adapt to others and, over time, incorporate them into behaviour. They tend to transform these behaviours in line with the changing needs of the society, as the older forms in turn become obsolete. For instance, we have come a long way from the stage of the printing press to the versatile mobile which does everything and is all in one, denoting a high level of technology to which humans adapt. Therefore, the Indian, requires to know how to manipulate technology to serve his needs at a faster pace more efficiently and more effectively.

Individuals learn early, through constructing and reconstructing the stimuli around them, to anticipate the expected outcomes of their actions. They learn by experience, the ways in which they need to change their behaviour to cues within their social environment, which fit their own needs. In urbanised ecologies, where extra-familial care of the young is available, varying styles of child care management are desired: some of them in different quality.[30] (Khalakdina, M.,1998) In common everyday life there is a likelihood to perceive members of a cohort of peers alike, as in a formal classroom situation, without an understanding of individual differences.[31] (Woodhead, Martin, 2001: 78) If we extrapolate such a concept to the Indian situation, we see similar scenes within varying age groups. For instance, when the young child is able to vocalise his needs he is indulged in, but in later years such expressed needs are conditioned by adult caretakers. In later growing years, individual differences are observable when each child uses different and alternate strategies of how he is expected to behave. He learns to live with an inner self and an outer self, moving from concentration on self-needs or ego-centricism, to considering the needs of others or socio-centricism[32] (International Society for study of Behavioural Development, India, 1995). Over time he learns to internalise the need to conform to expected social behaviour. Harsh and authoritarian disciplinary measures only serve to bring about a schism between the adult's expectation and the individual child's needs. This is especially marked when communication by demands, commands and physical punishment accompany the expressed and expected behaviour. In the Indian situation since the bond is strong between the nurturer and the nurtured[33] (Ainsworth, D.S., 1972), it provides cues for casual interaction in disciplinary measures used. For instance, it is quite common for a mother to impose a punishment, and on the continuous pleading crying or tantrum of the child to give in, and allow the child to have his own way. In this respect the authority of the father is more consistent in using disciplinary measures. *Over time, because of the close proximity of living, the adult and the child grow to learn from each other from their body language. Even when there is no communication,* vibes from one to the other are quickly understood and either adapted to or ignored. For, in the area of communication of cultural modes, it is important to underscore that it is not only the child who is persuaded or directed to learn a certain type of behaviour, but that the adult on his/her part learns to anticipate behaviours from the child and learns the cues to prompt the required behaviour. For example, parents, especially urban, usually have set goals for the academic achievement of their children. They frequently need to remind their children to study to achieve. The nurturer is often aware that if he insists, the child baulks and reacts negatively. Therefore, the parent may need to find alternative strategies for motivating the child to study, and thereby meet the parents' goals. These interactions are learned over time and are tactical in nature. Parents tend to be sensitive about perceptions of the management of their children as perceived by neighbours and friends and, therefore, tend to act according to societal expectations by being decorous in public with their children, so that the child is perceived as being "well brought up".

Over time and with increasing maturity, the child internalises modes of learned behaviour, communicated by adults which then become his personal cultural traits. To change or modify such cultural tendencies as growing independency in adolescent children, for instance, requires the adults to move from traditional methods of interaction, towards modes of democratic interaction, where the child is offered challenges to attain the communicated behaviour transmitted by the parent.

In all these milieus, it is important to recognize that children being quick learners also learn that parental behaviour should be in conformity with societal norms. For instance, if the parent is ill-mannered, sloppy and does not have a time consciousness, he cannot expect the opposite in his/her child. We are familiar with little children talking among peers about discrepancies in parental behaviour. They may be often heard to say, "My mother wants me to behave well, not shout, not get angry but she herself often does so". In translating these styles of communication, it is apparent that the child uses the parent unconsciously for the transmission of values. When there is a juxtaposition between what the parents say and what they do, the child perceives this inconsistency. This discrepancy in communication confuses the child's cognition of what is right and what is wrong. The child, thus, becomes hesitant and non-decisive in the performance of normative behaviour. For instance, children are very quick to observe when their parents are not being truthful. With their transparent nature, they eventually uncover the truth as children are frank and honest in the early nurturing years. Children also learn, like adults, to circumvent the truth when confronted. It is not unusual for a child to say, for instance, "but, why should I go to bed, when you are awake?" or "if you can use lipstick and nail-polish why cannot I." The child quickly learns that parents present two fronts, one for the public eye and one for the inward "household eye". In a later chapter, relating to personality, we will discuss social learning to understand how the child unconsciously models himself or herself according to the admired model of the same sex parent by the opposite sexed parent.

The above example is a simple illustration of a highly complex motivational analysis of the interaction between the parent and the child. This theory has been proposed by Bandura,[34] (Bandura, A., 1977) who explains this phenomenon on the basis of imitation and role-modelling, which is dealt with in detail in the chapter on "Selected theories relevant to the Indian psyche"

Several expected changes in the nurtured child may be met with resistance by the child, especially when the child grows into adolescence and is learning to become more independent. Internalised attitudes of the child in the modernising world destabilise authority and power structures prevalent over centuries.[35] (Suvannathat, C., D. Bhanthumnavin, L. Bhuapirom and D.M. Keats, 1985: 4-5) Further, as the child moves from the micro eco-system of the family into the meso system of interaction with others, there is a stronger attachment to the values of the peer group, who perceive heroes/heroines of the movies, of sports, of fashion-modelling world and such like as models to be imitated. Such roles models come and go off the "adolescent's screen", causing rapid changes in the models imitated. In family relations, it is acceptable that the child in the early stages learns to model behaviour, from the immediate family, but, later on, the sources widen to include many others, and are not only variable but also changeable, as the child grows through the many stages of development.

The phenomena of inter- and intra-cultural individualism occurs in interpreting generic characteristics. *Such generic characteristics are: the variables of socio-economic class, caste, religion, region and ethnicity, which interact in different degrees. The* outcomes of modulated behaviour are dependent to a greater level upon the motivation of the individual, rather than on the persuasive capacity of the micro ecology, whether familial or otherwise. It is perhaps true to say, however, that with a firm grounding in familial values, *the communicative themes, and the models to which the individual is exposed to are more likely to be internalised.* Each individual has a personal history of participation in social life, different from the others, even among siblings of the same family. There are also intra-cultural differences within the prism of "Indianess"; we can only assume a broad spectrum of conceptualisations for subcultures, as to how they give expression to cognise concepts like dominance, authority and such like attributes. *Each parenting adult may, for instance, have his/her own personal history, which he/she brings to bear on the parenting situation. This is especially emphasized in psychodynamic theories.*[36] (Horney, K., 1939; Maslow, A.H., 1970, Murray, H.A., 1936, Freud, S., 1964) It is not uncommon to hear, for instance, one mother telling her friend: "My mother did it this way, this is what I shall do", and so on. Often such conceptualisations cause researchers to present a picture of the reality of these interactions through ethnographic[37] (Whiting, J.W.M., and Child, I.L., 1953) and idiographic methodologies,[38] (Guba, E.G., 1990) rather than a nomethetic approach, as to what happens in social reality in actual familial settings.

It is often said that the general Indian public looks upon the disadvantage of the poor as being a part of the latter's *karma*. This is specifically the attitude of the rich towards the poor. It is often the perception of the rich, that the only way they can live with a non-guilty conscience about the difference between themselves and the disadvantaged, is to give *daan.* We commonly observe that when the rich pass by beggars, they tend to turn away, as if the beggars were non existent. It is neither apathy nor indifference, but simply a reversion to the rationalisation that we all have "*purana karma*" to undergo a destiny that is mandated from a previous life.

7. Communication and Societal Ethos

Since democracy has come into existence, there are policies to integrate scheduled castes and the scheduled tribes with the upper castes in the socio-political sphere. *Such a direction to implement "equality" which is one of the mandates of the Constitution brings about a covert struggle between socio-religious beliefs and secular-democratic beliefs.* These two sources of communication on socially sanctioned behaviour create a dichotomy in the learning patterns of the young. In schools, the young learn that all Indians are equal and yet at home, the lowly domestic servant in urban areas and a lower caste in the village is discriminated against. As the child grows, he has to come to terms with the fact that these two patterns co-exist. As he grows into an adult, he adopts a "compromise" attitude in simultaneously accepting these divisive perceptions.

It is increasingly evident that the children of this century are becoming more knowledgeable, experienced and self-confident in their occupational spheres, in comparison with *their parents when the latter (the parents) were young.* Whether this is due to the influences of westernization or modernization or both, we do not know precisely the patterns of relationships. There is also insufficient evidence to indicate what models parents hold up to their children to imitate, or what modes of communication are used for inducing socially approved behaviour in the children. *The fact remains that in increasing numbers, the new generation is moving towards a casteless society, especially among the urban elite young.* Although yet to have a "spread of effect", it is a fluid situation, given the homogenising effect of science and technology on behaviour. For instance, while there is still the practice of arranged marriages, there are also increasing numbers of self-selected marriages, and the use of the internet to find partners. We cannot state that this is happening across the board, yet it is unmistakably apparent in the upper elite, and the upper middle classes. The lower classes in their turn are imitating the upper classes in their behaviour as "imitative adaptation" in a spiralling effect.

Again, individual families have individual intra-culture diversities. For example, some parents disown their rebellious children who marry out of caste or even class. Still others reconcile to the situation and accept the inter-marriages. Personalities of parents differ. Some supervise their children rigidly, others are casual, still others are inconsistent. In families which adopt a democratic aura, it is marked with free and open communication. There are several strands of communication: with family members; with colleagues, in written communication or in inter-country conferences. The pressure to understand each other's language, even within India, from one State to another becomes a stressful situation especially in the orientation to achieve success. Increasingly even in the upper echelons of society emphasis is being placed on "how to convince others and manage business successfully". Achievement oriented individuals usually attempt to better their skills in order to rise in their profession, still others may not have the opportunities to do so. The modernizing of the economy, facilitated by technological advances, globalization of markets and liberalization of trade, has created the need for professional abilities and young adults find that they are earning beyond their expectations. However, with the present recession in the global economy, all countries, especially developing countries like India who work in the international sphere of businesses and commerce, are becoming destabilized, although it is said that India's GDP is growing fast. *Consequently, previously known roles both expected and performed are continually changing in the shuffling between modernisation and the old traditional styles of behaviour.*

Variability in communication of family ethics

Types of families	Communication	Modes of cultural communication
Traditional families (usually rural)	Infrequent usually traditional demands performance of roles	Submissive or rebellious
Modernising families (usually middle class)	Inconsistency in frequency and types of communication	Submissive and confrontation
Modernised families (usually upper class)	Free, spontaneous, liberal	Miscommunication inter generation gap in behaviour between parent and child

Paradigm 5.3: Expected and Performed Roles and their Variations

The expressions of emotionality are fairly high profiled in the Indian society.[39] (Paranjpe, A.C., and Bhatt, G.S., 1997: 130) Some societies are called stoic, as they are culturally attuned not to express emotions in their behaviour, such as in some of the east European societies. In the Indian society, informal learning inculcates habits like "it is alright for a woman to cry but not for men." It is not expected that women will mix freely with men. In rural communities, it is not expected that the daughter-in-law will be given to loud talk and laughter in the presence of male in-laws. It is permitted, however, that the younger brother-in-law is allowed to laugh and crack jokes with his older sister-in-law (Bhabhi). These are culturally approved behaviour which also intuitively give to the individual his cues as to the forms of approved emotional communication. When listening to a *Geeta* discourse, one should not talk, that is disrespectful. In a wedding, the more you eat and laugh and talk and even dance with the *baraat,* the more the hosts feel you are having a good time. When the subordinate wants to talk with his boss, he is quiet and submissive, but with his wife he need not be. These cultural frames give an individual the utilization of verbal and non-verbal behaviour at appropriate times, and with the appropriate peoples, adding emotive tones to his expressions.[40] (Argyle, M.,7)

8. Cultural Relativity

In traditional psychology, growth and development were explained on the basis of intuition, instinct, innate potentials, folk theory and naïve psychology.[41] (Murray, R., 2001) In those days, when life systems were routine and simple and the family system was extended and community-based, there was little consideration given to ecological influences. This was acceptable in the pre-Independence era. However, the variability in the social and economic flux over the past fifty years renders it necessary to understand the importance of environmental influences impinging on human behaviour.

In the previous era, growing demands were being amplified by informed explanations that the individual in the family is also accountable to the rest for his actions. Social change has increased this mode of thinking and behaving. The trend is that rural and tribal individuals migrate to urban areas in search of new avenues of occupations. The growing individual is increasingly in a household where both parents are working or where due to family disorganisation, there is only a single nurturer, who is to manage the economic aspects. These are relational correlates of a culture, which over many years bring about change in the size, shape and types of impact on the society at any given time.

The concept of relativity implies a relational linkage between one time frame and another and between one group and another in terms of cultural modes of behaviour. Time and space may not indicate that even adjacent groups will have the same social norms even at the same time. For instance, a businessman in a high-rise apartment and a construction worker lives at the construction site very close to the businessman's apartment, tend to live side by side but have different cultural modes of behaviour. What one group subscribes to may be radically different from those of the adjacent groups. By the same token, although in the current era, the old and young generation live together, the norms of one need not necessarily be subscribed to by the other. *Thus, cultural relativity taken as a cultural phrase implicitly means that culture over time and space is relative.*

For example, the cultural norms of the North-Eastern states are quite different from that of Gujarat, so when we speak of patriarchy or matriarchy, we know that this term is relative, as some States in the northeast are matriarchal in structure. Therefore, the types of behaviour within the family towards maternal and paternal loci differ. In the highly dense metropolis areas of Mumbai and Delhi, there is an inter-mix of cultures jostling side by side. For example, the Dharavi slums in central Mumbai have a completely different culture than those in sophisticated high-rise apartments nearby. Although it must be said that even in the slum areas several types of gadgetry are similar to those of the upper socio-economic group. For instance, television, cellular and such like are familiar items in migrant slum areas just as in high-rise apartments. In Delhi, a similar pattern exists as pavement dwellers live under flyovers, adjacent to posh residences. Therefore, to explicitly state that India has a distinctly homogeneous culture may be accepted as a generic statement. Culture is relative from one geo-ecological area to another, and from one sub-culture to another, as the operationalisation of culture is differentially available in each one of these.[42] (James, A., and Prout A., 1990) The dynamic process of normative behaviour can be conceptualized by assuming that there are norm-transmitters in the adult generation, namely, the parent, the teacher, and the *guru* and the norm-taker, namely, the younger in the cultural group. The norm-giver has to have many attributes, namely, control (emotional and economic), and power (decision-making, delegation and supervision of tasks) over the various members of the household/ kin group/organization.

Those subservient to the locus of power and control, assess the need and value of the norm in terms of self-fulfilment and self-advancement. For example, it is not uncommon to see small businesses run by fathers who are the patriarchs, but managed by the younger generation. These are delegated to younger relatives (sons, nephews and others), who work in the niche of control and power of the patriarch during which time they also parallely seek their own pathways and careers, although the final decision maker is the *Bauji* (the patriarch). In a somewhat different manner, this is also obvious between a child and a parent. The father is a norm giver. He sets down the rules for his unmarried adolescent daughters and there is a list of non-verbalised do's and don'ts. In traditional families, young and married girls are allowed geographical mobility in so far as they move around with young girls who are known to the family and within the geographical vicinity. Norms are instilled in the young by the adult norm givers so that the institutional infrastructures have continuous systemic role. It is not unusual, for instance, for parents to say, "you may go with Gita and Sheila to the movies since we know them and their families." However, "you have to come back straight home after it is over. You should not wander around after dark, it is not safe." *There may be discussions and arguments, but eventually a point is reached where either the norm taker redefines her need or the norm giver modifies the norm.* This process is a transaction of norms or transmission which are accepted fully or modified through negotiations. In highly conservative traditional families, however, there is hardly any room for such negotiation. The child either follows the rule or is punished for violation. In modernizing strata, family members communicate their stances and each attempt to understand the other and finally there is a via media adopted. This is more likely to happen in nuclear families. Where there is family disorganization (unhappy marital relations) among the norm-givers, the child tends to barter or takes sides or acquiesces with the weaker side. These dynamics are activated in microscopic family units. At the macro level, such types of transmissions of the culture of an organisation (organisation behaviour) are set down in the communications relating to staff and client interpersonal relations. These are communicated and monitored by HRD cells in most formal organisations.

On the other hand, moving to a different dimension, that of socio-religious norms, interactions among larger groups are accepted as being formal. For instance, different religious beliefs may operate in the same locality and there is usually a tacit acceptance and respect for such differing religious norms. For example, Sikhs and Muslims have lived together in the old city of Delhi and in the dense city areas of older Bombay, Hindus and Muslims live side by side. There is acceptance of and participation in the social rituals of each other. Conceptually, the dominant ethos prevails irrespective of the heterogeneity of these sub-cultures within the ethos of the dominant culture. For instance, while a Muslim does not enter a Hindu temple, neither does a Hindu enter a Muslim *dargah*, when Id and Diwali come around, each participate in the socio-cultural events of the other group. The Hindu religio-cultural symbols such as incense and flowers are also evident among the Muslims, the Parsis, the Sikhs and in fact most religious sects. Thus, transactions of valued behaviour move dynamically from one group to another. While not fully absorbed, they remain on the peripheral level as accepted and valued behaviour of the other. In India, therefore, there is a high level of tolerance of differences among the plurality of sub-cultures that exist adjacent to each other.

We have mentioned relativity about space. *Valued behaviour may be valid for a given time in the social history of a society, but changes may occur during the course of time.* We have seen civilizations come and go in the history of India, and while fine nuances may change, the core systems remain more or less the same. If we go back in history, we observe that in the phase of pre-independent India, Hinduism, in its variegated ethnicity, was dominant, and although there was strife between one feudal kingdom and another, they were mainly over territory. As the decades passed, these feudal kingdoms collapsed under the absolutism of the *zamindari* system, which fragmented the country into little principalities. During the current times, as the saying goes, "even a cabbage can look at a king." It is not uncommon to find erstwhile Rajas and *Nawabs* rubbing shoulders with lower socio-economic classes in parliamentary forums today, which give the latter equal status in the eyes of the law and democracy.[43] (Sharma, R.S., 1981) As one civilization moves into another, permutations and combinations take place, but the rootedness of the core culture remain cohesive in spite of variegations.

Transactions which change the nature of one sub-culture or the other do not validly alter their formats. They differ mainly in the socio-religious domain, in spite of the hackneyed phrase that India is truly a culture wherein there is "unity in diversity". Avoidance and acceptance exist conjointly, although differing in situations. Admittedly, modernising trends are slowly overtaking traditional public behaviour patterns, simply because the average Indian tend to separate work from home, in some measure or the other, perhaps less in rural and tribal areas, but more certainly in industrial and urbanised living spheres.[44] (Madan, A., 2003)

9. Multiculturalism in India

The Indian society is a unique mixture of ideologies and their practices, as affected by the ecological environment. Generically, being Indian is Indianism in the political sense. Socially and economically, there are vast differences, given the variable of differing ecologies. The differences are even wider in behavioural practices. There exists, as said before, structural differences among religions, among castes and classes, and more especially, in the identities of the variety of ethnic groups.[45] (Feagin, Joe R., and Clairece Booher Feagin, 2007) The intergenerational communication and their values have been the main tools in the social groups which differentiate one group from another. For instance, the Punjabi is distinctly different from the Bengali due to a nexus of differing ethos. The term 'ethnic' is both genealogical as well as socio-religious. For instance, there are Christians who live in North India, where they speak the same language as the Hindus, practice similar social customs but observe differing religious customs. Ethnicity in this context remains the same while religion varies. For example, among the people of Kerala, it would be difficult to distinguish who is a Christian or a Muslim or a Hindu from just the physical appearances. In other words, ethnicity is seemingly correlated to geo-ecological conditions. Thus, we find that ethnicity is dictated by the times in which small communities live in close proximity with each other. *This multi-culturalism has existed for centuries. However, there are alignments and realignments with the changing times that are brought about by new forms of science and technology*. Previously, for example, villagers had a civic entertainment mainly *melas*, *kathputli* and *demonstrations by travelling drama groups*. Now, a villager sits before a television set and learns about the world, thus, aligning him to the upper social group in this respect. The wealthy *Marwari* businessman's wife now goes to fashionable parties. In the past era, young girls were normatively not expected to display their bodies, but these days, commonly in urban areas, they dress even more skimpily than a westerner, whom they tend to imitate. Thus, multiculturalism in India has many combinations and permutations. Diffusion of characteristics from one culture to another is highly dependent upon the value attached to imitation of others, especially the socially elite, even though it might be alien to the value orientations of a traditional group.

Sociological theorizing has moved from evolutionary forms to functional forms. Functional analysis in turn has progressed to the process of what is termed social acculturation. This behaviour is an indigenous form of adaptation. The imitation of the upper by the lower caste, class is akin to Srinivas's conceptualisations of "westernisation" and "Sanskritisation". The latter refers to the process by which a low caste or tribe imitates the customs, rituals, beliefs, and ideology of a higher caste, particularly of the "twice-born", the Brahmin[46] (Carstairs, G.M., 1957).

What Srinivas termed as "westernisation" was the movement towards westernized modes of behaviour. *It is now accepted that the term westernisation in the current socio-political framework at the global level should be conceptualized as modernization or the adaptation to scientific and technological structures and systems.* Countries like Japan, Singapore, Hong Kong, Malaysia and the UAE all have adapted to modern technological changes and thus improved their economic and social statuses. They are not imitative of the west *in toto*, but have selectively changed their modes of lifestyles to be able to utilize the benefits of science and technology, while at the same time, maintaining their cultural norms. This process does not imply the adoption of the Anglo-Saxon ethos of living and thinking.[47] (Singh, Jaswant, 1997) Each nation has its own ethos, and its own perception of social history and culture. One nation perceives that having four wives is permissible, another insists on monogamy. Cults like the Mormons in the USA have their own perceptions on polygamy, and of what is right and what is wrong. The Pennsylvania Dutch to this day, till their land and prepare their food using the structures and technologies of the eighteenth century. Therefore, ethical values revolve around one's perception of one's own culture, and tend not to superimpose their ideologies on others. However, colonization also meant that the rulers attempt to superimpose their own ideologies as happened during the British colonisation of India before independence. However, the mass of people who made up rural India, who were mainly Hindus and were out of the range of the British eye, continued the socio-religious mores and customs of their forefathers. Over time, some sections which had adopted forms of the colonizing rulers in pre-Independent India had their influence in specific geo-ecological areas such as the Portuguese in Goa, the orthodox Coptic Church in Kerala and the scattered number of Anglo-Indians in the major cities where the British had their greatest presence as in Bombay, Calcutta and Delhi.

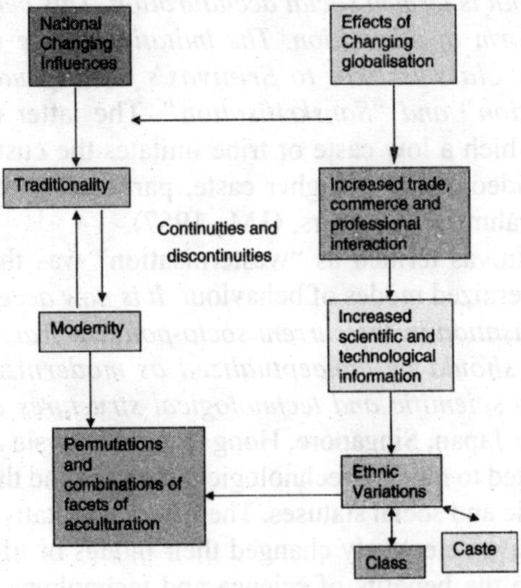

Paradigm 5.4: Socio-Economic Changes – Global and National

Ethnic groups live in varied ecologies as also are of varied religions, castes. These variables are in varied forms of intermix (multi cultured) in ethnic groups accultured to global and traditional changes.

With the inter-mobility among nations, there are cross-cultural marriages of differing nationalities, and within India, of different ethnic and religious groups. These again form a hybrid type of culture spanning both cultures of origin and adaptation, causing readjustment in modes of thinking and behaving in most patterns of sub-cultures. Part of the issue of adaptation is the pressure to conform, which need not necessarily be overtly observed. In the early years of colonization, orphanages were opened up for the poor children, and proselytizing took place. According to the colonialists, the Indian "natives" needed to be educated and converted. In spite of these efforts by the British, core socio-cultural patterns still continue and have not been eroded. In the world of today, money and power play a very significant role in manipulating existent patterns of lifestyles, where previously, routine and stagnation were the normal patterns. As is well-known, when change is imposed, it brings about a destabilizing period till absorption of the new norms are assimilated, as is happening with the tribals in remote parts of India today. These tribals are attracted by the money incentives of industrial cooperatives and are literally ejected out of their age-old habitats.[48] (Ghosh, S., 2008)

Belonging to a social group which has its own unique culture is essential for an individual's identity. Even though culture continues to have different operational definitions, in the last analysis, it gives the individual his unique social identity, and it answers crucial questions occurring to him, like: *Who am I? To whom do I belong?* What is my reference group? With whom do I share the same type of behaviour in group situations? What are the prescribed and the prohibited modes of behaviour that apply to my group? How should I behave when I am in situations similar to those of my group? If I behave differently from other members of my group, is there a system or are there systems by which my behaviour is judged? In which areas can I accept or tolerate differences? What happens to me if I transgress norms?"

Such self and in-depth analyses, helps the individual in a given culture to assess his position and to find his niche in a cultural group, which meets his needs more clearly, and to which he is easily acculturated. The catch, however, is that someone has to show the way and, therefore, in the rung of hierarchy, the individual finds his place as a follower, a leader or, a would-be leader. Studies in human organization indicate that the organization is based upon an individually known cognitive structure of positions in the hierarchy and, therefore, specifies the job tasks accruing to the particular position.[49] (Mirza, S., and P. Gupta, 2008)

India is a pluralistic society with 22 officially recognized languages, 250 major dialects, many other minor dialects, and their sub-dialects. Some originate from the Indo- European languages, some from the Dravidian, and some from the Sino-Tibetan culture. Many languages are unrelated to others in the country. English is spoken and understood by about 3 per cent of the population. Hindi has been declared as the national language, but is not as well understood in the south as fluently as in the north. In the rural, interior villages and tribal areas, the local dialect is the main medium of communication[50] (Mehta, D., 1970: 93), like, for instance, Bhojpuri is the language of the people of eastern UP and, although as a dialect it is similar to Hindi, it is not well-understood by people whose mother-tongue is Hindi, leave alone the South Indians. *Besides language, there are innumerable other patterns of distinguishing parallel strands in this pluralistic society.* Language is the major form of acculturation and understanding of the norms and beliefs of the others living adjacent to each other; for instance, the meat-eating Punjabi may live side by side with the *shudh* Brahmin but they practice their own beliefs and rites. Through oral tradition, each sect is aware of the do's and dont's in interaction with the other, while each keeps its own distance. In spite of the various wars fought across India from outside and within from time immemorial, the fabric of the continuously stable rituals and rites of each sub-culture continues more or less unchanged. Except for one fanatic Muslim ruler, Aurangazeb, by and large, most alien rulers did not force their religious ideology on the Hindu subjects and in fact during Akbar's regime there was an almost secular state.[51] (Berinstain, V., 1998) These variations in language are related to particular ecologies. *Thus, there is an intricate interweaving of variables in these ecologies of differing languages and socio-religious values and customs.* For example, Muslims are to be found in concentrations in States like Uttar Pradesh and Andhra Pradesh, while they may practice different religion, their ecologies are the same as of the Hindus, Christians and other religions in these areas. Again, while caste prevails in Hinduism as a divisive factor, it is non-divisive in other religious groups except for minor changes. Therefore, we may assume that there is a cohesive factor operating between language and ecology.

We also observe that the religions which were formed in protest against some socio-religious practices of Hinduism such as Buddhism, Jainism and Sikhism did not effectively alter the core of Hindu values. Even the influx of Christian missionaries hardly created a dent, except in tribal and interior villages. At the same time, it must be said that, the Christian missionaries brought with them the markings of education, nutrition and better quality of life. For the most part, even communal riots did not have much to do with religious ideologies, but are maneuvered to seem so because of political and territorial reasons. Often times religion is used ruse to create riots by political upsurges. The Babri Masjid conflict highlights the claim of territorial right for a place of worship, which is nowhere near resolution.[52] (Young, J.G., and D. Kaplan, 2003: 31) Islam came to southern parts of India immediately after its origin in Arabia through the channel of Arab traders and it spread to north-west and north India after the invasions of early Muslim conquerors beginning with Mahmud of Ghazni in the eleventh century AD. Paradoxically, most of the cultural practices of the Hindu and Muslim communities, especially in relation to family events, like naming, puberty rites and marriage rituals, seem to have similar trends. The merger of the two languages, Hindi and Urdu seem to be well understood as 'Hindustani'. Further, the idiomatic implementation of secular laws was by far mostly an integrative process, covering all religious and ethnic groups.[53] (Young, J.G., and Kaplan, D., 2003: 32) *Considering the vast differentials which related to difference in behaviour within the general Indian society, we must relate what we know of civilization from ancient times as documented. The available literature is mostly in traditional oral information and recorded documentation in Sanskrit and Arabic.* The *Vedas, Upanishads*, the epics of the *Mahabharata* and the *Ramayana* and such like religious texts form the written documents of Hinduism,[54] (Nath, V., 2001) while the *Quran* is the major document of the Islamic religion and culture. From religious texts like that of Confucianism[55] (Fairbank, J.K., 1992 : 51-52), Islam[56] (Cleary, Dr. Thomas, 1993) and Buddhism, we note that the practice of one religion did not debar one from respecting other religions. The respect for other religions has been further reinforced by the philosophies of Kabir, Tagore and Mahatma Gandhi. Plurality of religion is almost equivalent to plurality of sub-cultures that diversify India. Thus, we can trace the variations in the exo systems as related to identifiable religions. The following highlight the major conceptualisations regarding multi-culturalism in a pluralistic society:

(a) Critical Bases of Development

Development implies a progression, whether positive or negative. Unambiguously, it implies change in status. However, not all change is development, for development is a life-long process and fluctuations either way occur during the process. It is a continuous process with every phase subscribing to a set of unique traits.[57] (Valsiner, J., and K.J. Connolly, 2003) A stage is logically related to time-span. *Thus, time is the major criterion relating to change. Time dictates the degree and levels of change during the stages of development.* The stage is not progressive, regressive, or static. It is a process of elaboration, a system of interface and exchange in a contextual, dynamic system, in which each component influences the other towards adaptation.[58] (Anderson, J.E., 1957) The world of the individual is constructed through experiences of time during these stages. Some periods may be longer or shorter than the one before or after. Nevertheless, they follow a chronological order. For example, some mothers may get very anxious if the infant does not utter sounds, or if the preschool child is unable to comprehend simple instructions. Their anxieties provoke them to think that the child is retarded, whereas in actual fact these time periods, although successive, may differ for different individuals. Development is additive. There is no value judgement or epistemology, or spiritual dissonance akin to the concept of Descartes "I think therefore I am."[59] (Descartes, R., 1637/1980)

Pre-determinism and epigenesis indicate the potential to increase.[60] (Gottlieb, G., 2002) *Because of the unique individualism of development, qualitative dynamism is being increasingly analysed through systems of development.* These systems are also uniquely idiographic, idiothematic and localised *in situ* methodologies. For these reasons, current day thinking and writing on socialisation and other patterns of behaviour are elaborate idiothematic conceptualizations. Therefore, social scientists are increasingly emphasising biological and physical attributes of development, Expansion into the meaning and impact of epigenesis gathered interest in 1900s with the study of embryonic behaviour[61] (Gottlieb, G., 1998). This emphasis began in the revolutionary change resulting in the trend moving from homogenesis to heterogenesis[62] (Gould S.J., 1977). Gould discusses that the epigenetic knowledge in relation to physical knowledge is about contingent causal objects, spatial and temporal relations. These are also associated with other contingent relations, which are dependent upon physical conditions determining their occurrences. Therefore, physical phenomena are probabilistic and conditioned on events. For instance, the appearance of clouds in summer may portend the first rains of the monsoons, and the movement of smaller animals in the forest into hiding may portend imminent danger from larger animals. Closer to home, malnutrition can be responsible for stunted physical growth. On the other hand, necessary relationships are non-probabilistic as they depend upon invariant events such as the appearance of permanent teeth, the appearance of menarche in young girls, and now growing more evident, the use of drugs and smoking effects on the foetus and the lungs of the human[63] (Zuckerman, B.D., R. Hingson, H. Amaro, S.M. Devenson, H. Kayne, S. Parker, R. Vinci, K. Aboagye, L. Fried, H. Cabral, R. Timperi and H. Bauchner, 1989). On the other hand, cognitive development is a concept that is variant and a probabilistic event depending upon genetic potentials and environmental stimuli[64] (Langer J., S. Rivera, M. Schlesinger and A. Wakeley, 2003). Further, cognitive developmental processes as expanded by Piaget, whereby cognitive abilities are developed, include the socio-emotional environment. Some processes are invariant, for instance, stage-wise development indicates that abstraction in cognitive development occurs after concrete events are related to specific causes.[65] (Piaget, J., 1932) The Piagetian concept may be understood more fully through the explications of Vygotsky who included the socio-historical perspective, so as to present a fuller analysis of the totality of human cognition.[66] (Vygotsky, L.S., 1934)

(b) Control of Self and Self-adjustment

The process of adjustment appears to be high-profiled during the primary school years when relations within the micro-system and meso-system are cemented. Within these two initial eco-systems, the child's cognitive development from the sensory to the formal stages are relatively well established. *It is to be noted here that there is a congruence among theories of development regarding the construct of adjustment.* We see an amalgam of concepts in the various constructs such as those of "the latency period" formulated by Freud; the "period of industry", according to Erickson[67] (Erickson, Erik, 1959); and "the period of cognitive formal operations", according to Piaget.[68] (Piaget, J., 1954).

The processes of control and adaptation during these stages continue progressively, accumulating a complexity of traits indicative of maturity. One of the most significant domains of accomplishment is school achievement, which occurs in the meso-system of the school, the playgrounds and the neighbourhood in which the individual lives. For example, in these past two decades, more than ever before, there is a growing awareness of the need for success in school and avoidance of failure. Here we will describe briefly the cluster of concepts which go to make up the child's strivings towards adjustment with parental and school expectations. *Firstly, perhaps the most reinforced behaviour in the primary school years is the child's achievement in education.* It is observable mostly in urban ecologies, where it is a major parental investment. The child's performance is indicative of the parents' abilities to reinforce the child's scholastic ability. It is not as intense in rural ecologies, and perhaps hardly so in tribal ecologies, where the child is expected to become "a high school pass", irrespective of doing better than others, or of achieving a grade. The second aspect of adjustment is the way a child gets along with others in the meso eco-system: Is he cooperative, sharing, altruistic and obedient towards his elders, teachers and other adults? Does he work with other like a team member or is he a bully and aggressive or does he allow others to "stamp all over him?" Is he a *bahadur*, and is she a quiet feminine modest girl? Parents are anxious in most ecologies that their children get along with others in their peer group. Thus, we see a close interaction between the micro ecosystem of the family and its adjacent meso ecosystem in the development of the personality. *It is not infrequent that disharmony occurs within the micro and the meso-systems, as also between the two.* In the micro-system, as the child grows older, he attempts to be autonomous and to break away from his dependency on older generation. This creates disharmony. It is not infrequent that there are broken friendships, although they may be repaired again. Further, there may be disagreements between the micro and the meso systems in that parents may not favour the kind of friendships their children make. *The family situation and the characteristic of the parents, their relationships, their limitations and strengths also influence the child's adjustment processes.* An influential sphere is the working, non-working status of the mother. Apparently, working mothers have more extrovert male children whereas non-working mothers have more extrovert female children which implies that mobility of the mother also creates a wider vision of the "ecological givens". These areas in a study showed were social, educational, emotional and home areas of adjustment wherein these characteristics were exhibited.[69] (Seth, M., and U. Bhatnagar, 1979)

(c) Ethnicity and Identity

It is important to stress here that a well adjusted growing individual carries with him a fair concept of his identity in his social network. Perhaps, social distance was a factor that weighed strongly between the upper and lower ethnic groups.[70] (Majeed, A., and E.S. Ghosh, 1982) In a study, comparison of different ethnic groups regarding social identity, high class Hindus, namely Brahmins perceived themselves to have a more configured sense of social identity vis-à-vis lower class Hindus and Muslims. In extreme cases of feelings of inadequacy and loss of self esteem, other debilitating attributes appear in the personality of the child. In these situations, the child experiences a sense of loss of self-esteem and insecurity. This quality may continue well into the age of adolescence. This attribute of alienation is termed the "alienation syndrome" in the exploration of the negative attributes according to Erikson's life-cycle theory.[71] (Qureshi, A., and M. Dutt, 1979) Sex differences, do not make for any significant differences in the expression of these negative attributes of identity.[72] (Mohanty, N., 1984)

The growing infant and the preschool child are involved in gaining experiences in the ecological givens. At the same time, the child is interested in control of himself and in acquiring competencies towards adjustment with his human ecology. During this period, he may meet with several barriers within himself, with his ecosystem and more especially when the micro ecosystem is deprived, economically and socially[73] (Bronfenbrenner, U., 1975). What happens in the process of the child's interaction with the nurturant and other family members? The major traits of the nurturant which influence the child are: domination, punishment, reward, authoritarianism, or a referral to a higher authority like the father or the teacher. At times, the techniques of the nurturer may be inconsistent and creates confusion in the child's upbringing process. The tendency of the child is to comply with the wishes of the nurturant. When wills clash, the child complies with a resentful manner. Therefore, there is both: the opportunity and the choice; and confrontation with compliance, which may destabilise relationships within the human ecological network system. *During socialisation the child moves from dependency to autonomy, and towards taking responsibility for the self's actions. It is perhaps that males are* less *conforming than females, that brings about a duality in the gender roles, given the duality of socialisation in the patriarchal system.* This seems to be a general potential attitude irrespective of the socio-economic status of the micro ecosystem. For instance, in a study by Reddy *et al.*, it was found that males are more non-conforming than females, with the middle class indicating greater problems in getting the male child to comply.[74] (Reddy, N.Y., T.N. Rao, P. Sandeep and V.V. Padmakar, 1970) It seems females tend to be more conforming because of the restrictive norms and their lessened mobility. Social change is an intervening variable, in the perception and practice of control of behaviour by parents, exacerbating the distance between generations by the modernising trends, affecting especially male children[75] (Singh, S., V.V. Upmanyu and Rameek, 1982).

(d) The Role of Psychological Frustration and its Defence Mechanisms

The principles of adjustment in their generic form refer to the dynamics of how the individual, in essence, finds a via media between libidinal energy and the injunctions of the superego. The process that the individual tend to use is catharsis. Catharsis evolves and devolves upon the articulation or suppression of the libidinal energy. As such, the principles of adjustment are applicable to molar or goal-oriented aspects of behaviour.[76] (Thompson, G.G., 1952: 179) This paradigm consists of – (a) the organism which acts and reacts to needs, both of a primary and a secondary nature; (b) thus, a set of behaviour patterns, which are goal-directed, pursuing a pattern of cultural needs either minimally or increasingly as the individual matures; (c) the child's motivational level to satisfy these needs is dependent upon a hierarchy of needs, as related to their *press*.[77] (Maslow, A.H., 1966) These *presses* indicate the strength of the needs. However, each need has a different strength of pursuance and each has a competitive *press*. Reasonably, we may assume that these *presses* are related more to primary needs as the latter have priority; (d) *Needs are not satisfied fully at any given time, except in rare cases when they attain a point of satiation. Satiation occurs, for instance, when hunger is not only satisfied but the individual says,* "I have over-eaten." Children who are fond of ice-cream may want to eat as many types as they see in an ice-cream parlour. But then again how much of ice-cream can a child consume over and beyond need fulfilment at any one time?For instance, hunger is perhaps the major need that is to be satisifed, and is related to food availability either produced in the ecology or exchanged or bartered. Other needs also operate though at lower levels of *press*. Dynamically, the order might change, giving precedence to secondary needs, such as the need for affiliation, as demonstrated in Harlow's experiment with infant monkeys.[78] (Harlow, H.F., 1963)

Harlow demonstrated in an experiment that an infant monkey, when offered to choose between the options of having milk from a bottle or staying with its mother for bodily warmth and security, chooses the latter. Arising out of the difference between the need and its satisfaction is a pathway which is termed frustration. Frustration arises out of lack of need fulfilment. It is seen that frustration of primary needs are more intense in their effect than that of secondary needs. One cannot do without food or shelter, for instance, but one can do without wanting to eat ice-cream. *The libidinal energy of the individual to meet his need forces the ego to find a pathway to meet the need, which pathway is more forceful if the need is primary. This force is the id-directed energy that destabilises the individual, creating a situation of social and personal inadequacy to meet the needs*. When this frustration builds up to an extent that it cannot be controlled by the ego, frustration gains in strength till the need is met and satisfied. The description and functions of the Id, the Ego and the Superego have been described in the section on Freud's analysis of his psychodynamic theory in the Chapter No. 4 on "Selected Personality Theories Relevant to the Indian Psyche". To equalise the dynamic flow of energy between the id and the ego's attempt of striving to find resolution to the frustration, the ego turns to behaviour which is compensatory.

The mechanism which the ego uses for this compensation is a strategy which resists attempts to destabilise the ego's homeostasis. *The ego adopts a different strategy to deflate the libidinal energy by catheting the barriers that create a frustration anxiety.* Several psychologists have attempted to develop theoretical approaches as to the management of frustration, which, if uncontrolled, leads to extreme psychosomatic disorders tipping the individual over the edge of what is known as culturally acceptable normative behaviour. Sears[79] (Sears, R.R., 1943), a psychologist, gives a detailed overview of the psychoanalytic principles related to frustration management. These defences occur as unconscious mechanisms, which are spontaneously used without the individual being consciously aware of their mechanisms. These mechanisms also tend to stabilise reality to bring about a sense of homeostasis, even though this process might be temporary. It is important to remember that these defence mechanisms are not continuous. They occur intermittently to diffuse an immediate situation but it does not mean that the frustration itself is eradicated or attenuated completely. It might build up again when evoked through similar stimuli. For instance, a child may tell a white lie to avoid punishment, resolving that particular situation for that time. However, sequentially the child may experience a residual anxiety, and, therefore, conflict can reappear when the need reappears again.

Where an ecology has several alternative strategies to select from, a substitute is quickly found to suppress the given frustration, and to meet the need. Again, *interactional influences on development depend upon the dynamic reactions of the individual and the "givens" in his micro-ecology*. This influence of the micro-ecology is suggested by Bonfenbrenner[80] (Bronfenbrenner, U., 1979) and Vygotsky[81] (Vygotsky, L.M., 1978). While the former used the concept of "micro system", the latter proposed the concept of "the zone of proximal development".

(e) Dependency and Independency

Psychological and physical dependence upon the major caretaker for guidance and sustenance is well known. This is the first social linkage formed by the child, variously interpreted as "bonding", "close proximity" and the "first symbiotic relationship". *Physical dependency is reflexive and spontaneous and is symbolised by auditory sounds like crying when hungry or in pain. Psychological dependency occurs when the infant is cognitively aware of his surroundings and can discriminate and differentiate* between and among cognitive images. *In the infant, this behaviour is shown as avoidance of strangers and sources of pain and discomfort when in distress, or as movement towards the source of comfort. His sensory motor perceptual development is the first learning of ontogenetic behaviour in being able to discriminate and distinguish perceptually among various images.* The child's caretaker/s, usually tend to encourage the growing individual to take progressive steps towards self reliance and self responsibility. At about the preschool age, when about four or five years old, the child learns to modify and condition his dependency on others. For, by this time the superego has developed, so that the child is able to distinguish right from wrong.

Dependency is recognizable through attention seeking behaviour of the child. We may observe several situations in the child's behaviour where he incessantly seeks attention from the caretaker; objecting violently to attention given to others in the vicinity. He may even deliberately seek to destroy objects so as to catch the caretaker's attention. These are manifested in very overt mannerisms in the initial stages of early development, which then become muted into covert forms, like refusing to eat a meal, complaining of feeling sick (when not really) showing symptoms of withdrawal and lack of concern about the environment around. Illustrations are numerous: for instance, a mother might say, "Ankit, don't do that." The child will look defiantly at the mother and continue to do just that. The child will incessantly demand a chocolate, on the adult's refusal there is unprovoked screaming till the nurturant gives in. Discipline and consistency of discipline are the major instrumental learning strategies to guide the child towards socially approved behaviour and away from non-approved. *Dependency in early childhood occurs in most cultures, and is a phenomenon which is cut short abruptly as in some societies in the west when the child is made to sleep on his own, or allowed to scream, till he sobs himself to sleep.* If the child is older, he is "made to take time out", sent away, or is punished by non reward. Like the nurturant saying, "I don't love you, for your behaviour makes me unhappy." In the average Indian family, there are many other adults who intervene and say to the major nurturer: "Let him have his way, what does he know? He is yet a child." Children, who are used to this mind-set and behaviour in the mental workings of the nurturer, take advantage and use the same techniques to get what they want. There is, in essence, ways in which the child, who is unable to negotiate, meets his needs arbitrarily, in an egocentric manner. *For the young child the immediacy of a satisfactory response is an important factor. If the nurturant delays in gratifying the young child's needs, the child tends to become temperamental.* On the other hand immediate gratification of need creates a stronger bond of dependency between a child and his caretaker. Eventually, this cycle creates a habitual dependency formation on the part of the child towards the nurturer. The more severe the weaning process away from the dependency relationship the more traumatic is the consequence on the child. *The syndrome of strong dependency ties, abrupt and severe weaning away from this dependency bond creates an anxiety in the child, which is termed "separation anxiety."* This separation anxiety manifests itself in many ways on the child's part: listlessness, inability to eat, lack of interest in surroundings, reduced interaction with other adults and a highly anxious form of behaviour. The longer the separation the greater the anxiety, which in later childhood and even in adulthood, can be the source of those traits which we attribute to over-anxious people. The relationship between dependency and the dependency drive, undergo changes for when dependency is punished, having been a pattern of the child's life previously it heightens the drive, which continues throughout the chronological age spans. *Whiting and Child have hypothesised that the combination of rewarding and punishing dependency (intermittent positive and negative reinforcement) creates and establishes a stronger dependency drive, involving a conflict between dependency and anxiety which adds to the strength of the drive.*

(f) Negative and Positive Stimuli

A well-used model of conflict, termed "approach avoidance" occurs from early childhood. We see this clearly evidenced in young children watching a horror movie. They are riveted to their seats, flinch away from the screen and yet at the same time watch the movie in between their fingers held up to their face. When they observe that the horror increases, their reaction is one of fear and avoidance, and yet they will continue to watch the movie as if irresistibly drawn. Adults watching a horror movie react psychologically in a similar way; though the behaviour is not outwardly visible as in young children for they have learned to "control" their reactions. It is necessary, however, to underscore that when two drives occur in conflict the stronger one will prevail[82] (Miller, N.E. 1952).

The above assumptions occur when they are not competing with other drives, and require to be examined within their own constructs. For instance, if we examine the need for dependency, and there is a strong drive at any one time, it can be situationally and psychologically displaced by another stronger drive, namely the drive for a youngster to show that he can stand without his mother's support or feed himself. *This autonomy which he exhibits itself is, according to Erikson, either "a positive trait", like "autonomy" and "mastery" or a negative one, namely "shame" and a "loss of self esteem".* These traits continue through early childhood to the primary school years and into adolescence.

10. Cross Eco-cultural Considerations

The meaning of culture in its abstract form, can be operationally defined by several interpretations according to the variegated sub-

cultures in their varying ecologies. When we operationalise this concept of culture, we are specifying the various psychological, sociological and ecological dimensions of a society. People of a culture, by virtue of the traits they exhibit, indicate the simultaneous existence of homogeneous and heterogeneous traits in a pluralistic society. These homogeneous or "universal traits" are prevalent in the macro society of the country. For example, all Indians have mostly a patriarchal system and some matriarchal. All have ritualistic ceremonies for auspicious occasions. However, 'specific traits' are uniquely heterogeneous. *Therefore, an in-depth analysis will indicate that each of these variations have a rationale which justifies the belief and the practice.* For example, the veneration given to deities in the ecological givens such as those ceremonies related to the harvesting season in agricultural families, is an important period since the success of the produce is related to their survival needs.

All Indians have some common psychological attributes. The typical institutions like the family and the kinship structure are evident in some form or the other in most eastern cultures. Why do we need to know about cultures other than our own? Granted that it is educative to know about the dimensions and structures of other cultures, we do not have sufficient data from which to extrapolate the commonalities between the Indian culture and the other cultures, except to say that they are similar or dissimilar. The empirical data from existent samples of differing cultures are not adequate to make reliable comparisons, since each culture exhibits *in situ* phenomena, uniquely variant from others. There is much that is unknown about contrasting variables from one culture to another. Such cross-cultural contrast would be indicative of the variations in the macro system. Granted that this is true, we have to know also that the world is changing dynamically. Given this situation, knowledge of the repertoire of other cultures, increases the distinctions among these cultures, and increases inter-personal relationships among them. Communication, through media and travel, have increased interactive phenomena. For example, it is not unusual to find elderly relatives travelling from India to visit their children abroad and *vice versa. As science and technology increase, people of the world are becoming inextricably wired to each other in complex forms. The scenario, for instance, in India is that it is becoming more interactive with other societies which increases its trade profiles.*

The world is shrinking in this twenty-first century, and is likely to be telescoped further. The cognition and recognition of differences provides Indian scholars and professionals, an understanding of why other people do what they do, differently from their own. We have stressed these facts in the discussion on ethnicity and its diversity, in the ways in which the individual in India adapts to his ecology, whether it is the tribal or the urbanite in the chapter on "Ecology: its parameters". *Thus, adaptation and adjustments are self-initiated regulatory mechanisms*[83] (Markus, H.R., and S. Kitayama, 1991), *which direct the ways in which the human being acts and reacts with his environment efficiently or otherwise.* The same is true of other cultures, whose life styles, and their utilization of their environmental artefacts over the years and over generations develop certain typical customs and mores that characterize their national identities. In India, we call these indicators as attributes of "Indianness". Others use the religious criteria and call them the Indian ways of life, and still others use stereotypes. The fact remains that there are common patterns and heterogeneous patterns which gives the Indian a sense of acceptance of differences. For instance, a Sikh knows he is an Indian. He behaves with attributes which connotes Indianness and yet at the same time he can separate these from his form of ritualism and worship. He is also aware that unlike the Hindu, there is no caste system in his ethnic group. and that it is important he abides by certain ritualistic accoutrements such as a turban, a beard, and a *kirpan.*

The understanding of the variation among and within a culture is not easy as there are no reference points on a one-to-one basis with the Indian attributes. The major characteristics are those which an individual Indian shares with members of the same culture, like the ways of greeting and the celebration of major festivals like Holi and Diwali,[84] (Maidment, Richard and Colin Mackerras, 1998) which make for homogeneity in most subcultures in India. It is important to underscore that these are differentially interpreted in the varying national sub-cultures. For example, parents in the west are usually surrounded by a scientific support system such as paediatricians, obstetricians, guidance counsellors, community workers and such like, unlike the Indian society.

Added to these are the value-orientations among members of the Indian family and community, together with the transmission of these values through institutions like education, religion, governance, and occupational stratified structures.[85] (Kluckhohn, C., and F.L. Stredtbeck, 1961: 31; Elkin, F., and G. Handel, 1972: 27; Dubois,

A.J.A., and H.K. Beauchamp, 1978) These components/domains are similar in the abstract form in most countries. For instance, in the west the family is usually nuclear. In India, we have both the extended and nuclear family systems which interact more closely than is observed in western cultures.

A cross-cultural approach gives an insight into the understanding of the behaviour of other people in other ecologies. For example, we do not fully know why do the Chinese eat frogs, and why do the Indians eschew it. Why do the westerners use artefacts different from the easterners, like the implements and appliances for food preparation, and why they have different marriage rituals, and such like. In attempting to understand the way other people live we also see our own culture in a totality of perspectives, that there are others who live differently who are achievers, who live a good life, who practice different sets of beliefs but are as competent and as humane as in most other cultures. This sense of appreciation is also essential especially when we realise that India is open to the influx of many visitors of other countries who act and react differently to the Indian systems, but who themselves also learn to appreciate differences in these different ecologies. As Whiting puts it, such expansion of knowledge adds to our repertoire of variations in human behaviour.[86] (Whiting, B., 1963)

However, *documented knowledge is more comprehensible when it is derived from idiographic data rather than normative*. The latter only indicate general tendencies. There are a wide and varied number of differing variables in each culture which render comparability almost impossible, as the plateaux for comparison differ in nature and structure and, therefore, may be more reliably termed "contrastibility". For instance, the operational definition of religious behaviour in a catholic church is dissimilar from that in a Hindu temple. In the former, the rituals are guided by a priest according to a set format, whereas any Hindu can go to a temple at any time and do his or her *aarti* and give donations or offerings without a set format. In Christianity, Jesus Christ is the supreme Godhead, whereas in Hinduism, there are several godheads, each assuming a different *avatar* of the Supreme Being.

There is a lack of experimental control and measurement of variables that further preclude the validity of comparison among cultures. All cultural aspects, when viewed cross culturally, are often perceived tangentially by others, as they do not offer comparability among them. For instance, Malhotra states that in the Indian society "personal dependence is not a cherished socio-cultural goal", and the ideal value in Indian society is "dependability" and "interdependence". Whereas, in the west, independence is a highly cherished developmental goal.[87] (Malhotra, S., 2003: 6) In the colonial past, many patterns based on the ayurvedic conceptualisation and philosophy were looked at askance, like swaddling, breast feeding on demand, and holding and cuddling the child frequently. In fact in many traditional homes, especially rural and tribal the mother and infant are segregated from the rest of the family for at least forty days, after which the mother is given a ritualistic herbal bath, and after specific rituals are performed, both mother and child interact with the others in the family. The western world is beginning to observe the 'sense and sensibility' of these practices as various forms of bonding between mother and child, such as swaddling, and is inculcating some of these in their recommended practices.[88] (Sroufe, L.A., E.A. Carlson, A.K. Levy, *et. al.*, 1999)

11. Selected Parameters among Selected Varying Cultures

This section will contrast three studies indicating childcare: the first study was done by Bronfenbrenner[89] (Bronfenbrenner, U., 1974) in two different ecologies, namely, USA and Russia; in the second study, Doshi[90] (Doshi, S.L., 1971) describes the Bhil tribal culture in transition; and the third study was done by Munroe and Munroe[91] (Munroe, R., and Munroe, R., 1975) in three south-sea island cultures, namely, the Gusii, the Trobianders and the Ainu.

Contrasting Cultures

(a) The first is a study of childcare in USA and Russia done in early seventies. It describes the effect of ideology on childcare systems. The Russian is brought up according to a disciplinary code, the American according to a free type of democracy. In the Russian conceptual format, there is the umbrella of the collectivism *vs.* individuation patterns in the American system.[92] (Bronfenbrenner, U., 1970: 76-81) This concept emphasizes the fact that ecology is composed of the economic, the political and the ideological social systems, which have a significant part to play, either overtly or covertly, on the actions of the caretakers in the upbringing process of their children and, therefore, the inculcation of cultural norms.

(b) The second is the study of the tribal community of Bhils in transition from traditionality to modernity. The changes occurring in the community when they move from one ecology to another is also discussed in this study.

(c) The third study of three south-sea islanders offer insights into their commonalities or universals as well as variations, differentially interpreted by each island community. The domains of these south-sea islanders discussed in this study are: life stages; physical growth and motor skills; affect; language and perception; cooperation; gender roles; dependency; aggression; and motives for achieving.

All the above three studies focus on one domain, namely, childcare patterns. In the study of the south seas islands, the authors state that the most important aspect was to relate parenting and child behaviour, in these their cultural norms as contrasted with the western cultures. By serendipity, we may be able to avoid assuming too much about human behaviour, whether from documentation of other cultures, or in contrast to the Indian culture *per se*. *In the world today, there is much geographical mobility from one country to another, and while the Indian might know much about his own culture, when he travels outside the country, he comes across peoples with culturally differing values, which might initially create a dissonance in perception.* Apparently, this comparability does not work between such elementary forms of society as the south sea islanders, and the highly developed western cultures, of America and Russia. The authors of these differing cultures state that the western child's development arises from exposure to a regimen purposefully designed to maximise his developmental potential. In the western culture, he is trained to be smart, competitive, achieving, and self-oriented. These facets of what might be called "developmental hypertrophy", which seem to have at their roots, a kind of focused stimulation that is seldom found in a traditional elementary society"[93] (Munroe and Munroe, 1975: 150). The second comprehension about the difference between the Islanders of the South Seas and the tribals of India is that *their occupational tasks are mainly dictated by the geo-ecology in which they live:* the islanders are fishermen and the Bhils are hunters in their place of origin and casual labourers when they migrate to the plains. Whereas, when contrasted with the western societies, the basis of contrast of these varying cultures are different. *The two western societies live by standards systematised by their ideologies with their regulations and governance, which have a trickle down effect in affecting cultural behaviour of their peoples.*

The extent, type and range of behaviour in the Western societies has a greater impact in affecting values which consciously follow regimens[94] (Whiting, J.W.M., 1968) whereas upbringing is casual and informal in elementary societies of the three Islanders. *The world of the three islands is routine, conscribed and lack stimulating environments for creativity and innovativeness, whereas the western societies, as indicated by the author, Bronfenbrenner, emphasise achievement orientation.* The selection of the Soviet Union in contrast with USA was to provide a "contrasting perspective" provided by two societies which differ substantially in their ideologies in the process and context of socialisation, but at the same time face similar problems as industrialised countries with highly developed systems of technology, education and mass communication.[95] (Bronfenbrenner, 1970: 2).

These studies which are descriptive in nature, draw their conclusions on the basis of informal observation connecting them to psychological constructs. Even though they are ethnographic narratives, with some anecdotes sprinkled in between, they preclude co-relative assessment even though they might deal with common domains. *For instance, the study on south sea islanders, follows a systematic and specific accounting according to psychological domains.* The study of the Bhils is mainly anthropologically descriptive, and the study of the western societies follows psychological themes. Further, the diversity of variables among these studies, precludes synthesis and intensive probing into details. There is always the possibility of misconstruction. We can continue tabulating different customs of cultural behaviour, which may be construed as weird by other cultural groups, precisely because, we neglect the *in situ* context-specific nuances of each one of these cultures, which are appropriate only to that culture. Data from ethnographic sources are commonly viewed as being too variable, to offer adequate data for quantitative comparisons. They are narrative and subjectively reportive and, therefore, the validity of the findings is in question because of subjectivity. The observation of single incidents might lead to distortion of the given cultural customs and ways of life. The already existing knowledge of the dynamics of psychological behaviour, such as the role of dependency—independency in the socialization process might be differently construed in a traditional society vis-à-vis a modern sophisticated society. Therefore, we need to understand the *in situ* context-specific situation for concepts and their interpretations involved in behavioural outcomes in the cultures of these varying societies. For instance, the major assumption in all the three island societies is that, the child's behaviour is influenced mainly by the adults in the environment. The important distinction here is not the concept but its interpretation in social reality terms by the given culture. The islanders, for instance, guide and direct the child informally. The occupation of the Bhils is observed and imitated by their children, while in the western societies, there is a deliberate conscious and programmed effort to direct the child towards ideological behaviour.

In the area of empirical data gathering, *it is essential that there are standards of reference/norms which are used as stepping stones for studying different domains in behaviour.*[96] (Willerman, 1972) *For instance, we use the intelligence quotients of the west, as touchstones as standard references for testing intelligence in Indian children.* It would be far-fetched to use such tests for relatively elementary societies like the south sea islanders, and for even perhaps the Bhils, whose geo-ecological and human ecological environment offers those stimuli different from the west, wherein these standard tests are developed. Therefore, studying elementary societies in their cultural context, offers more insights. The use of case study or ethnographic methodology (participant and no participant observation and idiographic methods offer more insights into the life styles of elementary societies such as the south sea islanders).

In looking at major differences between the cultures of the islanders and the western societies, we may state the following:

(i) Early experiences influence adult behaviour significantly in the islanders' progeny. In the cultures of the USA and Russia, the adult practices relate directly to the regiment of formalized behaviour.

(ii) The islanders displayed a susceptibility to testing situations with which they were unfamiliar, whereas the westerners were familiar with testing experiences as they were culturally toned.

(iii) Inculcation into adult responsibilities and tasks, led to low levels of self-seeking behaviour among the islanders, whereas conscious attempts were made in the western societies to raise levels of confidence and self-esteem. In other words, among the islanders the individual is subsumed under the umbrella of adult responsibility, whereas in the western societies, the child is taught to be responsible for his own actions.

If we view the available theoretical frames emanating from the west, as to their relevancy to these elementary societies, there seems to be some relativity between Erikson's schema[97] (Erikson, E.H., 1958), and the developmental trends observed in the behaviour of the children of the islanders. Further, there seems to be also a similarity in the cultural processes of upbringing in these elementary societies and the three indices stated by Super and Harkness. Super and Harkness refer to the development niche of physical settings, culturally regulated customs of child care, childrearing and maintenance systems as comprising the niche for development of specific child practices.[98] (Super, C.M., and Harkness, S., 1986)

Since the major caretaker in all these societies is the parent, much emphasis needs to be laid upon how these parents transmit cultural norms to their children. In other words, what are the strategies the parents use? Thus, we arrive at the major premise that these strategies are culturally generated, transacted with the society, and transmitted through the repository of the adult caretaker.

The concluding premise we offer is that these studies point out to the variability of attributes, from one culture to another. Thus, developmental strategies in different cultures are poles apart. These forms of development do not lend themselves to comparability of cultures, but to contrastability as the premises on which they rest are differentially construed from the elementary to the technological milieu.

The elementary living of the islanders emphasise socio-religious normative behaviour shrouded in mysticism. On the other hand, western societies have well-developed socio-political governance emphasising law, order and justice.

When we examine the descriptions of these cultures individually, we find that there is an attempt to identify "universals" which are phylogenetic in nature, such as characteristic traits like independence and aggression. As stated by Saraswathi, "human phylogeny has been shaped by adaptation due to pressures of contextual demands"[99] (Saraswathi, T.S., 2003: 39). Are these universals generic concepts such as the concept of Phylogenesis? According to some experts of psychobiology, these are labelled into two categories: the broad sense and the narrow sense. *In the broad sense, psychobiology is the study of human species as a whole, revealing, the relationship between behavioural and biological aspects of the developing organism, that is, the genesis, control and consequences of behaviour. According to the narrow sense, psychobiology is physiological psychology or behavioural neurosciences*[100] (Dewsbury, D.A., 1991), *which focuses on the physio-psychological dimensions of the social being.* In describing human behaviour, we tend to rely on the broader sense of interpretation.

Generally, what we have gathered is that, there is casual but caring investment in early childhood among elementary societies,[101] (Bowlby, J., 1969: 427) *and seemingly unplanned, following the pace of the child, but in others like the developed societies there is much deliberate planning and objective investment, more from a consideration of civic sense and well-formulated societal goals.*[102] (Bronfenbrenner, 1962) With the elementary societies, there is non-verbal transmission of intergenerational goals, and well known modes of communication, most often non-verbally. Whereas in the developed societies, there is much discussion and implementation based on scientific thinking to meet the goals of these societies.

12. The Kaleidoscopic Development of the Individual in Varying Cultural Ecologies

In viewing human development in the twenty-first century, a beginning is being made on recognizing that, although there is still a tendency to represent western thinking in terms of quantitative empirical data, there is a shift in the paradigm of thinking in the human analyses. *Qualitative hermeneutic descriptions mainly emanating from cultural anthropology is influencing cultural psychology.* Often, there is an overlap in cross-cultural psychology in discussing cultural relativity. By force, cultural relativity define these social realities in the identified cultures. These social realities are embedded in what Brunner called 'co-constructed reality', by each individual in the given culture.[103] (Brunner, J., 1996) "Intentionality has replaced comparability" as a cross-cultural explanation of differences. However, currently, behaviour in socialisation is considered as a process of negotiation between the human and his ecology (both human and geo-ecology).[104] (Dasen, P.R., and R.C. Mishra, 2000) *In the present day world, there are two paradigms which are interlocked. One is post-modern individualism of the western capitalist hegemony, converging towards a global village. The other is a conglomerate of "little traditions," which are at various stages of combinations of traditionality and modernity.*[105] (Marriot, A.M., 1976) Frequently, analysts used both the types of approaches in studying societies cross-culturally. Again, the aim is not the confrontations between both the paradigms, but, as stated by Berry and Dasen,[106] (Berry, J.W., and P.R. Dasen, 1974) it is an effort to observe and explore new cultural system to discover cognitive variations and to compare them with the present day existent cultural hypotheses. Thus, *there is an interaction between local phenomena and global characteristics*. Whiting, for instance, studied the limits of his hypothesis-testing in local cultures in his attempt to identify commonalities in childrearing practices. The net result, however, does not cause major changes in the paradigms. The intercultural variations tend to precede the common features in the paradigms. In other words, in discerning these paradigms, there is an attempt to collate the varying premises towards encompassing universal premises. For example, the interpretation of rituals marking rites of passage at adolescence is towards a major tenant, namely, "passage into adulthood."[107] (Whiting, J.W.M., 1968) In the search for new theorizing on socialization, the constructs of Super and Harkness, namely; physical settings, maintenance of systems and cultural toned care-taking are used more frequently in describing socialization processes in societies of the developing world. Therefore, socialization might also assume a broader analysis of the concept of acculturation.[108] (Super, C.M., and S. Harkness, 1996) Within this acculturation process culture is constructed by individuals in interaction between cultural universalists and cultural relativists. A recently growing field of interest is utilization of variables of ecology,[109] (Greenfield, P.M., 1997) which in themselves use a qualitative methodological approach. *However, it must be stressed that the qualitative ethnographic approach gives in-depth analysis of realities, while at the same time moving away from universal attributes as we saw in the differing studies of three societies in the pacific islands.* Even though they discussed universals, for instance, dependency and sex roles, the outcomes of the analyses were local specific. Perhaps we will still continue to use paradigms, which examine domains such as aggression, competition, cooperation, individuation, collectivism, and such like; which will continue to offer variation among cultures. The practicality of researching these dimensions adds to the dimensions of social-psychology, in as much as they reveal three varying aspects, namely:

(i) The variation in the meaning of constructs by one group vis-à-vis the other.
(ii) The variation within group of varying individuals.
(iii) The variation within an individual over a life span (time-related and over a process of being influenced by social change).

It is precisely these variations that distinguish one society's culture from another. We observe that the Indians are more family-oriented when contrasted with western micro-ecological system. In fact, we need to view this conceptualization from the opposite angle. If the Westerner lived in the same social, psychological and ecological milieu, as the Indian, would he be more family oriented? We do not know. All we can say is, when describing the Indian, we tend to identify the elements that influence him to be family-oriented. While this conceptualization may be true today, but the context might change over time, as is happening in the globalization phenomenon of today. Similarly, if we examine thc culture of the Bhils in the Indian paradigm, we find they are living in traditionality but cheek by jowl with modernity in the coal mining areas of Birmitrapur, Orissa. Over time they might lose contact with their culture in the hinterlands due to the continued exposure to science and modernisation.

So no one Indian ethnic group is like the other in all respect of similarities. In the growing throes of modernity enveloping the metropolitan ecologies, the westernising young modern individual is less recognisable as the stereotype Indian. His parents are traditional but he is in the process of modernising. As he grows older, he might use the same authoritarian patterns with his children, as did his traditional father. *Thus*, we observe that *there is a large hiatus in describing a society's culture and in the operational understanding of it in its own idiomatic and teleological context, as* societies change *kaleidoscopically.*

13. The Lifestyles of the Majority

Who are the majority? In the families of orientation and procreation, the male head of the household has a strong commitment to patriarchal norms.[110] (Kakar, S., 2001) *The mother has a strong commitment to nurturance and household maintenance. Sociologically, the father's role is "instrumental" and the mother's role is "expressive"*. The young child expects and gets indulgence and sympathy, but as he grows older he is moulded into responsible role-taking. Structures and systems have thus their own linkages, both supportive and negative. The roots of cultural heritage are vested in the nurturant, and are explainable by symbolic forms such as the veneration of the female as "*mata*" and "*devi*".

The concept of development has also its flip side. Much research has indicated the relevance of poverty as an inhibiting factor in development, mainly physical.[111] (Pareek, U., 2001) While small scale studies have been done on economic action, mainly there has been a large-scale overview of consumption and deprivation since they are related to each other, which indicates that these two factors are more prevalent in an inverse ratio in the poor.[112] (Krishna Kumar, T, Shushanta Mallick and Jayaram Holla, 2009) Classificatory variables for finding relationships to deprivation, have been used more popularly such as socio-economic status, cultural and such like distal variables. However, the ramifications in the current knowledge of the underlying cognitive dependent variables such as motivation and apathy, are yet not fully explored in relation to economic deprivation.

Misra has made a strong case for examining variation from a holistic perspective, when discussing the probabilities of occurrence and the consequence of economic deprivation. The major conclusions he arrived at were: deprivation of a prolonged nature, both economic and social, depress cognitive functions.[113] (Misra, G.,1982) Elsewhere, we have analysed this phenomenon and suggested that deprivation, indicating poor performance, may also be due to the factor of little or no opportunity (experience) to exhibit these skills, to indicate high or low cognitive performance. Acquisition, storage and retrieval capacities are subject to enhancement through intensive experiences of the individual/s. The content of these experiences have yet to be fully explored, for tests only elicit a total packaged effect (of independent variables), and do not pinpoint specificity of the cognitive aspect. For instance, economic deprivation in one family might mean living on less food, whereas in another family while there may be enough to eat, there may not be sufficient economic resources for healthcare and educational needs[114] (Datta, A.K., and S. Sharma, 2002). The package of variables has yet to be unravelled in order to find direct and significant relationship to such cognitive elements, related to deprivation.

Therefore, if and when, there is little or no economic deprivation, then it is reasonable to assume that cognitive development increases proportionally given the inherent potential. If so, can we assume that the absence of economic deprivation, leads to an enriched cognitive development? Certainly not. For, there are other and perhaps more significant variables affecting cognitive development, as yet not fully explored. Therefore, what is empiricised is the economic aspects of deprivation. If so, what does this do to the differential positioning of class, caste, and ethnicity with these individuals who experience these specific effects on cognitive development. For example, in families of village craftsmen located in distant rural areas, traditional cultural practices of health strategies might be in vogue, and little is known of scientific practices. Or, take another family; with sufficient economic resources: it may be a high caste family but may also be a disorganised one. This form of family disorganization, is an example of social deprivation. Therefore, it is incumbent to specify in the total cultural framework what then is the meaning of the absolute term 'deprivation', what are its connotations from different viewpoints of disciplines, and what are the final combinations in academic enquiry? Can we term this a culture of deprivation, giving deprivation a sweeping umbrella connotation? Or are there insidious facets which require burrowing into, in order to unearth their effects? Even if we assume that the level of deprivation is homogeneous, then does it lower the potential of different individuals differently in that group? Perhaps, a holistic conceptualisation of deprivation requires an alternative paradigm, including the strengths of various affecting variables. We have attempted to describe a a diagrammatic picture of how the majority who are poor, live their life pattern, which are economically and geo-ecologically deprived as given in the paradigm below. The destabilising geo-ecological factors are floods famines and earthquakes, and man made wars also include social deprivation in terms of normal family life and its supportive systems.

The schism between the majority and minority in lifestyles is in stark contrast. Retarding factors for the majority are lack of education

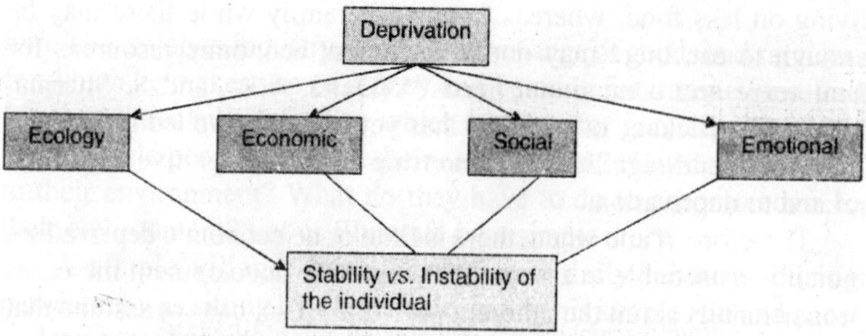

Paradigm 5.5: Characteristics of Deprivation

and opportunities to rise in economic status, and lack of social homogeneity given the caste divisive nature of the Indian society. The educated and socio-economically well off segment of the society tend to describe the Indian from merely viewing the economically better off urbanites who under no circumstances represent the poor majority.

14. Traditionalism and Scienticism: A pot-pourri of Relational Systems

We have so far focused on the individual in his human and geo-ecological setting. We will now focus on the situation of the individual's social realities to understand the forces that impinge upon him.

(a) Social Realities

(i) *The first and the foremost is the individual's relationship to his families of procreation and orientation: his immediate ecosystem.*

(ii) The second is to the individual's family network, the extended family and supportive network of close relatives and friends. (the meso system)

(iii) *The third is towards the individual's caste/gotra and the religious* attributes *of his family (socio-religious beliefs).*

(iv) Finally, the ideology of his religion, the limitations, the extensions of his privileges and the prohibitions, which his society expects him to comply with (societal norms).

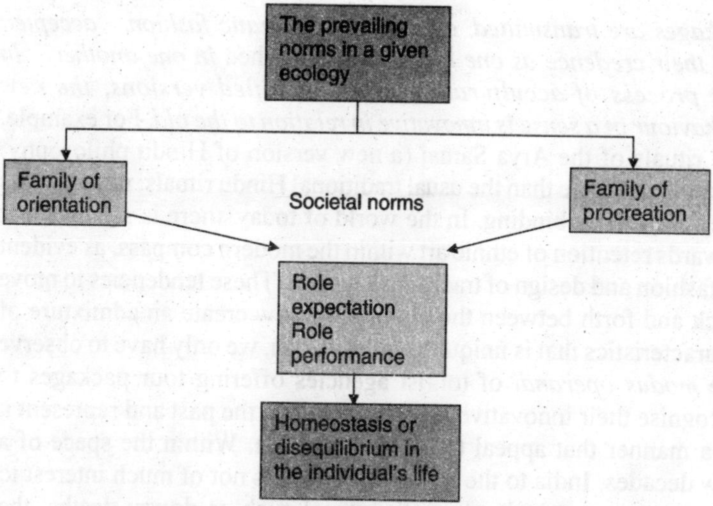

Paradigm 5.6: Responsibilities and Accountabilities of the Individual towards Society

To understand this paradigm, we turn to the knowledge of science and tradition, which is now being documented in India, mainly in its philosophical sense, rather than its empiricism. *This emphasis on the socio-historicity and cultural heritage of India is a positive sign that we are looking more intensively and sensitively towards our roots of origin.* The latter offer many hypotheses of reconstructing our identity and the three-fold axes of the Indian psyche: (i) the roots of "Indianism"; (ii) the expanding world of science; and (iii) the compatibility between science and tradition. The latter need not be anathema to the Indian perspective, for the Indian psyche, has the flexibility, by and large to respond to dynamic changes in its ambit.

(b) The Writing on the Wall

Witness the fact that in most cosmopolitan cities the illiterate or the neo-literate carries with him a cell phone, even though he may not be able to read or write fluently. *The relation of tradition to scientific knowledge is what links the past with the present. It is the past in the present. No society is created* post facto *by its present members. Ideas, beliefs and values are modified by oncoming generations. Cultural linkages are transmitted, often in an automatic fashion, "accepted for their credence as one layer after* enmeshed *in one another". In the process of acculturation to the modified versions, the new behaviour in a sense is innovative in relation to the old.* For example, the rituals of the Arya Samaj (a new version of Hindu philosophy) are less elaborate than the usual traditional Hindu rituals; nevertheless they are just as binding. In the world of today, there is a movement towards retention of ethnic art within the modern compass, as evident in fashion and design of traditional apparel. These tendencies to move back and forth between the old and the new create an admixture of characteristics that is unique to India. Again, we only have to observe the *modus operandi* of tourist agencies offering tour packages to recognise their innovative ability to reinvent the past and represent it in a manner that appeal to tourist attraction. Within the space of a few decades, India to the rest of the world is not of much interest to the west, except in its dramatic appeal such as dowry deaths, the lives of the poor, denigration of the girl child and such like phenomena. But in terms of its science and technological expertise and its rising GDP, it is being reluctantly higher profiled by the west; while its mysticism and myth is still a fascination to the western mind.[115] (Paranjpe, A.C., 2003)

Since the inception of documented traditional knowledge, little or no distinction was made between psychology, philosophy and religion in analyzing social behaviour which was and is viewed as holistic.[116] (Dalal, A., and G. Misra, 2001) The *Rig-Veda* and Gautam's *Dharma Shastras* around 600 B.C, stated that *dharma* is the duty of a human being on this earth towards his fellow men and towards himself, and is a continuity of philosophical thought and action. It has shaped the psychological and social behaviour of the Indian through the ages.[117] (Kakar, S., 1996) Inclusive in this precept is the concept of life stages and the life-cycle. Even to this day the concept of *dharma* interweaves itself intricately in all walks of life. It is one's *dharma* to feed the poor; to respect the elderly; to take care of the destitute in the kin group; to give alms to charitable organisations and to give *daan* to the poor at the time of religious events. These concepts translated into daily life is what some westerners euphemistically call "ritualism". In its deepest socio-religious sense, it has an inner sense of linkage with the past, the present and the future of one's life as in the belief of one's reincarnation. *If we examine these concepts dispassionately, they are not far from the philosophical thinking of the west from the days of the Greek philosophers: Aristotle and Plato: that "man is responsible for his fellow men".* Just as the *Bible* is a treatise of Christianity when Christ says through his apostle, "I say unto you... go out and do good", so also the treatises of the *Ramayana* and the *Mahabharata* contain concise and clear instructions on the behaviour of man to man, man to nature and man to the supreme being who lives in everything animate. *There are various but relevant conceptualisations, on how human beings are guided for their essential adaptation to the ecology so that they fit into their philosophical niches.*[118] (Kak, S.C., 1994) For instance, one such adaptation is the use of roots and herbs of the ayurvedic system to cure diseases and the practice of *yoga* for maintaining a healthy status,[119] (Rao, P.V.K., 1998) and a belief in the effects of cosmic energy on the human mind and body. These are deep-rooted philosophical beliefs. The word "*shantee*" has more meanings than just the term peace. It indicates being in harmony with God and nature, in an interdependent and inter-related manner.

15. Acceleration of Socio-cultural Change

In this, the twenty-first century, the socio-cultural face of India is changing. Urban elites in their adherence to cultural conceptualizations are becoming less dependent upon the family network, less socio-centrically involved, and perhaps less philosophically involved in the lives of others. The Indians are, as individuals, comparable with the western-oriented interpretations of acceptable abstract concepts such as individualism and imitative lifestyles of the western elite. It is not difficult to observe these phenomena in everyday life. Such identified groups live a life style of liberalised mobility, where their parents travel to other countries, and older children go on their own holidays with their peer groups. There is a protection of one's "private space," unlike previous years when people interacted at any time at any place in any context in an informal manner. Adolescents in the upper classes have a pop culture, and adults in these classes tend to have free sexual relationships. But, on the other side of the coin, such as in deep forests in the upper hills of Himalayas, social history has not changed much in the cultural traits of its inhabitants for over half a century or so.[120] (Berreman, G.D., 1970: 87). We have a deeply entrenched hiatus of those who have and those who do not, with the latter being proportionately much more.

Interpretations of abstract conceptualizations of variables, are differently operationalised even within a culture. India has many feudal/tribal cultures still living in the past. There are many sub-cultures in the rural areas of India that have not moved much from their social, occupational structures and still remain parochial in their world vision. We are, therefore, attempting to identify, however elusive, the concept of culture which is not definable in static terms. For instance, while it is contented that since human beings belong to the homo-sapiens species, they all have the potential to exhibit similar characteristics such as behaviour based on primeval needs. Be that as it may, they are generic abstract concepts and have meaning translatable in their own paradigms within a specific contextual framework of a unique culture of a specific group. What we are attempting to say is that these generic characteristics are only handles, which direct operational definitions of the characteristics as interpreted by the given culture. For example, with the spread of the electronic social media, astrology, as interpreted by the Indian sages, have meaning only in the Indian context of individual horoscopes, such as the positioning of the stars in individual horoscopes. For example, the trait dependency implies differential concepts in different cultures, and while we do not wish to go into lengthy explanations about semantic differences we do have to admit that social perceptions differ from one culture to another, from one era to another, and within an era from one generation to another.

It is the concept of "situational determinants" which dictate the interpretations of the abstract concept "the universe". These situational determinants are not easy to change. They refer clearly to the theme of "it is what it is". For instance, such concepts as caste behaviour differential, residential patterns of living, accessibility to services and institutions and the most important of all is economic viability (wealth); which are realistic factors which, therefore, monitor the interpretation of such abstract concepts. In a deprived economy, unlike non-deprived economies, dependency, for instance, is more under the control of the adult.[121] (Waxman, C.I., 1977: 6). In a deprived ecology where people spend their capacities and abilities mainly on the tenants of survival, there is no knowing how many geniuses have their capacities buried under depressed economic conditions.[122] (Dreze, J., and Sen, A., 1995) *Therefore, the interpretation of dependency, aggression, conformity, altruism, achievement and moral values are manipulable by situational determinants and, therefore, underlie the sources of social change which affect the contours of a culture.*

In the study of culture, whether mono-culture or multi-culture or the global culture, the psychology of development among cultures is dependent upon its numerous interpretations. *Their interpretations depend on how groups can cope with their situations competently given the level of physiobiological development.* This is essential to understand, whether it is the South African bushman's method of hunting game, the belief of the Chinese in herbal medications, or the Ethiopian mode of Coptic Christian worship where women stand against the outer walls of churches and pray, or the accelerating dynamo of industrialisation: all are equally and yet different elements of the contextual culture.[123] (Mandelbaum, D.G., 1949) *Therefore, at any given time, in these economically developing societies which are in a transitional stage, moving from traditionalism to modernism, different groups will act differently, and their observed behaviour is what gives the information to elicit the components of a culture in its psycho-social dimensions.* Curiously enough, an individual who is straddled between the two major types of systems, namely, traditionality and modernity, can act according to traditional concepts in one situation (ritualistic behaviour at births, marriages and deaths) and in a modern fashion in another situation (attending disco parties, entertainment in peer groups).[124] (Khalakdina, M., 1979: 24.-25) These are the situational determinants which monitor human behaviour. It may be illustrated dramatically by the behaviour of multi-million tycoons. They will return home from business after a cocktail party, dressed in their three-piece American suits and patent Italian shoes, but changes immediately into traditional *kurta/pyjama* and *chappals*, enter the *puja* room bare-footed, and conform to all the various rituals. They, then return from the *puja* room to easily slip into the role of a high-flying magnate attending to inter-continental conference calls, conducting financial business with his stock-broker, and leisurely consuming branded alcohol. The most remarkable type of this behaviour, is the ability of an individual to modify himself according to the given situational norms. *Therefore, it is not only the interpretation of culture, that forms linkages between subsystems and their concepts as culturally toned, but also differential interpretation of how cultural behaviour should be articulated from time to time by different individuals in the same cultural frame.*

This dynamically changing behaviour, is much more apparent when individuals move from one cultural frame to another, where they carefully carry their socio-religious and cultural behaviour forms to the new locales.[125] (Chaudhary, N., 2007) This is evident in the religious behaviour of migrants who move from countries of the east to the countries of the west. Indians, who are migrants in America, for instance, build temples, mosques and Gurudwaras to re-emphasise their religions. Some are deeply enmeshed in valued behaviour in the abstract forms such as religious philosophy, ethnic solidarity and kinship collectivism, which become more deeply ingrained in the new locale, than in the country of their origin. These are core values and, as expressed by the Lewinian theory[126] (Lewin, K., 1951) are more difficult to change than are the peripheral values of social behaviour. Kagitcibasi,[127] (Kagitcibasi, C., 2003) comments that: the adult's social cognition has an impelling influence on the child's cognition in particular behaviours. To illustrate this, commonly, the mother demands of her child, non-aggressive behaviour when other children wish to play with his toys. The child logically assumes that these toys belong only to him and cannot be parted with. In this impasse of dynamic non verbalised communications between mother and child, the child's ego-centricism is reinforced. Whereas with the mother, it is a package of processes: the child's negative reaction, the sense of failure to control, the reflection on the other children of her child's mean behaviour and most of all the reflection of others that her child is a 'spoilt brat' and so on. These are all fleeting thoughts except, here, that the mother is prompted by social norms, and the child has not as yet internalised them. *According to Kagitcibasi's analysis, a specific behaviour can be explained by the theoretical constructs of most development experts.* Most experts tend to use reference of standards of their own disciplinary connotations, such as Lewin's explanation of behaviour cumulating into habits.[128] (Lewin, K., 1951) *The human mind works like a computer with templates which record experiences in memory, stored as habits, repeated on being prompted, and become permanent expressions of the linkage between thought and action*[129] (Kelly, G.A., 1976: 38). Thus, the co-existence of traditionality and modernity in the Indian psyche is subject to dynamic situational determinants of a given human ecosystem and its given geo-ecological system.

REFERENCES

1. Weiss, P., 1959, 'Cellular dynamics', *Reviews of Modern Physics*, 31, 11-20.
2. Knight, R.G., 1992, *The Neuropsychology of Degenerative Brain Diseases*, London: Erlbaum.

3. Jennings, H.S., 1930, *The Biological Basis of Human Nature*, New York: W.W. Norton & Co Inc.
4. Jennings, H.S., 1930, *The Biological Basis of Human Nature*, New York: W.W. Norton & Co Inc.
5. Merke, F., 1984, *History and Iconography of Endemic Goitre and Cretinism*, New York: Springer Publications.
6. Cullen, J.F., and H.G. Butler, 1963 (June), 'Mongolism (Down's Syndrome) and Keratoconus', *British Journal of Ophthalmology, 47(4), 321-330.*
7. Singh, M., 2000, 'Animal Behaviour', in J. Pandey (ed.), *Psychology in India Revisited: Developments in the Discipline*, Vol. 1, pp. 19-57, New Delhi: Sage.
8. Singh, M., 2000, 'Animal Behaviour', in J. Pandey (ed.) *Psychology in India Revisited – Developments in the Discipline*, Vol. 1, pp. 19-57, New Delhi: Sage.
9. *Ibid.*
10. Mandal, M., 2000, 'Physiological foundations of behaviour', in J. Pandey (ed.), *Psychology in India Revisited – Developments in the Discipline*, Vol. 1, pp. 58-93, New Delhi: Sage.
11. Moorthy, K.S., 2008, *Child Psychology, Anti Social Behaviour*. New Delhi: Cyber Tech Publications.
12. Sears, R., E. Maccoby and H. Levin, 1957, *Patterns of Child Rearing*, New York: Harper Bros.
13. Stork, H., 1980, 'La naissance d' un fils dans la tradition religious de l'Inde' (The birth of a son in the religious traditions of India), *Journale de psychology Normale et pathgalogque*, 77 (2-3), 151-86.
14. Hartshone, H., and M.A. May, 1928, *Studies in the Nature of Character: I. Studies in Deceit*, New York: MacMillan.
15. Deutsch, M., 1975, 'Equity, equality and need: what determines which value will be used as the basis of distributive justice?', *Journal of Social Issues*, 31, 137-149.
16. Pandey, J., 1987, 'Effects of crowding on human social behaviour', *Journal of Social and Economic Studies*, 5(1), pp. 37-41
17. Adams, J.S., 1965, 'Inequity in social exchange', in Berkovitz (ed.), *Advances in Experimental Social Psychology*, Vol. 2, pp. 267-99, New York: Academic Press.
18. Leventhal, G.S., 1976, 'Fairness in social relationships', in J.W. Thibaut, J.T. Spence and R. Carson (eds.), *Contemporary Topics in Social Psychology*, pp. 99-131. Morristown, N.J.: General Learning Press.
19. Greenberg, J., and R.I. Cohen, 1982, *Equity and Justice in Social Behaviour*. New York: Academic Press.

20. Kagitcibasi, C., and J.W. Berry, 1989, 'Cross cultural psychology: Current research and trends', *Annual Review of Psychology*, 40, 493-531.
21. Krishnan, L., 2000, 'Distributive justice in the Indian perspective', in H.S.R. Kao, and D. Sinha, *Asian Perspectives on Psychology*, Cross Cultural Research and Methodological Series, Vol. 19, New Delhi/ Thousands Oak/London.
22. Krishnan, L., 2000, 'Distributive justice in the Indian perspective', in H.S.R. Kao, and D. Sinha, *Asian Perspectives on Psychology*. Cross Cultural Research and Methodological Series, Vol. 19, New Delhi/ Thousands Oak/London.
23. Piaget, J., 1930, *The Child's Conception of Physical Causality*, New York: Harcourt Brace & Co.
Kohlberg, Lawrence, 1981. *Essays on Moral Development: Vol. 1: The Philosophy of Moral Development*, San Francisco: Harper & Row.
Kohlberg, Lawrence, 1984. *Essays on Moral Development: Vol. 2, The Psychology of Moral Development*, San Francisco: Harper & Row.
24. Misra, R., 1971, *Mallukurumbas of Kappala*. Memoir No. 30. Indian Museum, Anthropological Survey of India. Calcutta: ASI, Government of India.
25. Benedict, R., 1938, 'Continuities and discontinuities in cultural conditioning,' *Psychiatry*, 1, 161-167.
26. Khalakdina, M.,1979, *Early Childcare in India*. London. Gordon and Breach p-212.
27. Kakar, S., 1981, The Inner World: Psychoanalytic Study of Childhood and Society in India. Revised ed., New Delhi: Oxford University Press.
28. Bowlby, J., 1981, *Attachment and Loss*, Vol 1, New York: Basic Books Inc.
29. Chatterjee, L., 1984, *Power Differences: Machiavillianism and Coalition Dynamics—A Sociopsychological Perspective*. Unpublished doctoral dissertation, Indian Institute of Technology, Kanpur.
30. Khalakdina, M.,1998, "In sight-on site: a study of mobile crèches", in M. Swaminathan (ed.), *The First Five Years: A Critical Perspective on Early Childhood Care and Education in India*. New Delhi: Sage.
31. Woodhead, Martin, 2001 'Psychology and the cultural construction of children's needs', in James, A., and A. Prout, *Constructing and Reconstructing Childhood: Contemporary Issues in the Sociology of Childhood*, pp. 66-77. Britain: Routledge and Falmer
32. International Society for Study of Behavioural Development, India, 1995, *Perspectives on Deprivation and Human Development: Implications for Intervention*, South Asia Workshop on Culturally

Relevant Intervention strategies for Psycho-social Development of Children and Youth in Poverty. Chandigarh, November 20-23, 1995

33. Ainsworth, D.S., 1972, "*Attachment and Dependency: A comparison*' in D.L. Gerwitz (ed.) *Attachment and Dependency*. Washington. D.C.: V.H. Winston, pp. 97-137.
34. Bandura, A., 1977, *Social Learning Theory*. Englewood Cliffs, NJ: Prentice Hall.
35. Suvannathat, C., D. Bhanthumnavin, L. Bhuapirom and D.M. Keats (eds.), 1985, *Handbook of Asian Child Development and Child Rearing Practices*. Bangkok, Thailand: Srinakharinwirot University, Behavioural Science Research Institute.
36. Horney, K., 1939, *New Ways in Psychoanalysis*. New York: Norton; Maslow, A.H.,1970, *Motivation and Personality*. New York: Harper & Row;

    Murray, H.A., 1936, 'Basic concepts for a psychology of personality', *Journal of General Psychology*, 15, 241-268;

    Freud, S., 1964, 'An outline of psychoanalysis', in J. Stratechey (ed.), *Standard Edition of the Complete Psychological Works of Sigmund Freud*, Vol. 23, pp. 144-20. London: Hogarth Press.
37. Whiting, J.W.M., and I.L. Child, 1953, *Child Training and Personality*. New Haven: Yale Univ. Press.
38. Guba, E.G. (ed.), 1990, *The Paradigm Dialogue*. Newberry Park, CA.: Sage.
39. Paranjpe, A.C., and G.S. Bhat, 1997 'Emotion: A perspective from the Indian tradition', in H.S.R. Kao and D. Sinha (eds.), *Asian Perspectives on Psychology*, pp. 127-143, New Delhi: Sage.
40. Argyle, M., 1976, 'Verbal and non-Verbal communication', in J. Wolfson, *Personality and Learning*, Vol. 2, pp. 77-93. London: Hodder and Stoughton (in association with The Open University Press).
41. Murray, R. Thomas, 2001, 'Theory trends' in Thomas Murray (ed.), *Recent Theories of Human Development*, pp. 1-26. Thousand Oaks, London, New Delhi: Sage Publications.
42. James, A., and A. Prout, 1990, *Issues in The Sociological Study of Childhood*, London: The Falmer Press.
43. Sharma, R.S., 1981, *Indian Feudalism*, New Delhi: McMillan.
44. Madan, A., 2003 (Nov. 1), 'Old and new dilemmas in Indian civil education', *Economic and Political Weekly*, Vol. 38, No. 44.
45. Feagin, Joe R., and Clairece Booher Feagin, 2007, *Racial and Ethnic Relations*. Englewood Cliffs, N.J.: Prentice Hall.
46. Carstairs, G.M., 1957, *The Twice-Born*. London: Hogarth Press.
47. Singh, Jaswant, 1997, "Modernisation *versus* westernization", *The Business Standard*, 10 March 1997.

48. Ghosh, S., 2008, *Tribal Development in India: Dimensions and Initiatives*. Hyderabad: Icfai University Press.
49. Mirza, S., and P. Gupta, 2008, *Business and Management: General Management Organisation and Structure Design — An Indian Perspective*. New Delhi: Macmillan Publishers.
50. Mehta, D., 1970, *Portrait of India*. New Haven: Yale University Press.
51. Berinstain, V., 1998, *India and the Mughal Dynasty*. New York: Harry N. Abrams.
52. Young, J.G., and D. Kaplan, 2003, 'The concept of culture', in J.G. Young, P. Ferrari, S. Malhotra, S. Tayano, and E. Caffo (eds.), *Brain, Culture and Development*, pp. 31-91. Delhi: McMillan.
53. Young, J.G., and D. Kaplan, 2003, 'The concept of culture', in J.G. Young, P. Ferrari, S. Malhotra, S. Tayano, and E. Caffo (eds.), *Brain, Culture and Development*, pp. 31-91. Delhi: McMillan.
54. Nath, V., 2001, Puranas and Acculturation: A Historic-anthropological Perspective. Delhi: Munri Publishers.
55. Fairbank, J.K., 1992, *China: A New History*. Cambridge, MA: the Belknap Press of Harvard University.
56. Cleary, Dr. Thomas, 1993, *The Essential Koran: The Heart of Islam*. San Francisco: Harper; New York: Collins.
57. Valsiner J., and Connolly, K.J., 2003, 'The Nature of Development: The continuing dialogue of processes and outcomes', In J. Valsiner and K.J. Connolly (eds.), *Handbook of Developmental Psychology*, pp. ix – xviii. London: Sage.
58. Anderson, J.E., 1957, 'Dynamics of development, systems in process', in D.B. Harris (ed.), *Concept of Development*. Minnesota: University of Minnesota Press.
59. Descartes, R., 1637/1980, *Discourse on Method* (trans. DA Cress). Indianapolis: Hackett.
60. Gottlieb, G., 'Probabilistic Epigenesis of Development', in J. Valsiner and K. Connolly (eds.), *Handbook of Developmental Psychology*. London: Sage, 2002.
61. Gottlieb, G., 1998, "Normally occurring environmental and behavioural gene activity: From central dogma to probabilistic epigenesis", *Psychological Review*, 105, pp. 792-802.
62. Gould S.J., 1977, *Ontogeny and Phylogeny*. Cambridge, MA: Harvard University Press.
63. Zuckerman, B.D., R. Hingson, H. Amaro, S.M. Devenson, H. Kayne, S. Parker, R. Vinci, K. Aboagye, L. Fried, H. Cabral, R. Timperi and H. Bauchner, 1989, 'Effects of maternal Marijuana and cocaine use on foetal growth', *The New England Journal of Medicine*, 12, 762-768.

64. Langer J., Rivera S., Schlesinger M., and Wakeley, A., in press, 'Early Cognitive Development: Ontogeny and Phylogeny', in J. Valsiner and K. Connolly (eds.), *Handbook of Developmental Psychology*, pp. 141-170.
65. Piaget, J., 1932, *The Moral Judgement of the Child,* New York: Harcourt Brace.
66. Vygotsky, L.S., 1934, *Thought and Language*. Cambridge, MA: MIT Press.
67. Erikson, Erik, 1959. *Identity and the Life Cycle.* New York: Norton.
68. Piaget, J., 1954, *The Construction of Reality in the Child.* New York: Basic Books.
69. Seth, M., and Bhatnagar, U., 1979, 'Personality factors in relation to the adjustment of children of working and non-working mothers', *Child Psychiatry Quarterly*, 12(2), pp. 48-56.
70. Majeed, A., and Ghosh, E.S., 1982, 'A study of social identity in three ethnic groups in India', *International Journal of Psychology*, 17(4), pp. 455-463.
71. Kureshi, A., and Dutt, M., 1979, 'Dimensions of alienation: A factor analytic study', *Psychologia: An International Journal of Psychology in the Orient*, 22(2) pp. 99-105.
72. Mohanty, N., 1984, 'Social and psychological correlates of alienation among adolescents', *Psychological Studies*, 299(2), pp.147-151.
73. Bronfenbrenner, U., 1975, 'Nature with nurture: a reinterpretation of the evidence', in A. Montague (ed.), *Race and IQ*, pp. 114-144, New York: Oxford University Press.
74. Reddy, N.Y., Rao, T.N., Sandeep, P., and Padmakar, V.V., 1970, 'Certain correlates of conformity behaviour', *Child Psychiatry Quarterly*, 12(4), pp. 93-102.
75. Singh, S., Upmanyu, V.V., and Rameekl, 1982, 'Psychometric correlates of modernity', *Social Change,* 12 (3), pp. 29-33.
76. Thompson, G.G., 1952, *Child Psychology*. New York: Houghton Mifflin Co.
77. Maslow, A.H., 1966, *Motivation and Personality*. New York: Harper and Row (2nd Edition).
78. Harlow, H.F., 1963, 'The maternal affectional system', in B.M. Foss (ed.), *Determinants of Infant Behaviour*, Vol. II, New York: John Wiley & Sons.
79. Sears, R.R., 1943, 'Survey of objective studies of psychoanalytic concepts', *Soc. Sci. Res. Counc. Bull.*, No. 51. New York: Soc. Sci. Res. Council.
80. Bronfenbrenner, U., 1979, *The Ecology of Human Development*. London: Harvard University Press.

81. Vygotsky, L.M., 1978, 'Development of higher mental processes', in M. Cole, V. John-Steiner, S. Scribner, and E. Souberman (eds.), *Mind in Society*. Cambridge MA: Harvard University Press.
82. Miller, N.E., 1952, 'Comments on theoretical models', in D. Krech, G.S. Klein, Duje, *Theoretical Models and Personality Theory*. Durham NC: Ubui Press.
83. Markus, H.R., and S. Kitayama, 1991, 'Culture and the self: Implications for cognition, emotion and motivation', *Psychological Review*, Vol. 98, 224-253.
84. Maidment, Richard and Colin Mackerras, 1998, *Culture and Society in the Asia-Pacific*. London: Routledge.
85. Kluckhohn C., and F.L. Stredtbeck, 1961, *Variations in Value Orientations*. Evanston Ill: Row Peterson & Co.; Elkin, F., and G. Handel, 1972, *Child and Society: The Process of Socialization*, p. 27. NY: Random House; Dubois, A.J.A., and H.K. Beauchamp, 1978, *Hindu, Manners, Customs and Ceremonies*. Delhi: Oxford University Press.
86. Whiting, B., 1963, *Studies of Child Rearing*. New York: Wiley.
87. Malhotra, S., 2003, 'Sociocultural diversity and ethnocentricism in child mental health', in J.G. Young, P. Ferrari, S. Malhotra, S. Tayano, and E. Caffo (eds.), *Brain, Culture and Development*, pp. 3-13. Delhi: McMillan.
88. Sroufe, L.A., E.A. Carlson, A.K. Levy, *et al.*, 1999, 'Implications of attachment theory for developmental psychopathology', *Developmental Psychopathology*, 11 (1), 1-13.
89. Bronfenbrenner, U., 1974, *Two Worlds of Childhood: USA and USSR*, New York: Russell Sage Foundation.
90. Doshi, S.L., 1971, *Bhils: Between Social Self-awareness and Cultural Synthesis*. Delhi, Sterling.
91. Munroe, R., and R. Munroe, 1975, *Cross Cultural Human Development*, Monterey, California: Books/Cole Publishing Company.
92. Bronfenbrenner, U., 1970, *Two Worlds of Childhood: U.S. and U.S.S.R.* New York: Russel Sage Foundation.
93. Munroe, R., and R. Munroe, 1975, *Cross Cultural Human Development*. Monterey, California: Books/Cole Publishing Company.
94. Whiting, J.W.M., 1968, 'Methods and problems in cross-cultural research', in G. Lindsey, and E. Aronson (ed.), *The Handbook of Social Psychology*. Vol 2, 2nd edition, pp. 693-728, Reading, Mas: Addison—Wresley.
95. Bronfenbrenner, U., 1970, *Two Worlds of Childhood: U.S. and U.S.S.R*, New York: Russel Sage Foundation.

96. Willerman, 1972, 'A review of H.J Eysenck's The IQ argument', *Contemporary Psychology*. 17, 585-586.
97. Erikson, E.H., 1958, *Childhood and Society*. 2nd ed. New York: W.W. Norton & Co.
98. Super, C.M., and S. Harkness, 1986, 'The developmental niche: A Conceptualisation at the interface of child and culture', *International Journal of Behaviour Development*, 9, 1-25.
99. Saraswathi, T.S., 2003, 'Introduction', in T.S. Saraswati (ed.), *Cross-cultural Perspective in Human Development*, pp. 23-47, New Delhi: Sage.
100. Dewsbury, D.A., 1991, 'Psychobiology', *American Psychologist*, 46(3), 198-205.
101. Bowlby, J., 1969, *Attachment and Loss*, Vol. 1, London: Hogarth Press.
102. Bronfenbrenner, U., 1962, 'Soviet studies of personality development and socialsiaion', in Raymond Bauer (ed.), *Some Views of Soviet Psychology*, pp. 630-86. Washington D.C.: Am. Psych. Assn.
103. Brunner, J., 1996, *The Culture of Education*. Cambridge, MA: Harvard University Press.
104. Dasen, P.R., and R.C. Mishra, 2000, 'Cross-cultural views on human development in the third millennium', *International Journal of Behaviour Development*, 24, 428-434.
105. Marriot, A.M., 1976, 'Hindu transactions: diversity without dualism', in B.C Kapforer (ed.), *Transaction and Meaning: Directions in the Anthropology of Exchange and Symbolic Behaviour*, pp. 109-142, Philadelphia Institute for the Study of Human Issues.
106. Berry, J.W., and P.R. Dasen (eds.), 1974, *Culture and Cognition: Readings in Cross-cultural Psychology*, London: Methuen.
107. Whiting, J.W.M., 1968, 'A model for cross-cultural research', in G. Lindzey, and E. Aranson (eds.), *Handbook of Social Psychology*, 2nd ed., Vol. 2, pp. 693-728, Reading, MA: Addison-Wesley.
108. Super, C.M., and S. Harkness (eds.), 1996, *Parents' Cultural Belief Systems*, New York: The Guilford Press.
109. Greenfield, P.M., 1997, 'Culture as process: Empirical methods for cultural psychology', in J.W. Berry, Y.H. Poortinga and J. Pandey (eds.), *Handbook of Cross-cultural Psychology, Vol. 1: Theory and Method*, 2nd ed., pp. 301-346, Boston, MA: Allyn and Bacon.
110. Kakar, S., 2001, 'The themes of authority in social relations in India', in A.K. Dalal and G. Misra (ed.), *New Directions in Indian Psychology*, pp. 132-140, New Delhi: Sage.
111. Pareek, U., 2001, 'Poverty and motivation: Figure and ground', in A.K. Dalal and G. Misra (ed.), *New Directions in Indian Psychology*. pp. 262-279, New Delhi: Sage.

112. Krishna Kumar, T, Shushanta Mallick and Jayaram Holla, 2009, 'Estimating consumption deprivation in India using survey data: A state-level rural-urban analysis before and during Reform Period', *The Journal of Development Studies*, Vol. 45(4), pp. 441-472.
113. Misra, G.,1982, 'Motivational structure and prolonged deprivation', *Indian Journal of Social Work*, 43(1), 11-18.
114. Datta, A.K., and S. Sharma, 2002, *Facets of Indian Poverty*, New Delhi: Concept Publishers.
115. Paranjpe, A.C., 2003, 'Contemporary psychology and a mutual understanding of Europe and Indian', in J.W. Berry, R.C. Mishra and R.C. Tripathi (eds.), *Psychology in Human and Social Development: Lessons from Diverse Cultures,* pp. 18-30, New Delhi: Sage Publications.
116. Dalal, A.K., and G. Mishra, 2001, 'Psychology in India: Evolution and emerging trends', in A.K. Dalal and G. Mishra, *New Directions in Indian Psychology*, pp. 19-49, New Delhi: Sage.
117. Kạkar, S., 1996, *Culture and the Psyche, Selected Essays*, Delhi: Oxford University Press.
118. Kak, S.C., 1994, *The Astronomical Code of the Rigveda*, New Delhi: Adiyata.
119. Rao, P.V.K., 1998, 'A note on yoga as a system of psyhcotherapy', *Journal of Indian Psychology*, 16(2), 10-13.
120. Berreman, G.D., 1970, 'Pahari Culture: diversity and change in the lower Himalayas', in K. Ishwaran (ed.), *Change and Continuity in India's Villages*, pp. 73-103. New York: Colombia University Press.
121. Waxman, C.I., 1977, *The Stigma of Poverty: A Critique of Poverty Theories and Policies*, New York: Pergamon Press.
122. Dreze, J., and Sen, A., 1995, *Indian Economic Development and Social Opportunity*, Delhi: Oxford University Press.
123. Mandelbaum, D.G., (ed.), 1949, *Selective Writings of Edward Sapir in Language, Culture and Personality*, Berkeley and Los Angels: University of California Press.
124. Khaḷakdina, M., 1979, *Early Childcare in India*, London: Gordon and Breach.
125. Chaudhary, N., 2007, 'The family: Negotiating cultural values', in J. Valsiner and A. Rosa (eds.), *Handbook of Social Psychology*, pp. 524-542. Cambridge, M.A.: Cambridge University Press.
126. Lewin, K., 1951, *Field Theory in Social Science: Selected Theoretical Papers*. (Edited by D. Cartwright). New York: Harper and Row.
127. Kagitcibasi, C., 2003, 'Human development across cultures: A contextual functional analysis and implications for interventions', in T.S. Saraswathi (ed.), *Cross-cultural Perspectives in Human*

Development: Theory, Research and Applications, pp. 166-191, New Delhi: Sage.

128. Lewin, K., 1951, *Field Theory in Social Science: Selected Theoretical Papers*. (Edited by D. Cartwright), New York: Harper & Row.
129. Kelly, G.A., 1976, 'Constructive alternativism', in J. Wolfson (ed.), *Personality and Learning*, Vol. 2. pp. 34-47, London: Hodder and Stoughton (in association with the Open University Press).

6

The Inter-Linkages between Personality Development and Ecology

The chapter consists of the following sections:

1. Introduction;
2. The major differences and linkages between human ecology and geo-ecology and the distinguishing exchanges between them;
3. Psychogenic development and the human ecology;
4. Selected correlates of the Indian psyche;
5. Cognition of the self in the ecological environment;
6. Ecology and socio-cognitive development;
7. The linkages between cognition and ecological derivatives;
8. Interactions among the eco-systems;
9. Interactions in the meso system;
10. Major linking theories;
11. The emergence of cognitive neuroscience with psychological constructs;
12. Cohabitation of social development with technological development;
13. Eco-cultural variability in personality development; and
14. Major overarching linkages.

1. Introduction

In this chapter, we will look at several important characteristics of the individual, and the socio-economic ecology in which he grows into a "personality". The latter process occurs mainly through the socialisation processes used by the nurturer/s, especially in the initial foundational years, when values and habits are inculcated, mainly through the social learning and imitation processes[1] (Bandura, A., 1977; Miller, N.E., and J. Dollard, 1941). These processes were described in detail in chapter 4. The geo-ecology is a system with which an individual in the micro-system negotiates to meet his needs. The various systems of this interaction will be discussed in the following sections.

2. The Major Differences and Linkages between Human Ecology and Geo-ecology and the Distinguishing Exchanges between them

Human ecology is intertwined in situations and relations with other human beings in the various networks of family and kinship *in the micro system and the increasing contacts in the outer* ecosystems[2] (Alan Sroufe, L. Robert Cooper and Ganie Dehart, 1996). *Geo-ecology refers simply to the givens of nature, in climatic geographical areas: the tropics, the* tundras, the hills, *ocean sites* which delineate geographical characteristics. *These two ecologies, namely, the human and the geo, act and react upon each other and consequentially affect* human behaviour *in varying degrees*[3] (Huggert, Richard John, 1995). Human ecology is limited to the social interactions spread over a large radius from the family to the global spheres of the various countries. Every individual has his own specific ecology comprised of two major parts – his residential ecology and his interactive ecology of other places, small or large. For example, the villager's orbit is mainly his village and other adjacent villages and perhaps occasional visits for special events to other ecological areas. The urbanite, especially the elite executive of an MNC is more in the air and in conferences than the villager. Therefore, there are many extremes in ecologies and in between these extremes there are numerous in-between individual ecologies.

The following paradigm depicts the major factors of ecology, and the various influences on the human micro-system of, the family. The human ecology in this micro-system; the family is influenced by the ecology, technology, and organised institutions. The organisation specifies role expectations and role-performances, where each individual is interdependent upon the other.

Over the past decades, increasing science and technology are breaking down barriers between the human and the geo-ecologies.[4] (Gadgil, M., and PRS Rao, 1998).

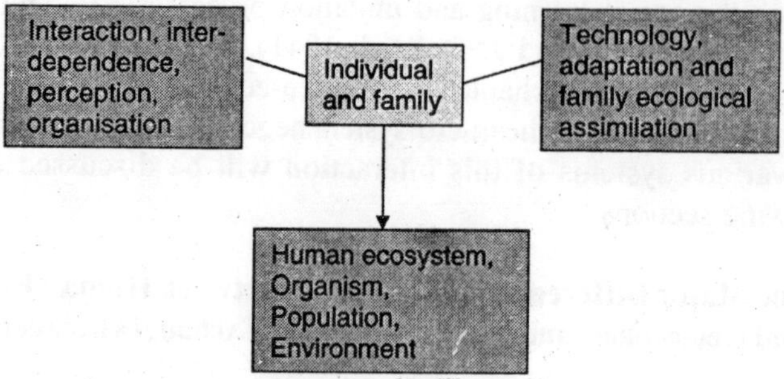

6.1 Paradigm: Major Factorial Inputs into Ecology – Human and Geo-Ecology

Thus, it is important to analyse how the surrounding geo-ecology influences the development of the human individual into a personality. In the above paradigm, the intricate interactions of the human ecology and the given geo-ecology exhibit observable interactive processes. Nature and its products are malleable according to human volition. *The human dominates over other species, and particularly so in the* territorial ecology he occupies. *He exercises* physical, social and political *rights in his territorial space, just like lions do in the jungle.* Any violation of territories creates destabilisation. Human beings by civilisation and by race have occupied different geographical spaces over the world, and have forged themselves into nations and, citizens of nations. Within countries, the citizens inhabit varying ecologies such as urban areas (urbanites), rural areas (ruralites), tribal areas (nomadic), coastal areas (fishermen), arid deserts, fertile plains and such like, all belonging to the nation and, therefore, have different constructs of the relation of human to geo-ecology, where interaction takes place within and among these categories. Take the instance of oil for energy. The industrial development in the 'developed' nations require more oil, but the geo-ecologies within these nations cannot meet the growing demand of their industrialisation. Therefore, oil-producing countries are being exploited for the benefit of the richer nations. In this century, however, there is a juxtaposition occurring. The previously less economically developed countries, like China and India, are increasing their energy demands as their economy is developing at a higher rate than before. This leads to global power politics between countries and destabilisation of harmony among them[5] (DeSombre, Elizabeth R., 2006). This may be viewed as a reflection of the phenomenon that while the ecologies remained stable in size, populations in the developing countries grew faster than in the developed. The population of India and China together total 2.4 billion, which is 2/5th of the world population.[6] (Barry Eichengreen, Poonam Gupta and Rajiv) This clearly indicates that their needs are growing in relation to their population growth. Further, the current recession has created an imbalance in world trade: the US Dollar has fallen in value while other developing counties are increasing their economic conditions. The tendency, however, is that, nations attempt to find a balance between needs and demands into a mode of equilibrium. The hardest hit countries are now seeking to address the problems of deleterious climatic changes, to remodify their budgetary allocations and to gain territorial power in the economically emerging nations.[7] (Charles Brownell, 2008) *The implications here are clear that ecology is related to a nation's economy, its GNP, its consumer index and such like parameters* which illustrate the quality of life in the given nation. Here again, however, *these larger populations in the developing world have less resources and, therefore, are not only economically poorer, but also have lower social indices like infant mortality, maternal mortality, educational levels, nutritional status* and such like. These low indices are available in countries like Bangladesh, India, and Nepal in Asia and Somalia, Ethiopia and Sudan in Africa. What this means is that in developing countries like India there are more human beings than the ecology can provide for, while the situation is *vice versa* in the economically developed countries like the Netherlands where there is a little more than zero per cent population growth and, therefore, an ecology that comfortably sustains human living patterns.

In the civilisations of hunting and pastoral lifestyles, there was a relative balance between geo-ecological produce and human ecological needs, which worked in tandem. When natural disasters occurred and humans were exposed to the ravages of nature, they had little scientific knowledge but much "traditional wisdom" as to how to deal with these disasters. In India because of the various and changing rulers in the pre-colonial days, little industrialisation could take place, unlike the sophisticated fast-paced industrial development in Britain, other countries of Europe and, in America. The original inhabitants of America, namely, the Red Indians, and the aborigines of Australia, were literally pushed into the background by the British migrants and, therefore, they were little affected by industrial development. Thus, technological advancements in agricultural and industrial economies proceeded at their own different paces and in their social historicity created their own inroads.[8] (Adams, C., 1935)

Over the years, India experienced a successful green revolution (agriculture) and then a white revolution (dairy) contributing to self-sufficiency in staples and dairy products. On the other hand, countries which were moving along the path of industrialisation were already self-sufficient, and were able to export their surplus to developing countries like India like the PL 480 programme which supplied surplus and sometimes poor quality wheat to India in the 1960s and 1970s.[9] (Haq, M.U., 1995) India is ranked 134 among the countries of the world.[10] (UNDP, 2009) Thus, India has a long way to go to rank higher on the Human Development Index of the UN which measures countrywide data regarding life expectancy at birth, adult literacy rate, combined gross enrolment ratio in education, and per capita GDP.

Therefore, since most Indians live in sparse ecologies they have to work harder with less well-nutritional bodies and high morbidity rates to wrest from the ecology what is required in increasing quantities, while at the same time attempting to control destabilising natural phenomena. The individuals in modernising ecologies like India are faced with the consequences of high industrialisation, such as unpredictable climatic changes and global warming caused by greenhouse gas emissions, increase in crowding in urban areas and unhealthy surroundings.[11] (Joel, B. Hagen, 1992)

As further destabilisation of the human lifestyle occurs, it requires further technological and scientific innovations to right the situation. In India, for instance, although limited to metropolitan cities, the change to the environment-friendly Compressed Natural Gas (CNG) instead of Petrol and Diesel as fuel for the public transport and the use of paper and cloth bags instead of plastic has to some extent decreased pollution. Unfortunately, India's increasing population tends to de-equate the relationship. *The human ecology is witnessing this phenomenon in a return to a "greener environment" concept; a concept now occurring in the very countries which had a high level of technological inventions.* These industrial activities create a vicious problem – namely, the degradation of natural geo-ecologies and destablisation of natural resources. This requires additive innnovations to stem the destabilising effects of technologies. In India, we have several examples smaller in complexity than those of the developed world, but nevertheless alarming. For example, in the Alwar District of Rajasthan the "marble" barons are decimating the hills for the marble requirements of cities like Delhi. Consequently, during the monsoons the ponds, lakes and '*jhoods*' lack adequate water to stabilise the requirement between man and nature and deplete the necessities of life for the villagers. To remedy a situation like this, projects like water harvesting are being implemented by NGOs so as to retain monsoon waters for the rest of the year.[12] (Pandey, D.N., A.K. Gupta and D.M. Anderson, 2003) So also other forms of bio-technology have increased their activities such as the use of solar panels, Methane gas from cow-dung, use of waste products of forests for village arts which are exhibited in several State emporia in every large city so as to garner State revenues, which feed back into these village entrepreneurs. It is well-known that in the Indian government system, those not working in organisations both private and State, do not pay taxes. Therefore revenues for States are limited, to provide for facilities such as hospitals, schools and such like public amenities meant for the less advantaged, for whom these facilities are free or subsidised. Yet, the pity of it is that there are too few facilities for too many.

What happens to the traits of the individual in the course of the changing nature of ecologies, which, as technological development progresses, creates unintended or serendipitous debilitating consequences? In what way does a given ecology contribute to such regressive factors, since the main intent of innovative technology is to create a better lifestyle? Within these shifting paradigms, we do perceive the simultaneous effects of cures and causes between geo-ecology and human ecology. At the geographical level, these disconcerting inequalities between human ecology and geo-ecology are observable, in that regressive ecological conditions like floods and famines ravage the human lives. For example, the melting snows of the Himalayas add to flood waters during the rainy season. They often sweep away whole villages and even urban settlements, causing huge losses to the people and requiring the governments to spend huge amounts in the rehabilitation of the flood-affected peoples. Thus, the more unstable the geo-ecology, the higher the range of imbalance between human and geo-ecological harmonious conditions. For instance, in an earthquake-prone geo-ecology like Haiti, the insecurity of the individual increases. Similarly, the more the threat of increase in nuclear weapons, as is happening in North Vietnam and Iran, the greater the insecurity in the world-widening ecology. For instance, the once stable Iraqis are now living a life of insecurity and tensions because of the continuance of war and fighting.

Thus, we need to know how the development of the individual in his ecology, whether normal or otherwise, is being affected, and as to how a human being develops into a person with or without equilibrating *traits in his ecology*. Therefore, what are the foundational properties of a developing person, which are subject to uncertain ecological factors? The difference is that human beings can communicate their problems when stressed whereas stressed ecologies are silent "undertakers".

3. Psychogenic Development and the Human Ecology

The psychogenesis of human development provide the bases for the individual's personality formation in terms of his mental and physical growth. The latter form the foundation of the individual's traits, characteristics and values. In the ecological setting, they stabilise to become habitual patterns. Maturation forms the basis of the normally developing human being in such specific settings, which, in turn, act and react upon the organism. Changes in development are qualitatively modulated by these situational factors, such as the human network encompassing the individual.[13] (Altman I., and Wohlwill J.F., 1977) *However, ecology is not something static. It changes on its own* through *evolutionary processes.* In the previous chapters, there have been several allusions to the close interactivity that occurs almost unconsciously between an individual and his surroundings. This interactivity is operational throughout the lifespan of the individual and during the process the ontogenetic traits of the individual are nurtured or otherwise by his human ecology[14] (Richard L. Mosher, D.J. Youngman and J.M. Day, 1999). This process, in turn, is affected by the geo-ecology[15] (Richard L. Mosher, D.J. Youngman and J.M. Day, 1999).

How does the individual in India become influenced by his human ecology? Like all individuals in all cultures, an Indian works towards his goals, *communicated by his human ecology, which are socially approved.* In attempting to move towards such goals, he perceives socially approved models in his environment, and he is motivated to imitate the indicated models. *Ecologies, however, are innumerable, and so are the models and the human* frames *surrounding the individual. Consequently, the norms of behaviour vary.* They do so from one caste group to another, from one ethnic group to another, and from one religion to another. If we analyse the operationalised meanings of these concepts, many of them relate to several theoretical concepts of personality development. For instance, in relation to the theory of social learning and imitation, there tend to be closed circuits for modelling, where models exist in the same/known eco-systems. For example, in tribal areas, the tribal head may be held up as a model. In business circles, a Tata or a Modi or an Ambani may be held up as models. In other words, models may be distal or proximal in the ecological space. The model has the ability to attract imitative behaviour by virtue of possessing characteristics that are admired.[15] (Bandura, A., 1962) The strength of attraction towards modelling behaviour depends on the innate potentials of the individual's motivation to imitate. In elementary societies, mythological figures are held up as models to be imitated or avoided, such as *devis* and *raakshasas*, respectively. A child is perhaps deliberately guided towards the model in the growing-up process. This may be because the model is a socially revered figure, like a *Guru* or *Sant*, or a teacher admired by the parent. Alternatively, it may be just as possible that the imitated behaviour may be disapproved by the socialiser and as the behaviour might be in opposition to social norms. Frequently, anti-social behaviour is on the basis of ontogenetic dispositions rather than societal directives. However, it is quite possible that a child brought up in a family which has non-ethical values like evading payment of taxes, might learn that such unethical values should be imitated. There is, however, lack of adequate data to empiricise such phenomena, as the imitation of a model in India, may range over a wide variety of choices from a school teacher to the president of America or even some villain or socially disapproved figure like autocratic rulers of countries. For example, parents often bemoan the behaviour of adolescents turning out to be delinquents when they were such good, well-modelled children in their younger days. Parents may be unaware of unknown variables which are psychodynamic in nature which may be influencing their children's behaviour adversely. These factors occur in the meso ecology of the child, consisting of peers and neighbourhood friends, influencing their child towards inappropriate "gang behaviour". These tendencies may vary according to the degree of harmony between the child and his parents, and between the parents themselves, which may as the parents are models of approved behaviour in the family. Disharmony between the parents and among the relational groups may cause confusion and frustration in the child as he grows into an adolescent, where he has to choose between societal norms and familial norms of behaviour. On the other hand, due to some malfunctioning in the individual's perception of what is approved, he may use defence mechanisms to justify his anti-social behaviour just as much as a traditional family might also unintentionally let the child go astray. Like saying, for instance, "my friends smoke, so why cannot I try?" or, "my school mates go out in gangs over the weekend, if I do not go with them, I shall be isolated". Thus, a human ecological network may be composed of any number of pro- and anti-social re-enforcers. It is not unusual for a slum-dwelling child to indulge in anti-social behaviours. It can be seen that the child is influenced and reinforced not only by his interactions within the family, but he is also influenced by anti-social elements in his wider human eco-system and the meso-system, which may lead him to anti-social behaviour. *There is no one to one relationship*, however. It is quite possible that the traditional middle class child may become delinquent and the slum-dwelling child may be highly reinforced by familial ethical values. It is, therefore, the type of tendencies communicated to the individual by his human ecology which reinforces the individual to go either way, law-abiding or anti-social.

The individual's need, as is psychologically known, is an internal energy which is relatively unknown to others in the human ecology, unless it is communicated. It is frequent to hear mothers say, "Make friendship with the boy next door" or "Do not make friendship with the boy next door", when they themselves are unaware of the characeristics of the neighbour family. It is often observed that families which make up a community are approximately of the same socio-economic status and contribute to similar values. The parents might assess the similarity or dissimilarity of attitudes of others in the human network, assuming a rapport between them and other members in the group. For instance, it is rare to observe a child from a high-rise luxury apartment building making friendship with the children of the adjacent construction workers, which may vitiate the patterns of life styles in both types of families.[16] (Khalakdina, M., 2008: 214) In other words, "The like seeks out the like". Thus, in social psychology, we are able to categorise or classify groups by similarity of values and behaviour like the division of members of a society into different socio-economic classes.

Neither personality nor geo-ecology are neat compartments. They interact in varying degrees according to situational determinants.[17] (Berry, J.W., 1978) We often hear the saying he must be a good boy since he comes from a "good family background". The catchword here is background, if we disassemble this phrase, it goes back to the variables of human and geo-ecology.

Personality is foundationalised on the biological concepts of orthogenetic derivatives of specific genetic constructs of the individual. Ecology is a composite of human and natural components of differing personalities of differing chronological ages, with varied experiences in varied geographical areas. These personalities have varying experiences, living in urban, rural and tribal ecologies and different make-up of the human and social networks. All these combinations and permutations are both affective and effective factors in influencing traits of development.

Personality is an abstract concept and is perceivable in overt behaviour as indicated in the chapter on "Selected Personality Theories Relevant to the Indian Psyche". We notice the operation of their conceptualisations in everyday life. If an Eskimo perceives an African without much clothing, he will conclude that this is not normal, since he himself is overly clothed. This is an outcome of an eco-cultural perspective. If, on the other hand, the perception of a person is placed in his own ecological context or eco-culture, then the logical analysis is context specific. An example is the relationship of an African to his environment, namely, a tropical climate as opposed to the Eskimo's relationship to his Arctic surroundings. Mead in her study of Samoa adolescents arrived at a hypothesis that there is both continuity and discontinuity that configure the personality of the individual as influenced by his human ecological network.[18] (Mead, M., 1928)

4. Selected Correlates of the Indian Psyche

The writings of Locke in the early twentieth century were the earliest in knowledge of how learning takes place, restricted to studying elemental forms of behaviour, as conceived by the mind. The ideas of the mind are expressed by language, which is a major correlate of personality development. Language causes the action to be initiated by the mind, wherein the environment plays a secondary role, in that it can only stimulate such ideas.[19] (St. John, J.A., 1902) The major correlate is the ontogenetic potential of the individual. For example, personal pronouns such as "I', "me", and "mine" related to the "self" which is the first ego-centric step towards recognition of self-identity in relation to "the surroundings". Early in the explanation of the working of the mind, pre-scientific thinking attributed "I" to a *Homunculus,* a little being residing in the head.

The identification of the object, acting upon by the organism, was the main emphasis of the Behaviourists. They believed that the basic processes are the action by the organism evolving from the mental structure responding to the selective aspects of the ecological environment. This theorising is the beginning of the recognition of the importance of a unique environmental ecology interacting with unique personality/personalities. In a deductive way, Behaviourists believe that if an act is intelligently reasoned out, it must reside in the genetically determined physiological makeup that makes one person act more or less intelligently and differently from another. Behaviourists recognize that intellectual ability is covert from the real world, and it mainly originates from thought processes. Some Behaviourists, who adopt the structural themes, assume that thought processes are the outcomes of the structural codes\decodes in the mind, and that, it is, therefore, an object of the mind like the mental decision-making modes which become overt only when expressed. Behaviourists, therefore, have emphasized the need for overt expressions of covert thoughts. The verbal mode is the act of talking to oneself as when one speaks to himself: "*I must get to the exhibition on time*". This may involve sub-vocal movements of the vocal chords. In some instance, the "inner speech" is said to occur within the central nervous system.

The major correlates of personality indicated here are:

(a) Moral judgments, which have relevance to the ecosystems of the interaction with family members in the micro-system and kinship, peer groups and others in the meso-system.
(b) The relationships with peers and the formation of values arise from contact with them.
(c) Self-control adjustment which connotes the personality's inherent competency to interact with his human ecology.
(d) Cognition of relationships among ideas and objects of the ecology.

In all the above four aspects, the framework in which these occur is the socialization process in which the chief articulators are the family members of the micro-system. The development of moral values is central to the socialization process, as explained in Kohlberg's theory.[20] (Munsey, Brenda, 1980) This theory has been used in Indian samples. For example, some studies of school children using an adaptive version of Kohlberg's test examined the moral issues of life, punishment, father-son relations, promised contract and trust. Using age frequency as a variable, there was noticeably significant age-trend progression in the cognitive understanding of right and wrong in the issues presented in the study. Moral judgments as a whole showed similar trend in both sexes.[21] (Saraswathi, T.S., J. Sundaresan and K. Saxena, 1977) When socio-economic differences were viewed between the sexes, on a moral judgments test, it was found that the capacity to make such judgments increased with age. Sex and economic status showed no significant difference regarding moral judgment. Within the age-groups, there were some significant differences. The within age-group fluctuations and within-sex fluctuations of differing ages were attributed to different modelling and socialisation techniques.[22] (Tripathi, D.K.M, and Misra, G., 1979) This study is given as an example of the few available in the Indian context. It is important here to state that morality is a very wide area wherein all attributes can be exemplified. Much of our understanding of moral behaviour arises from the scriptures of religion, since the Indian child is firmly rooted in socio-religious norms beginning from the early stages to adulthood where the individual tires to find his place in the family ecology and to find his identity in the interactive processes with his human ecology.[23] (Woodward, Kath, 2003) In a study of school-children from two different types of schools—missionary and vernacular, it was found that truth, purity, *punnya* (virtuous deeds) and respect were more acknowledged by older children, increasing at each age-level, irrespective of the type of school. Sex differences or mental abilities also had no effect on differences in moral judgment, especially on the positive aspects of moral judgment except in the area of respect. It seems that the home environment and the social ambience of socialisation were more significant variables in the development of a sense of moral judgment than the effect of the meso-system.[24] (Tripathi, D.K.M., and G. Misra, 1979).

5. Cognition of the Self in the Ecological Environment

In cognitive theorizing, the neural and physiological mechanisms are important adjuncts as neurological and motor maturing are related to the formation of cognitive schemas. For instance, sensory motor development has been stressed by psychologists such as McGraw[25] (McGraw, M.B., 1940) when discussing sensory-motor coordination as part of the infant's physical and cognitive growth processes. These processes provide a conjunction of physiological maturational sequences which then become more apparent during the latter part of the Piagetian pre-operational and the early part of the concrete operational stages of development. For instance, in the concrete stage of the cognitive schema, there is an increasing ability to conserve mass and convert mass into compressed and non-compressed material by experimentation.[26] (Rao, S.N, 1976)

That there is recognition of the operation of genes in behaviour is evident from such idioms as *like father like son, the black sheep of the family, the apple doesn't fall far from the tree*, and so on. Here, we limit ourselves to the description of psycho-social characteristics, which predispose individuals to behave in distinguishable and socially sanctioned ways. The most obvious example is one of defective physical and mental characteristics. It is said that because of the hereditary nature of the doubling of genes, and their transmission of physical and defective characteristics, these become obvious in the progeny, because of the pairing of paternal and maternal defective genes.[27] (Jennings, H.S., 1930) Such examples indicate the tendency towards behavioural disorders. These disorders affect the social cognition of the individual which is a fractured perception in relation to his human micro-ecological environment. The environment is mainly composed of other individuals. Some like the members of a family are perceived as emotionally linked, others are perceived as friends, and still others are acquaintances or unknown. Therefore, social perception directly is related to the cognitive skills of the individual.

Such defects are clearly seen in defective formation of the brain, in brain damage, leading to retarded intelligence of various degrees, or the inability to use senses such as speech, hearing and motor coordination. Brain damage is also evident in imbalance in hormones. For example, in malfunctioning of the thyroid and its relation to cretinism, abnormal hypothalamic growth and retardation, micro cephalic, macro cephalic and neural deficiencies might occur. Mongolism is believed to be caused by 'faulty mutation' of the ovum, that is the foetus is seen to be 'pathological' in some form or the other.[28] (Chaudhuri, A., and K.C. Chaudhuri, 1966)

There is a close relationship among the psycho-social dimensions of perception, its acuity and frequency of repeated perceptions which form mental images. Such mental images are cognized as to their parameters and can be repeatedly retrieved so as to enhance consequent such experiences.[29] (Purohit, A.K., 1984) For instance, the relationship between occupation and skill is well-known. A computer specialist is expected to know eye-hand coordination with perceived images at the same time decoding their meanings in relation to the technological configuration. He also needs to be aware of his social world while working at computers in an office situation. In an elementary society, on the other hand, a fisherman has to know signs of weather related to the growth and concentration of fish likely in certain parts of the ecological water space, whether sea, lake or river. At the same time he has to be aware of the relationship between the end-product, the marketed fish and his survival needs.

Cognition plays an extremely important part in elementary societies as individuals *have to be aware of the close nature of ecological symbols in relation to their occupational tasks.*[30] (Karen, A. Cerulo, 2001) Such cognitive developmental processes begin from the early pre-school years along a track of simple to complex perceptions of objects and their cognition to the extent that with repeated skill the success of the performance increases.[31] (Reese, E., and Brown, N., 2000) For this reason, *Piaget describes the relationship between* the individual's perception, the object and his cognition *in relation to the immediate ecology of the child, which fulfil his needs especially primary needs.*[32] (Piaget, J., 1954) *Vygotsky has* expanded cognition *to include the importance of the social and cultural ecology and the symbolic use of communication as completing an understanding of the relationship of cognition to geo-ecology.*[33] (Vygotsky, L.S., 1978) In this respect the acuity of the perception of the self is also directed towards perception of the social environment, both the human ecology and the geo-ecology.

6. Ecology and Socio-Cognitive Development

Sociology and anthropology, through some of their idiographic studies like that of Ishwaran[34] (Ishwaran, K., 1970: 6-8), gave glimpses of the vast resources of information existent in ecologies. In the West, Parsons wrote about social action, mainly in theoretical terms of structure, systems, organisations and the generic functional description of human interaction within an environment[35] (Parsons, T. 1937). In this sense, human ecology is influenced by the social text of human behaviour. Super and Harkness, for instance, described that physical settings of the various cultures had their impact on the ways the childcare systems operated in the several cultures they studied[36] (Super, C.M., and S. Harkness, 1986).

Bronfenbrenner[37] (Bronfenbrenner U., 1979) presented an innovative approach to the study of this interactive process in an explanation of the model of the ecology and the human being. He also used a construct of proximal and distal variables interacting with each other. An example of this interaction is the frequent and focussed interaction of the family members among themselves. This is the first level of social interaction which multiplies in communication and reciprocal activities to the extent of the number of members in any social group, the frequency of which is symbolised by the matrix $n(n-1)\div 2$. That is why frequently it is said that social gatherings which also employ the pattern of meal-sharing is an important situation where face to face communication takes place in a human ecological setting. In the Indian culture, such settings occur frequently at meal times among parents, children, the kinship group and at times of such significant social gatherings like marriages, births, deaths, and other events.

Postulates of development depend heavily upon phylogenetic origins. All men are social animals — they seek comfort with their own kind (affiliation), they also seek the opposite sex and procreate (sex drive). They tend to develop their environmental settings to meet their goals. They are aggressive or regressive, depending upon the power or the supremacy of one over the other (the use of defence mechanisms). The individual's spatial ecology *influences the development of certain abilities and represses others, to form a grid of accordance (aligning one's abilities to situational provisions)* In elementary societies it was considered manly for a male to have a hand-to-hand fight and for a girl to be feminine.The ability to use the sword has now been replaced by the ability to precisely target the minutest object from overhead fighter planes or drones.

Thus, the ontogenetic potential remains an abstract construct till such time as articulated by individual behaviour. However, phylogenetic traits are the foundation from which such ontogenetic traits spring. For instance, the given phylogenetic ability to cognise perceptually and auditorily is latent till they are used. Thus, cognitive development is related to maturity of ontogenetic traits which are based on the phylogenetic potential. If, for instance, the ability to target a specific object is exercised, repeated and practised, it increases the sharpness of the needed cognitive ability. The latter, however, is dependent upon the ontogenetic potential as to how the individual cognises his environment. For example, a life-term prisoner can only cognise those who live in the same ecological prison space. He also cognises that there are two different layers of people: prisoners like himself and the guards/warden of the prison. Translated into the social world, this means the individual is socialised to understand the differences between one group and another.

As such those traits which are more nearly physical are more predictable than those which originate in the mind and are not as apparent in perceived outward traits. For instance, it is difficult to assess the relationship of mental processes to intelligent behaviour. Neural mechanisms occur more prominently in early learning behaviour, which become consolidated as chronological age progresses and as cognition of the outer world becomes more complex. The relationship between the child and his initial cognition is said to be related to breast-feeding which stimulates his cognition of his mother and other such nurturers,[38] (Mortensen, E.L., K.F. Michaelsen, S.A. Sander and J.M. Reinisch, 2001) but the evidence is still insufficient. Correspondingly, different ecologies monitor patterns of living differentially, when generic skills are the same. For example, a hunter in a forest needs to have the same perceptive cognitive skills as a golfer or a cricketer to relate time and space to his ontogenetic skill of perception, the object and the target. Yet, the hunter lives in an elementary society, while the golfer lives in a highly sophisticated ecology.

In the mechanism of the brain, rapid response for enhanced identification also activates social adaptive responses. This is called "significance detection" where evaluation of the stimulus is completed and the behavioural goal is linked to response strategy, where response systems are stimulated from the outer world. Thus, it is possible through encephalographs to detect low and high speed activation of different domains in the brain responsible for perception, memory lapses, heightened hyperactivity and low mobility in responding to situations in the environment. For instance, the origins of intelligence are not well-known and, therefore, are assumed to be phylogenetic in nature. Evolutionary theory which states that behaviour in human beings is more focused than in the primates, does not afford much insight into the origins of intelligence, or how any individual's intelligence level is related to interactive social cognition. However, genetic endowment indicates that even in the case of twins, monozygotic twins are more similar than dizygotic twins in their cognitive patterns of intelligent behaviour.[39] (McCartney, K; M.J. Harris and F. Bernieri, 1990) In other frames of theorizing (with the exception of the cognitive experts), we find that explanations about social cognition are either descriptive as in Erikson's theory or indirectly referred to in Lewin's topological model. The latter is related to regions of priority in dynamic thought processes, indicative of habits and values. It is perhaps Bronfenbrenner's theory which more specifically implies social cognition as the individual moves from the micro to the other eco-systems and back. In the psycho-dynamic theory of Freud, the constructs such as, social perception and cognition are mentioned only by inference when dealing with the individuals who have distorted perceptions due to dysfunctional social thinking.

Thus, development is a repetitive pattern of behaviour where there is a simultaneous absorption of the cultural traits of the society in which the individual lives. This is because of the inculcation of skills (both mental and physical) learnt in the specific society. We might even say here, that while all men are born equal, inequality results from differentiation of one ethnic group to another, one race to another, and/or one region to another in terms of socially differentiating cognition.

7. The Linkages between Cognition and Ecological Derivatives

It is admitted that effective information processing is essentially a part of intelligence, and, therefore, is a cognitive process. While the outcomes of cognitive processes are seen in behaviour, the latter is articulated within a given environment and, as we have stressed in many places in this book, the Indian ecological context is heterogeneous and, therefore, cognition of the same process may be heterogeneously interpreted. No one situation is totally applicable in another. Therefore, there are variations towards which the cognitive processes require to be aligned. Cross-cultural studies and, therefore, heterogeneity of ecology indicate these variances.[40] (Bruner, J.S., R. Olver and P.M. Greenfield,1966) In these cross-cultural studies, Piagetian schema were used to test the tasks of "conservation", "invariance", and the perceptual appearance of the object in various settings. These studies indicated that social class variations lowered the level of performance, but not the pattern of abilities (cognition/ intelligence). Ethnicity, was also related to variation. The variables were: schooling and no schooling from African, Americans, Algerian and Hong Kong children as also the type of schooling. The findings were:

(a) There was no time lag in either technologically oriented ecologies or traditionally oriented ecologies in conservation tasks.
(b) Spatial or perceptual aspects of the tasks indicated some surprising results. Disadvantaged children or those from poor ecologies showed little or no difference from the advantaged children in verbal or abstract tasks.
(c) Differential pattern of skills were more likely to occur among children of similar formal schools, when ethnic backgrounds were different. Thus, these findings underscore the ecological influence on cognitive thought processes.[41] (Lessor, G.S., G. Fifer and D.H. Clarke, 1964)
(d) Ethnic background and class were more stable for indicating homogeneous Piagetian task-behaviour within the group studied, where, differences in intelligence were minimal.[42] (Goodnow, J.J., 1962)

Thus, it seems that these types of experiences validate the assumption that tasks are homogeneously performed by specific age-groups, according to the Piagetian conceptualisation, with little or no significant differences among advantaged or disadvantaged groups in task performance. Ecological and cultural background variations were, however, significant in modulating tasks in the ecosystems. In a study by Anandalakshmy of the manual skills of potter's children, it was found that potters' children informally learned conservation of weight, volume and mass in the making of pottery items.[43] (Anandalakshmy, S., and M. Bajaj, 1981) The Piagetian schema, however, lacks explanation into cultural conceptualisations like the influence of the culture, the ecology and language on the development of these "operational tasks". Occupational tasks which involve manipulation of concrete or ideational experiences, together with innovative deductions, apart from the schema, are yet to be fully explored especially in relation to the Indian situation. Vygotsky attempts to expand the theoretical assumptions of the Piagetian schema to include language and social cultural aspects of the society in which the child lives[44] (Vygotsky, L.S., 1978), namely, the micro and other relevant expanding eco-systems.

8. Interactions among the Ecosystems

The interaction of the ecological systems is the core of the relationships between one ecology and another, in influencing behaviour and development. We suggest the following theoretical concepts that affect such relationships:

(i) Erikson's theory, as we have seen in Chapter on "Selected Personality Theories Relevant to the Indian Psyche", emphasizes domains of development across the life cycle.[45] (Erikson, E.H., 1980)
(ii) With the beginnings of life outside the womb, the trusting relationship between the nurturer and the nurtured forms a bonding of attachment.
(iii) If this symbiotic relationship is destabilized, as in the separation of the child from the mother, then mistrust developed in the detachment from the nurturer is generalized to the human ecology, and is transferred to the geo-ecological environment, if the trauma is severe. For, the child is predisposed from the early years to continue these values learned into the years of adolescence, where there is a tendency to feel a loss of identity. This loss is also contributed to by exposure to other ecological factors, like when one moves from one ecology to another unknown ecology, it may create a sense of "anomie" and a loss of identity.

If we examine the Field theory of Kurt Lewin, the analogies he uses are concepts of space, energy, valence and forces typical of a topology of psychological domains of the human being. He specifically mentions regions, core and peripheral traits, akin to the individual's psychological distance from his core values to his peripheral values, similar to proximal and distal variants from the ecology influencing his behaviour.[46] (Lewin, K., 1951) For instance, it is usual that a strong emotive bond exists with one's place of origin, and his original habitat. He is used to eating those foods, with which he has been socialised, available in his ecology of childhood, as food represents a core valued object in his psychological domains.

From the viewpoint of Behavioural theory, the stimuli emanating from the environment are manifold. A villager, for instance, will be non-plussed when he visits a bustling city and he is accosted by varying and multiple stimuli different from those in his village, where stimuli are few, similar and routine. Urban children have many min-ecologies in their micro ecosystem, like playgrounds, going to the movies, attending events, shopping at malls, and handling electronic equipments. Stimuli from the environment can be oppressive and cause stress especially in high-tension occupations, or bring about serenity if it is a peaceful and soul moving place. Psychodynamic theories are reflected in their major proponent namely, Freud's description of psycho-sexual development. While data are scarce in this aspect in India, we may speculate as to the relationships in the development of the person with his ecology, explainable by Freudian insights, as observed in his theory discussed in the Chapter on "*Selected Personality Theories Relevant to the Indian Psyche*". We at once see a distinction between overt and covert theories, the former being observable and the latter, as in Freud's theory, within the human mind, unless expressed.

One might extrapolate on an assumption basis, the effects of ecology on personality using the themes of severity of training and oral and anal fixation as explained in the Freudian analysis of the study by Whiting and Child. The conceptualization of child training in the oral stage relates to ingestion of food and toilet training. If there is severity in weaning or in toilet training, they are related to fixation at the oral and anal stages of psycho-sexual development[47] (Whiting, J.W., and I. Child, 1953), which affects the development of personality in ecologies where socialisation is rigid vis-à-vis the societies where socialisation is casual and informal. In the Indian situation there is hardly any severity in toilet training and in weaning. Therefore, such ecologies which are less technologically oriented and time is not stressed, socialisation brings about a casually developed personality. We notice, for instance, that in village ecologies, time is not stressed, the performance of tasks are not pressurized and there is hardly any severity in the punishment for failure to perform tasks, which then tend to be leisurely oriented. The expressions "*aise hi hota hai*" (it happens like that) or "*ho jayega*" (it will happen), "*koi baat nahin*" (it does not matter) and such like. They, thus, usually say "*jaane do, woh abhi bacchha hai*", which means let him be, the child is still young. In urban areas children have to go to school on time, attend classes on time, are reprimanded if they do not do their homework and when they come back home they continue to be reprimanded if they do not do their homework. The more sophisticated the ecology, the more time-bound are the growing child's tasks and the more attracted he is to the various ecological stimuli. In later adolescence the child may go out with his peers to pubs, hang out at malls, which detract the child from his daily tasks and cause increasing stress. This may result in his tasks not being accomplished on time. There is conflict between wanting to enjoy his attractions and having to perform to please his family and society. This again takes us back to the mini theory of motivation, and Maslow's classification of primary and secondary needs.

Various systems of human ecology are perceived as interlinking in Bronfenbrenner's thesis of theoretical constructs. If we *relate the various human ecosystems to the geo-ecology, each is related to a unique habitat of geo-ecology.* The immediate habitat of the person is his family and kin group. The geo-ecological parameters widen with the increasing concentric circular systems of the meso, the exo and the macro systems as related in the chapter on "Selected Personality Theories Relevant to the Indian Psyche". In a largely, generic manner, we might say that Bronfenbrenner's thesis is based on the foundational theory of stimulus-response. We may justify this by saying that *as individual's experiences widen and become varied in contact with the larger and larger groups at further distances, the cognitive map becomes also enlarged, and as Kurt Lewin's theory implies the greater the contact with experiences, the more habituated value system becomes.* We might say that the greatest interaction of the individual is in his micro system which then becomes valued as a core system, and, therefore, the individual is more attached to his micro rather than to other eco-systems. We have made several assumption in attempting to link one personality theory with another. With increased empirical data it will not be too extraneous to say that eventually there are constructs of each theory that are similar to each other in their analysis of the same object: the personality.

9. Interactions in the Meso System

Friendship patterns of the individual in the meso system form an important influence on personality characteristics, as they are one of the secondary sources of socialisation on the growing personality. Moreno who developed the technique of sociometry used a scale to measure affiliative patterns among groups of individuals who congregated at different times according to different situations, and for different purpopses.[48] (Moreno, J.W., 1977) *His major theme was to document the formation of groups through a sociogram of friendship patterns*, by using interviews to ask the members of the group as to whom they would choose in differing situations. Those who were over-chosen were labelled as "stars" (members most sought after) and those who were hardly chosen and remained on the fringes of the group were termed "isolates". The aim of this technique was primarily to identify leaders in the group for the purposes of directing the goals of the group. This method has been used several times in India for identifying leadership and followership patterns. For instance, in a study in Delhi, it was found that in 50 per cent of the schools, few persons were over-chosen, indicating that leadership patterns are marginally perceived, and that in 10 per cent of the schools, 50 per cent were under-chosen. The overly selected or "stars" evidenced more positive personality characteristics as compared to those under selected or "isolated". Patterns of friendship were thus scattered.[49] (Rao, T.V., and D. Banerjee, 1973) This technique is a fairly reliable method to quickly estimate friendship patterns, where people choose others on the basis of affiliations.

Socialisation per se *in India is different from other societies, especially the west; where socialisation patterns are more peer group oriented than family oriented.* However, there is a caveat. This pattern is mostly in traditional families and sparse ecologies. The upper crust of society in India, however, continues to ape Western modernised patterns of interaction in the meso and exo systems. The child in the early years of upbringing, tends to stay closer to the family in the Indian situation. It is mainly in primary school years and later that the child tends to gravitate towards peers, but since many in rural and tribal areas either go infrequently to school, or tend to drop out earlier from school, the micro family is the major orbit of interaction.

During adolescence, while it might be expected that the individual grows to be less under the dominance of the family, empirical data indicate that, contrasted to the western counterpart, the Indian adolescent spends less time alone, more time with peers but still prefer to spend more time with the family of orientation, than do children in the west.[50] (Larson, R., and M. Csikszentmihalyi, 1984) Over the years, while other resemblances change, as influenced by extraneous variables, the family ethos still exist in the Indian psyche.[51] (Saraswathi, T.S., 2003: 42-43) This is more true of females than males, especially in close ties of the parent with the same-sexed child. In the Indian culture there is an added phenomenon of over-protection of adolescent girls (so as to preserve their femininity and virginity) which adds to their restrictive movements in comparison to their male counterparts. The latter have a larger orbit of circulation and mobility than do the females. *As yet in most subcultures in India, the free interaction among adolescents in heterosexual groups is* still frowned upon, and is often a bone of contention between the generations, especially in the parent-daughter relationships, where more strictures prevail than with parent-son relationships. The pattern of 'space privacy' which is a common phenomenon in the west is less so in India because of the informal frequent interaction with children who from early childhood spend much time under the supervision of family adults. Free interaction between female and male children in the family and kinship circles of the meso system is taken for granted.[52] (Kumar, K., 1993: 69) In fact, cousins are not labelled as such, but are still called brothers and sisters. This cross path interaction is especially true of rural and tribal areas where families share the same space with their children, and work closely together in the same family chores. However, in other developing countries, this pattern may not be similar. For example, in some sub-Saharan cultures, as in Somalia, which is mainly nomadic, from primary school years, boys and girls mix freely in their allotted job tasks so long as they are within the perceptual range of the elders.[53] (Bledsoe, Caroline H., and Barney Cohen, 1993) With the acceleration of modernisation, there is a growing movement in the middle and upper classes in India towards accepted co-educational activities, which then spawns out into the social activity spheres.[54] (Verma, S., and Saraswathi, T.S., 2002) *Because of the variety of the multicultural nature of Indian sub-societies in their sub-ecologies, the combinations and permutations of patterns of cohesion are also myriad*, depending upon conventional customs. If one looks at wider patterns of relationships, with the exception of the family, leadership and follower-ship patterns in the meso and exo systems still exist as in many small communities in rural and tribal areas. Leadership in these communities is the main driving force to set the goals, the societal mores and the structural systems in the community[55] (Bales, R.F., 1958), as reflected in the Panchayat system, where the leader is elected to the office of the Pradhan. Leadership, however, in a group situation is not a generalized ability: some individuals perform better at one set of organized activities rather than another. For instance, in a college, one who is a good student union leader may not necessarily be perceived as a good student in his class room activities. Therefore, different situations call for different abilities which may not be present in the same individual, deemed as a leader in one group vis-à-vis another.[56] (Messick, David M., and Roderick M. Krammer, 2005)

Where there is a dissonance in perception of and attitudes on authority, as measured by the adapted Californian F scale (a test on personality attributes), there is a likelihood of disharmony between leaders and followers. When we relate this to everyday patterns of friendship, we observe that there is a likelihood of impermanence being given in group friendships, where cleavages are likely to occur and "sides" are taken.[57] (Haythorn, W., A.S. Couch, D. Haefner, P. Langham and L.F. Carter, 1956) On the one hand, this type of discordance may be observed in differing ethnic groups who live adjacent to each other in informal bonds of community friendship in the same geo-ecology. Yet, on the other hand, the likelihood of discordance may occur on the basis of claim over territorial rights or privileges. Some of this type of discordance may be observed in slum-dwelling areas where different ethnic groups settle down adjacent to each other, and where dissonance might occur over the apportioning of scarce resources like water and other shared amenities. Norms are essential in the formation of groups, whether temporary or permanent affiliations.[58] (Newcomb, T.M., 1947) *Friendships formed on the basis of affinity, similarity in likes, dislikes and interests cement friendship patterns.* These patterns tend to hover around the same local ecology, as in same schooling systems, neighbourhood events and such like. There are others who need not necessarily contribute to the formation of affiliated patterns as in formal groups such as acquaintances in a formal conference. The pattern of being elected a leader of a group may be based on objectivity (rules and norms of an organized group), but more often than not, they are biased on the basis of affinity. Apparently, attitudes towards authority, especially in reference groups, play an important part in the sustenance of group formations. These may be in proximate geo-ecological areas or at geographical distances where individuals may be based temporarily such as hostel students.

Included in this meso system of the growing individual is the profile of the schooling system, particularly teachers. *Teachers are known to have a significant influence on the developing personality of the child, positively or negatively as the school going child spends a large part of his time under the influence of teachers.* Teachers are the secondary nurturers of school children as they direct and monitor much of the thinking and acting processes of the child. These interactions may be either positive or negative and have lasting influences on the child's development.[59] (Ellis, Sue and B. Rogoff, 1982) The reality of the situation is that many children, especially from the deprived ecologies, drop out of school and, therefore, may not be influenced as such by the teacher community in the meso system.

Therefore, group formation can be either informal or formal depending upon the mutuality of personal relationships or the focus on the goal of the group. Interactive patterns play an important role in the formation of group structures which cover an ecology that has a human network. Science has advanced to such a stage that the internet and web-based social networking systems like the Face Book, Skype and Twitter have offered a wide scope for maintenance of group relationships.[60] (Christian Fuchs, 2008) However, this type of interaction is limited mostly to the upper classes; the majority who live in rural, tribal and disadvantaged areas have no such access to micro-chip-based social networking. In the latter, there is more oral communication where friends take and give counsel and have a strong bond of loyalty. A more structural friendship as coming together for studying or for a team game does not necessarily connote the emotive quality of cohesiveness. *There are, thus, degrees of affinity.* Also, it is not essential that one should be in a dominant role, while the others are in submissive roles for the group goal to be successfully achieved. It is not essential that there should be a continuous uniform submission/dominance pattern, authority, or followership of authority. *These affiliations may occur on the basis of perceived goals in any combination or permutation and change in a dynamic fashion.* Affinitive roles may assume different structures according to the needs of the individuals in the given ecology. For example, children of pasturers band together while pasturing small animals on a more frequent basis than if they were urban children living in a condominium complexes.

The strength of the goals also need not necessarily be uniform.

There are various traits that bind peers together, either temporarily for a particular goal, or more permanently like in long-lasting friendships, wherein each accepts the other for each other's strengths and limitations over long periods of association. In cases where one is more demanding and the other is more giving, the relationship may be lopsided. If one says, "I hate this hero", the other submissive friend is more likely to agree than disagree. Such referencing occurs in close-knit groups. For, socialisation does not occur only in the family alone, but also in other meso groups: the school, the neighbourhood or specific others, such as a celebration in the family or going on a *yatra* or a vacation with school-mates.[61] (Newcomb, T.M., 1958)

10. Major Linking Theories

We present below a paradigm of linkages among major theories which we assume are relevant to the Indian psyche, with the proviso that their concepts are conditioned on the basis of the Indian being uniquely different from other societies.

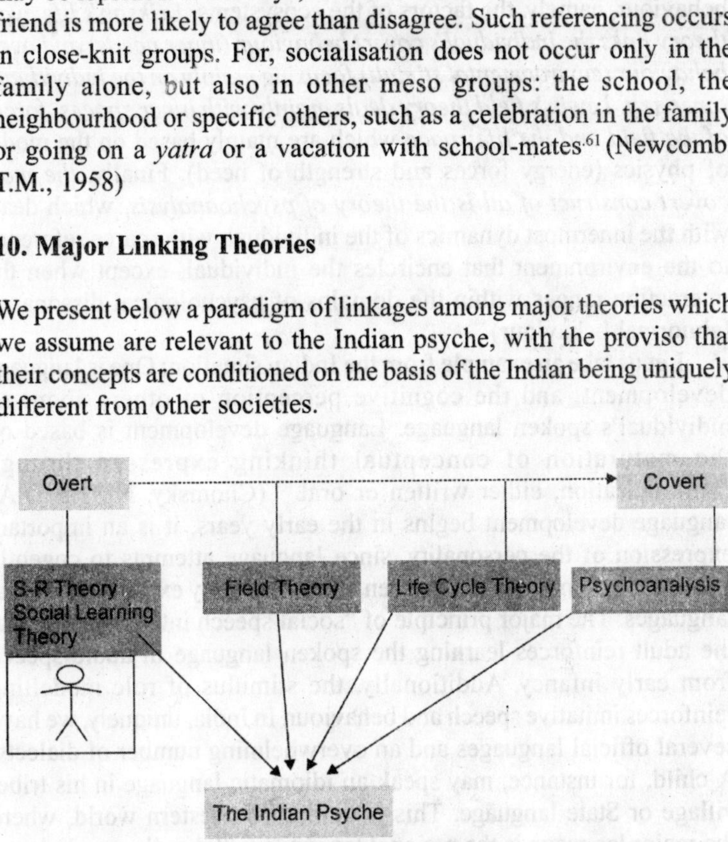

Paradigm 6.2: Key Markers of Selected Theories of Personality

The paradigm above *differentiates among theories which are interpreted on the basis of observed behaviour,* such as the outcomes of stimulus-response theories and the interpretation of covert behaviour as elicited by psychodynamic theories. We move, therefore, along the dimension where *stimuli are both overt and covert,* such as inner dynamical constructs like drive and need. Therefore, *social learning concepts find their source in these domains* and are elicited as such. From the point of ecology, Bronfenbrenner who is one of the primary experts on human ecology, deals with the environment of the human being. He analyzes overt stimuli emanating from the ecology, which affect changes in behaviour and this theoretical framework offers an understanding of what influences overt behaviour, namely, the factors of the ecosystems. *Erikson's life cycle theory links the individual's covert behaviour (inner needs) and overt behaviour (environmental stimuli) focusing mainly on the individual's inner self. Lewin's field theory deals mainly with inner spaces, forces of the field and the life space* which are mainly based on the model of physics (energy forces and strength of need). Finally, *the most covert construct of all is the theory of psychoanalysis,* which deals with the innermost dynamics of the individual, with scarce reference to the environment that encircles the individual, except when the interaction ranges within the domains of psychological dissonance (abnormal behaviour).

Let us take an example from the Indian situation: One is language development, and the cognitive perception of others about an individual's spoken language. Language development is based on the maturation of conceptual thinking expressed through communication, either written or oral.[62] (Chomsky, N., 1965) As language development begins in the early years, it is an important expression of the personality, since language attempts to cogently express ideation. In India, children are increasingly exposed to several languages. The major principle of "social speech interaction" is that the adult reinforces learning the spoken language in audio-speech from early infancy. Additionally, the stimulus of role modelling reinforces imitative speech and behaviour. In India, uniquely, we have several official languages and an overwhelming number of dialects. A child, for instance, may speak an idiomatic language in his tribe, village or State language. This is unlike the Western world, where the major language is the national language with hardly any dialects. For instance, in America, English is the homogeneous language throughout the country, although there are migrants from different parts of the world. Thus, from this illustration we can extrapolate that the exposure to an increasing complexity of languages (multilingualism) has the potential of increasing the coding and decoding of the same ideation from one language to another which takes place covertly and simultaneously. In India, most children are usually bilingual, and in some cases multi-lingual. For example, a Keralite might use his own idiomatic village language, know his State language and, because of his schooling, also learn Hindi. The coding then gets reassembled into idiomatic configurations which have meaning in the relevant ecology. It is, therefore, not unusual to observe educated individuals especially those exposed to a worldly vision expressing an idea using more than one language. For example, in common everyday parlance "*lets go yaar*," "*wahan pe itna hot nahin hoga*," "*problem mat uthao*," and "*kya tension hai*" are commonly expressed sentences using an intermix of Hindi and English, which is popularly called "Hinglish". If the mother tongue has a typical intonation, for example, vowels are mainly emphasized and consonants suppressed, it gives rise to language that is neither Hindi, Malayalam, nor Gujarati but is compounded by the typical intonation, like "*istason*" for station and *fiss* for fish (mostly in north India). Thus, the transference from covert to overt and overt to covert communication is so dynamic, that it is difficult to pinpoint the source of the spoken word arising from the original context. In the Indian scriptures, the aspects of identifying heroes, villains, morality and immorality, are reflective of the characters and characteristics in Hindu scriptures such as the *Ramayana*, the *Mahabharata*, the *Panchatantras*, mythology of *Devis*, *Rakshases* and so on. For example, a chaste feminine woman is likened to 'Sita' and a villain is likened to 'Ravana'. Thus, language is related to the acquisition of knowledge and often times uses scriptural figures figuratively. These affect the life style of the individual and, therefore, his meaning and understanding of self and others in the specific ecology.[63] (Roland, A., 1988; Chaudhary, N., 1999) However, the self is more easily explainable in concretely measurable terms such as self worth, self esteem and so on. But their concrete interpretation from Hindu philosophy is relatively more difficult to measure and evaluate.

Thus, ecology is a potent influence in the individual's development into a personality. This concept includes both human and the geo-ecology of the individual's habitat. Several authors have shown how ecology is an intervening variable, when it modifies the individual's behaviour. In addition, ecological pressures can frequently suppress the development of a personality such as the ravages of war, famine and flood.[64] (Berry, J.W., 1976: 112) Using basic ecological influences as enunciated by Berry and his associates, we can extrapolate the following ecological concepts as related particularly to habitats such as the tribal areas and rural villages removed from the urban, where occupations are mainly related to the natural ecology. Therefore, in the above example, the variable of ecologically influenced language assumes importance in affecting personality. To carry the example further, in tribal areas, where the mode of sustenance is hunting, the ecology impacts on perceptual skills as an intervening variable in moderating awareness of detail, in sharpness of visual range, and in enlarging the spatial periphery of perception. These types of moderations are honed by cultural aids such as language cues, encoding of non-verbal messages, practicing the art of shooting and crafting tools, and assessing weather conditions, so that there is alignment between perception, cognition and language expressing ideation. This "functional adaptation" is set to the limits by the ecology (terrain, footprints, and odours of animals). For functional adaptation is a need for survival, especially in elementary habitats.[65] (Cole, M., Bruner, J.S., 1976: 173) There are some data from the Indian situation which trace such socio-perceptual and occupationally perceived skills.[66] (Mishra, R.C., D. Sinha and J.W. Berry, 1996) We may extrapolate from studies by Berry who found that visual spatial skills vary systematically with a cluster of ecological and cultural determinants among tribes.[67] (Berry, J.W., 1966) On the basis of these findings, we may hypothesise that, given the ecology in urban areas, a primary school child, for example, hones his skills in order to be competent in his school environment. He increases his perceptual and mental skills to use cellular phones, to use calculators and to be skilful with the computer (the intermix between covert needs and overt stimuli). These are the strategies by which he is in equilibrium with his ecological habitat just as the tribal is in equilibrium with his tribal habitat by using tribally known perceptual and language skills.

11. The Emergence of Cognitive Neuroscience with Psychological Constructs

In this, the twenty-first century, there is a gradual progress to interlinking cognition with the neurosciences in terms of the hemispheres of the brain and the location of thought processes relating to memory, to verbal reasoning and so on. It is said that modern cognitive psychology began as a reaction to the anti-mentalist excesses of Behaviourism and the latter's major dependence upon stimulus-response and experimental control.[68] (Thomas, R.M., 2001: 19) Thus, *cognitive psychology seems to mesh with experimental psychology, especially in basic concepts such as perception, learning, reaction time, and motor skills*. However, other recent developments are progressively influencing cognitive psychology. For instance, computer science not only provides the metaphor for information processing, but also in the form of artificial intelligence and computer simulation for the modelling aspects of human code and behaviour.[69] (Warm, J.S., 1988)

As far back as the *Vedic* period, the four methods of acquiring knowledge were said to be sensory perception, reasoning, testimony and *tapas* (meditation). The *Upanishads* provide an elaborate description of consciousness. The *Brihadaranyaka Upanishad* has attached importance to the development of consciousness. The *Mandukya Upanishad* describes various levels of cognition, and also mentions that the state of dreaming is inverted cognition. *The oldest school of learning which is the Samakhya presents the cosmic as well as individual principles of evolution.*[70] (Singh, I.L., R. Parasuraman and G. Matthews, 1998). The existence of the *ampramosa* doctrine of memory has been experimented on.[71] (Dwivedi, C.B., 1987) It is also stated that the *vaisheshika* theory of perception expands on the interaction of perception of material objects related to cognition. Even Gestalt psychologists[72] (Wertheimer, M., 1923) concluded that cognitive phenomenon must proceed experientially. This is *akin to the conscious experience advocated by the Indian schools of philosophy such as the Advaitya Vedanta, the Nyaya and the Mimamsa schools of philosophy.* These continue to be of current importance, even though western experimental behaviourists like Watson[73] (Watson, J.B., 1916) and Skinner[74] (Skinner, B.F., 1938) discounted introspective psychology. However, it has to be said there is a gap between the potency of Indian philosophical thought, its fundamentals and its relationship to demonstrate abilities in a direct manner in life situations. It is only by operationalism of curative medical science that we are able to demonstrate the cognitive mechanism underlying thought processes.

Neuroscience, for instance, involved studies of neuro-systems aided by techniques like MRI to image changes in the brain during the thinking processes and the Encephalograph which tracks images in the body and the brain to discover inter- and intra-relationships. Methods are used to elicit localisation, circulatory nature of the images, the modulation of attentiveness and plasticity of imagery in relation to cognitive skills.[75] (Posner, M.I., 1994) These methods of cognitive neuroscience are under active development for it is possible to analyse a number of cognitive tasks, under the neurological aspects of anatomy and physiology of the brain. There are also other experimental studies where the pharmacological approach has been used to discover the neuro-chemical systems in the brain that mediate specific human behaviours.[76] (Russel, R.W., 1987) The major problem in the studies is that manipulation of a single neurotransmitter may affect levels of activities in other parts of the neurological system. Therefore, multi-behaviour strategies are used in order to control the transmitted activity of the neurotransmitter systems.

Experiments on human volunteers between the ages twenty-one to thirty-one years were attempted, which indicated that time estimation when acted upon by pharmacology tends to produce memory impairment. These studies state that there is a strong interplay of the basal ganglia in temporal processing. They also state that idiopathic has long been known to be a disorder of the basal ganglia where patients experience extremely low levels of the activity triggered by the ganglia.[77] (Hornykiewicz, O., 1972)

The domain of attention has also been studied within the framework of the neurosciences. *Recently with the aid of instrumentation like EEG, Events Related Potentials (ERP), Positron Emission Tomography (PET), and Magnetic Resonance Imaging (MRI), cortical functions are better understood.* The role of the sub-cortical neuro-chemical systems, however, is still not fully researched upon, and their functions are to be further experimented with, as they influence the sub-cortical zone of the brain. Further, dementia, Alzheimer's, schizophrenia and attention deficit disorders of the hyperactive type are presumed to be due to underlying neuro-chemical imbalances,[78] (Parasuraman, R., and P.M. Greenwood, 1998) which are assumed to be genetically propelled (genetic mutations in chromosomes from the inception of the individual). Studies in reasoning and problem solving in medical practices under the rubric of medical cognition, are of recent interest. In a review where specific emphasis on data-driven reasoning was tested, the latter was found to be related to the diagnostic ability of the individual.[79] (Patel, V.L., and G.J. Groen, 1986) Experts tended to use the field situation for testing their hypotheses on data-driven processes, unless these data came in conflict with clinical results. Although still in the nascent stages, these techniques suggest intriguing trends of the linking of cognitive processes with the neurosciences,[80] (Patel, V.K., J.F. Arocha and D.R. Kaufmann, 1994) demonstrating the linkage between psychology and neurology.

12. The Cohabitation of Social Development with Technological Development

It is often stressed that there is a comparable economic development process taking place in India as in Japan and China. Perhaps, the process styles termed "modernisation" covertly implies a comparison with the western modes of living. There is still a lively debate about the observability of "modernized behaviour". Already the computer age has taken over in India, shopping malls, eateries and metros compare favourably with the west. So in what way is Indian different? The main deflecting construct is that there is not one India but several little Indias, the greatest proportion being the lower classes where such technological advancements are not available. What is observable is the behaviour of the upper crust of the middle class which is aping the upper class, which, in turn, is aping the western mode of behavour. *Added to these concepts are the peripheral behaviours relevant to each habitat such as consumption patterns, leisure-time activities and such like.* These differences between the miniscule rich and the majority of poor are perhaps tolerated in the Indian milieu because of the belief in *Karma*, namely, the allocation of duties to one's status in life and also because the buffer of democratic values are profiled so that the phenomenon of rags to riches is accepted as a destined or *Karmic* happening. We have given several examples of the phenomena of the same individual behaving traditionally, at one time, and in modernized ways, at another. *Then, we need to identify several parallel strands of development: the "fully modernised" and "fully technologised" (the* khandani *elite), the partially modernised and fully technologised (the nouveau riche), the partially modernised and partially technologised (the rising middle class) and the vast majority who are the non-modernised and non-technologised (the illiterate rural in the hinterlands of India).* These are further influenced by the intervening phenomena of class and economic status. Granted that these assumptions do in fact exist, then we need to ask ourselves: *does economic development automatically give rise to social development? Does social development mean the retention of the roots of cultural heritage*? True, one might protest that these two situational scenarios might go hand-in-hand, harmoniously, but already we are seeing signs of cultural differences between parent and child generations, the jostling of *dharmic* values in the face of commercialized influences on traditional values as observed in the television serials to which millions of Indians are glued. For instance, the joint family structure is crumbling, yet there are traces of its ethics still valued, but for how long? Already nuclearisation of families has brought in its wake, stresses and strains, which have "leap-frogged" into dalliance with hierarchical lineage.[81] (Sontheimer, G.D., 1977) For example, there are signs of parental neglect and even parental abuse in the current day picture of elderly parents being abandoned by their adult children.

The fact remains that spiritual values are still strongly embedded in the Indian psyche of the parental generation, but there are also signs that they are being eroded in the younger generation. *Belief* in cosmic causation, a tendency to fatalistic helplessness that human experience is transitory and illusionary, continue to hold sway in core beliefs. Hinduism which places emphasis on mysticism and astrology also emphasizes man's need to achieve in social and economic pursuit. On the one hand, from the western point of view, it is felt that the rigidity of fatalistic beliefs precludes human endeavour in achieving better economic levels.[82] (Kapp, K.W., 1963; Mishra, V., 1962) On the other hand, it is felt that these conclusions are based on a superficial understanding of the Indian philosophy. The latter, in fact, advocates a balanced approach to both aspects. A non-Indian perspective might argue that the Indian society is based on differentiation among categories arising from socio-religious values such as casteism. *Therefore, the contention of India being secular is an ironical confrontation between the concepts of democracy which is equality for all and the concepts of conservatism, which emphasizes the maintenance of caste and ethnicity.* However, *a little more incisive insight will reveal that each caste is cohesive within itself and is linked one to the other in a linking manner*, in order to stabilize the community of castes and occupations in a reciprocal manner, stabilizing duties and obligations. From the philosophical view, caste is not a confrontational issue, unless it is politicised, which has occurred, is occurring and will continue to occur. The values of the *Vaishya caste* are encased in economic concerns, and that of the Brahmin in religious rites. The major area where it is fragile is the differentiation between the *shudh* and the *ashudh* (the pure and the non-pure) and the *oonch* (upper) and *neech* (lower), differentiating between the "higher" and the "lower" in the caste structure.

Equality and secularity are constitutional principles implemented by governance, through policies and programmes for raising the status of the scheduled castes, scheduled tribes, religious and linguistic minorities, and other "disadvantaged" sections of the Indian society. Further, *the injunctions within a caste are not immutable, given the impact of flexibility in scientific logic. There are, for instance, six systems of Indian philosophy beside the three non-Vedic schools, and the meaning of the terms used in the Vedas differ from one system to another and one interpretation to another.*[83] (Rao, M.S., 2004) *All, however, have emphasized the core values of balance and harmony.*

Similar spiritual ideals exist in the offshoots of Hinduism, namely, Buddhism and Sikhism. Buddhist and Vedantic psychologies have since their inception bonded the mind and body in unison, a phenomenon acquiesced with in the western thought but not fully discussed in developmental processes, except to acknowledge the biological aspects of cognition and its relationship to the functions of the brain.[84] (Patel, V.L., R. Glaser, J.F. Arocha, 2000) In the Indian context, '*Mann*' *and 'roop' are the terms used for the conjunction of the mind and body, which are ever changing but which operate in tandem.*[85] *(Malhotra, S., 2000: 2-7) In the vedantic view, 'jiva' or the living being is a multi-layered entity.* Consciousness is vested in the self and is the major focus of psychological thinking. The Hindu philosophy goes beyond the conscious state to other frames such as sleep, dreams, and the astral body which link these frames to the human being. Thus, culture from the Indian point of view goes beyond the realm of practicality and the supernatural to include various forms of the tenants of Indian philosophy, dealing with the spiritual world. For instance, horoscopes written on *Palmyra* leaves have existed from the time of writings of Hindu mythology, dependent upon astrological configurations, which are important guides to the patterns of living. It is also said that such horoscopes exist in thousands in selected temples which can be related to other humans so long as the date, the time and the configuration of the plans are matched in the libraries containing these horoscopes.

As stated by Rao[86] (Rao, M.S., 2004) many of the Hindu conceptualizations exist also in parallel forms in Japanese Zen philosophical thought, and in thoughts like emancipation, enlightenment, and the notions similar to *nirvana* in Chinese Confucianism. *As Kakar states that the socio-religious thought is the conscious of the Far East, the self in the Indian Vedic philosophy, and the Zen in the Japanese*. *Chetna* or consciousness are conditions of *sukh* and *dukh, dharma, karma, samskar, jeeva, atman, nirvana* which together imply important linkages, akin to the concepts of cognition, ideation and self-identity in socio-psychology.[87] (Kakar, S., 1966)

It must be admitted that while these are socially relevant to understanding the Indian psyche, much attention has still to be paid to their empiricism. There seems to be many individualized interpretations of the cosmos and the components of the cosmos, namely, the Godheads, the *Avatars* and the formulation of conceptualizations of the "*jeeva*". Nevertheless, these philosophical and socio-religious beliefs continue to form the unconscious layer that motivates Indian behaviour in its various ecologies and its personality according to the theorizing of concepts on the *Gunas*.[88] (Jerath, J.M., and Anjum Sibia, 2009)

13. Eco-Cultural Variability in Personality Development

It is apparent that within a social group, the various factors affecting lifestyles seem to cohese and present a picture of a culture which evolves its own spectrum. The latter is dependent upon available resources, both concrete and human in the Indian context. We cite here a few generalizations based on inter-cultural variability among the ecologies of India.[89] (Super, C.M., and S. Harkness, 1996)

(i) *If there are changes within sub-cultures* such as in the non-Hindu in the secularism of India, *they tend to take on the parameters of the dominant culture*. For example, the "Parsis", who now form a very small minority in India, their ancestors having originated from Persia, practise their faith using fire as symbolic of God, have fire temples, wear *Saris*, and use flowers, incense and fruits at religious events just as much the Hindus do in performing "*aarti*". However, the roots of core values of Hinduism remain relatively unchanged as the dominant culture, such as value for family and religion and their correlates. Where changes occur, they are mainly spearheaded by the younger generation who are more resilient to change.

(ii) In viewing the various cultures of the world, there is no culture that is deficit in the phylogenetic characteristics. It is mainly the ontogenetic differentials which make for the differences among these cultures.

(iii) *Cultures do not remain static. As the rate of exchange of knowledge and skills improve, so do the statuses of these cultures*. Each starts at different level with a tendency for proceeding towards upward level simultaneously with others or singly. Priorities in values differ. Some give priority to religion, others to ethnicity, and yet others to industrial development. Religion and ethnicity are the roots of the individual. However, increasingly value is placed on economic power and territorial rights in the modernized world.

(iv) Ethnographic studies give a more comprehensive picture of the life styles of cultures, while nomethetic data give general characteristics. *Rarely do comparisons of cultures move along similar dimensions to give a "social reality picture" of the given cultures. They are usually described in constructs, which are themselves variable in their operationalisation.* While the points raised above refer mainly to generic culture, they may also as easily be applied to sub-cultures within a culture.

(v) *Criteria used in the description of cultures vary over time and within the same space*. What is existent today may not be tomorrow. Therefore, studies of cultures across similar dimensions, or even dissimilar dimensions, will differ over time. In India, viewing the psycho-social dimensions of adolescents in this century, we realize how they differ from the past. Longitudinal studies of Indian sub-cultures are few and far between, though some small community studies like Mishra's study of Jaunpur[90] (Mishra, P.S., 1994) and Seymour's study in Bhubaneswar,[91] (Seymour, S., 1986) attempt to find changes over a time period. Both studies indicated progressive changes indicative of modernising trends.

(vi) Conceptualizations of behaviour of values and attitudes have been discussed under the umbrella of the concept of universals. What is *a universal trait (value, behaviour, attitude, interest), do not necessarily have the same connotation from culture to culture.*

We have consciously viewed a variety of different sub-cultures from elementary to transitional to westernized modes of culture, and have highlighted the contrasting platforms on which they rest. It is from these foundational platforms that variations have been described. These variations index the contrastibility of the domains which are relative to one sub-culture and not the other.

In attempting to view different groups simultaneously, ultimately the description settles down to the variations of the existent patterns of sub-cultures in their ecosystems in India. Each of these in their own framework differ from others in a dynamic fashion. *Ethnographic studies seem to present these social realities for a better understanding of cultural behaviour in an ecosystem, in contrast to quantitative data approaches.* This is not to say that quantitative data are not equally important as qualitative data, but that the idiographic data are more related to ground-level realities of how people live in their specific ecologies. The ecologically influenced behaviour systems change dynamically as influenced by vicissitudes in social behaviour, along the dimension of traditionality towards modernity. However, not all aspects of modernity are invariantly adopted. Since India is a pluralistic society, multiculturalism is a common phenomenon of behavioural types. This concept of multiculturalism is a package of varying regions, religions, ethnicities, caste and community variables in varying degrees.

Therefore, *cultural relativity is accepted as a perceptual process, and adaptation to new ways is a generational variant, the younger being more amenable to relativity of roles and role diffusion.* There is also a tendency of confrontation between conformity and non-conformity with the younger generation adhering more to the latter. There are various permutations and combinations of the variables engulfing the Indian society. These are globalised trade, high-profiled information technology and the differential speed of industrialisation. The movements towards trying to preserve what one has and to predict what one has to face in the oncoming years, is both a frustrating as well as a stimulating challenge.

Socially approved behaviour is transmitted through communication, both verbal and non-verbal, both scientific and traditional. The latter exemplify the core values that continue from one generation to another in a rooted manner, although muted in the peripheral context. *Therefore, communication is perhaps the most pervasive and continuous process of transmitting cultural models through valued behaviour from generation to generation*, even though the process and styles of communication are not immutable. As greater technology impinges upon it, communication adopts fine nuances as influenced by impacting sources such as media, sophisticated technology and man's ability to utilise them for both preserving what is core and adapting to what is new. We have observed in this generation, for instance, that ethnic groups are interacting more homogeneously. As geographical mobility increases communication and decreases heterogeneity, the younger generation are becoming more informed than the previous. Since India is a country of several sub-cultures, abiding side by side, in a sense of tolerant acceptability, we would expect that all classes would be travelling up the social ladder and increasing their economic power. *Thus, we observe that social change piggy backs on time changes in affecting lifestyles, such that westernisation and modernisation are creating their own transformations in the domains of the global culture.*[92] (Mittelman, James H., 1996)

14. Major Overarching Linkages

In the overarching conglomeration of psychological domains, spiritual domains and sociological domains, although not overtly known, indicates a covert linkage among them as reflected in the following:

(i) *We have leap-frogged into western conceptualizations of childhood carrying with it post-facto psychological explanations of western-oriented data on childhood.*

(ii) *Taking this "borrowing" of concepts into cognizance, we may reinterpret them within our contextual framework, to better understand them* within the context of the Indian psyche.

(iii) *It is essential in this age and stage, to divest ourselves of thinking of the child as an empty slate, or an entity to be subordinated to adult maneuvers.*

(iv) We require to think in a forward proactive manner the contributions that the child himself makes to the emerging content of his development as a process. *The individual creates and recreates his own societal frame, which is his perception of culture and ecology with which he has the freedom to modulate according to his needs.*

From the late 1950s onwards, with the freedom given to Indians to develop their own potentials, there began a spate of investigations on themselves, their ecology, their environment and their culture. Scholars like Dube, Srinivas, Marriot, Singer and others[93] (Singer, Milton, 1955-56; Srinivas, M. N., 1962: 42; Dube, S.C., 1965; Vidyarthi, L.P., 1961: Marriot, McKim, 1961) examined the validity of the concepts of universals propounded by western scholars. This gave rise to alternate conceptualizations, such as Srinivas's thesis on Sanskritisation and Westernisation[94] (Srinivas, M.N., 1962). *Over time, there have been many themes analysed; the latest being a combination of concepts of cultural psychology and socio-technological changes, moving towards more heterogeneous socio-psychological patterns.*[95] (Sebastian, J. Jayakiran, 2003) *However, Indian themes retained the homogeneity of their intrinsic value systems,*[96] (Kakar, S., 1999) *while themselves living in differing socio-cultural ecologies.*

REFERENCES

1. Bandura, A., 1977, *Social Learning Theory*, Englewood Cliffs, N.J.: Prentice Hall;
   Miller, N.E., and Dollard, J., 1941, *Social Learning and Imitation*, New Haven: Yale University Press.
2. Alan Sroufe, L., Robert Cooper and Ganie Dehart, 1996, *Child Development: Its Nature and Course*, New York: McGraw Hill Education.
3. Huggert, Richard John, 1995, *Geoecology: An Evolutionary Approach*. London: Routledge.
4. Gadgil, M., and P.R.S. Rao, 1998, *Nurturing Biodiversity: An Indian Agenda*, Ahmedabad: Centre for Environment Education.
5. DeSombre, Elizabeth R., 2006, *The Global Environment and World Politics (Continuum Studies in Global Politics)*, London: Continuum International Publishing Group.
6. Barry Eichengreen, Poonam Gupta and Rajiv (eds.), *Emerging Giants: China and India in the World Economy*, Oxford University Press, under publication.
7. Charles Brownell, 2008, *Sub-prime Meltdown: From U.S Crisis to Global Recession*, U.K.: Createspace
8. Adams, C., 1935, "The relationship of General Ecology", *Ecology*, 16, pp. 242-63.
9. Haq, M.U., 1995, *Reflections on Human Development*, New Delhi: Oxford University Press.

10. UNDP, Human Development Report, 2009—Overcoming Barriers: Human Mobility and Development. New York: Palgrave Macmillan.
11. Joel, B. Hagen, 1992, *An Entangled Bank: The Origins of Ecosystems, Ecology*, New Jersey: Rutgers University Press.
12. Pandey, D.N., A.K. Gupta and D.M. Anderson, 2003, "Rainwater Harvesting as an Adaptation to Climate Change", *Current Science, 85*, 46-59.
13. Altman, I., and Wohlwill, J.F., 1977, *Human Behaviour and Environment: Advances in Theory and Research*, Vol. 2, New York: Plenum.
14. Richard L. Mosher, D.J. Youngman and J.M. Day, 1999, *Human Development Across Lifespan*, New York: Praeger Publishers.
15. Bandura, A., 1962, 'Social Learning through Imitation', *Nebraska Symposium on Motivation*, 10, pp. 211-269.
16. Khalakdina, M., 2008, *Human Development in the Indian Context: A Socio-cultural Focus, Vol. 1*, New Delhi: Sage.
17. Berry J.W., 1978, *Human Ecology and Cognitive Styles: Comparative Studies in Cultural and Psychological Adaptations*, New York: Sage/ Halsted.
18. Mead, M., 1928, *Coming of Age in Samoa*, New York: William Morrow.
19. St. John, J.A., (ed.), 1902, *The Philosophical Works of John Locke*, New York/London: George Bell & Sons.
20. Munsey, Brenda, 1980, *Moral Development, Moral Education and Kohlberg: Basic Issues in Philosophy, Psychology, Religion and Education*. Birmingham, Alabama: Religious Education Press.
21. Saraswathi, T.S, J. Sundaresan and K. Saxena, 1977, *Age, Sex, and Social Class Differences in the Development of \Moral Judgement of Indian Children Between the Ages 10-15 Years*. Baroda: Faculty of Home Sciences, M.S. University, Dept. of Child Development (mimeo).
22. Tripathi, D.K.M., and Misra, G., 1979, 'Development of Moral Judgement in Indian Children', *Psycologia*, 22, pp.164-160.
23. Woodward, Kath, 2003, *Understanding Identity*. London: Hodder Education.
24. Tripathi, D.K.M., and Misra, G., 1979, 'Development of Moral Judgement in Indian Children', *Psycologia*, 22 pp.164-160.
25. McGraw, MB., 1940, "Neuromuscular development of the human infant as exemplified in the achievement of erect locomotion", *Journal of Pediatrics*, 17, pp. 747–777.
26. Rao, S.N, 1976, 'An experimental investigation of children's concept of maths and volume', *Indian Journal of Psychology*, 51 (3), pp. 212-220.

27. Jennings, H.S., 1930, *The Biological Basis of Human Nature*, p. 3, New York: W.W. Norton & Co. Inc.
28. Chaudhuri, A., and K.C. Chaudhuri, 1966, "Clinical and cytogenetic findings in twenty patients with mongolism", *Indian Journal of Pediatrics*, 33, 298-306.
29. Purohit, A.K., 1984, "An Experimental study of the role of environmental context in memory", *Indian Journal of Psychology*, 59, 49-52.
30. Karen, A. Cerulo, 2001, *Culture in Mind: Toward a Sociology of Culture and Cognition*, New York/London: Routledge.
31. Reese, E., and Brown, N., 2000, "Reminiscing and recounting in the preschool years", *Applied Cognitive Psychology*, 14, 1-17.
32. Piaget, J., 1954, *The Construction of Reality in the Child* (M. Cook, Trans.), New York: Basic Books.
33. Vygotsky, L.S., 1978. Mind in Society: *The Development of Higher Psychological Processes*, Cambridge, MA: Harvard University Press.
34. Ishwaran, K., 1970, *Change and Continuity in Indian Villages*, pp.105-127, New York: Columbia University Press.
35. Parsons, T., 1937, *The Structure of Social Action*, New York: Free Press.
36. Super, C.M., and Harkness, S., 1986, 'The Developmental Niche: A Conceptualisation at the interface of child and culture', *International Journal of Behavioural Development*, 9, pp. 545-569.
37. Bronfenbrenner, U., 1979, *The Ecology of Human Development*, London: Harvard University Press.
38. Mortensen, E.L., Michaelsen, K.F., Sander, S.A., and J.M. Reinisch, 2001, 'The Association, the Duration of Breast Feeding and Adult Intelligence', *Journal of Adult American Association*, 287, 2365.
39. McCartney, K; M.J. Harris and F. Bernieri, 1990, "Growing up and growing apart: A developmental meta-analysis of twin studies". *Psychological Bulletin*, March (1990),107(2), 226-237.
40. Bruner, J.S., Olver, R., and Greenfield, P.M., 1966, *Studies in Cognitive Growth*. New York: Wiley, 1966.
41. Lessor, G.S., Fifer, G., and Clarke, D.H, 1965, 'Mental abilities of children from different socio and cultural groups', *Monograph of Society for Research in Child Development*, Series 30, Vol. No. 102.
42. Goodnow, J.J., 1962, 'A test of mileu differences with some of Piaget's tasks', *Psychological Monographs*, 76, No. 36, Vol. 555.
43. Anandalakshmy, S., Bajaj, M., 1981, 'Childhood in the weaver's community in Varanasi: Socialisation for adult roles', in D. Sinha (ed.), *Socialisation of the Indian Child*, New Delhi, Concept.
44. Vygotsky, L.S., 1978. Mind in Society: The Development of Higher Psychological Processes. Cambridge, MA: Harvard University Press.

45. Erikson, E.H., 1980, *Identity and the Life Cycle*, New York: W.W. Norton & Company.
46. Lewin, K., 1951, *Field Theory in Social Science: Selected Theoretical Papers*. (Edited by D. Cartwright), New York: Harper & Row.
47. Whiting, J.W., and I. Child, 1953, *Child Training and Personality: A Cross Cultural Study*, New Haven: Yale University Press.
48. Moreno, J.W., 1977, *Who Shall Survive? Foundations of Sociometry: Group Therapy*, Boston: Beacon House.
49. Rao, T.V., and Banerjee, D., 1973, 'Sociometric structure of the pre-adolescent classrooms and the personality differences among high-choice receiving by children', *Indian Educational Review*, 8(1), pp. 215-225.
50. Larson, R., and Csikszentmihalyi, M., 1984, *Being Adolescent Conflict and Growth in the Teenage Years*, New York: Basic Books.
51. Saraswathi, T.S., 2003, *Cross Cultural Perspectives in Human Development*, pp. 42-43, New Delhi: Sage.
52. Kumar, K., 1993, *Political Agenda of Education: A Study of Colonialist and Anti-nationalist Ideas*, p. 69, New Delhi: Sage.
53. Bledsoe, Caroline H., and Barney Cohen (eds.),1993, *Social Dynamics of Adolescent Fertility in Sub-Sharan Africa—Population Dynamics of Sub-Saharan Africa.* Working Group on the Social Dynamics of Adolescent Fertility, National Research Council). Washington D.C.: National Academy Press.
54. Verma, S., and Saraswathi, T.S., 2002, 'Adolescence in India: Street Urchins or Silicon Valley Millionaires?', in B.R. Brown, and T.S. Saraswathi (eds.), *World's Youth. Adolescence in Eight Regions of the Globe*, pp. 105-140, New York: Cambridge University Press.
55. Bales, R F., 1958, 'Role and role conflict', in Maccoby, E.E., Newcomb, T.M., and Hartley, EL., *Readings in Social Psychology*. pp. 446-447, New York: Henry Holt & Co.
56. Messick, David M., and Roderick M. Krammer (eds.), 2005, *The Psychology of Leadership: New Perspectives and Research*. Mahwah, NJ: Erlbaum Associates.
57. Haythorn, W., Couch, A.S., Haefner, D., Langham, P., and Carter, L.F., 1956, 'The effects of varying combinations of authoritarian and equalitarian leaders and followers', *Journal of Abnormal and Social Psychology*, 53, pp. 210-219.
58. Newcomb, T.M., 1947, "Development as a function of reference group: The Bennington study", in Eleanor E.; Newcomb, Theodore M.; Hartley and Eugene L. Maccoby (eds.), *Readings in Social Psychology*. 3rd edition. New York: Henry Holt & Co.
59. Ellis, Sue and B. Rogoff, 1982, "The Strategies and efficacy of child *versus* adult teachers", *Child Development*, Vol. 43, 730-735.

60. Christian Fuchs, 2008, *Internet and Society: Social Theory in the Information Age*. New York: Routledge.
61. Newcomb, T.M., 1947, "Development as a function of reference group: The Bennington study", in Eleanor E.; Newcomb, Theodore M.; Hartley and Eugene L. Maccoby (eds.), *Readings in Social Psychology*, 3rd edition, New York: Henry Holt & Co.
62. Chomsky, N., 1965, *Aspects of the Theory of Syntax*, Cambridge, MA: MIT Press.
63. Roland, A., 1988, *In Search of Self in India and Japan: Toward a Cross-cultural Psychology*, Delhi: Ajanta Publications;
Chaudhry, N., 1999, 'Language Socialisation: Patterns of Caregiver speech in young children', in T.S. Saraswathi (ed.), *Culture, Socialisation and Human Development*, New Delhi: Sage.
64. Berry, J.W., 1976, 'Ecological and cultural factors in spatial perceptual development', in J. Wofson (ed.), *Personality and Learning*, London: Hodder and Stoughton/Open University Press.
65. Cole, M., Bruner, J.S., 1976, 'Cultural Differences and Inferences about Psychological Processes' in. J. Wolfson (ed.), *Personality and Learning*, p. 173, London: Hooder and Stoughton/Open University Press.
66. Mishra, R.C., Sinha, D., Berry, J.W., 1996, *Ecology Acculturation and Psychological Adaptation: A Study of Adivasis in Bihar*, New Delhi: Sage.
67. Berry, J.W., 1966, Temne and Eskimo *Perceptual Skills*, *International Journal of Psychology*, 1, pp. 207-29
68. Thomas, R.M., 2001, *Recent Theories of Human Development*, California: Sage Publications.
69. Warm, J.S., 1988, 'Foreword', in I. Singh, and R. Parasuraman, *Human Cognition: A Multidisciplinary Approach*, pp. 15-16, New Delhi: Sage.
70. Singh, I., Parasuraman, R., and Matthews, G., 1998, "Diversity in cognitive theory", in I. Singh and R. Parasuraman (eds.), *Human Cognition: A Multidisciplinary Perspective*, 21-39. London: Sage.
71. Dwivedi, C.B., 1987, 'On Yogdarsana Doctrine of Memory' *Journal of Indian Psychology*, 6, pp. 1-6.
72. Wertheimer, M., 1923, 'Untersuchungen zur Lehre von der Gestalt, II', *Psychol. Forsch.*, 4, pp. 301-350.
73. Watson, J.B., 1928, *Psychological Care of Infant and Child*, New York: Norton.
74. Skinner, B.F., 1950, 'Are theories of learning necessary?', *Psych Rev.*, 57, pp. 193-216.
75. Posner, M.I., 1998, 'Current Research in Cognitive Neuroscience', in I. Singh, and R. Parasuram (eds.), *Human Cognition*, p. 41, New Delhi: Sage.

76. Russel, R.W., 1987, 'Drugs as tools for research in neuropsy-chobiology: A historical perspective', *Neuropsyco-biology*, 18, pp.134-143.
77. Hornykiewicz, O., 1972, 'Neurochemistry of Parkinsonism', in A. Lajitha (ed.), *Handbook of Neurochemisrtry*. Vol. 7, pp. 465-501, New York: Plenum.
78. Parsuraman, R., and Greenwood, P.M., 1998, Attention and Brain Function in Aging and Alzheimer's Disease', in I. Singh, and R. Parasuram (eds.), *Human Cognition*. pp. 126-143. New Delhi: Sage.
79. Patel, V.L., and Groen, G.J., 1986, 'Knowledge based solution strategies in medical reasoning', *Journal of Cognitive Science*, 10, pp. 91-116.
80. Patel, V.K., J.F. Arocha and D.R. Kaufmann, 1994, 'Diagnostic reasoning and medical expertise', in D.L. Medin (ed.), *The Psychology of Learning and Motivation*, 31, pp. 185-252. San Diego: Academic Press.
81. Sontheimer, G.D., 1977, *The Joint Hindu Family Evolution as a Legal Institution* (South Asian Studies), New Delhi: Munshiram Monoharlal Publishers.
82. Kapp, K.W., 1963, *Hindu Culture, Economic Development and Economic Planning in India*. Bombay: Asia Publishing Mishra, V., 1962, Hinduism and Economic Growth, Bombay: OUP.
83. Rao, M.S., 2004, 'Religion and Economic Development', in R. Robinson (ed.), *Sociology of Religion in India*, New Delhi: Sage.
84. Patel, V.K., Arocha, J.F., and Kaufmann, D.R., 1994, 'Diagnostic reasoning and medical expertise', in D.L. Medin (ed.), *The Psychology of Learning and Motivation*, 31, pp. 185-252, San Diego: Academic Press.
85. Malhotra, S., 2000, *Child Psychiatry in India*, Delhi: Macmillan.
86. Rao, M.S., 2004, 'Religion and Economic Development', in R. Robinson (ed.), *Sociology of Religion in India*, New Delhi: Sage.
87. Kakar, S., 1966, *The Indian Psyche*, Delhi: Oxford University Press.
88. Jerath, J.M., and Anjum Sibia, 2009, *"Trends in Personality Research: An Overview"*, in G. Misra, *Psychology in India, Vol. I: Basic Psychological Processes and Human Development. Introduction*, pp. 263-306, Delhi: Indian Council of Social Science Research/Pearson Education in South Asia.
89. Super, C.M., and S. Harkness (eds.), 1996, *Parents' Cultural Belief Systems*, New York: The Guilford Press.
90. Mishra, P.S., 1994, *Changing Pattern of Village Family in India: A Sociological Study*, New Delhi: Radha Publications.
91. Seymour, S., 1986, 'Changing families in India: adaptations to urbanization in Bhubaneshwar during the past twenty years',

Proceedings of the Eighth Conference of the International Association of Cross Cultural Psychology, Istanbul, Turkey.

92. Mittelman, James H., 1996, *Globalisation: Critical Reflections*, Boulder and London: Lynee Reinner Publishers.
93. Singer, Milton, 1955-56, 'Cultural Pattern of Indian Civilization: A preliminary report of methodological field study', *Far Eastern Quarterly*. No. 15, 230-327;
    Srinivas, M.N., 1962, 'A note on sankritisation and westernisation", in M.N. Srinivas, *Caste in Modern India and Other Essays*, pp. 42-62. London: Asia Publishing House;
    Dube, S.C., 1965, 'The study of complex cultures', in T.K.N. Unnithan, Indiradeva and Y. Singh (eds.), *Towards a Sociology of Culture in India*, pp. 421-423, New Delhi: Prentice Hall of India;
    Vidyarthi, L.P., 1961, *The Sacred Complex in Hindu Gaya*, Bombay: Asia Publishing House;
    Marriot, McKim, 1961, "Changing channels of cultural transmission in Indian civilisation", *Journal of Social Research*, Vol. 4., Nos. 1-2, p. 22.
94. Srinivas, M.N., 1962, 'A Note on Caste in Modern India and Other Essays sanskritisation and westernisation', in M.N. Srinivas, pp. 42-62. London: Asia Publishing House.
95. Sebastian, J. Jayakiran, 2003, 'Believing and Belonging: Secularism and Religion in India', International Review of Mission, April (2003).
96. Kakar, S., 1999, *Culture and Psyche: Selected Essays*, Delhi: Oxford University Press.

7

Proactive Perspectives

This chapter consists of the following sections:

1. Introduction.
2. Critical areas of enquiry.
3. The systemic linkages among the eco-systems.
4. The interactive dynamics of the individual in his eco-systems.
5. Differential experiences leading to different ontogenetic traits.
6. Homogeneity and heterogeneity of India's people.
7. The need for indigenized theorizing.
8. Ecological dynamic changes affecting patterns of living.
9. Assumptions and hypotheses.
10. An integrated holistic Approach.
11. Sustainability in Development.

1. Introduction

As this book is being written, we have witnessed in India far-reaching changes, written by the moving finger of time. On the 16th May, 2009, a unique General Election took place to the 16th Lok Sabha leading to the formation of a Government with its mandate as sustainable development. The comments by politicians, both those who lost and by those who won, and by media commentators reflected the movement from traditional to modernised thinking. They emphasised inter-linkages with the world in many spheres of enterprise — economic, technological and the newly emerging acceptance of international social exchange. In the first decade of the twenty-first century, there is an increasing rapidity of travel to and from between

India and other countries, trade, commerce and intellectual exchanges. "Sustainable development" and "democracy" indicate the government's determined efforts (once again) to de-emphasise existing discriminations of caste, ethnicity, religion and even ideological themes, so as to remove barriers impeding to progress and accelerate the ethos of "equitable and sustainable development".[1] (Dreze, J.D., & A. Sen, 2002) However, we cannot veil the fact that "saying is not the same thing as doing".

The Indian public have their own mandate as to what constitute sustainable development, which for the majority continues to be simply *Bijli, Sadak, Pani*, meaning energy, roads and water to imply the need for providing basic facilities to the majority.[2] (Bates, D.G., 2001) This is not to say that technology in India is lagging behind. In Mumbai and Delhi, for instance, solar panels are being used in hospitals for years, and in the early 1960s solar cookers and biogas plants were experimented within villages in North India. The major problem still remains: there is too little for too many in spite of innovative measures in biotechnology. Sustainability in development is possible, if the ecology has the potential. *Unfortunately, population growth has out-spaced supply and, therefore, contributed to the short-change in strategies for development.*[3] (Haq, Shamsul, 1999) India's rank in Human Development Index (HDI) has fallen from 124th in the 2004 UNDP report to 134th in the 2009 report. The latter report has used data of 2007 on life expectancy at birth (63.4 years in India), adult literacy rate defined as percentage aged 15 and above (66% in India) and combined gross enrolment ratio in education (61% in India) and per capita GDP (2753 pp US$ in India) as components of HDI.[4] (UNDP, 2009) Obviously, due to the growing population, differing mobility and migrating habitats, the human resource niche does not seem to have the capacity to keep up with industrialised countries which, with their high levels of technology and low proportions of populations, tend to have adequate and better facilities in comparison to other developing countries. Unlike the countries of the ASEAN complex like Singapore and Malaysia, India has not concomitantly accelerated its quality of life.

The chapters which went before offer insight into the telling conceptualisation of the role of man (human ecology) in interacting with the hemispheres' potentials (geo-ecology).

2. Critical Areas of Enquiry

In the light of the developmental conceptualisations of personality and nature's development in India, the analyses in the chapters indicate further areas of proactive enquiry, as mentioned below:

1. As India is composed of many large poor States with a higher proportion of less educated, less economically well-off and marginalised groups (women, Dalits, Tribals and poor Muslims),[5] (Desai, Sonalde B., Amaresh Dubey, Brij Lal Joshi, Mitali Sen, Abusaleh Shariff, and Reeve Venneman, 2010) the focus of enquiry should also high profile these groups.
2. The enquiry should *incorporate political and economic sciences in empiricising the social reality of the Indian,* especially those who are identified as being fragile in the fabric of social integration.
3. The social science disciplines need to move out of their hackneyed unidisciplinary approaches to view the holistic personality in a holistic frame of the social and political sciences.[6] (Bergman, L.R., R.B. Cairns, L.G. Nilsson & L. Nystedt, 2000)
4. Since the Indian's capability is dependent upon his skill at utilising the potentials of his geo-ecology, *strategies are to be well-targeted on the situational givens*. If these vary from ecology to ecology so also should the strategies of each level of governance. Otherwise attempts to bring about uniformity will be tangential to the needs of the various Indians in varying ecologies. Therefore, the importance of a multi-sectoral, multi-disciplinary and multi-centric approach / approaches all used conjunctively may be examined to create further areas of enquiry.[7] (Rahman, Tanhidur, Ronc Mittelhammer & Philip Wandschneidan, 2003)
5. The Indian, who in the *past decades lived within well-structured and well-known systems of Jaat, Jaati, Jajman, panchayat and, above all, the diversification in caste and class, was encased in a human ecology, wherein he adjusted to these differences*, as they were well-established accepted norms. *This human ecology for most Indians is now changing its contours.* It is gradually being drawn into a vortex of

dynamic changes, which began to show its face in the early years of the 1980s, as indicated by sociologists like Singh and Srinivas.[8] (Singh, Y., 1977; Srinivas, M.N., 1966) Such movements imply that the Indian is exhibiting a tendency towards present and future orientations at the same time. The issue of value orientations between generations, therefore, requires enquiry as to their dissonance within the micro systems of human ecology.[9] (Kluckhohn, F.R. & F.L. Strodtbeck, 1961)

6. The Indian is progressively being exposed to modernisation, bringing with him his core traditional systems.[10] (Kumar, R., 1999) How does he adjust to these simultaneous patterns is an important area of further empiricism.
7. In this, the twenty-first century, *many of the social structures and systems are rearranging their parameters*. For instance, a tribal or a ruralite who before knew only the forests or hills or rural hinterlands, is now being exposed to other frames of references in other ecologies.[11] (Ellen, R. F., P. Parkes & A. Bicker, 2000) Such new ecologies are for most migrant ruralites and tribals are overcrowded cities and mushrooming slum colonies in urban areas.[12] (Cash, D.W., W.N. Adger, F. Berkes, P. Garden, L. Lebel, P. Olsson, L. Pritchard & O. Young, 2006) Academic sensitivity may be directed towards an increasing and concerning trend in social demographics affecting human and geo-ecologies simultaneously. This is the new phenomenon of migration with its consequent overcrowding in slum-dwelling in already bursting urban ecology. The disjuncture between the ecology of origin in the hinterlands and the temporary ecologies of work situation for the travelling migrant creates dissonance in many spiralling patterns.[13] (Ramaswamy, S., & G. Sathish Kumar, 2009) These are the temporary geo-ecology, the permanent geo-ecologies in their hinterlands and the cohabiting of differential value systems of urban to rural / tribal and *vice versa*. Does this create dissonance or does the migrating Indian learn to adapt to two different frames of reference in a harmonious manner?
8. Another challenge that will confront psycho-social enquiry is in the uncovering and collating new empirical data. These data, the science of which are appearing on the horizon are:

the criss-crossing nature of socio-political and neurological information bases. With the acceleration of media strategies available in most micro-systems, with the interactive nature of global communication, trade and commerce, the Indian psyche is being increasingly stimulated. There are now increasing science of experimenting through computers in village Panchayat Ghars on providing updated information on agriculture technologies to the farmers. *Political and economic scientists should figure substantially in the analysis of personalities and their related ecologies.* The vertical geographical transmigration affecting personality characteristics is also subtly influenced by other parameters, such as new configurations of governance of the meso and exo systems, and even global factors.[14] (Najam, A., D. Runnalls & M. Halle, 2007) The rebounding effect of more trans-ecological movements, whether they cause resilient adaptation or displacement are growing avenues of analyses. With the increasing proclamations for improving the conditions of the poor and discriminated, the system of reservation in educational and professional institutions, creates a rebounding effect.[15] (Galaz, V., P. Olsson, T. Hahn, C. Folke & U. Svedin, 2006). For, individuals who originally come from poorer ecologies with their depleting effects find it difficult to cope with those seek admission on a merit basis. *Therefore, the reality of the situation is a jostling of poor ecologies with sophisticated ecologies in adjacency.* How do the disadvantaged groups cohese with the advantaged groups in educational institutions and in work situations with others who are more advantaged? Do the disparities lead to lessened quality or do they overcome the disequilibrium between the meritorious and the non-meritorious who seek the same portals of education and profession. *Such situation of social reality can be multiplied. Cognisance needs to be taken of to the serendipitous effect of such interactions.*

9. *These concerns of such analysts indicate the need for devising theoretical constructs that have relevance to the Indian* in situ. No longer can we assume that feeding patterns, toilet training, sleeping patterns and such like, are of major importance in child-care practices. *It is the emotionality, the attitudinal motivation, the personality attribute of the*

caretaker that impinge upon the personality of the young. A tribal mother tends to be traditional, superstitious and given to mysticism in her childcare practices. An urban mother tends to consult updated magazines and the trained personnel. Academia requires turning its sights to these varying patterns and devising such strategies as will reflect the indigenous nature of such socialisation practices which affect the young.

10. *Changing structures and systems require closer enquiry.* The structural systems of the close relationships in the family of orientation, the fracture of the joint family system, the growing self-orientation that is occurring in the coming generations, requires a more intensive analysis of factors affecting them. Further, the increasing ambiguity of the caste system which is rearranged by the diffusion of economic status, are challenging concerns for pro-active enquiry.
11. In the face of *lacunae of indigenous personality development theorising, further analysis should reveal other theoretical bases*, as for example the theory of *gunas* related to personality development according to the Hindu philosophical thought.[16] (Jerath, J.M., & A. Sibia, 2009: 267) It might be argued that this theory is related to the Hindu religion. Be that as it may, Hinduism is the dominant religion and for ages minorities have been dovetailed into their socio-economic spheres, if not the religious sphere.
12. Given the cultural and socialization patterns of the Indian individual as a growing personality, attitudes accrue which indicate two sides of the coin: *some are challenged, achievement-oriented, and aspire to better their living conditions and become more ecologically mobile. Others are passive accepters of their given situations and tend to continue with a sense of tolerance and resignation to destiny.* This is apparent between professional and an agricultural farmer.
13. An issue that deals directly with the *work ethic in public ethos is the way the Indian in his various ecologies learns or does not learn to abide by the norms of the polity and governance.* It is not unusual that the time dimension is low-profiled in the villager's acumen in contrast to the high-flying professional in multi-national companies. Thus, ecology plays a significant part in the contouring of attitudes and values.

14. It is well-known that *infrastructures and their systems of maintenance are unable to keep pace with the needs of the growing society, especially the under-privileged.* It is well-known also that a miniscule few pay the taxes that contribute to revenue or public facilities. The larger mass is not taxable and, ironically, those who are very wealthy private enterprises accrue a great deal of unaccounted cash so as to avoid paying taxes. Therefore, if *infrastructures and personnel are poor,* then services will have little impact on the poor. Assessments are essential to indicate what happens to the poor in further destabilising their status when such poor facilities exist.
15. There are *several erudite essays on the disadvantaged in theoretical terms*. It is essential to know whether the results of such assessments prompt the *government to re-arrange its parameters of* assistance. Therefore, further field studies of an action oriented type are required to be fed into programmes of alleviation and at the same time offer hypotheses which are relevant to such programmatic concerns. One such concern is that invariably the benefits do not trickle down to the most needy. They are siphoned off by the most powerful at the top. How does a policy implemented in order to be in tune with the neediest?
16. The vicissitudes of changing patterns of geo-ecological mobility, economic deprivation, and the state of the political ethos, *occur in various patterns in varying ecologies.Their differences should correlate theory with implementation process. The latter* need to be examined in tandem to assess the status of human ecologies in various geo-ecological areas.

The above points are merely illustrative of further areas of enquiries into parameters of human ecology as related to the geo-ecology.

3. The Systemic Linkages among the Eco-systems

The systemic parameters of the eco-systems are summarised as follows:

1. Generic dimensions of the micro, the meso, the exo and the macro eco-systems form concentric circles of interaction with and among themselves.

2. The development of the individual personality is in the micro system, namely; his family.
3. This centralized individual is centrifugally positioned in the micro nexus of the radiating other ecosystems.
4. Each ecosystem interacts with each other, dependent upon need satisfaction of the individual in his micro system. The interaction is reciprocally satisfying or otherwise dependent upon the needs of the individual in these systems.
5. The intensity of the interactions among these ecosystems, with the centrifugal individual, is in relation to the distance in terms of geographical space. It is also related to the frequency of contacts. Thus, degrees of intensity, distances in space and frequency of contact interact to high profile the individual's behaviour in his human ecosystem.
6. The interactions close to the individual are *proximal* and those at distances are *distal.*

*These six systemi*c characteristics in the context of the changing paradigms of relationships indicate new areas of investigation as to the overlapping cohabitation of the varying eco-cultural frames. Pro-active thinking in academic circles needs to combine disciplinary frames to view the growing individual through what is called a "single window" approach. By now, it may become apparent to the reader that as the saying goes "all roads lead to Rome" and, therefore, whether a psychological or a sociological or an anthropological approach to studying human behaviour in differing ecologies, they should lead to similar conclusions about the development of the individual. For example, psychology combines with the neurological science to study behaviour which is non-normal, while anthropology studies the normal behaviour from the point of view of the social cultural setting of a group. We feel that there are gaps in understanding how the other systems monitor and modify the individual's behaviour in his psycho-social group. There are only two known ways by which we may know more about the Indian in his habitat. One is the repetitive nature of sociology and psychology and their derivatives in explaining human behaviour. The other is to expand the parameters to include demographic, economic, political and other related dimensions. The inclusion of neurosciences is occurring at a rapid rate in the study of the human.

The economics of human behaviour are mainly available through studies indicating different degrees of wealth, otherwise known as economic classes.

4. The Interactive Dynamics of the Individual in his Eco-systems

On the horizon of India's progressive society in this century, there are several significant problems that are in need of academic attention. We specify them into three categories:

1. The quality of ecological factors (human and geo) contributing to economic poverty statuses in most Indian ecologies,[17] (Gupta, K.R., 2008) one major geo-ecological factor being productive land availability, its type and its management.[18] (Bodkin, D.B., 1990)
2. *An emerging factor in this geo-ecological spectrum, is the massive and growing unpredictability of geo-ecological changing resources, endangering human ecology, for instance, earthquakes of high intensity, and drought, especially in tribal areas, where entire tribes are dependent upon natural resources.*[19] (Ellen, R.F., & P. Parkes & A. Bicker, 2000) For example, the people who live around the Amazon, the largest river in South America, are in a fragile state exacerbated by industrial inroads into their ecologies.[20] (Onser, L.E., 1995) Another example is of the forest lands in Madagascar (Malagasy) where denudation of hillside of the ecological givens, which in turn, create issues for the wellbeing of its inhabitants.[21] (Harper Janice, 2002). Similarly, the melting ice in the North and South pole is causing imbalances in the sea's tidal waves.[22] (Metal, M., 1998) The same scenario is easily perceived in India where industrial inroads deplete agricultural lands and tribal forests and where the effects of climate on the productivity of land and the health of its people goes relatively ignored.

India probably has a larger spectrum of such dangerously fragile ecologies, beset by heterogeneous variables which negatively affect the quality of life.[23] (Gamely, P.J., 1998) To give a few of the countless examples, floods which are common occurrences (even in urban areas like Mumbai during the monsoons); the famine in Andhra Pradesh (which caused farmers to commit suicide), melting of the Himalayan glaciers and the flooding of the rivers, the over-crowding slums of the migrants, attrition of poorly managed programmes for the disadvantaged.[24] (Gole, Prakasa, 2001) These factors lead to permutations and combinations of the dynamism among and within the ecologies of the human, and in this case, the Indian.

Lacunae exist also in the knowledge of what happens to an Indian's psyche when he moves frequently between one ecosystem and another in comparison to another individual who is *status quo* in geographical mobility. A very familiar illustration is the differences in experiential knowledge, between the migrant who works in a city and visits his village-bound brother occasionally. He is more urbanised than his stay-at-home brother, and the difference is more striking, every time he visits his village. What happens to the psyche of the professional whose occupation in the inter-global market makes him travel to different geo-ecologies interacting with other nations. How does he react when he returns home, when he makes a right about-turn several times?

5. Differential Experiences Leading to Different Ontogenetic Traits

The growing individual himself changes according to circumstances and events, which repeatedly accrue in his ecology. An individual in an urban family develops tendencies which are different from children growing in more ravaged areas, as in the NEFA region. An individual living in such disharmonious situations may not exhibit the characteristics of tension, anxiety and fear, which is more dramatically observable in war devastated areas such as Dafour, in Sudan and Baghdad, in Iraq.[25] (Hoffman, Bruce, 2006) The kind of feudalism which existed in the days of the Nawabs and *Rajas*[26] (Sharma, R.S., 1981) is now no longer visible since India's ideologies have changed. However, differential forms of communication in governance now occur through media, and global interaction, indicating that the power locus has shifted its paradigm to international spectra, such as comparative GDP's, stock exchange indices, and territorial ownership. Therefore, problems differ between the developed and the developing nations *per se*.[27] (Uma, S. Kambhapati, 2004) In the telescoping of nations in globalisation and increased frequent international events, nations experience the spill over effects of interaction, which affect individual in their ecological habitat. In this case the Indian living under these changing ecological systems, even though they emanate from the macro systems is simultaneously affected.

Consequently, both the geo-ecology and the human ecology are changing their contours in relation to each other. There are two domains which could be further explored, to meet the challenges of this century.

1. The social sciences need to move out of their hackneyed unidisciplinary approaches and magnify their scopes on the total human being in his total ecology. How the individual develops socially and psychologically depends upon the availability of the "situational determinants" in the individual's environment for a quality of life that is sustainable.[28] (Rahman, Tanhidur, Ronc Mittelhammer & Philip Wandschneidan, 2003)
2. *If sustainable development is a priority, then human habitats in the given ecology should be the front runners, and not the followers in political acumen of governance.*

6. Homogeneity and Heterogeneity of India's People

If we look at the wider picture of the human homogeneous ecologies of the Anglo-Saxon west and the heterogeneous mixed races of the east (middle-east, far-east, south-east), attempting to find systematic patterns defies analysis. Homogeneity implies commonality, while heterogeneity implies variability. Therefore, it is easier to trace commonalities among the countries of Europe and North Americans. On the other hand, there is a tremendous variation in the lifestyles of the people of the east who compose races that are Arab, Aryan, Dravidian and the Mongols of the far east. Within a country itself there are variations. In India, for instance, there are tribals living off forest produce at one end of the dimension of traditionality-modernity and, at the other end, there are individuals who imitate the west without having the required abilities to adapt to an extraneous ideology. Therefore, which India can be analysed? Is it possible to extricate those dimensions of a personality which are immutable, resistant to change from those which are easily changeable? All theories of personality, in some measure or the other, attempt to deal with finding explanations, but like horses on a race track, they run in parallel lines, with blinders on, dealing with the generics of their theories. The specifics are laid by the wayside when applying them to the varieties of geo-ecologies contouring human ecologies in the Indian context. The traditional family living in an isolated community, in an elementary geo-ecological territory, tends not to change its traditional lifestyle, as there is no better alternative to their current setting which gives them a secure identity. With the widening of their horizon to include more of the other ecosystems in relation to its own changes are likely to occur. For instance, as indicated by Bronfenbrenner[29] (Bronfenbrenner, 2001) and according to the Lewinian concept[30] (Lewin. K., 1936) of valences, vectors, regions of life space, it may be deduced that the greater the exposure to other life styles which are of an improved quality, the likelihood of change may be accelerated. It may thus be inferred that the micro system of the individual's family and the core-centrifugal, habitual values and traits of the individual are perhaps resistant to change, as they are significant attributes of the individual's identity.[31] (Bronfenbrenner, U., & G.W. Evans, 2000) Yet, parenthetically we talk of an Indian, as if an Indian is a homogeneous package of traits, values and beliefs, where cognitive functions are influenced by variation in the ecologies.[32] (Berry. J.W., J.A. Bennet & J.B. Denny, 2000). However, irrespective of whichever country this Indian settles in, especially if he is a first generation migrant, there is a consistent core of quality of 'Indianness' in him. He tends to form or join a group especially if they are from the same ethnic/religious group. Co-relatively, for instance, there are many little "Indias" in America. It is precisely this retention of Indianness that distinguishes an Indian from a Chinese or a Sinhalese. *Enquiries into these phenomena should take a quantum leap into the future and build up a regimen for what are essentially the qualities of Indianness.* Therefore, the urgent need to keep abreast with the times and to also include into focus the Indian in the diaspora is essential. Academicians perhaps need to develop alternate paradigms to include such changing contours of the Indian in his varying ecologies, especially from India to other countries.

Therefore, all ecosystems which are composed of smaller circular interactional systems, by necessity, have to subscribe to the one macro system that encapsules all others. *It is necessary, therefore, to explore how a macro system is perceived.* To an illiterate individual, it is the world out there, where its qualities are unknown. On the other hand, an international corporate executive is supposed to know the intricacies of the dynamic world around him. How do these differential perspectives attune the behaviour of the individual for the best fit with his ecology? Perhaps there is a sense of spiriticism in the illiterate villager and a greater scepticism in the international traveller. *There are, thus, myriads of differential perspectives of the cognitive map-systems they are related to, depending upon the radial of contact and knowledge.* These facts are of importance when developmental conceptualisations are made about the growing individual personality. To close the heterogeneity of the gap of knowledge among individuals living in different ecologies in India, it is essential that first priority should be given to education, at the right time in the right place for the right chronologically aged individual, the child. For, an uneducated adult is a short-changed individual for the rest of his life[33] (Kashinath, H., 2003) in a growing technological world.

7. The Need for Indigenized Theorizing

As we have mentioned at several times in the foregoing chapters, the Indian repertoire lacks a knowledge of indigenous explanations about the human behaviour in the Indian context. *There is thus a need for a continuous search for indigenous conceptualisations*. This leads to the next issue, namely, theoretical constructs. The epistemological issue is: in what ways are human beings alike and in what ways are they different, not only between identifiable groups but also within a group from one individual to another? Indians as a group cannot extricate themselves from others in developing and behaving according to epistemological rules of phylogenesis.[34] (Fuller, J.S., 1960) Indians live in separate environments and different ecologies with differing sub-cultures. This is what makes them uniquely different from other races. So are there different theories of personality development? If we attach ourselves to the *emic* principle, then Indians also subscribe to the same developmental themes which are generic the world over. However, this is not completely enveloping. From the various readings and a search for theoretical postulates, which attempt to define Indians, it is observable that from available empirical data that Indians have their unique specific attributes like being more collectivistic-oriented than individualistic; that they can be or become just as familiar with a technological environment just as they are familiar with their traditional one. There are millions of such individual illustrations. For example, traditional *pujas* are performed in elitist families which then can easily adapt to cocktail parties and display sharp business acumen in dealing with world trade matters.

If the constructs operationalising the Indians are distinguishable, such as by cultural attributes, values and beliefs, and we believe that, if we stay within this axis, we might be able *to develop theoretical constructs typical of the Indian: both generically as the so called "average Indian" as well as the million of other Indians in heterogeneous ecologies.*

Except for a few analyses of certain personality structures, such as those by Paranjpe and Kakar there are few empirical data or views or idiographic material on the personality of the Indian in his socio-cultural and ecological habitat.[35] (Kakar, S., 1996; Paranjpe, A.C., 1975) Their works and the documentations by other academicians[36] (Saraswati, T.S., & R. Dutta, 1987) have contributed to an understanding of the socio-religious dimensions of the Hindu psyche. Paranjpe's exposition is heavily based on the Hindu philosophy and Kakar's is a combination of psycho-analytical concepts and the Hindu way of life. In a scattered form, other micro-constructs give a patchwork-like effect on understanding segments of the Indian psyche such as the interpretation of justice or morality and in annotated bibliographies collated by a few scholars. What is theoretically known about the psychosocial bases of personality is mainly from western sources. We are short-changed, therefore, in the availability of theoretical knowledge as applicable to the Indian psyche.

As we have said before India has many little Indias and what is researched in one little India has little applicability to the rest of the many Indias. We have attempted to bridge the knowledge that is available on the Indian psyche as related to different theories from the west. Most of the time, we have to admit that such bridging is based on suppositions and extrapolations. Attempting to apply research concepts to philosophy has been inadequate, as philosophical beliefs are more ethereal and not reliably related to the nomothetic approach. As, religious beliefs are more qualitative and heterogeneous in nature. For instance, God has several *avatars;* the belief in Krishna as God in one household is also like the belief in Shivji in another household.Other nations of the east like Japan and China offer such constructs which pertain to their indigenous socio-religious philosophy. However, most eastern countries are moving towards patterns of modernising life styles. In other words, we are believers in their traditional values at the same time subscribing to technologically influenced characteristics.

While, there is no alternative to the use of theoretical concepts and theories from the west, we need to specify that India like all other nations has to subscribe to the stimulus response theoretical constructs whether overt in behaviour theory or covert in psychodynamic theory. In Freudian theory, it is the moulding of the domains psychodynamic experiences. Socio-religious beliefs and attitudinal attributions which mould personality, but certainly do not offer adequate experience as to what he is in terms of socio-religious beliefs. What makes up the traits of an individual, whether he is Indian, Chinese or any other? As such we need to utilise these constructs as the foundational bases for theoretical reasoning for a particular society's individual. Wherever appropriate, we have used the constructs of theories of behaviour, especially social learning, of topology, of life cycle and ecosystems, with extrapolations to the ecologies which are Indian in nature.

Be that as it may, when we conceptualise the Indian as a personality, the picture is kaleidoscopically changing. These changes are not only more observable when vertically conceptualized as in different socio-economic classes, different ethno-religious groups, but also at different chronological ages.[37] (Mosher, Richard L., D.J. Youngman & J.M Day, 1999) Such changes are being experienced at the levels of both the micro and the macro systems.

8. Ecological Dynamic Changes affecting Patterns of Living

From whichever vantage point of personality theory we might view the individual, the quantity and quality of stimuli affect his behaviour in various ways. If the stimuli around him are unvaryingly routine, there is hardly any new stimulation for reinforcement and motivation to change lifestyles. *The greater the quantity and quality of stimuli the individual is faced with, he is forced to make choices, to use alternative strategies, pre-plan and develop the ability to make decisions and mentally hypothesise as to what the expected outcome might/should be.* It is, therefore, obvious that different individuals are living with differential amounts and qualities of stimuli to act and react with the ecology, and for this reason we find individuals at different levels of cognitive experiences. *If a crisis occurs, the individual is unable to cope when he has no experience with the stimuli causing the crisis. Some individuals are less prepared than others in coping with crises.* The less prepared are subject to using more defence mechanisms and are liable to exhibit greater inconsistencies in behaviour patterns.[38]

(Taylor, E., 2009) In ecologies where stimuli are scarce as in desert areas, the individual's capacity to deal with the situation in his ecology is highly developed to a high level. If he is transported to an urban ecology, his experience being limited, he would be limited in dealing with the situations in that ecology. Individuals in tribal areas, when faced with crisis, tend to resort to ritualistic propitiating measures to protect themselves from evil spirits.[39] (Troisi, J., 2000) Thus, adaptation to differing ecologies occurs in different ways. The characteristics common to individuals in varying ecologies are:

(a) The Consequences of Traditionality and Modernity of the Human Ecology

The situation of the Indian, based on his sub-culture, is affected by a variety of heterogeneous variables. This require local approaches to the study of the personality.[40] (Bornstein, H. Marc & Michael E. Lamb, 2005) *It is well-known by now that India has embarked on the train of globalisation with its attributes of westernisation and modernisation.* To give an illustration, the movement towards accruing the benefits of science by the Indian population may be compared to the rate of movement of trains. There are fast trains which the upper class quickly catches up with, while there are slow moving trains which are used by the majority as their need to achieve greater wealth than those moving in the fast trains. For instance, if an NRI returns to his village with an answering machine his relatives would be dumbstruck at the voice on answering machine and not know what to attribute the voice to. These families are ignorant of the products of modern technology. This difference is an index of the difference in ecological experience, where one environment has a surfeit of technological aids while the other does not. This brings into focus the differences in socialisation as affected by the ecological environment. *These factors which are serendipitous require analysis as to what affects socialisation. The phenomenon which is new and requires examination is the plight of the elderly who are proportionately increasing in numbers.* Gerontology is, therefore, a needed area for academic enquiry.

(b) The Combination of Poverty and Changing Demography on Patterns of Living

Almost unconsciously and covertly, the long-standing systems of societal structure and relationships within this structure are becoming fragile. What are the structures? They are for example the disintegration of the joint family, the delinking of castes from their traditional occupations with the emergence of new production structures and relations, and the dissonance between the parent and child generations in value systems. The adverse effects of these changing demographic factors are more prevalent in the mass of the urban, rural and tribal poor who are unexpectedly faced with technological changes.

Additively, *the structural changes, such as the financial structure related to multinational corporates, privatisation, globalisation and increased interactions are occurring coupled with transactions among the countries of the world. The levels of sophisticated knowledge* are changing *which occur mainly in the urban elite ecologies.*[41] (Metha, A., & S.A. Shepherd, 2008). The economically deprived are out of the circumference of such technological parameters, except, perhaps, the television. Further, the demographic pattern in India is changing drastically. There are some startling revelations from the analyses of data from the last two Indian censuses. These are:

(i) Decreasing number of productive individuals (young adults) who bear the burden of responsibility of the other generations, the younger and the older.
(ii) The increasing adaptation of the young generation to the products of technology *vis-à-vis* the older generation who lag behind.
(iii) The continuous transmigration of individuals both horizontally among ecologies, and vertically in moving up the ladder of social wealth. Such transactions need proactive investigation.
(iv) *The movement towards the macro sphere and the diaspora of professional Indians implies a losening of ties with the countries of origin,* in this case, India. This delinking may have consequences of various types: the movement of highly trained professionals out of the country to disorganised relationships when the parent generation is fixed in a time-frame of traditionality and the child generation becomes modernised and the rubbing of the high castes with the low castes in work places denudes caste-barriers.
(v) Even the illiterate in urban cities and district towns is learning

to use a mixture of national and English words producing a kind of "Hinglish". These illustrations of the effects of globalisation on the differing ecologies implies differential patterns of lifestyles, and, therefore, the need to understand human organisation / group formations from one ecology to the other and their interactions.

(vi) *The awareness of developmental programmes for early child care and female' education in hitherto disadvantaged groups is increasing.* There still needs to be quantification.

(vii) The growing proportion of educated females who in a sense now form a threat to the hitherto invincible patriarchal system has a domino effect on other relationships in the micro and exo systems.

(viii) While the major causes of diminishing females in the sex ratio is well-known, the major barriers to stemming wastage of females is yet to be fully analysed in terms of the families' interactional values regarding the profiling of their children of either sex in social values.

(c) Changing Socio-Political Ideologies Affecting Ecologies

The growing global disorganizations such as wars, floods, famines and man-made disasters are affecting the changes occurring in the geo-ecologies.[42] (Juma, C., 2002)

An individual in a normal family ecology develops tendencies which are different from children growing in ecologies which are destabilised by civil strife, as in Kashmir. In fact, the individual living in harmonious situations may not exhibit the characteristics of tension, anxiety and fear, which is more dramatically observable in areas where there is civil strife.[43] (Hoffman, Bruce, 2006) Although warring existed in India in the feudal days[44] (Sharma, R.S., 2006) it did not destabilise the majority of the poor who were mainly rural and tribal and were removed from ecologies devastated by wars. But, today destabilisation even at the global level has their fallout effect on most nations, changing the political exchange between nations and at global forums.

The feudalism which existed in the previous era is now transposed to be bureaucratic system of governance. Peculiarly, *although declared a democratic system, the difference between those in power and those powerless is increasing alarmingly.*

The problems of developed nations are different from those in developing nations.[45] (Uma S. Kambhapati, 2004) For example, the developed countries because of the triad nexus of (a) dominant profiles, (b) territorial power, and (c) the exercise of sophisticated covert international subterfuges create instability in nations at the international level which has its trickle-down effect to national political activities.[46] (Khanna, D.D., 2000)

The rate and type of change in modes of behaviour are affected by the amount and type of technology and scientific know-how in differing societies and their ecologies. Venezuela and the Congo, for instance, are rich in oil, but because of lessened power and the domination of differing ideologies, they are unable to come out of the stranglehold of lack of wealth and power and internal strife. Wealth is inextricably linked with power. While this is a sketchy appraisal of how changes over time and space affect world societies in their concomitant behaviour, there is a micro level perspective within each country. If we telescope the same processes onto the Indian landscape, these differences continue to be reflected in the several sub-societies that live in heterogeneous ecologies, which for the most part are populated by the poor and the powerless.[47] (Kohli, A., 1989) For example, fluctuations in oil prices at the international level affect the ordinary individual in terms of energy availability.

There is a caveat to this in that a few powerful politically engendered groups have accrued to themselves power, domination over wealth and autocratic feudal attitude towards the poor masses within their political jurisdiction. Strikingly the *jajman* system continues to work in these politically manoeuvred pockets. It is not unusual for a disgruntled worker to say I will go and ask my MLA or my brother-in-law who is in the Lok Sabha to help me.

(d) Analyses of the Causes and Consequences of Economic Deprivation

Given the occurrence of intersecting dimensions of power, wealth and territory, the latter, namely the territory, may operationally imply the scope of environmental ecology and its products. The existence of these variables should challenge academicians to examine the type of empirical data to evolve indigenous theoretical concepts. These considerations should ultimately revolve around those barriers which restrict the potentials of a developing society. We may ask several questions which indicate hypothetical strategies and domains that could be explored. Such questions are: does economic deprivation diminish or deplete the potential abilities of the growing personalities?[48] (Misra, G., & Tripathi, L.B., 1977) Do ecologies which are capable of only providing survival facilities affect the individual's need to achieve his innovative capacities? What are the permutations and combinations of an individual, living in a micro system (the family and kinship) which affect his personality attributes when he moves to an exo, a meso and a macro ecosystem? Does the fact that an individual's human ecology is a nuclear family contribute towards his different ontogenetic skills than when his human ecology is an extended family, or when he has mother surrogates, such as teachers, physical trainers, extra-familial care givers, like grandparents or, in several rich households, maids who are the major caretakers?[49] (Kurtz, S., 1992) Therefore, what differences occur in styles of living between the rich and the economically deprived? Do factors in the changing ecology such as depleting resources like water, petroleum, food, transportation and erratic power supply affect the living patterns of the deprived and, therefore, compel personality adjustments in the individual? For example, several decades ago there was no electricity, no power-driven industries, no energy-driven vehicles and no modernised communication in the rural hinterlands. Yet, the Indian in deprived ecologies lived and developed adjusting his lifestyles to the ecological situations. Since the last century we have become used to electronic media, electronic means of communication, high-tech vehicles, and transactions on the internet of all kinds and such like scientific and technological products.

If an individual is deprived of any or many of these facilities of living, what happens in the adjustments of the individual's traits? Does he become aggressive, join protest rallies, and ask for a better India or does he find an easier way of falling into delinquency and crime, or, even worse, fall into a state of apathy and tolerance of evil around him? Does living in a deprived ecology, develop more adaptations, create a better resilience to deprivation and, therefore, a general sense of tolerance of differences with the advantaged people in other ecologies? What do geo-ecological changes do to an individual's coping mechanisms?

9. Assumptions and Hypotheses

We may in this process of analysis assume many hypotheses, which may be difficult to handle but an attempt must be made to uncover the traits of several Indians in several ecologies. Already academicians are exploring ways of researching with social groups of various categories in their living parameters of "social reality".[50] (Anandalakshmy, *et al.*, 2008). Such academic attempts try to relate the Indian individual in a contrasting manner with other nationalities not as a matter of discrimination but of understanding that *differences exist and that these differences are legitimate and should be acceptable for a world to live in the global context of differences. Communication has broken barriers of isolation and complacency.*

While generally speaking the poor remain poor and the socially disadvantaged even so. There is no bar to crossing social barriers. We have witnessed the rise of leaders from socially restrictive conditions in many parts of the world. In India, homage is still paid to those who live as Gurus in ascetic conditions. *Thus, there is still recognition that excellence knows no barriers.* Therefore, while academicians may suggest measures for the removal of such barriers if the bureaucracy is not in tandem, academicians remain as *preachers on a lonely planet.*

Economic wealth and power are blood brothers. Any de-stabilisation within a country of these two domains as to the division between those who have and those who do not compel deeper analysis. Within India, the caste factor which served its purpose in the days of traditional feudalism, as specified by Marriot,[51] (Marriot, Kim, 1961) is now becoming defunct in the growing economic sphere especially in urban elite areas. Caste was then related to an occupation. Now this distinction is becoming blurred but ironically is used as a strong factor in the political arena. It would be no surprise that in future a *dalit* might become the Prime Minister or the President and the Brahmin the underling.[52] (Bayly, Susan, 1999) In a democratic country the possibility exists for anybody to aspire to be somebody. Such transactions in the political sphere need to be related to personality development of different types. A District Collector in his district ecology wields much power as relative to his position at the State level with other District Collectors. This implies that *powerful positions indicate different meanings in different ecologies.* Does an educated polity make for better assessment of leadership, or does a kind of feudalism prevail over illiterate masses?

What we are attempting to say here is that economic deprivation or class barriers do not automatically deny access to opportunities.

Through enterprise, through knowledge, through education and the development of the ontogenetic potential, an individual can surpass these rigid barriers of discrimination. It is not, however, a one-sided affair. The governance has much to do with it, for, policies are proclaimed in a democratic fashion but in the traditional sphere of family, caste and community, authoritarianism and autocracy have a stranglehold on maintaining this *status quo*. Individuals might want to achieve, might want to break barriers and seek opportunities but debilitating customs and conventions act as strong deterrence. We are aware of movements such as the feminist movements against discounting the female, the protest movements against corruption, against deforestation, against depletion of the ecological environment and so on. There are also well-meaning institutional policies such as the right to information, citizens' court, protection of the rights of children and anti-discrimination laws (anti-dowry, anti-child labour and such like). We still have to ask the question what has been the effect of these various attempts to improve the situation or to eliminate the impediment at the grassroot level?

The occurrence of such movements implies increasing public awareness. Therefore, a significant area for analyses of newer dimensions of enquiry and, therefore, new paradigms, for development in the Indian ecology/ecologies calls for an understanding and examination of the attributes of socio-political systems, interacting in the human eco-systems.[53] (Ray, R., & M.F. Ketzenstein, 2005). The social sciences would need to look at the components of the public ethos and its ethics in offering a developmental platform for the developing individual in his Indian context, where there seems to be a disconnect between what is said, what is done and the social reality of the deprived and the disadvantaged. An integrated holistic approach

For the reasons mentioned above social scientists may themselves attempt to look at the same social problems from different points of view related to their area of expertise. They may use the same hypotheses but operationalise it differentially. Eventually experts from different fields may arrive at a fragmented approach to the same problem. If the fragmented consequences of discussion or research on the same problem arrive at differential results then, obviously they need to be culled together. It then becomes important to look at the basic theoretical constructs of each approach and utilize them to put together an integrated theoretical paradigm.

Sitting at their bureaucratic tables of files composed of reviews, reports, evaluations, recommendations in absentia of ground level experience of the daily lives of the reality of the relevant samples, much of the finer innuendoes of the results might be lost in complete understanding of the problem/evaluation/reports. Therefore, the outcomes of these fora tend to be tangential to social reality.

Scientific analysis from the social sciences may focus on the idiographic and ethnographic data regarding the quality of life of different socio-economic classes. The segments who are powerless and most needy, and who do not really benefit from several palliative programmes, are the scheduled tribes, scheduled castes, women, the urban poor and the minorities. There is no denying that most of the alleviative programmes and infrastructures are poor in quality and personnel and what is more unfortunate is that there is indifferent implementation, monitoring and evaluation.[54] (Amartya Sen, 1992; Dreze, Jean and Amartya Sen, 1996) Women are discriminated by a double discount in the family micro system and in the exo system of governance.[55] (Dixit, P., 2008) Therefore, greater attention to women especially, in the fragile sections of the population needs further analysis.

In the *Human Development Report, 2009 Overcoming barriers: Human mobility and development*[56] (UNDP, 2009) an instance of the difficulties that female migrant workers face is given in the following idiographic example:

"*Now consider Bhagyawati. She is a member of a lower caste and lives in rural Andhra Pradesh, India. She travels to Bangalore city with her children to work on construction sites for six months each yean earning Rupees 60 (US$1.20) per dcy. While away from home, her children do not attend school because it is too far from the construction site and they do not know the local language. Bhagyawati is not entitled to subsidized food or health care, nor does she vote, because she is living outside her registered district. Like many other migrants, she has few options for improving her life other than to move to a different city in search of better opportunities.*

Bhagyawati is in an ambiguous position, registered in one place to be eligible for subsidies and benefits and working in another as a migrant and a stranger in the urban area stranger migrating labourer. The problems of displaced tribals whose lands are appropriated for a pittance by industrial projects need to be empirically analysed on a priority basis. The Indian Social Institute has estimated that there are about 21 million development-induced displaced persons in India, many of whom belong to Scheduled Castes and tribal groups.[57]

Unless academia examines these issues and presents such empirical data, and unless media communicate such concerns and planners address them, these disadvantaged groups will continue to be so.

Another distressing area of concern is the stranglehold of the patriarchal system on the poor working women and female householders. No amount of feminist shouting from the roof-top will have any satisfactory effect to redress the situation of women. It is only when men of households of such women are "re-educated" to realize and release them for opportunities for self-development that any effect would be discernible. This is an important gender issue for social scientists.

The relationship between the developing individual as a personality within specific ecology should be presented as a series of scenarios depicting the action and interaction of the personality and his/her ecosystem.[58] (Lars, R. Bergman, D. Magnusson & Bassan M. El Khorri, 2003). Such analyses may in truth show wide differences. For example, a nomad's child may be unlettered formally, living in the Rajasthani desert, but he accrues a great deal of traditional wisdom by learning from his arid and harsh environs, unlike the rich man's child cocooned in his luxurious flat, in his upmarket school and in the elite gatherings of his parents. Children of these two groups are at the two ends of the dimension of development, both in terms of the ecological effects on them and the contouring of their personalities. The nomad's child relies upon traditional wisdom for education while the city child has a surfeit of electronic gadgets and information systems.

Another area of concern in the light of the predicaments mentioned by Governments, both central and State about compulsory school education has not been intensively explored, from the point of view of ecology influencing personality attributes. The fisherman, the hill tribal and the inaccessible villager will be motivated to continue an education if it is related to their environmental ecology. The child in these groups is better able to understand educational concepts if it is linked with his ecology. A State-wide uniform school curricula with western-oriented illustrations even from the kindergarten stages will be of little interest and, therefore, create less motivation in the child, therefore depletes motivation in the child. This is true also in the case even of educational institutions in cities where early foundational teaching of concepts is highly sophisticated. To instil in the kindergarten children nursery rhymes from the west like "Twinkle, Twinkle Little Star", and "Jack and Jill" is irrelevant to their socio-psychological beliefs and ecologies in which they live.

Given the easy mode of mobility, a fisherman from Kerala may, through the channels of relatives, get to go to the middle-east, while the Pangi of the Himalayan hills may find it also profitable to work on the building sites in the Kangra valley and, thus, widen their socio-psychological spheres and increase their ecological knowledge. These changes in residential habitat are not without their negative repercussions. Frequently, such *transitioning individuals suffer from social anomie, depression, lack of the nurturant care available in the previous original ecology. Indeed, if prolonged, these factors may affect personality domains, leading to psychological consequences such as greater frustration, lessened drive to achieve because of barriers and the relevant conflicts and such like.* On the other hand, when an individual moves among different ecosystems, it is likely that he may be challenged to achieve more dependent upon his ontogenetic frame or, as said before, he may fall into a situation of alienation and loss of self-esteem.[59] (Kashinath, H.M., 2003, p. 3)

Integrated perspectives from the social sciences may be illustrated as below:

Children from a particular schooling system exhibit different levels of need to achieve. Psychologically the micro ecosystem, namely, family and kinship, have much to do with the foundation of these differences in these particular psychological domains. Sociologically, *the societal norms prevailing in the community framework of these children influencing their development is also significant.* Anthropologically, the given variants in the geo-ecological system may affect such like characteristics differentially. A child from a villager Pradhan's micro economic system has perhaps been positively reinforced through socialisation in contrast to the scheduled caste family living apart from the former. With the farmer's child these reinforcements may be discontinuous, sometimes negative, sometimes positive and, therefore, hardly imprint on the farmer's child who also has other occupational tasks in the micro economic system.

Frequently, nomethetic data tend to present averages. *Since most individuals are not average what is more important is to know about the characteristics of the below average and the above average.* These differences are hardly illustrated in such parametric data.

Further, how the global vision interacts with the local vision is an important area of investigation. The world is opening up to the Indian individual with a panorama of international exchanges, both in personnel and products. India is now flooded with foreign made commodities even at district levels. Bollywood and Hollywood interact with each other. NRIs come and go more and more frequently. Tourist packages to other countries are on the increase and are available on the internet. However, while most villagers are familiar with viewing television channels, others from the educated elite go beyond this passive viewing and explore further information from the internet.

Politics of the nation and the world, economic markets of the nation and the world, terrorist intrusions into India and other countries are now wellentrenched into the Indian's world vision. However, there are several far-flung ecologies which are only faintly aware of such distal factors, to give weight to a fuller knowledge of how a person develops in his ecology, both the centripetal and the centrifugal factors are required to be taken into account in these widely differing ecologies with their specific eco-systems.[60] (Taylor, E., 2009)

We have yet to understand the equation of social well-being to economic well-being.[61] (Mudacumura, Gedeon M., Desta Mebratu & M. Shamshul Haque, 2005) *We have deliberately emphasized this point of dubious correlation between economic and psycho-social development, because India is facing this paradox. Over a period of the last two-three decades, with some exceptions, the Indian's perception by and large is focused on "acquisition".* In families that concentrate on this phenomenon, becoming overly rich, family interaction is diminished and children with much money tend to experiment and indulge in drugs and other anti-social behaviour with little heed to parental guidance, or what is more concerning parental neglect towards these behaviours. The increasing phenomenon of drug-addiction in young adulthood is of concern in the urban areas and requires further investigation. *Thus, from the ecological point of view it is necessary to examine the centrifugal and centripetal areas of influence of the developing adolescent into a wholesome adult personality.*

In the horizon of India's society in this century, there are several significant problems that need the attention of academicians. In the above paragraphs we have briefly indicated them. Here under we specify them into two categories:

(i) The Maintenance of the Micro System: The Family

The family, the fundamental micro system is the nexus of our enquiry. How it survives and meets its aspirations given the increasing hiatus between the rich and the poor, with the latter increasing phenomenally. *The most fragile segments in the micro system of the family, namely, children and women will continue, at an accelerated pace, to be further deprived, especially those in chronic poverty and in poor agricultural ecologies.*[62] (Mohammad Ali, Abdul Munir, Shamsul Haque Siddiqui & Rocket Ibrahim, 2006) Academicians, planners and stake holders will, in such "reality situations", require to frame and monitor activities for fragile segments. This implies that academicians will need to present field tested empirical data and diminish desk-bound activities. The planners will need to monitor the field situation for themselves and not depend entirely on desk reviews.

(ii) Nurturance of the Growing Personality by the Contingent Eco-systems

As such, nurturing patterns that socialize the child should be understood and studied in the present milieu of economical and technological changes. The dissonance of living in an autocratic micro ecosystem is now no longer tenable given the fast-paced technology to which most families, whether urban or rural, are being increasingly exposed to. The emergence of new innovative indigenous information upon the child upbringing in such ecologies which are democratic in polity but traditional in upbringing under patriarchal societal norms requires to be studied for their impact upon the growing individual from both the democratic frame and the autocratic frame in which the individual coexists.

10. Sustainability in Development

In India, sustainability in development can occur if the geo-ecology has the potential, the individual has the developed skills, and the latter is knowledgeable about systematic relationships among the ecosystems. India's polity through its Five Year Plans and programmes for such sustainable development has attempted to improve the quality of life. There is, however, a curious mismatch. *Development occurs rapidly in the already developed sections of society, while those for whom it is really targeted fall by the wayside.* In the agricultural sector, the government's plans are increasing yields, water harvesting and the use of agro-technology in processing. As an adjunct of the task of preservation of land and its sources, the government's undertakings are in prevention of deforestation, biotechnology development, and more especially in finding alternate sources of energy. In the industrial sector, the Government's emphasis is mainly on entrepreneurial activities, mostly in small scale and cottage industries. However, the private sector through its own volition has gone far ahead of the public sector.

This is especially important given the fact that India is mostly an agricultural country with great acreage of land: fertile, arid and non fertile, with long lines of coastline and hill ranges. These are mostly inhabited by rural and tribal families. Throughout the over six decades of such geo-ecological development strategies, the task is unequal to those living in the rural and tribal habitats. The attempts of the polity to find ways and means to develop these larger and relatively disadvantaged sections has not produced desired results. This is because less is done for too many. Given the current enquiry into the scams by both the polity and the bureaucracy, these attempts have been fragmented.

So what is sustained? Are the people who are the beneficiaries sustained? Or is it the large unwieldly bureaucratic apparatus from the top to the bottom that is sustained? Where does most of the expenditure on these so-called alleviative programmes disappear?

How can these attempts be sustained and not fall into disuse? *Paradoxically many of the more knowledgeable segments of these sections voluntarily use their own initiatives for bettering their prospects, rather than depending upon highly bureaucratised, long-winding and little giving palliative governmental programmes.* This is currently the situation although governmental efforts have been going on for the past six decades. The work of NGOs is only those that have sustainability because of the commitment of their workers who live with the participants and share their problems, issues and have the credence of the beneficiaries towards such work.

It is now more imperative than ever, that academic research

explores these avenues at ground level. This must be related to 'social realities' before planning and programming developemental features.

This implies a three-pronged approach on the planning and programming process, the implementation and then the evaluation for the redress of assistance programmes in which all the three categories above are involved in an interactive face-to-face discussion to find the "realism" of these suggested programmes. There have been desultory programmes of peoples' participation, but very little of the participation of the academicians.

In the Indian context, sustainability does not just mean economic sustainability which implies that the masses should be economically motivated and assisted, but that there should also be social sustainability. *Social sustainability implies that there is no incongruity between political ethos and public ethos.* The fact is that an originally feudal country had the cognisance of adopting a secular and democratic ideology, which is highly commendable. However, over the years the development have not been compatible with the expectations. The efforts of the political policies have not been commensurate with expectations. We have in this book stressed the importance of geo-ecology and human ecology, implying a supportive network for each which interacts between each. These ecologies are countless and, therefore, require countless variegated measures. In the sociological context, *Indians are still embedded in their core socio-religious beliefs, cocooned in traditionality.* If any effort has to sustain them, then it has to be three-pronged. One, experienced personnel trained in the occupational channels available irrespective of caste, creed or ethnicity. *This education should also include the education to overcome caste differences, especially in areas of employment and interaction, where real equality can prevail and not just be a spurious, verbalised idea.* Two, the focus should be on the majority, namely the poor. Unless the majority is focussed upon, the operation, identification of sustainability will remain less attainable.[63] (Puthenkalam, John Joseph, 2004)

Three, the parameters of sustainability should be well defined. When these are operationalised, they indicate the commitment of the Government, responsibility and accountability of the bureaucracy and the willingness of people to enter into the domains of their own improvement. If these three are less than expected, sustainability over a period of time is less congruous. Yes, industrial development, government projects and the inroads created by the private sector into the landed property of the poor do not bode well for sustainability except those who are the directors/managers of such activities at all levels. Currently most beneficiaries view assistance programmes as the responsibility of the givers and in many respects this interaction appears as feudal charity.

Therefore, proactive perspectives imply the furtherance of social scientists' wisdom to look at the developing human being in his various ecologies, which then will provide a picture of social reality as it exists and pro-actively provide a future look into the consequences of the sustainability of developmental programmes.

REFERENCES

1. Dreze, J.D., & A. Sen, 2002, *India: Development and Participation.* New Delhi: Oxford University Press.
2. Bates, D.G., 2001, *Human Adaptive Strategies: Ecology, Culture and Politics*, Boston, M.A.: Allyn and Bacon.
3. Haq, Shamsul, 1999, *Restructuring Development Theories and Politics: A Political Study*, New York: State University of New York Press.
4. UNDP, *Human Development Report 2009, Overcoming Barriers: Human Mobility and Development*, New York: Palgravge Macmillan.
5. Desai, Sonalde B., Amaresh Dubey, Brij Lal Joshi, Mitali Sen, Abusaleh Shariff, and Reeve Venneman, 2010, *Human Development in India: Challenges for a Society in Transition*, New Delhi: Oxford University Press.
6. Bergman, L.R., R.B. Cairns, L.G. Nilsson & L. Nystedt (eds.), 2000, *Developmental Science and the Holistic Approach*, Mahwah, N.J., Erlbaum.
7. Rahman, Tanhidur, Ronc Mittelhammer & Philip Wandschneidan, 2003, A *Sensitivity Analysis of Quality of Life Indices Across Countries.* Agricultural and Applied Economics Association Annual Meeting, July 27-30, Montreal, Canada.
8. Singh, Y., 1977, *Modernisation of Indian Tradition. A Systemic Study of Social Change,* Faridabad, India: Thomson Press.

   Srinivas, M.N., 1966, *Social Change in Modern India*, Berkeley: California University Press.
9. Kluckhohn, F.R. & F.L. Strodtbeck, 1961, *Variations in Value Orientations*, Evanston, Ill.: Row, Peterson.
10. Kumar, R. (ed.), 1999, *Colonisation and Modernisation in India*, New Delhi: Anmol Publications Pvt. Ltd.

11. Ellen, R.F., P. Parkes & A. Bicker (eds.), 2000, *Indigenous Environmental Knowledge and its Transformations: Critical Anthropological Perspectives,* Amsterdam Harwood Academic.
12. Cash, D.W., W.N. Adger, F. Berkes, P. Garden, L. Lebel, P. Olsson, L. Pritchard & O. Young, 2006, 'Scale and cross scale dynamics: governance and information in a multilevel world', *Ecology and Society, 11(2), art. 8.*
13. Ramaswamy, S., & G. Sathish Kumar, 2009, *Energy, Environment and Sustainable Development: Issues and Policies*, New Delhi: Manohar Publications.
14. Najam, A., D. Runnalls & M. Halle, 2007, *Environment and Globalisation: Five Propositions*. Winnipeg MB Canada: International Institute for Sustainable Development.
15. Galaz, V., P. Olsson, T. Hahn, C. Folke & U. Svedin, 2006, *The Problems of Fit between Ecosystems and Governance Systems: Insights and Challenges*. Paper presented at Institutional Dimensions of Global Environmental Change Synthesis Conference. Dec 6-9, 2006. Bali.
16. Jerath, J.M., & A. Sibia, 2009, 'Trends in personality research: an overview', in G. Misra (ed.), *Psychology in India, Vol. 1: Basic Psychological Processes and Human Development*, Delhi: Dorling Kindersley (India) Pvt. Ltd. (Licensees of Pearson Education in South India).
17. Gupta, K.R., 2008, *Poverty of India*, New Delhi: Atlantic Publishers and Distributors.
18. Bodkin, D.B., 1990, *Discordant Harmonies: A New Ecology for the Twenty-first Century*, New York, Oxford University Press.
19. Ellen, R.F., P. Parkes & A. Bicker (eds.), 2000, *Indigenous Environmental Knowledge and its Transformations: Critical Anthropological Perspectives,* Amsterdam Harwood Academic.
20. Onser, L.E. (ed.), 1995, *Indigenous People and the Future of Amazonia: An ecological Anthropology of an Endangered World*, Tucson: University of Arizonia Press.
21. Harper Janice, 2002, *Endangered Species: Health, Illness and Death among Madagascar's People of the Forest*, Durham NC: Carolina Academic Press.
22. Metal, M., 1998, *Protecting the Arctic: Indigenous Peoples and Cultural Survival*, Amsterdam, Harwood.
23. Gamely, P.J., 1998, 'The human development index in 1994: impact of income on country rank", *Journal of Economic and Social Measurement*, 21, pp. 253-267.

24. Gole, Prakasa, 2001, *Nature Conservation and Sustainable Development in India*, New Delhi: Rawat Publications.
25. Hoffman, Bruce, 2006, *Inside Terrorism*, New York: Columbia University Press.
26. Sharma, R.S., 1981, *Indian Feudalism*, New Delhi: MacMillan.
27. Uma, S. Kambhapati, 2004, *Development and the Developing World*, Cambridge: Polity Press.
28. Rahman, Tanhidur, Ronc Mittelhammer & Philip Wandschneidan, 2003, *A Sensitivity Analysis of Quality of Life Indices across Countries*, Agricultural and Applied Economics Association Annual Meeting, July 27-30. Montreal, Canada.
29. Bronfenbrenner, U., 2001, "The theory of human development", in N.J. Smelser & P.B. Baltes (eds.), *International Encyclopaedia of the Social and Behavioural Sciences*, Vol. 10, pp. 6963-6970, New York: Elsevier.
30. Lewin. K., 1936, *Principles of Topological Psychology*, New York. McGraw-Hill.
31. Bronfenbrenner, U., & G.W. Evans, 2000, 'Developmental sciences in the 21st century: emerging questions, theoretical models, research designs and empirical findings", *Social Development*, 9 (1), 115-125.
32. Berry. J.W., J.A. Bennet & J.B. Denny, 2000, *Ecology, Culture and Cognitive Processing*. Paper presented at the 15th Congress of International Association for Cross culture psychology. Pulturk, Poland.
33. Kashinath, H., 2003, 'Interactive effect of mental health school adjustment and SES on academic achievement', *Indian Journal on Psychometry and Education*, 34 (2), July 2003, 150-164.
34. Fuller, J.S., 1960, 'Behavior Genetics', *Annual Review of Psychology*, 11, 41-70.
35. Kakar, S., 1996, *The Indian Psyche*, Delhi: Oxford University Press; Paranjpe, A.C., 1975, *In Search of Identity*, Delhi: McMillan.
36. Saraswati, T.S., & R. Dutta, 1987, *Developmental Psychology in India 1975-1986 : An Annotated Bibliography*, New Delhi: Sage Publications.
37. Mosher, Richard L., D.J. Youngman & J.M Day, 1999, *Human Development Across the Life Span*, New York: Praeger Publishers.
38. Taylor, E., 2009, *The Mystery of Personality: A History of Psychodynamic Theories*, New York: Springer Publication.
39. Troisi, J., 2000, *Tribal Religion: Religious Belief and Practices among the Santals*, Delhi: Manohar Publishers.
40. Bornstein, H. Marc & Michael E. Lamb, 2005, *Developmental Science: An Advanced Edition*. New Jersey: Lawrence Erlbaum Associates.

41. Mehta, Aasha Kapur and Shepherd Andrew, 2006, *Chronic Poverty and Development Policy in India*, New Delhi: Sage Publications.
42. Juma, C., 2002, 'The global sustainability challenge: From agreement to action', *International Journal of Global Environment Issues*, 2(1/2), 1-14.
43. Hoffman, Bruce, 2006, *Inside Terrorism*, New York: Columbia University Press.
44. Sharma, R.S., 2006, *Indian Feudalism*, Delhi: Macmillan Publishers India Ltd.
45. Uma, S. Kambhapati, 2004, *Development and the Developing World*, Cambridge: Polity Press.
46. Khanna, D.D., 2000, *Democracy, Diversity, Stability: 50 Years of Indian Independence*, New Delhi: Macmillan India.
47. Kohli, A., 1989, *The State and Poverty in India*. Cambridge: Cambridge University Press.
48. Misra, G., & Tripathi, L.B., 1977, 'The Concept of Prolonged Deprivation and its Measurement', *Indian Journal of Behaviour*, 1 (2), 48-60.
49. Kurtz, S., 1992, *All the Mothers Are One: Hindu India and the Cultural Reshaping of Psychoanalysis*, New York: Columbia University Press.
50. Anandalakshmy, S., Nandita Chaudhary & Neeraj Sharma, 2008, *Researching Families and Children: Culturally Appropriate Methods*, New Delhi: Sage Publications.
51. Marriot, Kim, 1961, "Changing channels of cultural transmission in Indian civilisation", *Journal of Social Research*, 4(1-2), 13-25.
52. Bayly, Susan, 1999, *Caste Society and Politics in India from the Eighteenth Century to the Modern Age*, Cambridge, Cambridge University Press.
53. Ray, R., & M.F. Ketzenstein (eds.), 2005, *Social Movements in India: Poverty, Power and Politics*, Lanham, MD: Rowen Littlefield Publishers Inc.
54. Amartya Sen, 1992, *Inequality Re-examined*. Cambridge, Mass.: Harvard University Press.
Dreze, Jean and Amartya Sen, 1996, *India: Economic Development and Social Opportunity*, New Delhi: Oxford University Press.
55. Dixit, P., 2008, *Politics and Political Culture*, *Vol. 15*, Asheville, Carolina: VIP House Publishers.
56. UNDP, *Human Development Report 2009, Overcoming Barriers: Human Mobility and Development*, New York: Palgravge Macmillan, p. 1.
57. *Ibid.*
58. Lars, R. Bergman, D. Magnusson & Bassan M. El Khorri, 2003,

Studying Individual Development in an Inter-individual Context: A Person-Oriented Approach. Mahwah, NJ: Lawrence Erlbaum.

59. Kashinath, H.M., 2003, 'Interactive effect of mental health, school adjustment and SES on academic achievement", *Indian Journal of Psychometry and Education*, July, 2003, Vol. 34(2), 159-164.
60. Taylor, E., 2009, *The Mystery of Personality: A History of Psychodynamic Theories*. Springer, New York.
61. Mudacumura, Gedeon M., Desta Mebratu & M. Shamshul Haque, 2005, *Sustainable Development Policy and Administration*, New Delhi: CRC Press.
62. Mohammad Ali, Abdul Munir; Shamsul Haque Siddiqui & Rocket Ibrahim, 2006, *Environment, Agriculture and Poverty*, (3 Vols), New Delhi: Concept Publishing Company.
63. Puthenkalam, John Joseph, 2004, *Empowerment: Sustainable Human Development Strategy for Poverty Alleviation*, New Delhi: Rawat Publications.

Glossary

Achoot	"Untouchable"
Avatar	incarnation
Ayurveda	The word "Ayurveda" means "complete knowledge for long life and is a popular ancient indigenous system of medicine in India.
Bahadur	a brave person
Bania	a person belonging to any one of the Vaishya or mercantile group of castes
Baraat	the bridegroom's party
Basti	a group of hutments where Scheduled Caste people live in villages
Bhoot	evil spirit
Bhoot chada hai	the possession of the individual by the evil spirit
Brahmin	The highest Hindu caste group traditionally assigned to the priesthood; a person belonging to this caste group
Chappals	slippers
Chawl	tenements of labourers in cities; in India these are inhabited by Scheduled Castes
Daan	charity-giving
Dargah	a Sufi shrine built over the grave of a revered religious figure
Dehat	Village
Devrani	younger sister-in-law
Dharma	righteous living, one's duty (see Purusharthas).
Dosha	dosha means "dysfunction" or "abnormal" — a

	divergence from the perfect balance for which Ayurvedic medicine strives. The central concept of Ayurvedic medicine is the theory that health exists when there is a balance between three fundamental bodily "humours" or doshas called "Vata", "Pitta" and "Kapha".
Devi	a Goddess from among the many venerated in different village households
Gaddi	A tribe in Himachal Pradesh
Garibi Hatao	The political programme of eradication of poverty
Jat	Caste
Jati	Sub-Caste
Jethani	elder sister-in-law
Jharra	village medicine man who use traditional methods for healing
Juggi	Slum dweller's hutment
Kathputli	puppet
Kshatriya	kshatriya, meaning warrior, is one of the four *varnas* into which the Hindu society is divided into; the other *varnas* are Brahmin, Vaishya and Shudra
Kundli	horoscope
Mahabharat	a Hindu epic story
Mahua	a deciduous tree found in the central and north Indian plains and forest areas. Its flowers are used to brew an alcoholic drink. It is considered holy by many tribal communities because of its usefulness.
Manusmriti	Laws of Manu, an earliest metrical work of the Hindus
Marwari	a Vaishya sub-caste whose occupation is trading
Mata	goddess mother
Mela	community fair
Nawab	A Muslim feudal lord
Purana karma	old deed
Ramayana	a Hindu epic story
Roti Sabzi	Bread and vegetable
Samkhya	One of the six schools of classical Hindu philosophy
Shudh	Pure
Tulsi	A medicinal herbal plant (Basil) considered sacred in the Hindu religion
Turban	headgear

Kirpan	a ceremonial sword or dagger carried on the person by orthodox Sikhs
Veda	A holy Hindu scripture. There are majorly four *Vedas*: *Rig Veda*, *Yajur Veda*, *Sama Veda* and *Adharvaa Veda*.
Vedic time	the period when the Vedas were written
Vedanta	A System of Hindu philosophy based on the *Upanishads*, the *Brahma Sutras*, and the *Bhagavad-Gita.* Includes both dualist (*dvaita*) and non-dualist (*advaita*) schools as well as others, but all believe in transmigration of soul (*samsara*), the desirability of escape from it, the authority of the *Vedas*, *Brahman* as the cause of the universe, and the law of *karma*.

Index